Reflections from a Glass House

A Memoir of Mid-century Modern Mayhem

I0104487

Carol Sveilich

Copyright © 2020 by Carol Sveilich

All rights reserved. In accordance with the US Copyright Act of 1976, the scanning, uploading, and electronic sharing of any part of this book without the permission of the publisher constitutes unlawful piracy and theft of the author's intellectual property. If you would like to use material from the book (other than for review purposes), prior written permission must be obtained by contacting the publisher. Thank you for your support of the author's rights.

Text: Carol Sveilich
Illustration: Jeannie King
Editor: Amanda Owens
Cover Design: Dennis Spear
Cover Layout: Danielle Smith-Boldt
Interior Design and Layout: Danielle Smith-Boldt

ISBN: 978-0-578-69096-4

This book is a memoir. It reflects the author's present recollections of experiences over time. Some names and characteristics have been changed, some events have been compressed, and some dialogue has been recreated. While all the stories in this book are true, some names and identifying details have been changed to protect the privacy of the people involved.

Early Praise for

Reflections from a Glass House

The author's candid life story is really a love story about life. Much of it wraps around her family's mid-century modern castle built by master developer Joseph Eichler. One cannot read about Sveilich's life without becoming immersed in her story and wanting to be her friend. Only great writing can achieve that. And if no legacy is so rich as honesty, as Shakespeare once said, then with the publication of this memoir Sveilich's legacy is set in stone.

—Rich Ross, Emmy award-winning comedy writer (Hollywood Squares, creating jokes for Joan Rivers and Steve Allen); writer on The Nanny television show; writer on comedian/actor Phil Hartman's NBC specials

Sveilich writes with the breezy wit of Bill Bryson, the forensic eye of Joni Mitchell, and the voice of a middle-class mid-century kid describing the dreams of that time.

Reflections from a Glass House is a hilarious, but highly touching read. The author dives deep into childhood wonders and awkwardness, and captures the birth of a "Modern" American landscape, casting an observant eye on her family life and the social dynamics of the adult world around her. She does so with love, loathing, and a boatload of fear intact.

Sveilich lovingly describes her Sixties glass-paned Eichler home in California's pre-tech Bay Area, the main locus of her childhood, and discovers in it a metaphor for modern idealism and a self-reflective mirror. That home reveals the inner angst and the joys of a girl who would later become a counselor and published author. A joyful read from beginning to end, highly recommended for all who remember America's promise.

—Dave Blackburn, music producer

I was born and raised in San Francisco. Sveilich shows us the journey the Bay Area traveled musically (jazz, soul, rock and roll) and socially in the City and suburbs. Conservatives were trying to resist the coming changes brought on by the counterculture. A soulful look at the ever-changing area seen through a young girl's eyes and her unique household. Highly recommended.

—Johnnie Bamont, saxophonist, Huey Lewis and the News

CANDID. SMART. WILD. Sveilich nailed it! The descriptions of early Santa Clara Valley, the fumbles through school and the passage through adolescence near the "City of Love" resonated with me and thrilled me. There's so much here to identity with and the memoir was a continual surprise. Highly recommended.

—"Krazy George" Henderson, professional cheerleader for Houston Oilers, Kansas City Chiefs, New Orleans Saints, and others, and author of Still Krazy After All These Cheers

With comedic prose and broken dreams, Sveilich writes with candor and delicious detail. Revealing, maddening, witty as hell, and at times bleak, Sveilich writes with observant precision about nostalgia, the joys and pitfalls of youth, and the darkness of growing up in a family of disconnected souls that had humor as its connective tissue.

A gifted writer can turn even the most transient encounters and dire circumstances into pure gold. Sveilich delivers. *Reflections from a Glass House* is both courageous and deeply funny. There's no better recipe for a great memoir.

—Richard Scopelli, psychotherapist

Here at *CA Modern Magazine* and the Eichler Network, where everything is "Eichler" 24 hours a day, Sveilich and her family are seen today as pathfinders. They helped to lay the ground floor for Eichler Homes' Fairglen tract of San Jose some 60 years before it was aptly named to the National Register of Historic Places.

On this thoroughly entertaining joyride through California's mid-century glory days, Sveilich recalls the intimate details of her childhood in Fairglen as if it were yesterday. We've interviewed hundreds of Eichler families over the years, but Carol is the first to transcend the mere interview to officially bring the joys of living Eichler modern to book form. It's about time!

—Marty Arbunich, Publisher, CA Modern Magazine; Director/Publisher, Eichler Network

I was there, starting my career opening for the likes of the Grateful Dead, Janis Joplin, Jefferson Airplane, and Donovan, thanks to the amazing and brilliant Bill Graham. By now, I remember a bit, forgot a lot, so it was fascinating to read another young woman's evocative takes on her experience back in the day. *Reflections from a Glass House* was a WONDERFUL READ.

—Tracy Nelson, multi-Grammy Award nominee, whose 40-year career reached from the Fillmore scene of late Sixties San Francisco to Nashville's top studios. She has recorded over 17 solo albums and several with the group Mother Earth

As a specialist in mid-century modern design and Eichler homes, I appreciated and thoroughly enjoyed this book about the birth of the Eichlers in mid-century modern America. The author's coming-of-age story with so many relatable moments was an added plus. She touches on the uniqueness of the home as well as many major pop culture moments that defined the lives of millions. I highly recommend *Reflections from a Glass House*

—Troy Kudlac, developer of the Desert Eichlers in Palm Springs, California, and real estate broker for KUD Properties, Inc.

In *Reflections from a Glass House*, Sveilich takes us on her journey from east coast to west coast through the lens of an inquisitive, adventurous child and teenager. Written in a style reminiscent of Mark Twain's *Huckleberry Finn*, her memoir brings us into her unique mid-century home with her mid-century modern family in a mid-century time period—1960 to 1972—with hilarious, nostalgic and poignant stories on coming of age in the turbulent era of the "sex, drugs, and rock and roll" circus. I was living in Laurel Canyon during the same period. In this era, we were breaking all the rules.

This page-turner reveals that life during these times was not always as neat and tidy as the *Ozzie and Harriet* or *Father Knows Best* television series suggested, but rather an often prickly and perplexing period in our nation's history. Whether you're a Baby Boomer or not, you won't want to miss this compelling and highly recommended memoir.

—Jay Rudman, former President and CEO of Trillium Health

I grew up in the same cultural "Ka-BOOM!" as the author—the Bay Area during the Sixties. My first band was forged in the midst of the melting pot that the Eichler neighborhoods became. We segued from the suburban middle-class utopia to the stages of the Fillmore and the Avalon at a dizzying pace. Say what you will about us baby-boomers; we knew exactly the right time to be born. We had it all: color television, a booming economy, and the greatest damned music ever played. Like Sveilich, I was right at Ground Zero.

I was becoming a musician and a man at a wondrous and often really scary time in American history. Rock and roll, drugs, and lots of craziness led me to a life that I look back upon and wonder: how did I go so far in the music business and how did I live through it? Thanks, Carol, for sharing your journey with another Bay Area brat with such honesty, humor, and insight. What a ride.

—Greg Douglass, American rock guitarist, toured and recorded with Van Morrison, Duane Eddy, Link Wray, Hot Tuna, Dave Mason, and Eddie Money, among others. In addition, he co-wrote and played on the Steve Miller Band hit "Jungle Love"

Sveilich brings so many memories back with detail, grace and a personal sensitivity that makes you feel like you're a part of her heart and soul. A highly recommended read.

—James Callner, MA, educator and filmmaker

I came of age in Sunnyvale, California, during the same time period as Sveilich. The best part of living in Santa Clara Valley was escaping into music with my friends, just as the author did. We would drive to San Francisco to see the likes of Jimi Hendrix, Sly Stone, The Electric Flag, Cream, and Tower of Power at Winterland or The Fillmore. For kids growing up in the Bay Area, music made up a healthy portion of our glory days. I lived a block away from an Eichler neighborhood and would play music after school in various garage bands. Sveilich writes about her own brother being in such a band. Reading *Reflections from a Glass House* brought back a flood of my own memories—both the challenging and blissful times. A fun, but poignant read.

—Paul Nagel, pianist and music arranger on Boz Scagg's But Beautiful album. In a 40+ year career in the music world, accompanied artists on piano such as Bobby McFerrin and jazz musician Eddie Harris

Who doesn't want to read about sex, drugs and rock 'n' roll? The book conjures up images of California's Glory Days, that pageant of sun, freedom, and playful existentialism. This humorous first-hand and soul-wrenching account of a girl's rocky road to adulthood evokes a personal and collective shock of recognition.

—Charlotte Daigle, former magazine editor (Antiques and Fine Art, Cowboys and Indians), author, and painter who once dated Jerry Garcia, lived in an Eichler, and still wants to ban the bomb

Sveilich writes with a flowing honesty and priceless observations that draw the reader in and never let go. I grew up in San Jose before beginning my music career. Some of my friends lived in Eichler homes. I could relate to so much of this engaging story. The music of that era stands as the soundtrack of our lives to this day and the author artfully weaves it into her own story. Cannot wait for the movie!

—Joe Sharino, Bay Area entertainer who opened for such acts as B.B. King, America, Chuck Berry, David Lindley, Emmy Lou Harris, The O'Jays, Charlie Daniels, The Drifters, and The Temptations

Sveilich lived in an innovative Eichler home saddled with parents stumbling forward to make sense at the pre-dawn of the digital and information age. Neither the author nor her parents were aware that their lives were at the epicenter of a metamorphosis of a new America they had no idea was coming.

This exploration of the reluctant reinvention of a family is compelling and speaks to all who grew up in the Sixties. It was a time of newness, exploration, discovery, and puzzlement. This mid-century modern tale speaks to Sveilich's "brave new world" that was unfolding with hidden thorns.

Reflections from a Glass House is a compelling version of an American experience that affects us all to this day. It's a powerful story that paints the era with a personal brush that's both compelling and heartfelt.

—Dennis Spear, publisher of N magazine and former PBS design director

Sveilich has a unique take on coming of age in the nuclear duck-and-cover era. Her memoir is a feast of hilarious and poignant slices of life and culture, served up fresh like mom's homemade meatloaf. The way the author draws the reader into her personal world, it's easy to imagine being a part of her family ... or perhaps a long lost sibling.

—Jim Soldi, called "the best guitarist in the business" by Johnny Cash, has played with Cash's live band as well as Ricky Skaggs, Kenny Loggins, and B.J. Thomas

Sveilich writes about a mysterious place, the Eichler. I remember them, being a Bay Area kid myself. The houses looked different—weird, in my eyes—and the kids seemed different, more worldly and wise. Every summer they held this groovy event called the Fairglen Art Festival, that I missed as a kid but attended as an adult. The author writes about the history of that event and reveals a backstory that few knew ... until now.

Reading Sveilich's story, I realize I missed a whole lot! Her memoir is a time capsule covering a period in history that may be unique to the Bay Area, but also transcends that uniqueness. I felt like an insider reading *Reflections from a Glass House*, and a bit of a voyeur. I lived the mayhem from the safety of my own couch. Thoroughly enjoyable read.

—Laurel Doud, author of This Body

What a great trip through an American slice of heaven I never even knew existed. You can taste the art and culture in this exquisite prose. Sveilich's memoir should be included as a standard U.S. history class in every high school.

—Todd Pyke, Guitarist, Instructor, Founder of Encinitas School of Music

I have friends and relatives in the Bay Area who still live in Eichlers. In 1992, while working as an architect, I did a remodel of an Eichler home, and I did my best to honor its integrity. *Reflections from a Glass House* brings back that feeling of wonder, naivety, and curiosity, when everything was in front of our generation. Sveilich captures that time capsule—our time capsule—perfectly and beautifully.

—Merle Axelrad, San Francisco-based architect and artist

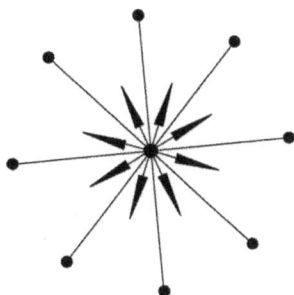

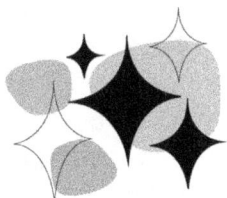

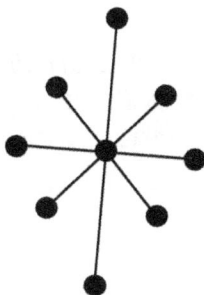

Acknowledgments

Memoirs are a mish-mosh of experiences and reflection. Sitting before me was a 10,000 piece jigsaw puzzle rattling around in a box. I needed a village to guide me after I dumped out all the jagged pieces.

I'm grateful to those who have assisted in making this book possible. They aided me in popping the proper pieces of the puzzle into place and ignoring the bits that didn't quite fit.

A personal note of appreciation to the early readers of this memoir for their support, frankness, and keen eyesight: *David Hardwick, Rich Ross, Charlotte Berney, Bob Goodman, David Watkins, Michael Schoenholtz, Steve Schlesinger, Jennifer Bradley, J.C. Wing, Chris Hassett, Sahar Abdulaziz, Rebecca Newlin, Laurie Henderson, Regan Karstrand, Jay Rudman, Richard Scopelli, Dave Blackburn, Joanne Conger,* and *Amanda Owens.* You have my deepest gratitude. A special thanks to *Dennis Spear, Jeannie King,* and *Danielle Smith-Boldt* for their mid-century modern design work and to *Glenn Smoak, Dennis Spear,* and *Brad Petersen* for their photographic restoration magic.

Dedication

This book is dedicated to the wonder, humor, and vivid memories of my parents, Joe and Blossom Sveilich, and to Pushka the wonder-cat.

Illustration: Jeannie King

Table of Contents

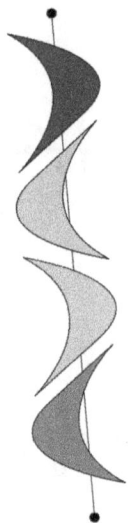

The past is the only dead thing that smells sweet.
—Poet Edward Thomas

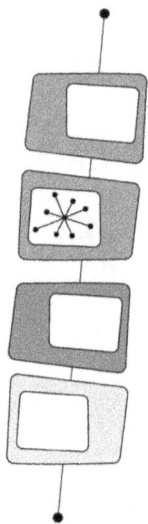

Prologue
Setting the Stage

I spent a good part of my early years saturated in angst. Worry was my primary skill, and I honed my craft daily. Luckily, the dangers of sinking in quicksand or contending with atomic bombs landing near our cherry trees in the backyard didn't turn out to be the big problems I assumed they would be.

My family of four was like one of those sets of *matryoshka* dolls, also known as Russian nesting dolls. Just as the wooden dolls decreased in size and were placed one inside another, so were our places in the family. My father, our resident in charge of comic relief, was born of Russian Jewish immigrants. He was the largest doll. Inside of him was my practical and chatty mother who sprang from Polish and Romanian parents. My brother, Harold, was next. Two years older than me, Harold was a mutt of DNA, with strands of Russian, Polish, Romanian—and traces of bologna sandwiches. I was the smallest doll with bony arms wrapped around a cat. Or perhaps Pushka, our house cat, could be the smallest doll housed inside me.

The reality is, we were raised by two wildly exuberant but distracted parents, their feet firmly planted in some strange mix of naiveté and irresponsibility still going on in their late twenties and well into their thirties and forties. They preferred to party rather than prepare meals for two offspring. They were not up to the task, but my father's quirky childlike nature and my mother's musical talent kept us entertained, even gleeful at times. I would toggle back and forth between feeling great affection for them to feeling great bewilderment.

When I was a teenager, I found out that my mother used to lock Harold in the apartment's coat closet during daytime hours because she couldn't deal with his bouncy energy and needs. Locked in the closet? It was like a wicked fairy tale from the Grimm brothers. My father would come home from work and holler, "Where's Harold? What the hell!" Then he'd release Harold from his cubbyhole cage in the hallway. My father would yell, but my mother saved face by hiding out behind a mask of pleasantness and a chatty persona. And she was beautiful. Nature had carefully constructed that mechanism to keep her in my dad's good graces.

I have often imagined my life as a play in the theater of the absurd. It's a play about a coddiwomple: a purposeful journey toward a vague destination. That obscure and ill-defined journey's end is adulthood. I have the lead role in this play.

If my existence could be transposed into script form—and taking into account the total history of stage and screen—who would fill the remaining cast? My father? That's easy. The part would go to Groucho Marx. He was equated to Groucho Marx so often that it's difficult to imagine anyone else in the role. There would need to be one slight prop modification, however. My father's curvaceous pipe would replace Groucho's stogie.

My mother's part would be more challenging to cast. Even though she looked a bit like Laura Petrie on *The Dick Van Dyke Show*, and certainly had the capris to fit the part, Carol Channing, with her too-wide mouth and ability to provide hours of blather, might be a better choice.

I'll be playing myself. The role of my brother? Dennis the Menace. Let's begin.

Summer 1962; The Willow Glen Neighborhood of San Jose, California; in a mid-century modern subdivision known as The Eichlers.

My father doesn't have a single worry in the world. He has a million of 'em. He's deep into it—pacing himself through the pre-vacation ritual of twisting oven knobs back and forth to make certain they are turned to the OFF position.

On, then off.

Off.

OFF!

He checks them a dozen times before moving into another room. He examines every corner of our home, making certain all the plugs are unplugged, lights are switched off, and the cat dish is not only filled, but overfilled. He checks not once, but a dozen times. Even Elvis doesn't touch up his pompadour this repetitiously.

Our days in New York are as distant as a train straining to be heard through the fog. It's now summer in Santa Clara Valley.

The warmth of the morning makes the scent of the rich soil rise even faster. There's no hint of the bits, bytes, or Silicon Valley chips that will arrive in a couple of decades. The pungent aroma makes us feel as though we are farmers, even though we are suburban pioneers plowing the streets with our behemoth Buicks and Plymouths.

We've been living in San Jose two years. My father's worry and restlessness is contagious. At age eight, I'm twitchy and fretful in a similar fashion. I worry, like him. For instance, what about our cat, Pushka? How will she know when we'll return home? Will she stop eating if someone else comes in to feed her? Will she become miserable and die? Will she miss us so much she'll want to hide in the thorny lantana bushes in the backyard and never come out?

I'm fidgeting in the back seat of our family car, a white Dodge Dart made gray with dust and grit, and not yet moving on the road. The valley heat makes the waiting tiresome. Restlessness and perspiration are setting in. I squirm in my seat, watching my father from the driveway as he eloquently demonstrates the art of worrying in its most pristine and Judaic form. It's a familiar scene and ceremony. I see his shadowy figure through the glass panel between the carport and atrium. The setting's all part of the dream of indoor/outdoor living in our Eichler home, a striking mid-century modern home in the Bay Area.

Three out of the four riders in our posse are settled in their respective saddles. My mother sits in the front seat and stares out the window, humming a few notes of an imaginary and nameless tune. Mom's humming feels incomplete, certainly not a finished product. Her fingers, sporting chipped pink nail polish, repose in patient prayer atop a suitcase-sized purse, her spirit seemingly filled with the sort of tolerance I'll never possess. She checks the contents of her bag. "Carol, did you bring the Wash 'n Dri? We're not going to be bathing for a while." We'll wipe our sweaty body parts, launder our sticky fingers, and cool our foreheads with soap-dampened Wash 'n Dri Towelettes. My mother has packed some stale Chex Party Mix and my father's blue and yellow can of Planters Peanuts. Three hours later, she'll ask, "Who wants to nosh?"

My brother, always on the verge of a taunt, is with me in the back seat. He's wedged between two overstuffed suitcases. We are usually separated by something massive to discourage him from teasing me. Barriers do little good. We laugh too loudly and too easily and fight too ferociously during these long car trips.

The car is becoming a searing kennel, where the cage door is a roll-down side window. The only escape from this brutal humidity is visual freedom. I stare at our patchy front lawn and the small shrubs planted in each corner of the yard. I fidget impatiently as I wait for my father to back our car out of the driveway. Let's go already!

It's been 45 minutes. My father is still in the house triple-checking. Check, check, check. He's moving out of the room where the cat bowls sit. Now he steps back in again ... just in case he forgot to see if they're filled properly. He's cleaning, wiping, correcting, and checking again. That's it! I jump out of the back seat and jiggle my legs, like drumsticks thrashing about in a Shake 'n Bake bag.

Our Dodge Dart is the base model with no radio and no air-conditioning, just roll-down windows operated by chrome cranks. Harold slinks out of the car for a moment and puts himself in a trance practicing tricks with his Duncan yo-yo. He disconnects from the car, the family, and the promise of an adventure. The yo-yo drags, then flies over his head and around the world, his world. "Did you see that? I got it to go from sleeping to cradle to around-the-world. Carol, did you see?" He jumps up and down. He's always jumping, running, twirling, anything but sitting.

I crawl back into the car and anticipate our overdue departure. But I just sit. It's stifling inside our hunk of baked metal. I swing my legs to the side. A geometric imprint remains on the bottom of my underweight thighs. I'll be the only one who notices the impressions that have chiseled themselves into the backs of my legs. I'll finger feel the braille texture every once in a while. I'll discreetly check my reflection in the glass window of whatever coffee shop we finally stop at to see if the imprints are still evident. As if reading my mind, Harold hollers, "Carol's got chicken legs!"

I watch my father's anxious silhouette move through the glass beyond our front door. He's trying to bring himself back to center, bouncing back and forth like one of those steel balls in Newton's cradle. He strikes a match and lights his ever-present S-curved pipe and draws in a lungful of smoke. The red embers glow brightly as he inhales. I can see their light, even from the back of the car. My mother shifts slightly to the left and looks towards the house. "Come on, Joe!" She's patient, but insistent. Standing in that doorway, my father is as imposing and enormous as the Jolly Green Giant, even though he stands only five feet eight inches tall.

It feels odd to call my father anything but "Dad," or, as I often call him, "Da-." I am too timid and terrified to form that three-letter word in my mouth. I can only manage to mumble two of the three letters. I am a piece of dust, a morsel of nothingness, an empty jar in his presence. He can't even see me sitting here. I'm convinced of it. "Da-? Uh ... Dad!" If I say it with two Ds, will you hear me? More importantly, will you see me? Not a chance. You'll walk right through me, as translucent and fleeting as smoke from your pipe.

My brother, the Yo-yo Master, has managed to crawl back into the car. He squirms and turns around to see what's going on in our 10-house cul-de-sac. He's an ever-twirling top, even in the confines of the back seat. Sweat forms on Harold's forehead. He's perspiring like Nixon at the presidential debate.

If I try with all my might, I can make my vision penetrate the facade of our house, the opaque glass that hides the atrium, and the walls inside. If I had those X-ray glasses sold on the back pages of comic books, I'd be able to see my father standing at the kitchen sink, dropping his pipe ashes into the basin and wondering what else needs to be turned off or on. Or turned on, then off again. None of us know what the correct number of times to check everything is except him. Check, check, check. Now? No. Check. My father's smoke sticks to his clothes and body, reminding me of the Peanuts character Pigpen and his puff of dust. My father often stops in mid-inhale, lips parted, seemingly distracted, his mind catapulting off to Planet Elsewhere. He's lost in thought, memory, worry, or just pausing a moment to take in his surroundings. I'm dreading the instant he climbs into the car. His pipe exhaust will trail his physical body by several cloudy seconds.

My mother begins to hum a made-up tune. For a car filled with music aficionados, it seems odd that there is no radio on these road trips. Music is the singular shared interest of this nuclear family of four—that and good deli. My mother is neither *miserable nor impatient. She is not in sweaty distress. But her offspring are. Harold's a sodden mess. And just look at me: I'm glistening. I'm Sonny Liston collapsed in the corner of the ring staring down Cassius Clay after the sixth round. I'm Cool Hand Luke spending the night in the box. Either let me out of here or let's get going! I need to feel the wind on my face through the rolled-down side window, even if it's only blowing sweltering air. If my father doesn't shuffle out of the house in the next two minutes, I will scream.*

He finally emerges from the Eichler and walks towards his family seated in the steamy car. He stops for a second, refills his pipe, gazes into infinity, then heads back to the house to check again.

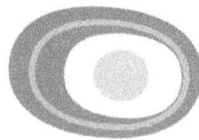

SECTION I:

Twisted Family Ties

Snowballs in Hell

The year was 1958 and winter was throwing a cold punch. After a wet sneeze of snow fell on Long Island, our driveway became indistinguishable from the yard and the slushy street. Everything was nestled under that weighty white blanket, and my parents desperately wanted to crawl out from under the miserable mess. Eventually, they packed up everything, including Harold and me, and journeyed to the West Coast, specifically Santa Clara Valley in California. But before then, snow and more snow was Long Island's whipped cream. You couldn't have an East Coast winter without the white stuff. Snowflakes danced and swirled at pedestrians' ankles like hungry house cats. The powdery flakes always felt magical, like something whooshed in from a fairy tale.

A blanket of goose bumps spread over the winter flesh of our limbs. It snowed like a son of a bitch in the winter, and my father shoveled it. And he said "son of a bitch" a lot when he did. He had to shovel, or he couldn't get his car out of the driveway. It was a ritual that was new to both him and to my mother. They grew up in small apartments in the city and took subways everywhere. Walking the city sidewalks was as necessary as breathing. New York City workers plowed their streets. But now, Dad was plowing our own driveway on Long Island in cookie-cutter suburbia. So much for fairy tales.

Above all else, everyone was cold. We could feel the change of seasons in our bones and outerwear. The leaves fell in the autumn, and there were no worries or decisions to make except where to jump into them to make the greatest mess and generate the most happiness. My father raked them into colossal piles that Harold and I would run and dive into with a lot of whoopin' and hollerin'. We all sweltered in the East Coast summer's heat and humidity. My parents had had enough of the elements, and my father wasn't keen on shoveling, raking, or sweating. But both parents were keen on adventure. They had their eyes on the prize, and although it seemed like there wasn't a snowball's chance in hell of getting out from under their weighty past, the prize was getting the hell out of the Big Apple.

For a long while, however—along with millions of people all over the globe, including Cole Porter and the incomparable Bobby Short—my parents loved New York. Perhaps because it was all they knew, my parents thrived in this dynamic city. My father was born and raised in Brooklyn. He met my mother at a downtown singles dance a few years after the war ended. They continued to dance, then married, and soon made their home in a one-room apartment in New York. They loved living in the city. They went to concerts. They saw The Weavers play Carnegie Hall. They protested in the streets. They applauded cool jazz. My father went to clubs for the music, while my mother, sipping a gin and tonic, was there for the vocalist belting out a jazz standard. Her long-held wish was to become a jazz singer. So my mother learned to sing and play every song she had ever heard in her life, but only in the key of C. She stopped singing when my brother came along a couple of years later. Before Harold arrived, my mother's friends in Queens, SoHo, and Greenwich Village were going to dances, bars, and parties, and my parents were living it up in the big city with music clubs, cocktails, and in summertime, the Catskills. When their friends started having babies and pushing strollers, my parents scratched their heads, looked at one another with uncertainty about what they were now going to agree to, and then decided to go along with the rest of the flock.

Ambrose Bierce once defined the word *sweater* as a "garment worn by child when its mother is feeling chilly." He must have known my mother. She always felt a draft. As a result, the entire lot of us had to change booths, chairs, rooms, or restaurants on a continual basis. And we were never to be seated near a fan, window, or door. If we were, my family of four would shuffle in unison to another restaurant table like a small army of ants with menus.

To avoid the horrors of cold moving air, my mother overdressed us for every kind of weather. In our snowsuits, we stood as wide as we were tall. We couldn't breathe, let alone move in a forward direction unless we fell face first into the icy piles of slush. We were enveloped so tightly—and under so many layers of sweaters, coats, mittens, and hats—that bending was not an option. This would be a theme for the rest of my life: my mother always making certain we were wrapped tighter than a wonton.

Beyond suffocating her children in outerwear, my mother always had to locate the person who gave us, or her, a cold or flu. Where did it come from? How did we get it? Whose germs had invaded her immune system ... or mine ... or whoever happened to be ill? It wasn't enough to be miserable with swollen, leaking mucous membranes. Someone out there had to take the blame for this ghastly crime and for my mother's having to buy a pallet of Kleenex. Someone or something had to be held responsible and dragged to Contagion Court for an unpleasant sentencing. Was the draft in the restaurant right over our particular table? Then it was the waiter's fault. Was it the breeze from the east? Blame the weatherman. Did I pick up some stubborn germ and carry it home from school on my blue binder? Call the principal's office. Who placed the exhaust vent too close to our booth? Get a court order and have the café owner arrested. Or the guy sitting next to my mother on the bus who was coughing and sneezing. Off with his head ... cold!

We shivered. We caught colds, and we caught the flu. We muddled through ear infections and strep throat. My mother was not keen on nursing children through scraped knees or sickness. She didn't know how. So our grandparents came by and wiped us down with a cool cloth when the fevers ran high.

My family lived in a series of New York City apartments when Harold and I were just babies. The living room window in one of these apartments looked out on a graveyard. In that dwelling, the dead of winter was literally the *dead* of winter. My parents didn't mind. They said it was nice and quiet. I fell down a long flight of stairs in Queens in my parents' walkup apartment. When I landed, even I was quiet. My mother was on the shared community phone in the hallway when I took that long tumble. She shrieked. She was certain I was gone, and she'd have one less mouth to feed. I lay there unfazed, pushed myself to my feet and walked away. No tears. No harm. No foul.

One rainy afternoon in our Long Island house, Harold and I were playing a game that he made up: he'd throw a ball, and I'd run and slide across the wooden floors after it. Genius! And it was fun. Then it wasn't. After one particularly long toss, I slid after the ball using my knees like a pair of roller skates and skimmed the wooden planks of our living room floor. My brother hollered, and I didn't know why. I looked down and saw that a foot-long, rather thick piece of wood had entered the front of my knee. Blood was pouring out like Hershey's chocolate syrup. Mom hollered as she lowered me on the top of the toilet seat and chanted, "I don't know what to do! I don't know what to do!" My father, whom I thought could solve every problem in the world, said he couldn't get it out safely as it was too long. Off we went to the hospital. I was quiet as I lay in the back seat. Quiet as a cemetery in Queens.

A blood-soaked bath towel hugged my leg while my parents exchanged hysterical and loud expletives in the front seat of Champion, a family vehicle shaped like an enormous black jelly bean on four wheels. We rushed down the road like an ambulance without a siren, just the screeches and moans coming from the front seat.

Emergency rooms are the last place anyone wants to be. You can tell because no one has a smile on their face or pep in their step. The flash and crisp curve of nurse's hats, white walls, and bright lights whirled around my head as they sat me on a gurney, made me lie back, and numbed my leg with an angry needle. I didn't feel them extract the long sliver of lumber from my right leg, but I could see a physician's needle and thread as I peered downward toward the lower end of my body. The surgeon must have gotten it out of my grandma's sewing kit, I thought. But this time the needle was larger and longer than expected, and I was the torn Raggedy Ann doll being stitched back together. I still have a long wide scar on my knee from all that commotion. It still looks like the train track that ran behind our Long Island home.

Everything Is Relative

My grandparents often came to visit us on Long Island. They were always happy to see us, and we were happy to be seen. I had two full sets of grandparents, both referred to as *Bubbie* and *Zaide*. In the Yiddish vernacular, all grandparents were referred to as Bubbie and Zaide. Jewish grandparents had a wide range of names to choose from, each of which came with its own history—and its own baggage. *Saba* and *Savta* were Hebrew, but I never heard my grandparents referred to with those names. In my family, there was Bubbie and there was Zaide, or the more familiar Grandma and Grandpa. But Bubbie and Zaide are the most traditional names for an Ashkenazi Jew's grandparents and evoked a sort of old-world vibe. Oh yes, we were Ashkenazim. It sounded like an act introduced on the old *Ed Sullivan Show.* "Ladies and Gentlemen, presenting the Ashkenazi Jews!"

The ethnicity of *Ashkenazi* originated in medieval Germany, but the term now refers in broader terms to Jews from Central and Eastern Europe. Eventually, the majority of Ashkenazi Jews relocated to the Polish Commonwealth (today's Poland, Lithuania, Latvia, Ukraine, and Belarus). I didn't learn any of this from my relatives. I learned it from a maroon-colored hardbound edition of *Encyclopedia Britannica* borrowed from a neighbor.

Max and Anna were my father's parents. For decades, they occupied the same cramped one-bedroom apartment in a merciless section of Brooklyn. The living room with high-gloss turquoise walls gave off an odd sheen that reflected the minimal light that shone through their two small living room windows. The apartment consisted of a doll-sized kitchen, one bedroom and bathroom, and a small living room always well stocked with ribbon candies displayed in an ornate glass dish. No one had the *chutzpah* to reach for a piece or come in close enough to rearrange the order. Those ribbon candies were stuck together for all eternity and had likely been gathering dust since WWI.

In another corner of the room sat a black canister with colorful images of hard candies that reminded me of meteors flying through space as black as licorice. That distinctive tin, with a sheen like Aladdin's lamp, held not wishes, but pastel-colored hard candies rolled in snowy sugar. It was the canister, not its contents, that caught my eye.

During their childhood, my father and his sister, Evie, would share the living room of this same apartment on Legion Street. The living room was their bedroom, and two cots were their beds at night. The living room was proportioned like a pen for raising veal, where creatures butted shoulders and stumbled past each other. But I always looked forward to going to Brooklyn and spending hours in their corral.

The crowded apartment buildings in Brooklyn looked like a bunch of crisscrossed radiators. A steady stream of hooligans lurked on the walkway outside my grandparents' living room window. The scent of urine forever embedded in bricks and asphalt was one of the telltale aromas of an impoverished neighborhood. But inside it was warm and smelled of carrots and celery treading in chicken broth. Grandma Anna would go to the living room hutch and pull out a handful of colorful satin ribbons. I would marvel at the different colors and play with those thin shiny tails of cloth all afternoon. Those bright ribbons were state-of-the-art playground equipment, at least to me. I still remember the excitement of streaming them through my small sausage fingers. It would start me giggling, then springing around my grandparents' small living room like a Slinky. Their small space magically morphed into a festive carnival with streamers. No toys. No Slinky. No dolls. No board games. Just ribbons, falling through five-year-old fingers for hours on end.

Grandma Anna had a Ph.D. in misery. She would wring her hands in that stereotypical Jewish grandmother manner, then sigh and display a straight-faced expression of pain like every day was worse than the last. Her wrist would bend and one hand or the other would be thrown in a quick downward motion, accompanied by "eh" or "oy" with each movement. Heavy sighs were in her job description. As soon as my father was able to do so, he fled from his mother's clenched hands, her pleas to come home, the wearisome worry, and the constant insistence on multiple layers of heavy clothing. First, he ran to the U.S. Army for four years and served on active duty on the ground during World War II. Then he ran to the state of marriage—and eventually to the opposite coast.

As much as my father liked to tell stories about things that had happened to him, people he had met, and situations he had witnessed, he never told tales about his parents or his childhood.

I learned more from my aunt—his sister—than from anything my father shared. He went to Hebrew school and was raised on the downtrodden streets of Brooklyn, but it's as if he had a massive chalkboard eraser that took out all the details, characters, trials, and joys of his boyhood and banged them against the nearest wall to scatter the chalk dust.

My father's father, a Captain Kangaroo look-alike, was no one you would want to run from. Max was adventurous, with a mischievous side that emerged when he was around Harold and me. Max had worked as a shipping clerk in a men's suit factory. The job didn't bring in much income, but it was steady. When my father bought our first house on Long Island, Grandpa Max was flabbergasted. "You each have your own room? And a yard too?" He could not have imagined such a life for his own young family, who were crammed into that Brooklyn apartment so tightly there was no place for an apple to fall.

One afternoon, when I was four or five, and when no one else was around, Grandpa Max sat me in the driver's seat behind the wheel of our family car, a black Studebaker Champion. There were no seatbelts or kid's car seats to restrain me. We powered down the road together with me in the driver's seat and his foot tapping on and off the pedal. Accelerate. Brake. Accelerate. And ... brake! I'm sure it was illegal in most states, but at the end of the 1950s it was our pretend-time and our own personal amusement park ride. There was an invisible protective bubble around our car and around our world. Nothing could go wrong.

We resided in Glen Head on Long Island, a safe haven several attitude adjustments away from the frantic flutter of New York City. It was a bedroom community of red brick and mortar, with a sprinkling of stores and small cafés. A sparkling green oasis splattered with holes in the ground sat directly across the street from our house. This sizable golf course contained acres of perfectly tended and tenderly manicured grass. The function of this vast plot of land was lost on my family. My father couldn't swing a nine-iron if it was his only means of defense against a mugger diving for his wallet. But those rolling hills outside our living room window were a playground of unimaginable beauty. They were a brilliant green in the summer months and sparkling Disney-like wintry white during the season of Santa and menorahs. I grew up believing golf courses were specifically created and designed for snowsuits and sledding.

Our Long Island home was Mr. Toad's Wild Ride on LSD. The décor was perfectly tolerable, but only if you happened to be Ray Charles or Stevie Wonder. Each room had a distinct and frightening color palette and wallpaper pattern featuring suspended objects with their own vertigo-provoking effect. Fast-moving gold geometric lines and designs drag-raced up and down the living room walls; records and dancing figures jitterbugged across an upbeat red background in the family room; and cowboys and Indians galloped over my brother's bedroom walls. The kitchen had a gray and red brick pattern with kettles and kitchen tools haphazardly floating through space. It must have been the inspiration for the opening sequence of Rod Serling's *The Twilight Zone*. The designs were so chaotic and distracting; I don't know how we kept our dinners down.

On Long Island, the fireflies would sparkle around my backyard swing set at night while I pumped myself higher and higher, trying to reach the stars, listening to the distant chords my mother's fingers produced as she played "The Lady Is a Tramp" and "Sentimental Journey" on our upright piano.

On the second level of our home, walls awash in pink wallpaper supported watercolor ballerinas who danced across my bedroom. I'd stare at each figure and marvel at its costume and grace. With the snow drifting outside the bedroom window, or as the sun tried to break in burglar-style, I'd lie in bed fingering the wallpaper and picturing myself as a dancer. Dancing signified freedom, beauty, and storytelling. I was going to be a ballerina. I was going to twirl, coil, and leap in a fluffy pink tutu. My future was an empty stage. It needed a pink figure prancing and pirouetting across it, someone like the willowy, womanly spirit in a Jules Feiffer cartoon. I would dance to spring, to American optimism, and against the dreaded realities of recession, deficits, poverty, racism, and sexism, all in a form-fitted leotard and overstretched tights that gathered at the knees. I would have the discipline and delicacy of a waifish bun-headed ballerina. Others would applaud my dance and call it precise, flawless, moving. More than that, they would watch me. I would be visible. I would be noticed in my Capezio tights. I would retire to my pink bedroom after each performance. Pink everything. Pink rug, pink dresser, pink socks. Pink, pink, pink.

My father was a confounding mix of sweet and sour. He liked precision, but he adored the anarchy of jazz and thrived on a steady diet of Hershey's Mr. Goodbar and Nestlé Crunch. We rarely saw him in those early years. In fact, I can't remember one frame of memory in New York that featured my father's presence. It took him ten years of night school at Cooper Union to get his drafting degree while working at Lily Tulip Cup Company. He was the first in his family to earn a degree, and the first to eventually break away from New York State.

In the morning, my father would hop the train that ran directly behind the back fence of our Long Island home. The tracks would take him straight to his drafting table, where he'd sit in a sizable room filled with triangles, number two pencils, a set of French curves, one clear plastic ruler, dozens of other designers, and endless mugs of coffee. Then he would ride the subway straight from work to night school to fine-tune his drafting skills and become a design engineer using the GI bill.

We start out with a large bucket of time. I have always thought of time like the view out the window of a moving train. When you look directly out the window, everything speeds by in a softened blur. But look back at what you've passed, and the world seems to slow down. You can make out all the details that you easily missed before. Look too far ahead, and you can't see what's in front of you.

I don't remember seeing either parent for more than a minute here or there before our family moved to the West Coast. My father was busy building his career and attending night classes, and my mother was MIA (Mom's Inevitably Absent). She was not one to touch or be touched and hadn't had any experience or interest in burping, feeding, or raising blanket-wrapped bellowing babies. Instead, she hired an old woman she referred to as "grandma-the-nurse" to care for us. In those days, even if you were just scraping by on a low income, such a person could be employed at an affordable rate. Neither a nurse nor our grandmother, she nevertheless changed our diapers, fed us baby gruel, and slapped our infant backs to encourage belching.

My own grandparents, Max and Anna, would often stay at our house. They slept in the living room's pull-out sofa bed, which was fully equipped with a mattress stuffed with rock candy. But to my grandparents, who were used to sleeping on mattresses the thickness of a potato chip, it was a lofty retreat. In the morning, we'd jump into bed with them for a tickle tournament until breakfast was served.

Grandma Anna would tuck me in at night and sing a song while dressed in one of her oversized cotton housecoats. As she shuffled across the floorboards, she seemed like a house tented for termites. My mother would soon be wearing similar unflattering frocks but would refer to them as dusters. What is a housecoat but a cross between a bathrobe and daywear? It states quite clearly, "I don't care enough to get fully dressed today because I'm staying inside with soap operas and a pound of Lay's potato chips."

I'm not certain if Grandma Anna made up the song or if it was some traditional Russian nursery rhyme, but I have never heard it since. She'd plunk her palms down at the edge of my mattress, push up and down in some rhythmic rocking ritual on my single bed, and sing in tortured a cappella:

"Aww aww, baby,
Momma is a lady.
Daddy is a gentleman.
All fall down!"

She'd repeat the nonsensical refrain over and over until I was fully hypnotized and finally asleep. I didn't know what it meant then, and I don't know what it means now. But that up and down pushing motion was like the rocking of a cradle, even though my particular cradle was a bed as hard as a stale *hamantaschen* prune pastry. It would barely move. But the monotone and repetitive verse of that ludicrous lullaby lured me to sleep. I drifted off, unafraid. I was being tended to. Someone was watching over me and keeping me safe. It was Grandma Anna from Russia with a bonnet of coarse wavy red hair, soft smile, laughing eyes. Anna and Max were from Minsk. I was from Long Island. But life in New York was as permanent as the pile of freshly raked leaves waiting for the wind.

Soon, we wouldn't have Grandma Anna or Grandpa Max around to engage us in a tickle fight or rock us into slumber. We'd scatter apart as we stepped on a mammoth hunk of metal that streamed across the sky from the right to the left coast. Soon, I'd be rocking myself to sleep in a different and faraway state, remembering that simple "Aww aww, baby" tune and cinching it around my shoulders like a soft blanket. And in a New York minute, I'd discover that we're never too old for a lullaby. In fact, we require them more frequently as the years march on.

Nuts roll downhill, so the saying goes, and that's why Florida is so full of them. Many of them rolled down the coast from New York. But Floridians would argue that this maxim is meant to explain the population of California. We'll settle that debate in a bit, but I can tell you that those nuts started to rattle around in our first house on Glen Cove Avenue, Long Island. If you shook my family tree, you could watch the nuts fall out and blanket the ground below.

Of all the places we lived on the East Coast, I can only tease memories out of that one home on Long Island. It sat at the end of a row of identical houses, lined up like ceremonial guards from one end of the block to the other. Before Long Island, my family played house in a number of cramped and forgettable apartments in and around the Big Apple. But that house on Glen Cove Avenue held us steady for twenty-four months. And steadiness was not my family's strong suit.

Pansies popped up all over that expansive yard. Perhaps it only felt expansive, as I was so small. Those fanciful purple and yellow faces quickly became my favorite flower. Their mournful expression shifted slightly with each burst of wind to their petal-wings. My father, who was always taking photographs, took several frames of two bright yellow and purple pansies that grew beneath a woody sugar maple tree outside the front door. He turned them into Kodachrome slides. Those pictures in a carousel have remained filed in the back of my memory all these years. I can still see them as clearly as when they were projected on the fraying screen propped up in our living room. They were not just two flowers with mustached faces that looked like Groucho Marx, but two delicate kindred spirits huddled together in the elements, boogying with each breeze.

Mama's Family

My mother's parents, Murray and Mae, were the polar opposites of one another. Grandpa Murray, a Polish immigrant, with his broad Charlton Heston physique, tall stature, and massive hands, was a world-class hugger and cheek schmusher. He had words of affection for everyone, and they were often in Yiddish. He was always fussing and *kvelling* over us. "Oy, look at the *punim* on that one!" he'd say as he grabbed our cheeks between his thumb and first finger and shook them until the skin would redden. That flesh would remain flushed for half an hour. Then he would disappear into the living room, door slightly ajar so that we could watch him pacing back and forth, back and forth. He was talking in some strange Jewish gibberish, yelling at the top of his lungs, and tossing his fist to the ceiling as if he were angry at God and giving him what for ... but I never knew what for. Then he'd return to our company with two languages we could finally understand: English and hugging.

Mae and Murray made their home in a basement apartment in the Bronx. Their living quarters smelled of mothballs, Downy fabric softener, cigar smoke, and baked goods. *Holishkes* (stuffed cabbage), *tzimmes* (stewed carrots, sweet potatoes, and prunes), *knishes* (potato and flour dumplings), and *kasha varnishkes* (a buckwheat groat mixed with bow-tie noodles and loaded with slow-cooked onions and quarts of chicken fat) were always baking in the oven. Ashkenazi Jews were not much for health food.

To get to my grandparent's apartment, we'd step off the lobby's cool marble flooring into a wobbly elevator and press B for basement. We felt our stomachs drop up, not down, as the floor beneath our feet took on a mind and destination of its own. We'd brace ourselves against the handrail as the floor shook under our feet and dropped us to what felt like the bottom of the world.

Grandpa Murray was an Orthodox Jew. He called my mother, his only child, *mamaleh*, meaning little mother. Their house had dust-magnet *tchotchkes* scattered throughout, and the walls were strewn with gaudy oil paintings of fruit baskets that glistened like they were marinated in olive oil. Dogs playing poker would have fit right in. These unnerving artworks were displayed between the hard-cushioned, floral-print couch and the forest green doilied upholstered chair. Colorful perfume bottles huddled together on a tray in their bedroom. For all these modest people didn't have, they had a plentiful array of unnecessary belongings that didn't belong.

The Yiddish word *babushka* is sometimes used to describe a crazy lady who has been around forever and who chases people with a stick … or a rolling pin … or a massive meat cleaver. To some, she is known as "grandma." To us, it *was* our grandma. Mae Grabowitz, my mother's Romanian mother, was a substantial woman, nearly breaking the scale at over 300 pounds. She was built like a delicatessen case with cankles.

Grandma Mae always wore a sour expression on her face. It was a face cursed with jiggling jowls, a downturned mouth, and a protruding bulldoggish underbite. Her eyes looked like they had plowed one too many fields and were ready for a nap. She was a perpetually annoyed drill sergeant, and she hovered around us like an unfriendly ghost. Whenever she'd come to our house on Long Island, my brother and I would flee the fearsome presence by running under the closest table or locking ourselves in the coat closet. Her tongue was sharper than a deli meat slicer, and her disapproving voice could summon Satan. Neither a hugger nor a touchy-feely type, Grandma Mae *always* seemed irritated. We didn't know why. We only knew she was very scary.

In the summertime, Harold and I would run outside with a bottle of bubble juice in one hand and a wand in the other. We would try to blow the biggest bubble ever. If one of us had success, and a massive bubble emerged from our bubble wand, we'd yell out, "Look! It's Grandma Mae!" We would never do this in her presence, of course. It was not mean-spirited. Just kids having fun and making light of things that frightened them. She terrified us. What she lacked in affection, however, she made up for in delicious, freshly prepared chopped liver and onions smeared on a matzo cracker.

My mother didn't inherit the cooking gene, even though her mother cooked throughout the day, every day. Our kitchen was devoid of the usual clank of pots 'n' pans and food perfume. But Grandma Mae was always at one with her kitchen table, like Itzhak Perlman with his Stradivarius. She did nothing but cook and yell at my grandfather in a vocal tone akin to a tormented violin.

Her wide buttocks filled the entire seat cushion at the kitchen table from early morning until suppertime as she'd conduct her dinner symphony, with her peel, cut, and core movements.

My mother's parents fought incessantly throughout her childhood. Maybe Grandpa Murray had too much time off from work. Maybe Grandma Mae had too little patience. But to my mother the holy state of matrimony seemed to be two people living together in too little space, arguing about everything, and asking one another what they wanted to eat for supper until one of them died. My mother would often run to her friend Joyce's house to get away from the frequent and foul exchanges between her mother and father. Joyce lived a short distance away in a walkup in the Bronx. In many ways, she took my mother, an only child, under her big sister wing.

I always hoped cooking was Grandma Mae's JOY, like the famous cookbook title, but I never saw any cheerfulness or serenity on her sourpuss puss. She was so enormous that she couldn't stand at the kitchen counter for long. She'd remain seated on that plastic-covered red kitchen chair with her kitchen utensils. Like a seasoned drummer ready to play her instruments, she was the master of the butcher knife and soup ladle. While her husband would pace back and forth in the next room, mumbling in Yiddish, shaking his fist at God, throwing kisses to his Hebrew books, and prattling on with the Lord, my grandmother would be mumbling and mixing it up with the peeled potatoes, brined poultry, and celery stalks.

Their apartment housed a noisy radiator that heated the entire living space. This obtrusive piece of metal sat in the living room and often sounded like a gassy relative making intermittent body noises. There was no refrigerator in their musty basement apartment, so Grandma Mae would go to the meat market and grocery store every day and buy fresh produce and poultry. Outside the living room window of that damp apartment was a wide alley where neighbors would drape their laundry from ropes and pull them back and forth. Even in wicked weather, garments were strung like colorful Christmas lights. A girl with red pigtails used to bounce a ball along the alleyway. I wanted to go outside and play with her, this potential new pal who was a doppelgänger for Pippi Longstocking, but I was stuck inside with the scent of Grandma Mae's chicken stock marinating the air like a room freshener and Grandpa Murray squishin' in my left cheek until it hurt from all the lovin'.

My grandparents never went to the dentist. They seldom went to a doctor. Not only was there no insurance, there also was no money. Soon, there were no teeth. My grandfather worked a small part of the year as a furrier, dealing in the acquisition and sale of animal fur. This makes me cringe more than a little, as I'm an animal activist. But in the Forties and Fifties, fur coats were a hot item. Think Mae West, Marilyn Monroe, and Claudette Colbert, who accepted an Academy Award from Shirley Temple with a white fur coat draped on her arm like a sleepy Persian cat. In the early Fifties, fashionable women would wear animal skins around their necks like a scarf. Quite often the head and paws of the animal were retained for decoration. But the fur markets hit a downward spiral in the early Forties, mostly due to World War II, when the industry suffered a shortage of equipment and material. Although the business provided jobs, my grandfather worked only a few months during any given year, and his occupation didn't pay much when it did pay. As a result, my mother's family existed in near-poverty.

Raised in her parents' tiny apartment, home came to represent my mother's prison cell. She always had a "run away from home" streak. I didn't inherit that. I always wanted to stay put. I was the *yin* to my mother's *yang*, the introvert to her extrovert. Home remains everything to me. According to the astrological charts and traits, late June babies like me have a home-loving nature, appreciate the nest, and are continually fluffing and feathering its contents. It keeps us grounded and makes us feel safe. Astrological Cancers consider their home a necessary retreat and need order and calm to reign and rule inside its walls so they can recharge their inner battery after a hectic day. But unlike me, my mother was a Pisces and a woman of the outside world, not the indoor jail. To my mother, home was not where the heart was. It was where the shackles were. She flourished on the sidewalks of the city. She loved being in crowds, deeply embedded in the hustle and bustle of urban living and thumbing through clearance racks with hoards of other bargain seekers.

Although my mother grew up on delicious home-cooked meals, my brother and I grew up on TV dinners and chicken pot pies. Sometimes there was a can of SpaghettiOs with round noodles swimming around in a watery tomato base. I don't remember a dinner that wasn't canned or heated from a frozen state, except liver and onions and an occasional pot roast that smelled divine. My mother also whipped up a mean chopped liver. She would use shallow, splintery wooden bowls with built-in bacteria along with her metal chopper tool with a wooden handle to chop-chop-chop. Maybe she was chopping out her angst about having to be in the kitchen. It was her least favorite room in any place we lived.

Chopped liver has come to mean second best ("What am I, chopped liver?"), but it originally meant to express a feeling of being overlooked, as in "side dish." As far as I was concerned, this appetizer should have won first prize as a main course. New York Jews used chicken fat to moisturize their concoction of chopped liver. In fact, when we lived on Long Island, we'd scoop chicken fat out of a thick glass jar and spread it on bread. It was pale yellow and tasted like ... well ... fat. My grandparents used to spread chicken fat on matzo crackers. If they could see my radically healthy diet plan now, they would scratch their heads, hunch their shoulders, wave one hand in a downward motion, mutter "eh," and leave the room.

Gefilte fish often sat in an unopened jar in our kitchen cabinet. It had a peculiar pale hue and consisted of an irregular blob. It looked like a contained brain that had been sitting too long on the shelf. But I happened to find gefilte fish tasty and not at all fishy, despite its dreadful appearance. Think fish meatballs. It beat TV dinners and pot pies housed in aluminum.

Let's Get Going

My parents were skilled escape artists. Although they had a close-knit extended family on the East Coast, a city full of synagogues, hot pretzels, and Italian lemon ices in the small squishy cups, my mother and father wanted out. They wanted a fresh start; a new landscape; kinder, milder weather patterns; a different diet from a platter full of salami and pastrami. Man cannot live by deli alone. They longed for weather conditions that were partly optimistic, with a chance of accomplishment as opposed to shoveling snow and cursing at the bitter cold of a New York blizzard. My father was Houdini, and he was about to perform the biggest trick of his life. One minute we were snuggled up in our warm beds on Long Island. Then, without warning, we were boarding a plane for the West Coast.

I wasn't used to leaving people. But when we left New York, I left my grandparents in Brooklyn and the other set of grandparents in the Bronx. I don't remember if I said goodbye or waved from the car thinking I'd return shortly. When you're six, you don't have an accurate grasp of time. When you're sixty you still don't, but you want more of it. More, more, more, like it's some rich dessert topped with fresh whipped cream that you can't get enough of on your spoon.

I rarely saw them again. My grandparents were chained like snow tires to the streets of New York while we were flying off to the West Coast on steel wings with in-flight magazines and complimentary peanuts. In 1960, passengers dressed up to fly, not like today, where everyone's wearing baggy shorts and sandals. Air travel was an occasion, a privilege, and anything but routine. We landed in San Jose and stayed downtown for the first few nights in the De Anza Hotel. The moving van was on its way with all our furniture, clothing, and jarred deli. We had landed on fresh terrain and were awaiting a new house and new employer for my father. There wasn't a Jewish temple or overprotective relative in sight. My restless parents loved change and nonstop adventures. Why they thought they'd find it in a sleepy suburb on the West Coast, I don't know. But guess what? They did. My father's spirit was larger than life and needed a new landscape. New York was old and gray. California was fresh and green. My father muttered a phrase I would hear again and again throughout my life: Let's get going! And so we did.

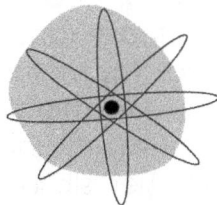

How the West Was Fun

Flight of the Russian Dolls

My mother's only childhood friend in the Bronx was Joyce. They were inseparable, and both had a lackadaisical, matter-of-fact demeanor and sluggish pace that must have sprung from growing up in the Bronx. Otherwise, I couldn't fathom why both women moved through the world with such a lethargic energy and stride. There must have been something in the water near Fordham Road.

Since Joyce was slightly older than my mother, she became a big sister of sorts. Joyce was a virtuoso at big-sistering. She had loads of little brothers and sisters packed into her small apartment. In contrast, my mother was an only child. Her family of three lived in that small one-bedroom basement apartment. There was no getaway except through the escape hatch into the alleyway and onto Fordham Road, straight to Joyce's apartment. My mother ran there on a daily basis, just as I would run off from my home when I was a teen. I couldn't manage my parents' loud battles either.

If my mother's house of discontent was one side of the coin, Joyce's home and her extended family were the other. Joyce's mother was the Jewish equivalent of Julia Child; bold in expression, vivacious, and bosomy, all neatly held together behind a gingham apron. At Joyce's bustling apartment, my mother found an environment where she was always welcomed with open arms and a plate of steamed knishes fresh from the oven. My mother never left those familiar arms. Their friendship would span a lifetime. In fact, my mother would eventually grant me her friend's name as my own middle name: Carol Joyce.

Every waking moment of my mother's childhood was spent at Joyce's apartment with her siblings, cousins, nieces, and nephews. There she felt grounded and alive. It was such a grand family and vibrant space, and missing the dreaded animosity of my mother's apartment. But beyond being a big sister stand-in for my mother, Joyce was the California Whisperer. When Joyce decided to leave New York for the California coast, my mother was eventually pulled into her slipstream. My mother still needed a big sister beside her.

Joyce was also the Eichler Whisperer. If it weren't for Joyce and husband Chuck locating a section of peculiar homes in Palo Alto called The Eichlers, we never would have found ours. And our new home would become much more than a structure. It would soon become akin to a protective family member. Joyce wasn't working for the Chamber of Commerce, but she would place frequent long-distance calls and make sales presentations to my mother reporting on the glories of California. She urged my parents to get away from the East Coast snow and cold and take a leap of faith westward.

Joyce had met a wonderful and highly creative artist, Chuck, while looking for a job in Los Angeles. She gobbled him right up. They were best of chums and perfect lovers all rolled into one. I've held up every tender relationship next to Joyce and Chuck's perfect union. They were young married comrades soon raising their own brood of three children in a warm, nurturing home, complete with frequent stolen kisses collected in the kitchen. They teased one another and discussed world events. They were romantic and sarcastic and connected. They seemed to have mastered the fine art of compromise and continual care. They had it all. Chuck and Joyce would land in Palo Alto, California, and remain there for the rest of their days.

"Tell Joe to find a job out here, then move to Palo Alto. It's paradise," Joyce urged. My mother nudged my father to look for a job in Santa Clara Valley. It was probably more like a shove. He flew out for an interview at Food Machinery Corporation (FMC) and was hired immediately as a draftsman. But where would we live? By the time he got out to California, the Palo Alto mid-century modern housing development that was close to where Joyce was living, had sold every home.

"Joe Eichler has built a subdivision over in San Jose," suggested Joyce. "It's called Willow Glen. Check them out. The houses are smaller, but affordable."

My father, with his usual bravado, drove over, saw a rough drawing of our Eichler home, and purchased it sight unseen. Before we knew it, he was moving us, lock, stock, Harold, and

Carol to San Jose in the summer of 1960. If it hadn't been for Joyce, the daring explorer scouting out these special homes, we never would have heard of The Eichlers, certainly not on Long Island.

Everything about Joyce said Mother Earth. She was a big-boned gal with thick, short brunette hair cursed with untamed waves, like my own mop of tangled hair. Her lips were full and her eyelids were heavy, like my mother's lids. Did everyone who originated from the Bronx appear half asleep at all times? Joyce had an embrace like a boa constrictor and open hands as welcoming as a Thanksgiving Day platter. She would squeeze the love right out of you or into you. Joyce moved leisurely and assuredly through her world with a knowing and peaceful dignity.

Joyce's husband, Chuck, worked in advertising and graphic design in San Francisco. He was the one who created, among many other designs, the original Swensen's Ice Cream logo and characters for the sugary Funny Face drinks, a cooler beverage than Kool-Aid. They were simple, but they crowned Chuck with a celebrity status, at least in my book. Those little packets of artificially colored, unnaturally flavored powder sweetened with calcium cyclamate stared out at us from the pantry shelf. Calcium cyclamate was later banned in the United States and replaced with saccharin. Eventually the drinks were offered unsweetened.

Chuck had a doughy face and a bulbous nose, two stocky animated hands, and a big heart. His tummy was always a bit rounded and soft, like the raw contents of Pillsbury Crescent Rolls after the container had been banged against the edge of the kitchen counter. Joyce kept him well fed. His head was oversized with unruly taupe-colored hair, and a bald spot on the back of his crown was hidden from view, especially if you were under four feet tall.

To me, Joyce and Chuck reigned as king and queen, with the royal secret of happy coupling. They celebrated Jewish traditions and put great importance on family life, always lighting candles, shoveling home-cooked meals into their family's mouths, and passing the gravy. They adored one another and were constantly hugging or holding hands. It was a sight for this young girl's sore eyes and a treat to witness such expressions of adoration. They shot each other knowing looks whenever they were together. Joyce would send a joking insult in Chuck's direction or make a sardonic remark about his baggy beige clown pants or his unkempt hair, and they would smile at one another, knowing that they would never hurt each other's feelings or damage the other's heart, ever. And they never did.

Joyce often wore muumuus with giant red and gold flowers and matching bold beaded necklaces. Big-boned gals did that to camouflage the consequences of too many stolen baked goods. I wanted to hide under that muumuu and never go home. I wanted to stay with Joyce and Chuck. I wanted them to adopt me. I wanted to live in their home with their family. Terms of endearment—such as darling, honey, and sweetheart—bounced off their wooden and glass walls. From age six through eighteen, I held them up as the ideal of romantic, ever-lasting love. I wanted what they were having. They made me want to get married. My parents, in contrast, made me want to divorce both of them and run away from home.

My family spent every Thanksgiving with Joyce's family of five. My father would bring home a free turkey from FMC, and we would all enjoy turkey and fixings—the adults seated at the dining table and the kids at the separate children's table, which was always an unsteady card table with one leg shorter than the rest.

Joyce had three children by the time we moved out to San Jose. Larry was two years ahead of me and my brother's age, Elayna was a year older than me, and Theresa was too young to play with unless we were forced to. We'd spend weekends at their house, or they would visit ours for a day. We passed the time hunkered down in our secret club. It was located in a makeshift tent in the front yard, fashioned with a stick and our own bed blankets or crumpled sheets from the linen closet. If the rain was coming down outside, we would shuffle the tent to a bedroom or vacant corner of the house. Our clubhouse tent would have a special secret word for entrance, or sometimes two words: STINKY FEET or GET LOST. Other times we'd jump up and down on the bed, intoxicated by the glee that comes from doing something you're not supposed to do. Joyce and Chuck's kids would visit our house for a few hours at a time, but we were often at their home for a weekend or a week, playing in their massive playroom, enjoying the toys we'd never have at our house, and making believe we were Gidget or Godzilla. Sometimes we'd play doctor with Larry's kid-sized doctor bag with colorful candies for medicine or mosey around the streets like we owned the neighborhood, which of course we did.

With Larry and Elayna at the "kid's table" during Thanksgiving. (From left to right, me, Harold, Larry and Elayna with the overbite that I coveted.)

I was mesmerized by the many magazines about monsters, science fiction, and horror films scattered around their enormous play area. Larry had an annual subscription to several monster magazines. He was usually paired off with Harold while I was paired off with Elayna, but I shared Larry's love of creatures from other worlds and times. Joyce's family had the means to spoil their kids rotten with every game, mask, and latest toy store gizmo. Our house had an atrium, but their home had a spacious area carved into the home and devoted to kids only. It was designated "the playroom." When Harold and I would visit, it was like having our ticket punched at the Disneyland entrance gate.

After spending time with Joyce and Chuck, I began to notice something rather curious. They genuinely liked their own children. They enjoyed having a *home*, a shared space where all commingled and cuddled. Joyce and Chuck would playfully chase their kids around the house, hold them close, quiet their cries, answer their questions, and acknowledge their presence. What strange planet was this?

Chuck had built a children's play area in the backyard for the three kids, but it wasn't just any play area. It had a stream that ran beneath a curved bridge, along with ropes, swings, and slides, all constructed from cool steel and long beams of lumber.

Each metal shape or piece of timber was painted in bright blue, red, orange, or yellow. A pathway ran behind their property that carried us over and through hills to a nearby shopping center, and there were vast open spaces across the street from their house. It felt like a fairy tale setting. The early days of Menlo Park near Palo Alto were paradise. Our modest Eichler didn't compare to their sprawling structure and half-acre backyard, but we didn't mind, as long as we could visit as often as possible.

One day when I was back in my Eichler home, I picked up one of the two telephones in our house and heard Joyce on the other end of the phone. She was talking to my father. Oops. Should I hang up now? Before I could, I heard her lecturing him about trying to be a better father, curtailing his angry outbursts, and having some patience. "After all, they're just kids." I was stunned to be listening to such an adult conversation. I quietly and carefully placed the mouthpiece of the phone back on the hook. Was I supposed to hear Joyce lecturing my father about parenting? Was she mad at him? Was he in trouble? I wish I had hung on the line a bit longer to find out.

* ⚛ *

My father's job at FMC was designing machinery that separated this from that: pits from fruit; stems from the produce portion of the food; and corn from the ear. He would later be reassigned and retitled "design engineer," but early on he was a draftsman among many other draftsmen who would be recruited to create machinery to help separate, process, and package food.

In the twenty-year period my father was employed by FMC, he would work on everything from broccoli machines, milk machines, desalinization plants (he got old beer barrels from a junkyard in Oakland to use on this project), an automobile alignment machine, and military bullets. He would meet author Ken Kesey while on a business trip in Oregon and assist him with a massive irrigation system on his property. In addition to designing a complex irrigation apparatus, my father's claim to fame was developing a massive meat slicing machine. FMC also had a wartime gear and supplies division. For a year or two, we had artillery shells lining our bookshelves, and no one in the family appreciated that, especially in the upcoming decade of MAKE LOVE, NOT WAR. My father eventually asked for a transfer out of that department. He had had enough of war games and wanted to focus on something without difficult memories attached.

My father marveled at food products that were shaped like the can they emerged from. Think Ocean Spray Jellied Cranberry Sauce and Swift Premium Canned Ham. He was responsible for the packaging of various food items, as well as the separating of produce. Truthfully, I never fully understood what my father did at work. He rarely talked about it—or anything else. He muttered a few incoherent and inconsequential words to my mother, then caved quietly inward, contorting and bending into a tightly closed knot.

Before my father began working for this machine-oriented employer, I always assumed meat emerged pre-sliced from a calf or a pig. I also assumed fruits, like berries, were too delicate to be picked by machine. I came to learn that every berry I have ever eaten and every piece of fruit or slice of vegetable I have ever shoved into my mouth had been picked by calloused human fingers. Every smear of jelly represented someone's aching digits and long days under factory lighting or out in the sun. Someone wrestling with those pieces of produce had to wipe their sweaty forehead every few minutes. Then why did fruit taste sweet, not salty? Where did all the sweat from pickin' go before the fruit and vegetables went into cans, packages, and bags? As I grew up, those tired hands would be replaced by indifferent machines, and my father would help design a good number of them. Fruit separators and meat slicers were on his resume.

His years at FMC were his glory days. Although he was distant with his children, he was well liked and greatly appreciated in the workplace. His coworkers worshipped at the Church of Joe Sveilich. At FMC, he was a god. At home, he mowed the lawn, fixed the roof, and waited out his time until he could get back to his desk at FMC. There he would tell bawdy jokes, flirt with the secretaries, and create another machine that would play with its food.

Eventually, my father would collect a number of patents for food machinery products and parts, all of which fell under the umbrella and into the pocket of his employer. But in his spare time, he would invent his own contraptions and develop his ideas. My father was an expert in math and algebra, although he had struggled with these subjects in school. Yet he used them in creating diagrams of his monthly inventions. One of his more interesting inventions that never came to pass was a colorful covered tube that slid over florescent lighting in stores and businesses. The colors would tell the shoppers or workers where particular things were located, and each cover would have a different cut-out pattern to catch the eye. If you wanted produce, head to the green section with clover designs placed onto the lighting tubes. If you were in need of panties or pantyhose, the orange section with the triangles would get you to where you were going. In my mind, my father was brilliant and could easily alter the world with his magic wand—or his drafting pencil.

My father happened to like New York, but he loved California. His past didn't follow him there. His overprotective Jewish mother didn't run after him, begging him to put on a warmer jacket or galoshes. The noise of World War II was now filtering into the background. He reinvented himself on this remarkable new coast. No one was checking up on him to see if he was too cold, too tired, too thin. No one was telling him what to do, where to go, and when. He was starting fresh. New York was a dreary distant nightmare. He knew New York City like the back of his hand, but it didn't offer the future; it offered glances back at the past, and the past looked gray, cold, and difficult—and included a snow shovel.

My father shuffled us from here to there. He started a new job on the West Coast in a city he had never heard of and a state he had never visited. His four years as a soldier in WWII had taken him all over the globe, but he had never been outside of New York while in the States until we landed in the small San Jose Airport, long before it was the San Jose International Airport. I was six years old and Harold was eight. And there you have it. Nuts roll downhill to California. Argument settled.

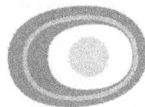

Act One
Scene 1

INTERIOR: {Fade in.} A residential structure called an Eichler, situated in a cul-de-sac among nine similar homes. The rear of the stage features a clear panel of glass looking out on a suburban backyard with two small cherry trees. The set reimagines the lived-in, ranch-style design of the Eichler. Long white horizontal wooden beams run across the upper stage, stem-mounted globe lights drop from the faux ceiling above, and a scattering of softly curved couches and chairs sit center-stage in bold hues of orange, pink, and chartreuse. A fireplace with a brick facade stands center stage rear. A white statue of a naked Venus de Milo sits on the fireplace mantel. Framed prints of Picasso's Three Musicians and Joan Miró's The Ladder hang slightly crooked on the wall. A television-stereo console finished in blond wood fills stage right.

Carol, a young girl, softly presses the back of her hand against her forehead and lifts her chin to the air, as if a single finger has been placed underneath and is propping her face upward. She peers to stage left, then stage right, studying the three family members who surround her.

MOTHER: If you're going out, take a sweater.

CAROL: No way, Mom. It's ninety-three degrees outside.

MOTHER: Take a sweater ... just in case.

CAROL: In case of what? We're attacked by the Soviet Union, and in the apocalyptic aftermath, the Earth is suddenly plunged into a nuclear winter?

MOTHER: Either you take a sweater or you're staying home with your brother and watching Lawrence Welk with your father and me. The Lennon Sisters are on tonight ...

CAROL: I'll take the red one.

Carol hunches her shoulders, grabs a sweater from the hall closet, and hurries out the door, stage left. {Fade out.}

End Scene

Bicoastal Linguistic

New York to California was a transition that brought with it more than a few hiccups. For one thing, we had to discover and adopt a different vocabulary for everyday items. On the East Coast, we never called soft drinks "pop." New Yorkers referred to these carbonated beverages as "soda," unless, of course, the carbonated beverage was seltzer water, in which case it was called seltzer. But Californians didn't know seltzer from club soda.

When it rained in California, my classmates would file through the classroom door and dampen the linoleum-tiled floor with their galoshes and brightly colored umbrellas dripping all over the vinyl flooring. Unfortunately, I sported practical winter wonderland shoe gear called rubbers. Yes, rubbers. My mother and I would pull these dreadful, semi-transparent, frosted gray covers over our shoes and secure a lone button on one side of the disastrous footwear. I would begrudgingly pull mine on while wearing a scowl on my face. There was nothing fashionable about them. Early in the morning, and before I'd begin my walk to school in rainy weather, I'd stash my rubbers behind the bushes in front of our Eichler home. By the time I arrived at school, my feet were soaking wet. Everyone else was placing their rainbow-colored rain boots near the coats. I desperately wanted rain boots. I wanted to blend in with my classmates—wear their raingear, go home to their parents, eat their home-cooked meals.

In California, tissues were called *Kleenex*. Three-sided kerchiefs or cloth hair covers on the head were *scarves,* not babushkas. Chopped meat from the New York butcher on the corner was now called *hamburger meat* in the grocery store. In New York, *cursive writing* had been referred to as script. My mother referred to her *purse* as a pocketbook. The words didn't match. I didn't know what "go potty" meant. I still don't. "Did you make?" That's what my grandma would ask as I exited the hall bathroom. I felt like I was learning a new language, certainly one that was not spoken in my home. In California, valises were referred to as *suitcases.* Until her dying day, my grandmother called her suitcase a valise. I was becoming bicoastal bilingual.

In many ways, it made perfect sense that my family of Russian dolls would make its way to an area of the country that included small regions collapsing inside a bigger region known as the Bay Area. This West Coast territory housed many smaller cities such as Los Altos, Berkeley, Palo Alto, Sunnyvale and Los Gatos, fitting one inside the other like matryoshka dolls. Inside the Bay Area nested a fragrant basin of orchards: Santa Clara Valley. Within Santa Clara Valley was an even smaller city: San Jose. And inside of that still undeveloped valley sat a suburb known as Willow Glen. Further imbedded in the Willow Glen community sat a tract of housing referred to as the Fairglen Eichlers. That's where we settled.

In the early Sixties, San Jose's Willow Glen community contained very few willow trees in its glen, but it did have an abundance of cherry and apricot trees. Santa Clara Valley was an expanse of orchards, and Willow Glen was the valley's sweet spot—an aromatic oasis of blossoms and pungent agriculture. A burst of azure painted the Bay Area sky, a blue typically found on those paradise-saturated postcards from Tahiti or Hawaii. But then the bulldozers came, and my family moved into one of the unique neighborhoods that sprouted amid the tread marks. The housing development we moved into was called The Eichlers.

My father had purchased our new Eichler home sight unseen. An artist's rendering was all he needed to sell him on this distinct spaceship of a shelter that materialized like something out of a Saturday morning episode of *The Jetsons.* What could possibly go amiss in a place that sounds as lovely as Willow Glen, where living promised to be as exciting as a moon landing and streets all had pleasant names. I lived on Fairgrove Court, which was off of Fairlawn Avenue, which was off of Fairglen Avenue, which was off of Fairorchard. You get the idea.

These unique homes, with their airy central atriums, were a space-age suburban oasis. In the Fifties and Sixties, Joe Eichler and his team of out-of-the-box architects designed and built homes unlike any others. They zigged where other homes zagged. Each dwelling was bathed in light. But the house was more than a structure. For me, it was a fifth family member with its own distinct soul. Our Eichler home was its own breathing being. A builder today couldn't replicate its spirit, because it was synonymous with a time when space travel and Jetson-style modern living was at our doorstep.

Blossom and Pushka—In the Eichler atrium.

My childhood home was in the cul-de-sac of Fairgrove Court in Willow Glen, a cluster of mid-century modern Eichler homes that mimicked Peyton Place; it was an alcove chock-full of nuts, drama, wild parties, babysitting co-ops, and infidelity. Neighbors didn't schedule their visits—they dropped in and shared juicy gossip or a fevered political outburst over coffee or cocktails. Everyone was acquainted with everyone else in this small community overflowing with children, creativity, and bicycles hastily abandoned on driveways at dinnertime. An intriguing cast of characters—including authors, artists, musicians, philosophers, poets, politicians, professors, and architects— became my neighbors. The ten homes in my U-shaped block circled like Conestoga wagons against the urban sprawl creeping across the south bay. My neighbors celebrated with block parties in the summer, Christmas caroling in the winter, and a variety of garden parties and evening shindigs all year 'round. Modern living in Willow Glen was trendy, yet easily attainable and certainly affordable. A down payment was $1,000. My family moved into our home in the Sixties, when a residence could be had for $19K and some pocket change.

Soft shapes, clean lines, dirty martinis, and cool Tom Collinses—that's what the San Jose Eichlers were all about. Even the phrase *mid-century modern,* coined by journalist Cara Greenberg around 1984, hinted at the new and old mixed together like rum and Coke. Only now, decades later, I realize that an Eichler life was for the fortunate few, the sons and daughters of the Sixties situated in this narrow slice of subculture. At the time, however, we had no idea how blessed the Flower Children of the cherry orchards were.

Each one of us can, at any time, be ambushed by an avalanche of recollections—a wave of nostalgia, rituals, and moments that used to be. One minute you're a fully fledged, productive grownup, then without warning and seemingly out of nowhere, a whiff of pot roast with garlic and onions sparks a fuse that snakes up the nostrils directly to the sense memory powder keg, igniting flashes of the past and ushering in uncanny detail from another time and place. In that moment, you're once again the younger, smaller, lighter version of yourself, re-experiencing your emotions from dread to elation.

It was a rare occasion when my kitchen-averse mother would cook up a pot roast in our rusty Presto pressure cooker, but I still recall that overwhelming scent of home. *Our* home. The jiggling top metal piece dancing on steam, and finally whistling away, would call us to dinner. But that was an uncommon meal, as our usual fare was Swanson or Banquet frozen dinners. My mother wanted food fast—and nothing too complicated. But the Sixties were complicated. Confounding. Coming of age in this Space Age home, in a unique and eclectic neighborhood housed in Santa Clara Valley during the sex-drugs-rock 'n' roll Sixties, was glorious and, in some ways, inglorious.

My mother, the Sweater Sheriff, sent out more Christmas cards than the White House, which was odd because we were Jewish. I was charged with licking all stamps, including postage, Blue Chip, and S&H Green Stamps. No self-adhesive stamps for those of us who came of age in the Sixties. We licked our postage. I couldn't feel my tongue for hours after the first lot of holiday cards were dumped in the mailbox.

Eichler Homes: Love 'Em or Leave 'Em

There were two types of people in the world: those who embraced the Eichler design and those who hated it. No one sat on the fence in this debate, and the deliberation continues today. Those clueless cads in the anti-Eichler camp had some kind of problem with the absence of windows on the front face of the home. Young mothers complained that they couldn't watch their kids playing out on the street. (Back in the day, children actually played on the street unsupervised and unaccompanied by cell phones.) The same naysayers also had something against a flat roof that collected rain till the ceiling bowed. And they had no patience for the Eichler home's heating system buried beneath the concrete slab foundation that could take an eternity to tease the heat up even one degree.

But "Eichler people" were and are quite willingly cats on a hot *thin* roof. To the pro-Eichler camp, the whimsical design of the home contributed to an outdoor/indoor feel, which more than made up for any of the design flaws. Our family, and many other homebuyers, were ready for something light and open after the Fifties, an era that was in many ways dark and closed. Eichlers were the answer to the question, "Sir, what do you have that's different?" With its windowless frontage, the home appeared drab from the street. But once you were inside, you'd be surprised by the lines, light, and colors exposing an assortment of geometric shapes. It was like standing inside a 3D version of a Mondrian painting.

On any given day, I could glide off the sidewalk in our cul-de-sac, through the front door, and into the safe haven of my home's center atrium. The heart of the Eichler was not the fireplace, nor the kitchen, but rather the airy open center courtyard that the rest of the home revolved around. Plants like Bird of Paradise and tropical ferns thrived in the atrium. It was a central patio area for families to gather, cats to roll in the sun and greenery to create a lush tropical oasis. Summer barbeques were held at the picnic table in our atrium, and special moments like a heart-stopping view of the moonwalk were viewed through my father's telescope in this open space.

In the Sixties, homes and showrooms featured lean, low couches and womb-shaped chairs. Today, those same styles are being mimicked in stores such as IKEA, West Elm, and CB2.

Sleek, simple Scandinavian designs featuring birch, beech, and ash wood finishes are old styles that are suddenly new again. So are the soft curves of chairs and sofas. The classic curve of Eames chairs began a flirtatious come-on and comeback with new consumers in the early 1990s. These were originally created by the husband-and-wife design team of Charles and Ray Eames in the mid-Fifties and became even more popular in the swinging Sixties. The Eames team were the gurus who developed the molded and curved plywood "chair of the century." Other bulbous, modern designs followed. Suddenly, the plastic curved kitchen and dining room chairs where I sat to drink my cherry red Kool-Aid and orange Tang were reappearing in furniture showrooms around the country.

Standing in the doorway with my brother on our way to the Eichler's fresh dirt backyard.

The running joke was that Charles Eames was an architect who never finished architecture school, while his wife Ray was a painter who never painted. But every space, curve, and design she created was like a three-dimensional art canvas for Ray. For a long while, Charles and Ray Eames were the holy matrimony of whimsy and whimsical designs. Fidelity in their marriage didn't last, as charming Charles was a world-class philanderer, but their designs certainly stood the test of time.

I honor the Eichler where our four orange Eames chairs sat at the kitchen table. I honor the fearlessness it took to create such an out-of-the-box boxy structure. It attracted its customers like a NASA recruitment center that was searching for the perfect Buck Rogers. The winning applicant had to have a great appreciation of space and a burning desire for a fresh and promising future. No others need apply. This home was searching for residents who were vision-seekers with *The Right (Eichler) Stuff.*

The Romance Dance

My parents met at a dance at the end of World War II. At that time, dance events were one of the few ways single people met and socialized, equivalent to online dating, a concept I'm sure they couldn't imagine at the end of the 1940s. Even when times were challenging and the tension between them was as massive as the Great Wall of China, my parents always enjoyed twirling and swaying together on the dance floor. Movement was a powerful language that enabled them to leave their tensions and troubles outside the dance hall.

Since their friends were getting married, my mother and father married in a frenzy. They didn't follow in the footsteps of their peers; they ran in them. Moving much too fast, they purchased their first home together, worked and went to school, and squeezed us into the schedule between homework and happy hour.

I never asked my parents how long they knew one another before they married. I don't think it was long. Why did they marry? They weren't very good at it. There was a lot of marrying going around in the late Forties and early Fifties. They jumped on the bandwagon. Besides, two incomes were better than one.

My parents needed one another nearby, but only within earshot. They needed to know the other was in the next room or down the hall. They had what I later labeled an "Orbit Relationship." They had to be flying and functioning around one another, but never close. They remained married. They were miserable together, but I believe my parents had simply carved out a different way of caring, mimicking their own parents and their unions. As the saying goes: whatever works.

If I could revise our lives, I would leave us on Long Island a bit longer, closer to our extended family and within reach of stimulating cultural events and a full-bodied education. I often wondered, if I had grown up in a more conventional setting than the San Jose Eichler, how would my life be different? We had many relatives in New York City. In California, we had none. I had one aunt and one uncle who lived on Long Island. They had adopted two kids, but all of them were my phantom extended family. I saw them a couple of times in childhood. Though they remained in New York, they were mentioned so often they permeated the ether around us. But they were also distant— not living and breathing, hugging, or squeezing, but someone caring from afar.

On the East Coast, I was unaware of my parents' presence. On the West Coast, I often felt I was living in a disaster movie where my father was Godzilla running after me with the girth and foul breath of an angry monster, a reptile that looked suspiciously like Groucho Marx. My mother had lost sight of me shortly after my birth. Things didn't shift after we moved from New York. She remained both distant and pleasant, but I needed her near to shelter me from massive fuming reptiles and drafty restaurant booths. My older brother was as agitated, bossy, and spastic as Jerry Lewis in *The Disorderly Orderly*. I was his part-time errand girl, taking direction and responding to his every wish and whim. In the wavering light of our new mid-century modern home on the West Coast, I became lost in the long shadows. My emotions became sealed in layers of my psyche, like sheets of glass in the transparent walls that held up our new house.

My parents were flying solo on the Gold Coast. They would never talk about their grandparents, cousins, uncles, and aunts. They barely mentioned their own parents. We were in a foreign country called Santa Clara Valley, where everything was ready for pioneers with the proper tools. New York had fallen away from our lives, broken off like a piece of Joyva *halvah*.

Seen Not Heard

Our detached Eichler house had a pint-sized backyard and a barking boxer next door. In the decades of prosperity that followed WWII, the single-family home came to epitomize the American dream. Suburbs sprouted up like weeds, and weeds sprouted up in front lawns in the form of dandelions. The days of several generations living under one roof were over. Now we were supposed to be an island unto ourselves. Ah, the circle of life ... and real estate.

Most homes constructed in the Sixties were the classic L-shape, with small kitchens, living rooms, and a dining area, all separated from each other for privacy. Our new house was shaped more like a doughnut with an open area—an atrium—in the center. Everything revolved around that open space, which had to be passed through in order to enter the living quarters through sliding glass doors.

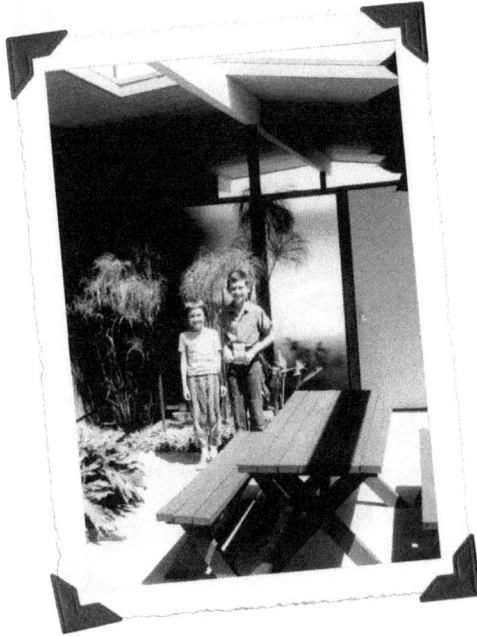

My brother and me loitering inside the atrium.

Transparent Eichler walls had a downside. Like many of the kids in our neighborhood, I ran directly into that glass, thinking the sliding door was open. So much glass; so little judgment. All kids do is run throughout their childhood and not pay attention. I was no different. Ka-boom! We all ran into the atrium's glass walls, but our bones were soft even if our heads were hard. We survived and carried on. Eventually, most of the adults stuck colorful decals on the glass to prevent such catastrophes. Those colorful decals never stopped birds from colliding against the glass walls. Head-on collisions, accompanied by indoor shrieks, were a regular occurrence. It was Bay Area barrier-free living at its best and most dangerous. Our Eichler model had a one-car carport and the coveted atrium with its open rectangular space. It featured a small garden and patio area. The atrium was the sun-infused light box of the entire structure. Large plate glass overlooked the backyard. Other models lacked an atrium. Instead, they featured a private fenced-off front courtyard and a two-car garage. No windows could be seen from the street in either model. They were all hidden behind the door or fence that led into the enchanting Eichler realm.

Mom sunning herself in the atrium.

The outdoors and indoors of an Eichler home blended seamlessly, and the post-and-beam construction showcased the clean lines of its architecture. An expansive beam ran above the living area like Atlas' outstretched arms. My father was like the house itself as he stood upright, a support beam who shouldered the financial weight for his family. Unlike the Eichler, however, he was anything but transparent. And unlike the central atrium, his core was nearly impossible to reach. I know. I would study him for the remainder of my life and would never find it. It wasn't for lack of trying.

From a very young age, I struggled to understand my father's actions and motivation. It was like studying for a test where there was no accessible answer key. My father was an impregnable mystery, but the Eichler was sunny and bright. Anyone who met my father would feel that he was just as sanguine. I was the spectator of the imbalance that needed to be carefully avoided. These shadowy fragments of my father's architecture would mold themselves into my own frame as I grew older.

If Glass Walls Could Talk

In San Jose I would gather acquaintances as easily as some people accumulate refrigerator magnets. True friends were harder to come by. My first true friend in the San Jose Eichler neighborhood was Sally Shoenstein. Her family moved in next door shortly after we arrived, and their stay was too brief. All the front and backyards were still mounds of the fresh, fragrant dirt that had so recently been an agricultural paradise. There were homes and neighborhoods springing up all around our hub of ten homes, but we were complete, ready to eat, sleep, mingle, and stay locked in our own little cul-de-sac world.

Sally had white-blonde shoulder-length hair. White, like eggshells. Pure white, as if every strand had accidentally come in contact with a jug of Clorox bleach, and wispy-fine as baby's hair. Sally's eyelashes were the same vanilla. All that was noticeable when you caught a glimpse of her pale six-year-old face were two ultramarine eyes surrounded by hair and skin as pale as a bed sheet. Her much younger brother, Carey, had the same startling, soft snowy white hair.

Beyond her otherworldly coloring, Sally looked like me. We were the same height with the same lanky limbs and the same sorry short, uneven bangs running across our upper foreheads. Sally and I were ballerinas together, parading about in our pale pink leotards and even paler skin. We invaded one another's girly bedrooms on a daily basis. I have no idea what we discussed at age six, but we never ran out of things to wonder about out loud. We were best friends until her parents decided to divorce and move away. Through a blubbery pout, I watched her station wagon pull away and her marshmallow-white family depart from the Eichler world. It was as if some soft ivory snowflakes had escaped from the protective snow globe.

Sally's family of four moved to a land far, far away: Palo Alto. Soon after, her mother married a man with several children even younger than Sally and Carey. We stayed in touch with frequent phone calls. My first friend now had a brand-new father and family, which seemed odd in the landscape of the early Sixties, where families seldom broke apart. Sadly, a short time later, my father came out to where I was playing in the street and told me the stunning news. Sally had died in a raging house fire, trying to save her siblings. Sally's mother and stepfather had gone out for the night, leaving Sally in charge of her brother and her stepsiblings. The stepfather's children accidentally set a fire. Sally ran inside to save her brother. They both vanished like a puff of smoke, turned to ash in the blink of an eye. Sally's and Carey's future was extinguished much too soon, and I didn't know how to wrap my small head around this immense news.

This tragedy was my first experience with death. I had never known anyone or anything that had died, even a pet. I had a vague and glossy television image of death, and I knew that when boys in the neighborhood sprinkled salt on a banana slug or snail, it croaked. This was very different. When I heard the news, I stumbled over to the small wooden bench that sat in my front yard near the carport. The prickly seat was chock-full of splinters, but I didn't feel them on my bare legs or through the bottom of my shorts. Not that day. I was too busy trying to wrestle with the sudden and surprising disappearance of my beautiful best friend and her brother. It all seemed too much to take in. I couldn't grasp death. My best friend had been here. Now she wasn't. How could that be? How could I know at such an age that we were all walking around with an expiration date stamped on the bottom of our foot in invisible ink? Death was a magic trick gone terribly wrong.

My second friend after we moved to San Jose was Marvin Reedy. He lived three houses down in the center spot of our ten house cul-de-sac. In the early Sixties, there was no shortage of fools and bullies, and Marvin had the misfortune of having M.R. as his initials.

"You're so stupid," the bullies would shout. "You're an MR!" MR stood for mentally retarded. He would shout back, "You're so lame. What a spaz."

The war of words had begun and wouldn't end for at least a decade. In 1962, "MR" was the worst thing you could call someone on the playground or on the block, other than calling them a fag. "Fag" came in second place in the name-calling division, but none of us knew what it meant.

Marvin was a live-action, walking, talking Charlie Brown. His head had design flaws. It was too round, his hair was too short, his mouth and chin were much too slight. He was neither masculine nor feminine. Prior to age ten, friends were friends. There was no sex drive, no division of boy toys and girl toys, no straight-line divide in interests. It seems we all had ambiguous sexual identities and interests for several years, and then suddenly ... we didn't. Until our interests divided, Marvin and I were the best of friends. We did everything together until we entered high school. Then we did nothing together.

His family of three moved to the cul-de-sac, but it quickly turned to two: Marvin and his mother. His birth father, Twain, divorced Marvin's mother, Lorraine, after hearing rumblings about her affair with the choir director at their local Mormon Church. No one knew if the rumors were true. Twain, a priggish, uptight, hum-drum architect, didn't know what to do with the likes of Lorraine and her wild ways. Lorraine and Marvin remained in the Eichler home while Twain went off to expand his new Mormon household a few blocks away.

Lorraine was a Chanel No. 5–scented, ginger-headed vixen, and she was the perfect Lorraine. She couldn't have had any other first name. Lorraine was a visual buffet and the hippest mother on the block. Her presence oozed sensuality and a seductive sizzle that I had never witnessed before. I didn't see myself growing up to be like Lorraine. She had something that seemed foreign and unattainable, so I watched and took notes.

Lorraine was part of the younger generation of parents in the cul-de-sac who would gather separately to have their afternoon happy hours on open card tables and play poker while sipping Chardonnay from striped plastic tumblers. My parents and their friends were ten years older, but occasionally the two age groups collided for block parties, fireworks, and weekend bashes.

While Marvin and I put together an airplane model in his bedroom, I could hear the sounds of Elvis' *Blue Hawaii* album blaring in the kitchen. Lorraine worshipped Elvis. Who didn't? I can't hear an Elvis song without being transported back to Marvin's galley-style kitchen with the evenly tanned Lorraine standing at the counter making peanut butter-and-jelly sandwiches in her low-cut orange summer top, matching tangerine lipstick smeared on her full lips, and tight-fitting leopard-print pants complete with stirrups hugging the bottom of her feet. They were called ski pants, even in summer. I had a pair of red ones that made my toothpick legs look non-existent. We would anxiously await the completion of our sandwiches so that we could run to the backyard hammock and swing in the late afternoon sun, talking endlessly about nothing and everything.

Lorraine was always walking around the Eichler with her dress half-zipped, or wearing a lacy pink or black nylon slip. Then again, half of the neighborhood housewives were walking around in slips. It was *Cat on a Hot Tin Roof,* Eichler-style, and it was not uncommon to be greeted at the door by your friend's mother in a half or full slip, bra, and panties.

"Come on in. Go back to his room" or "She's out in the backyard. Go!"

Years later, Country Joe and the Fish would compose and sing the song "Not So Sweet Martha Lorraine." I always assumed it was about lusty Lorraine Reedy.

Lorraine's bedroom was a curious love nest before I knew what went on in love nests. Marvin and I were repeatedly hollered at for entering her fortress, but it never stopped us from invading her private space. Lorraine's bed was covered with a white animal skin bedspread draped over the sides, teasing the floor below. That furry fabric beckoned to us, but in a much different way than it beckoned to adults. We would jump into the soft fur, roll around and around, and snicker until we fell off the edge and landed on their gray linoleum asbestos-backed tiles, identical to my family's Eichler flooring. We'd play for hours on that sumptuous fluffy surface until Lorraine caught and banished us again.

While his mother was still yelling at two snickering knuckleheads, we'd run out to Marvin's backyard and jump into the narrow hammock strung between two trees. His yard and bedroom was always jam-packed with toys, books, and the latest gadgets and games purchased by two divorced parents and their massive amounts of guilt.

Sweet Lorraine had an assortment of men coming and going through her front door and in and out of her bedroom. Her main squeeze for several years was Rob Newlin. As soon as she was done gobbling up every part of Rob on her white furry bedspread, Lorraine would put him to work. Handyman work. I could always find Rob up on the flat roof fixing the annual Eichler roof leaks, or repairing Lorraine's plumbing, or mending her fence, or trimming her juniper bushes. The kids in the neighborhood referred to him as Poor Rob. One afternoon, when he was fixing a hole on the roof, Lorraine jumped in another man's car and took off on a date. Rob watched, eyes small and squinting, as Lorraine and her date-of-the-week roared out of the cul-de-sac in a sports car with a high-pitched engine. Back to work Rob went. Lorraine and her orange lips and deep cleavage had Rob under her spell. There was nothing she could do to dim his devotion.

One year, she threw all of Marvin's friends a grand Halloween party, complete with dangling apples and spooky stories for a roomful of six-year-olds in their darkened living room. My family didn't have any traditions, so I clung to Marvin's. I dressed in a boxed costume labeled "Devil Cat" for the big Halloween party. The plastic cat mask made my face sweaty, so I took it off after a few minutes and wore it around my neck the rest of the evening. After we bobbed for apples from the ceiling, Lorraine's boyfriend Rob told ghost stories in the living room and scared us kids half to death. When the lights were lowered, his voice dropped an octave. We screamed in unison and then went home to shiver in our beds for the rest of the night while we relived the tales Rob told in his best Vincent Price voice. I spent so much time at Marvin's house that it quickly became my home away from home.

Marvin and I would often go out butterfly hunting with small nets and large Mason jars. I was fascinated with insects, especially butterflies. I'd prop myself up at my father's black wire desk in the study and examine each color photograph or drawing of butterfly wings and moths in my insect manual. My favorite book featured color photos of different species. When I found one in the yard that matched my book, it was like striking gold. I would throw my net, move these colorful creatures into a jar, and proceed with the slow process of suffocation. I was assured by various adult voices that they didn't suffer from this process. I believed adults never lied and knew everything, even about butterflies. That was my first mistake. In a few days, I would remove the butterfly's lifeless body and pin its wings to cotton balls. How could I? Someone should have pinned my butterfly net to the wall and left it there.

Marvin and I were inseparable. Best buddies. We watched monster movies together, caught insects, built sandcastles in his backyard sandbox, held hands, and kissed with clueless abandon. Then he got lost in a maze of bad behavior and drugs. Marvin transitioned from being a model child, good student, and best friend to getting into a heap of trouble. Not the sort of trouble Beaver and Wally Cleaver got into, but *real* trouble. After starting a few fires and tossing some small bomb-like devices on the streets of San Francisco, Marvin was sent to live with his father in a distant neighborhood. Drugs, acting out, anger. I couldn't fathom what had ignited these episodes. I wanted to be running with our butterfly nets in the sun once again, looking for the hidden splashes of colored wings in the greenery.

Meanwhile Lorraine went on hosting wild parties in her backyard. Simon and Garfunkel's "Cecilia" was blaring on the hi-fi, and she was strolling around wearing nothing but a multicolored paisley bikini and matching scarf. Correction: She was also wearing a colorful Virginia Slims cigarette in her navel as she began to belly dance. As one neighbor put it, some things seen cannot be unseen. If anyone had come a long way from a traditional marriage to Swingin' Singlesville, it was sweet Lorraine and her Virginia Slims.

Friends in the early years of cul-de-sac living included Ginger Cartwright and Gina Youngblood. Gina had yellow-blonde hair and a brushstroke of freckles on her cheeks. Her family drove to Squaw Valley nearly every weekend. I had no idea where Squaw Valley was and never did find out. The destination sounded mysterious, cold, and jam-packed with sweaters and snow boots. My family didn't ski, so the thought of going up or down a slope with sticks secured to your feet, or being carried off into the air by a lift contraption like the one at Disneyland, seemed too good to be true.

Ginger lived across the street from me and next door to Gina. I always thought they were in cahoots with those two G-names. Ginger had short-cut auburn hair and the same crooked bangs and smile I wore. I always wondered if Ginger Cartwright was related to Hoss, Little Joe, Adam, and Pa of the Ponderosa.

Ginger and Gina remained my friends until the solemn day when both of their families moved away, one right after the other. My kemosabes. *Hi-Yo, Ginger and Gina. Away!*

When the Youngbloods moved out, the Cockers moved in. We never stopped having fun with their last name. That's what you do when you're nine or ten years old—make fun of names that sound like something else. Every boy named Dick will know what I'm talking about.

The Cockers had two boys, Blaine and Tim, and one girl we called Little Wanda. This family also had golden hair, all in curls. Towheaded, fair-skinned kids were being delivered to our cul-de-sac on a regular basis. Blaine was my age. We would kiss without parting lips when we were twelve years old. Although a bit on the short side, his tight curly blond locks made him look like a miniature Adonis.

The Cockers maintained a shadowy household. Blaine, Wanda, and Tim's mother had become remarried to a man named Mr. Barnes. I rarely saw their mother, Mrs. Barnes, as she was always locked in her bedroom whenever I'd come over to play with Blaine. We'd have to keep very quiet if we played in Blaine's house, which was not often. They seemed protective of their mother and insisted she needed quiet. I never knew why. Did she suffer from depression, arthritis, migraines? I didn't know, and I never saw her emerge. She was locked away as mysteriously as Norman Bates' mother. Her husband, the massive and brusque Mr. Barnes, would pace back and forth on the driveway while his stepkids squinted at him with disdain, but always from a fair distance. If I asked questions about their home life, those questions were never answered.

Tim Cocker was the oldest brother. He, too, had soft curls piled high on his head. One afternoon in late summer, my brother and some neighborhood pals were teasing Tim. He was a softer boy, in both features and demeanor, who didn't fit into the usual gang. That gang was now taunting him with the deadly weapons of words. Brad Manners, a year older than my brother and the troublemaker of the cul-de-sac, yelled something about Tim being a fag, and others joined in with more insults. Tim stood slightly slumped over in his driveway, unaided by family members.

I watched as his limbs began to quiver. He was so injured and angry that his curls seemed to tighten. After the wrath collected in Tim's reddening face for several minutes, his emotions finally blew like projectile vomit being spewed across the street. At the top of his lungs, Tim hollered, "CHUCK YOU, FARLEY!" to every boy who was teasing him, including my brother.

The boys in that jeering crowd, including my own brother, began to point and laugh at the way the alphabet letters got switched around in Tim's mouth. I didn't. As his eyes teared up, my stomach dropped, then twisted. I couldn't laugh along with the rest. My heart hurt for Tim. I could feel his helplessness in my own body. I would always remember the retort Tim managed to release and how horrible teasing could tear pride apart and blow it to smithereens.

Living directly across the street from our Eichler was an unlikely family of Republicans named Churchfield. Even their name sounded conservative. I believed they all were placed in the cul-de-sac with an assignment to recruit members to their church. Hell, I didn't even know if they attended church, but with a name like Churchfield, how could they not?

Mrs. Churchfield paraded about the driveway in her three-piece coordinated outfits. They always looked like they had been purchased from a high-end store my family never shopped in and never would. Everything was tailored and matched perfectly. In contrast, my family's fashions came from Gemco, an early discount store similar to Kmart. Mrs. Churchfield's hair looked like an astronaut's wife's 'do. It was perpetually coiffed and curled into a massive brunette flip that looked crispy. Too much Aqua Net. I imagined those curls breaking off on her pillow at night.

The Churchfields had several small children, all of them younger than I was, and all with light hair and thin limbs. Both parents had dark hair, and were rather tall and hefty, but in an attractive way. But there was a shadow cast over the Churchfields' Eichler. Their mindset seemed radically dissimilar from the Liberal Democrats residing in our cul-de-sac and the Eichler neighborhood in general. I rarely saw Mr. and Mrs. Churchfield, but like weather, I knew they were always there.

My first and only recurring childhood dream guest-starred the nearly bald Mr. Churchfield, who looked like *The Dick Van Dyke Show*'s Mel Cooley. In the dream, he appeared in an Eichler garage across the street. His head was the size of the garage itself. Every time I had this nightmare, I would scream when I saw that massive head coming at me. It was only a head, no body attached. In my dream, I would run back to my family's Eichler for shelter from the colossal head that voted Republican. Then I would wake up, go back to sleep, and have the same dream. The nightmare was likely inspired by the many science fiction programs I was gobbling up around that same time.

The Sternfelds moved into the cul-de-sac a couple of houses down from us and gave our ten house hub some much needed class. David Sternfeld was a physician, and his wife, a socialite named Ellie, was a frequent wine sipper who never missed a chance to mix a cocktail of intoxication and obnoxiousness during one of their frequent adult parties. She could often be found dancing atop the kitchen table to some bossa nova recording, martini glass in one hand while the other waved gently through the cigarette and pipe exhaust to the sound of the beat.

Whenever my girlfriend would babysit for the Sternfelds' two young boys, Teddy and Jonathan, I would sneak over so that we could thumb through the thick, hardbound physician's books that lined the shelves of Dr. Sternfeld's study. It was our first glance at male and female naked bodies and body parts. We saw regions we didn't know existed. And not just livers and spleens, but penises and breasts and triangular hair riding high atop vulvas. Hair? Why does it grow in that shape? It looked like a slice of fur pie. We'd point and giggle and occasionally gasp at some of the revealing photos of inner and outer organs. Of course, we also viewed photographs of every unpleasant skin disorder known to man. My friends stared in disbelief. I covered my eyes. I decided right then and there that a medical profession was not my calling.

* ⚛ *

On a regular basis, I would orchestrate playtime with all of my friends. And by playtime, I mean we'd be in our own play with assigned characters and scenarios, usually involving imminent danger. Ginger would be Roger, and I would be Eloise, or she would be Rebecca and I'd be Robert. It didn't matter who we were.

We wanted to be someone else for a few hours in the afternoon. Our assigned adventure was always related to whatever comic book I had just finished reading. We would jump back and forth over on the sidewalks in the cul-de-sac pretending the concrete was a raging river. We had to skillfully maneuver through the forest of suburban flowerbeds and shrubbery in order to survive. One time, we were being chased by people from the Bizarro World. I was Supergirl, naturally. Sidewalk cracks and a plentiful supply of sticky lantana and bottle brush greenery couldn't stop me. Nothing could. The entire world of Bizarros, who resided on a cube-shaped planet called "Htrae" (*Earth* spelled backwards), were now running around the sidewalks in Fairgrove Court, always in imminent danger, always escaping in the nick of time.

I was the director, producer, and screenwriter of each afternoon adventure. At some point, I introduced the two-sided kissing sheet labeled HE on one side and SHE on the other. I instructed my friends that when we kissed at some appropriate and romantic moment in the plotline, we'd quickly insert a piece of lined paper to protect us from ever touching one another's lips. Eww. The setup, dialogue, relationships, and plot in this fairy tale fantasy were written, produced, and directed in my mind as we went along. Our bodies acted out the enchanted story of danger and intrigue, and like seasoned actors, we believed we were someone else. I finally had an outlet for my imaginary world, and my friends were the bit players in many preposterous suburban plotlines.

At some point, I lost my director's hat and sling chair and turned inside myself and away from the world. I felt dissimilar from my friends. My family was nothing like theirs. Their homes smelled different, looked different, and more importantly felt different. Suddenly, my friends and I were like dominoes that didn't match. I became shy and felt incompetent in social circles. I even began shrinking around my own family members. They were strangers, sometimes callous or lost in thought a million miles away.

As I lay in bed at night waiting for sleep to claim me, I was certain that nothing outside my bedroom was real. Only the grain on my wooden walls was authentic. I know because I ran my fingertips over its rough surface as though it were a living, breathing thing. Those mahogany vertical lines were blankets of comfort that made me feel sheltered. My family members weren't real, and I certainly didn't feel safe in their presence. They were a pretend family. I couldn't wait for daylight and the sounds of rustling in the kitchen to dispel the terrifying conclusions I drew at night.

When we were very young, my father picked up a couple of door locks at the hardware store and installed them on the inside of each bedroom door in the Eichler. We could lock ourselves away from sudden intrusions. It seemed an odd thing to give children the ability to lock themselves away from their own parents, but he must have found the mechanics of the locks intriguing. At least that's what I always told myself.

When I was age nine or ten, my father began mocking me relentlessly at the family dinner table. My chaotic hair. My unintentional pout. My stick-like figure. He seemed to revel in the slow, steady quiver of my lower lip, a telltale warning sign of the tears that would soon fall to my melamine dinner plate covered in cheery daisies. *Suck it up, girl.* My sense of worth had been reduced to the size of a molecule, like in the Disneyland ride Adventure Thru Inner Space, an attraction designed to simulate humans shrinking to a size smaller than "inner space." Now I was that minuscule and insignificant. I was no longer visible.

When I felt I couldn't hold back any longer, I'd run to my room with tears streaming down my face, never letting my father or brother see my eyes wretched and wet. I'd lock the door behind me. Like clockwork, my mother would arrive a few minutes later with a daisy dinner plate and glass of milk.

"You know how your father is." She always said the same thing in the same monotone delivery. I could almost say it with her as it came out of her mouth so often. As soon as she lowered the tray to the top of my bed, she'd disappear down the hallway. No touch of comfort. No soothing words. No parental figure as far as the eye could see.

This became an ongoing dreaded ritual. In those moments and whenever I felt fragile, I'd instinctively pretend that I was the opposite. Instead of being weak or hurt, I was strong and indifferent. I'd puff my feathers when threatened. When the enemy was near, I'd hike up my back and stand my fur on end in a threatening stance like our housecat Pushka in a fence fight. You can't hurt me. I'm THIS BIG. But that damn shaky lip. It would give me away every time. The next morning I would propel myself through my morning ritual feeling as small as Thumbelina.

What, Me Worry?

I was born in a state of discomfort, into a family tree just blooming with double-checkers and worriers. We worried about perfect strangers. We worried about the state of the union. We worried about polio and the effectiveness of the medicinal sugar cubes we had to gulp down to prevent it. We worried about the Soviet Union, and we worried that the duck-and-cover exercises we practiced in school would be inadequate to protect us. We worried about the frequency and consistency of our bowel movements. Most of all, we worried about one another. We never seemed to worry that we were worrying too much because we could never worry enough.

We didn't believe in fate. We believed in apprehension and discomfort. Whether we were facing a real or imagined obstacle, or dealing with a perplexing emotion, the trickiest thing to do was to let everything float. Surrender. It seemed so simple, and yet it was so hard to muster up and seemingly impossible to master.

My parents, grandparents, and brother were all terrific worriers. Nowadays, everyone is a worrier, but it seems to me that back then there was less to worry about. We didn't worry about the stock market. We didn't worry about our health and the foods we ate or how much mercury was in our tuna sandwich. Our parents didn't worry about whether their jobs were secure or whether they would have enough in savings as they approached retirement. They watched but didn't worry about who would get into political office and how it would impact them. They didn't worry about whether they should make an appointment with a therapist to talk about how much time they spent worrying, nor did they worry about whether they could afford to pay for therapy. No one we knew went to therapy. Not in the Sixties. But my relatives and I managed to worry about nearly everything. We had acres and acres of crops bursting and blooming with worry and not enough hours in the day to tidy and tame our concerns.

I was a tomboy. Most of my friends were boys, and I was drawn to active playtime activities, not Easy-Bake Ovens or playing dress-up. But I soon changed my mind about wanting to be anything but female. I didn't want to grow up and have to go to Vietnam. War was my greatest worry. The images on the television screen and the headlines in the newspaper terrified me. Battles, bombs, and being far from home—I wanted none of it. Suddenly being male was anything but an attractive option. It was good that I was born a girl. I didn't have to blow anything up.

The only thing I wanted to do with a newspaper was to roll it up, along with Harold and father, and have what we called Paper Fights! With tightly wrapped newspaper in a long roll, we ran towards one another and hit each other on the side of the arm with our newsprint weaponry, shrieked in delight, then quickly ran away. I screamed out in utter bliss! But Harold often hit too hard and turned my flesh pink. I didn't care. My father snorted with hearty laughter that washed away any pain. In those moments, he was childlike and enjoyed being with us kids. We were fun. We were silly, like him. It was one of my favorite regular activities when we first moved to California, along with having my father give me an occasional airplane ride.

When I was ages six, seven, and eight, my father enjoyed spinning me around the living room on outstretched arms. Lying across his arms on my stomach, arms in front of me like Supergirl, I was a superhero flying through the air. It was my own personal fantasy and splendid fairy tale. "Faster, Dad. Faster!" He heard my command and obliged. Both of us were spinning and roaring with laughter. Happy tears rolled from my eyes. I could hear his pleased chuckles. We were a team. We were connected. I adored him, and I felt adored. I could barely endure the faster speed and had to close my eyes until the spinning stopped. My head felt like it would explode from the speed. I assumed I was moving faster than the speed of light or sound. But like a terrifying roller-coaster ride, I never wanted it to end. I screamed with an equal mix of both glee and terror. In those moments, there was wild, unguarded, and unrepressed laughter. I loved my father so much I thought my heart would burst. He was my pilot. And in his arms, whirling around the living room, I mattered.

My mother wanted me to become a teacher so that I could have the summers off. That was her selling point: summer vacation for three months. She failed to mention that there was no paycheck while you had your toes in the sand or went hiking in the mountains.

I didn't know what I wanted to be when I grew up. My aspirations were as wobbly as a kite floating up into the clouds. I wasn't particularly good at anything. Not yet. I knew I didn't want to be in sales. Even now, when I see the people running kiosks at the local mall, my first thought is, that's got to be the worst job in the world. But of course it's not. It's not even close to being a sign twirler.

Oy Vey-Cation

Family vacations in the white Dodge Dart included everything except moving air. The stifling interior and the lack of oxygen was unsettling. As our steadfast vehicle lumbered through the waterlogged winters and steamy summers of the Sixties, we each assumed roles imposed on us in the confines of the Dart.

My mother, Blossom, was the blessed peacemaker in charge of shushing the residents of the back seat at regular intervals. My father, the commander-in-chief hardliner, was the barker of orders and buyer of burgers and Fresca at refueling stations. If any of his orders were disobeyed, even Blossom the blessed peacemaker could not intervene. My brother was the taunter-in-chief, assigned to provoke the commander-in-chief, but always playing the puppet master so that the anger was directed at me. His antics incited outbursts of laughter and much too much glee. The result? Two infuriated parents. Whether it was a spot-on imitation of Don Knotts as Barney Fife, or Wally mocking the Beave, or perhaps Elvis rocking his upper lip, the result would always be uncontrollable hysteria. Juvenile? Yes, but at the time—and under conditions of reduced oxygen—it was top-drawer entertainment, right up there with the Rat Pack playing the Stardust Lounge.

There were never many stoplights on our trips from here to there, but plenty of billboards appeared on the side of the road advertising faraway destinations, upcoming motels, and malt liquor. When we'd stop at a traffic light, I decided the red light radiated anger, the green dot was happy, and the yellow light was having one of those "Uh-oh!" moments. I was always seeing faces in inanimate objects. The grills and headlights on cars were the faces of the city crowd, some wearing braces, others a vicious smile, and a few as toothy as Milton Berle.

With no seatbelts to restrain us, Harold and I seriously needed a backseat restraining order. We were rambunctious monkeys in our spacious upholstered jungle gym. Boredom bred ants-in-the-pants nonsense. We couldn't help ourselves. My mother or father would eventually move one of us to the front seat for separation, silence, and sanity. I always wanted to be the one switching seat assignments. I could easily pop up to the front from the previous perch and lodge myself next to my mother. The scent of White Shoulders infused with perspiration was intoxicating.

Riding in the car's cockpit was an exhilarating experience. It was so damn adult. It made me want to throw my hands up in elation, as if I had an "E" ticket at Disneyland and was seated in the Matterhorn's front car. Here I was, propped up between two adults. I felt important and mature beyond my years. Now I would be visible. I would count. I would get to see where we were going before we arrived, which was much better than being cooped up in the back with my tormenter. Sandwiched between the commander-in-chief and the blessed peacemaker in the front seat, I'd swivel around like the ball turret of a B-17 and stick my tongue out at my former nemesis with no fear of being sucker-punched or knee-pinched. How deliciously satisfying.

During our car vacations, the minutes and hours ticked by too slowly like the sluggish and methodical drops of Chinese water torture. The scenery beyond the smudged side window flicked by, a grainy movie on a grimy screen. My father fidgeted and fussed while seated on one of those single, slippery, coil spring seat covers. It was supposed to keep the driver's bottom cool and comfy, but it would shift and flip with the slightest movement. Once I switch places with Harold, who now wanted to crawl into the front seat with my parents, I'd sprawl out in back, my luxurious loveseat, and watch the telephone lines shift up and down, up and down—hypnotic waves through gritty glass. I was always fascinated with telephone lines, long before

Glen Campbell sang "Wichita Lineman." They were hitched to pressure-treated pinewood poles, like I was hitched to this crazed and sweaty family.

Now laid out in the back seat, I would watch my father in profile. His once chiseled features were now beginning to collapse with age, taut skin now covered with soft lines matching a chaotic freeway interchange. My mother was the co-pilot beside him with a foldout map on her lap. A jet-black bob framed her porcelain face. Her strands were straight arrows of charcoal, unlike my chaotic, mousy brown head of hair feathers. Was she truly my mother? I wondered. Our hair didn't match. Nor did our coloring, our noses, our ease with my father or the outside world.

My parents didn't talk much in the front seat. When they did, their voices became lost in the bounce and echoes of wind noise or concealed by the holy dust of road racket. I would strain to hear but couldn't decipher too many of the words or whether they cared about what they were saying. Most of it was chitchat coming from the direction of my mother. So-and-so did this? So-and-so went there? Should we have such-and-such at our next party? My father would sometimes nod, but not often. For the most part, he kept his disinterest evident with a non-response stony stare at the road ahead, as if the road would save him somehow from all the external and internal chatter. He was in his own world with his own thoughts. I tried to imagine what was churning around in his head. Work and money worries? His parents back in Brooklyn? Subsidizing my aunt's income because my uncle had lost his job? How was he going to keep all the plates in the air spinning? He was competing with the guy on *The Ed Sullivan Show*.

How old they had become! Yet they were approaching their late thirties. How many more car rides would I take with them? Were these the same people who transported me from a hospital in New York City wrapped in a 100 percent cotton blanket, spoon-fed me, bathed me, ignored or cared for me? Their bodies were slowly falling apart; their interest in one another waning; their journey together was moving forward one tedious and unsatisfactory moment at a time. They were comfortable but not close. I would want something different for myself. I would want something more. I promised myself, lying in back of the Dodge Dart with the air whirring by outside the car windows and the sun playing on my upper thighs, I would get it.

As the day transitioned into cool dusk and the tires brushed the pavement like a Zildjian brush on the skin of a drum, I would silently imagine my favorite songs being sung to that rhythmic road beat. The sky would move from pale to midnight blue, and the moon would float up from the horizon like a helium balloon. I wondered if the moon would follow our car the way it always did. It was out the window, as if we pulled it along with us by an invisible string. It watched our family dysfunction and sporadic disasters from afar.

Are we there yet?

Peas in Different Pods

My parents had dueling temperaments. At one end of the spectrum was my father who could not only multitask but required constant stimuli and never-ending activity. My father was often spinning, swerving, and tumbling out of control. My mother, on the other hand, moved as leisurely as Heinz Tomato Ketchup. She was never concerned about what was going on in her peripheral vision. She had no peripheral vision. Whenever my parents would take a walk after dinner, a ritual they participated in every evening, my father would be a block ahead of my mother in his measured, rapid march. She would be strolling and humming, cleaning out her back teeth with the tip of her tongue, and looking down at the sidewalk while my father was on high alert, perusing front yards, passing the parked cars with his brisk steps, and greeting every neighbor and stranger in The Eichlers.

My mother's driving drove me crazy. She never attempted freeways. Not once. It's a good thing, as her driving was lackadaisical. How she passed her driver's test, nobody knew. Like Mr. Magoo or some other clueless cartoon figure, she was unaware of the cars swerving around her trying to dodge her lethargic acceleration—or at the very least avoid a collision. Her laid-back pace as she prodded our white Dodge Dart down the road in the direction of her workplace, maneuvering quiet side streets, talking and flailing her hand like she was conducting Beethoven's Symphony No. 9, made for neither safe nor sane driving. "Mom, watch out!" The backseat driver had to be on hyper-alert. I could barely wait for her car to finally lunge into the driveway so I could take a full breath.

My mother would impulsively purchase multiple packs of gum while she was standing in the grocery store checkout line. It was right there in front of her. She didn't think she wanted it, but there it was, in all its minty fresh glory, beckoning to my mother. She was always chewing gum. She was one of those shoppers who tossed every sort of knickknack into her shopping cart at the last minute. Pantyhose stuffed into a plastic egg now bounced into the cart. Resin beaded bracelets in a parade of blue and green hues were tossed into the basket.

My father, on the other hand, impulsively bought bad cars and had me pose beside them. Then he sold them a few weeks later. His cars never took us very far. His first impulsive purchase was a battleship gray Renault Dauphine. He bought it on a whim from his colleague at work while they were having a smoke in the parking lot. They were comparing notes on the new irrigation system they were developing, and suddenly, we had a new mode of transportation in our carport.

That pathetic excuse for an automobile sat in our driveway for no more than forty-five days. Then he was on to an apple red Austin-Healey Sprite, a minuscule convertible sports car with an engine that seldom woke up. When it did, you could hear it struggle from blocks away. That car departed the Eichler hemisphere more quickly than the Renault.

My father moved on from the diminutive Sprite to a sea blue Buick Roadmaster convertible the size of the Love Boat. Seated behind the wheel, my father was Captain Stubing. The back seat was the size of Shea Stadium. You could hit a fly ball and never see it land. In the Sixties, big was the new small.

Christmas Carols

My mother would play Christmas carols at holiday parties, but often flubbed up the words. We didn't know a hark from a herald or a yule from a tide, and we weren't familiar with angels or the faithful. Entering elementary school in this new West Coast city was jolting, but even more so when Santa and Christmas came to town. All my elementary school classmates would run to the walnut spinet piano wheeled into our classroom. The boys and girls would jump up and down singing one Christmas song after another. They stood at that piano like bees around a blossom. I had no idea what these songs were or where they came from, but more importantly, I didn't have a clue how everyone seemed to inherently know the words. Everyone except me. Not that I would have known the words to Chanukah songs. I was raised without religion and ritual. But how did everyone come to know about Jesus and John, Mary and Joseph, ye resting gentlemen, three wise guys, Bethlehem, and all this rejoicing except me? They were all foreign words and characters. I knew the Cat in the Hat. I didn't know the biblical cast.

As I sat at my desk across the room from the hootenanny and watched my classmates plow through "The First Noel," "Away in a Manger," "God Rest Ye Merry, Gentlemen," "Hark! The Herald Angels Sing," "What Child Is This?" and "The Little Drummer Boy," which I was quite sure wasn't about my brother the drummer, I kept wondering, *Who is this Jesus fellow they are singing about?* I felt ostracized, and I didn't know why I was rattling around in the dark when my classmates seemed to be born with these lyrics already programmed into their brains. Did they emerge from the womb with sheet music in one hand, a Bible in the other? The entire idea of Christmas seemed to be a mixture of symbols that made no sense to me. Bells, reindeer, coal? Really?

There must have been a couple of Jewish kids in the class who were sitting this shindig out. I don't remember them. I only remember mouthing the words to songs I didn't know and hoping no one noticed my cluelessness and mouth twisted into in the wrong shape for each word and phrase.

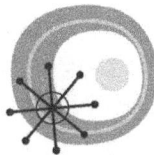

SECTION III:

Thoroughly Modern Mayhem
Elementary, My Dear

It was 1960. John Kennedy was elected President of the United States, and two Russian dogs became the first animals to survive a trip in space. That same year, my family survived a trip from the East Coast to the West Coast while Elvis Presley appeared on the Frank Sinatra television special. But we were busy appearing on the welcoming doorsteps of Willow Glen. When we moved into our Eichler, it was brand new. Evergreens and fresh air blanketed Santa Clara Valley. The sidewalks had just been laid; the yards had not yet been landscaped and were mostly dirt. The kids in my neighborhood were beginning school, and I was on my way to the first day of first grade. Booksin Elementary School sat half a mile from our front door, but it seemed like a long trek on short legs.

The school crossing guards were uniformed sixth graders and bored housewives holding CAUTION signs as we crossed the busy intersection of Curtner and Meridian Avenues. Every restaurant or park in our protective Willow Glen bubble could be arrived at by taking one of those main streets. But in September 1960, Booksin School, with its open field and line of portable classrooms, was the furthest I had ventured, other than flying from New York to California. I stood outside my classroom with a crowd of imperfect six-year-olds. There were round kids, tall kids, hyper and scared kids who wouldn't stop crying or let go of their mothers' hands. Some of them were sent home on day one. They would try again next year. Other kids were at ease or excited by the newness of the schoolyard and the transition ahead. I was strangely calm. It was not my usual.

The door to the portable classroom opened, and we were led into an airy space. Tables, chairs, blackboard, teacher's desk, tile flooring—all awash in neutral tones. I mentally and nervously organized myself for war. On the battlefield of making new friends, everyone must come equipped with the right gear.

A tough uniform to protect you from rejection, a warm smile to entice the enemy, and half of your peanut butter sandwich to bribe the comrades.

Our classroom had a wall of windows and long tables and small chairs where we'd sit until we graduated to the next grade. In second grade we'd have lift-top desks. Until then, we were seated at tables, our heads lowered to the tabletop for rest time, and our papers passed to the classmate on our left for collection by the teacher. Upper- and lower-case letters on a green background with white lettering wrapped around the top of our classroom wall. It was our decorative crown molding. Aa, Bb, Cc ... Would we learn to make those shapes? Would our pencils behave? I was left-handed. Desks in elementary school were made for the right-handed mates. So were notebooks, binders, and scissors. I started writing upside down to avoid the rings of my binder and to keep my elbow from falling off the desk.

We were seated in alphabetical order. Then the dreaded roll call began. I instantly knew this was not going to go well: or as my parents said, it would be a disaster. As the teacher moved through the roster of A, B, and C last names, then through the Ms and Ns, dread inspired spasms in my tummy region. She was at the R names, so it wouldn't be long now.

"Samuels?"

"Here."

"Stevens?"

A six-year-old hand went up. "Here!"

Here it comes. "Carol ..."

There was a long pause.

"Carol Ssss ..." Oh crap. "Uh. Carol Svees ... "

"Here," I muttered, hoping no one would turn around and look at the new student with the unpronounceable name.

"Schweee-leech?"

"Here!" I said it louder so she would hear me and leave me alone for the next nine months of the school year.

I went through school saying "Here!" as teachers fumbled my name in first, second, third, fourth, fifth, and six grades. "Carol Sssssssss ..." As soon as they started to struggle with the pronunciation of the letter combination "S-v" I got them off the hook by saying "Here!" so that they could move on to Swartz and Swenson.

Sveilich was not our original surname. It came from the name Shvaylekh. Who in their right mind would change their name from Shvaylekh to Sveilich? And why was I born with such a name? Why couldn't anyone pronounce it? It seemed simple to me. I mimicked my mother as she spoke on the telephone, spelling out her name to everyone: "S as in Sam, V as in Victor, E-I-L-L-I-C-H. Not litch. It's pronounced LICK." My mother hated our last name as much as we did. Years later, my brother would change his surname to his middle name, Laurence, and be done with "S as in Sam, V as in Victor ..." forever. I wasn't so smart. I retained the name, even throughout my first marriage.

Once inside the classroom, Mrs. Roubedeux, my first and second grade teacher, who looked exactly like a teacher should—she was tall, 50-ish, with specs creeping down the mid-section of her nose—passed out a drawing of a squirrel. Every six-year-old received this flimsy piece of paper with the black outline. We shuffled our butt cheeks in the hard chairs until she passed out our new weapon against restlessness: a red Crayola crayon. Like a sergeant in the U.S. Army, she barked out her only command of the morning: "Color the squirrel red."

One by one, we all began to scratch the rosy red waxy stick against the rough newsprint. My classmates were peering over the shoulders of their peers for instruction. I was no different. With great apprehension, we all started moving the colored stick across the paper this way, then that way. Up. Down. Sideways. There was no rhyme or reason to my own movement on the page. I dove in and began to fill in the empty space. I thought I was doing well. Coloring was fun. I already loved school.

With the first assignment complete, Mrs. Roubedeux held up Merle Axelrad's drawing and pointed to it as an example of what we *should* have done and how we *should* have attacked the paper. "See how she colored inside the lines, class? That's what you *should* have done." We collectively felt like crap. Merle was my only classmate on that first day of first grade, in a valley of cherry orchards, in the middle of our new home state of California, who colored inside the lines. Merle Axelrad had put her classmates to shame. Interestingly enough, she went on to become an architect and, later, a gifted artist whose mixed-media tapestries are recognized and applauded nationwide. Years later, the rest of us would be on Oprah or in our therapist's office trying to figure out where we fell off the beam. I had always crossed beyond the bold black outlines of coloring books with my fuchsia, sky blue, or burnt sienna Crayola. Now I had learned I was doing it all wrong. I felt awful. I felt stupid. I felt klutzy, dim, and amateurish. Welcome to the San Jose Unified School District.

* ⚛ *

The first time in 400 years that Neptune and Pluto aligned was in 1962. It was also the first time I aligned with other seven-year-olds in third grade—and when I assumed the exalted position of Milk Monitor. What responsibilities did that entail? I had to walk to the school cafeteria pulling a red wagon behind me, load it up with small cartons of milk, then wheel it back to my classroom. What could possibly go wrong? It was Friday the 13th, but what does a seven-year-old know about such superstitions?

I felt important: little red wagon, big responsibility. I followed the aroma of ketchup-smeared meatloaf and baked biscuits with my nose and feet, as though they were a line of seasoned bread crumbs on the pathway from my portable classroom to the cafeteria. Two Rubenesque cafeteria ladies in hair nets filled my wagon with the world's smallest milk cartons. I, too, felt small, but in charge and responsible for carrying out this decidedly urgent delivery. I felt honored as I scuffled past the invisible velvet rope and into the culinary world of food preparation and clanking dishware. I began enthusiastically—and much too rapidly—wheeling the little red wagon away from the scent of burnt cheese and baked apple cobbler and back toward my classroom. It seemed miles away. Suddenly one of my wagon wheels hit a rock. The entire load of dairy delights fell out of my cart and onto the sidewalk. I felt like Charlie Brown when yet another something went wrong. Aaugh!

As this horrific event occurred, the school janitor happened to walk by. He saw me standing there, staring at the white pools of Borden's milk laid out on the sidewalk. I was immobile with the steady expression of a sphinx as I looked at the mess on the pavement in front of me, but my brain was processing options at warp speed. Should I run inside and tell the bosomy cafeteria ladies about the soppy sorry mess I made, or … pick up each carton, toss the opened ones in the trash, and play dumb when the teacher asks why there are only seven cartons instead of fifteen?

The middle-aged janitor muttered with a half-smile, "Don't cry over spilled milk, kid." It was the first time I had ever heard the expression. I didn't even know it was an expression. I thought it was sage and specific advice for this messy occasion.

Eichlerville

In the early Sixties, change was rustling the soft air of Santa Clara Valley. Alaska and Hawaii had joined the forty-eight other states on Old Glory. Eisenhower, a former World War II general, had passed the presidential seal over to John F. Kennedy, a handsome and confident forty-three-year-old freshman senator from Massachusetts. Giants fans, with heavily mustard-upped dogs in hand, erupted into cheers that shook the bleachers as Willie Mays popped another one over Candlestick Park's left field fence. Those hollers could be heard as the Fifties tumbled into the next decade. In the early to mid-Sixties, many Americans were prouder and more intoxicated with hope than ever before.

I was growing up in the midst of the social and political hubbub of the Sixties. We resided in our Eichler from 1960 to 1972. No one suspected, certainly not me, a youngster in 1960, that the coming decade would explode like some Fourth of July firework cone into a mix of violence and love. We were on the threshold of change. And what was I doing? Balancing a Crayola crayon between sausage fingers and trying to color inside the lines.

At the same time, Joseph Eichler was riding the post–World War II housing boom. Eichler wasn't an architect. He was a real estate developer with a distinct vision. Inspired by the work of Frank Lloyd Wright, Eichler hired top architects to design homes with the goal of affordability for middle-class working Americans. But these homes were different. Very different. Our Eichler wasn't just a house to me; it was another character in my childhood that held more warmth than a bowl of Campbell's tomato soup and provided more shelter than a mother's arms, certainly my own mother's arms. In the Sixties, that house was my safe retreat from some of the chilliest days of childhood and adolescence. I became more myself once I was inside the structure or had it in view as I approached its windowless face and bright-colored entry.

The front beams on our home's facade were painted goldenrod, and the entrance door was a bold carrot orange. You had to walk through the outside carport to get to the front door, then move into the atrium, a sort of courtyard filled with greenery, bicycles, and a small barbeque grill. Beyond the atrium were sliding doors that led to the living room in front of you, the family room to the right of the entrance, and the fourth bedroom to the left. Three sides of the atrium featured glass sliders, and most of the walls facing the atrium were transparent.

Mom posing at the grill in our Eichler atrium. She never actually did the cooking, but she did pose for photos like an expert model.

The Eichler neighborhood attracted creative types who were ready, nearly ready, or trying-desperately-to-become-ready to buck convention and dive into something brand new. The unique design of the home and the racially mixed makeup of the neighborhood attracted an amalgamation of gifted occupants, including a Sociology professor who later became the first—and to date—only female president of San Jose State University, Gail Putney. She and her husband-at-the-time attended many of my parents' house parties. Hell, almost everyone did.

The groundbreaking design of the Eichler embodied change. From the outside, the neighborhood may have appeared like any other inexpensive subdivision, but inside the bright orange, turquoise, or gold doors, the homes revealed a wonderland of glass and rich mahogany walls and a bright, transparent, daring sort of living. The middle class was no longer reduced to L-shaped structures, cottages, or traditional lines. According to Chuck Elkind, a neighbor in our special pocket of paradise, beyond the racial mix, "The income levels fell neatly in the $20 to $30K bracket, and the median per family was 1.25 advanced college degrees, 1.5 cars, and 2.3 children." We were about as middle-class a group as one could find, but we were not middle-of-the-road in philosophy. We were ready and willing to challenge the status quo.

It's difficult to imagine that present-day Eichler owners are much different in their politics, but perhaps they are. In all likelihood, they have remodeled the kitchen and changed out the dingy but daring gray linoleum tiles that looked like the flooring of a rocket ship. Maybe they don't even know or talk to their neighbors. They've likely replaced the single-paned glass walls with something more shielding in the four-season climate of the Bay Area. By now, they've removed the then-modern gray and white Masonite cabinets of the Sixties kitchen and replaced them with stylish doors to go with new granite, concrete, or quartz countertops. And they likely take pleasure in the fact that their Eichler nest, with its ordinary shoebox form and facade, does not reveal the whimsy and spirit that lies beyond the mundane exterior. That's for some to know, and others, like myself, to remember.

Early in the Sixties, we cherished our blond wood and brightly colored plastic furnishings and modern slat benches with clean lines. As kids, we were swallowed alive by the oversized shag rug that sat in our wall-of-windows living room. Our nights were illuminated by the white planet-like lighting fixtures that hung from stems and dropped from our ceilings like upside-down lollipops. Why would we want to live like everyone else? We were Eichler people.

None of the Eichler homes came equipped with forced air heating or air conditioning. After all, we weren't mere mortals living in ordinary L-shaped structures. We required a unique living space with a radiant heat system buried like sunken treasure beneath the tile floors. That made perfect sense in the late Fifties and early Sixties when energy was inexpensive. After the energy crisis in the early Seventies, homeowners had to take out a second mortgage to pay for heating their Eichler home. Cats, however, adored the floor heating. The toasty warmth felt heavenly on chilly mornings, and the gray-speckled tiles provided ample coolness to the bottoms of our feet on muggy summer days. Eichlers were all about form-plus-function.

The home's flat gravel roof was lined with pebbles that would blow around with the slightest gust of air. I spent over a decade listening to that colony of rooftop nuggets relocating with every brush of wind. It was the Eichler version of soothing wind chimes. But when it rained or was blustery, it sounded like someone was rearranging furniture above me. And when lightning cracked, I'd count the seconds until thunder shook the glass walls of our Eichler.

But living in a house of glass walls during blistering summer months was no picnic. The rooms would become steamy and sauna-like. There was no escape from the sun. These were the days before dual-pane and low-e window glass. Eichlers had single-paned aluminum-framed sliding doors and glass walls. It was a modern open design that let you know quite clearly what season you were in. We shivered inside the Eichler through the Bay Area winters. Sweat moisture circles appeared in the armpits of our shirts in the summer. We didn't care. We could get used to anything and everything. We embraced the elements. We were at home in the indoor/outdoor atrium. We were like the Jetsons! We were in the Eichler, and the era was taking off like a rocket to the moon.

Living in an Eichler in the Sixties was like driving a classic car that was the envy of every driver on the road. We took great pride in the built-in kitchen table, the outside-in atrium, brightly painted front door, and the teenagers' escape hatch in the kids' bathroom. How many adolescents in the Sixties and Seventies slipped out of that exterior bathroom door late at night, much to the chagrin of their parents? My parents assumed the door would be a practical way to avoid muddy boots in the house. A children's bathroom that leads to the outside. Brilliant, except for the fact that adolescents had amorous expectations and raging hormones. It turned out to be my own personal revolving door of classmates and trouble. What was Joe Eichler thinking? As pre-teens and teenagers, we used that door to sneak out and get dirty, raunchy, stoned, and laid. We'd hang out with our friends, then slip back inside through our convenient passageway. I don't think Joe Eichler had teenagers. If he did, he didn't think like one.

The kitchen table was a bit different: it was semi-attached to the countertop of the kitchen and snuggled up against the stove area. The table could easily rotate this way or that, although we never moved it. It truly was a Jetsons kitchen. The cabinetry wasn't pine or oak or walnut. It featured gray frames with Masonite-type sliding kitchen doors in off-white.

In the Sixties, kitchens were thought to be the heart of the house. But since my mother seldom cooked, our hub was the living room floor, where we sat cross-legged on the rug or propped up with a TV tray in front of the Zenith console, our own version of a fireplace to gather around for music, weekly shows, warmth, and comfort. Sometimes we'd be swinging from an outdoor rattan chair that had been moved inside. My father had screwed it into the ceiling at the end of our kitchen table. When it came to these unexpected projects and notions, we never asked why.

The Bluebirds of Happiness

I was absent from the classroom one day only to return and find that my favorite classmates had already been recruited for Brownie troops. All that was left for me was to become a Bluebird. I didn't really understand the difference between Brownies and Bluebirds, and it turned out there wasn't much difference except that the more popular girls chose to become Brownies, and the ones who were floundering or less popular—or missed class due to a sore throat—became Bluebirds.

But it wasn't the end of the world. The Bluebirds' outfit was much cuter than the mousy brown Brownie attire. We wore red, white, and blue. We were walkin', talkin' American flags with tennis shoes. The Brownies were dressed in … well, brown. They graduated to Girl Scouts who wore Kelly green.

For those unfamiliar with the protocol, Bluebirds and Brownies are the "junior" levels to what will eventually be Campfire Girls and Girl Scouts. I was certain there was a similar graduation for boys, but I honestly didn't care. None of it sounded appealing, except perhaps singing on the way to the house where the meetings were held. "We're the Bluebirds, the jolly Bluebirds, we are happy all the time." Those were the actual lyrics. What I wanted to know was, who's happy all the time? We weren't. That was a damned lie. But I liked making pictures out of macaroni and greeting cards from pieces of felt. When you were a Bluebird, there was no shortage of craft projects.

Later, when I was a Campfire Girl, I enjoyed sewing decorative beads in assorted shapes onto my uniform vest when I performed a "positive task" that was listed in my Campfire Girls book. Complete a task, have a parent sign off on it, and be rewarded with a colorful bead. It was like a to-do list with a reward for each completed mission. Sometimes I lied. I didn't help my mother make dinner, clean the windows, or sweep the floor. How could I, when she didn't do any of those household chores?

Eventually we had to take part in some outdoor activity. I was not an outdoors type of gal. Jews don't camp. But my friend Julie was in my Bluebirds and Campfire troops. Julie wasn't too popular in school and in fourth grade developed a nervous condition in which she continually yanked at the hair on her head until it was nearly all pulled out. Her head looked like a stick of cotton candy with a few bites taken out of it. After a few months, she was bald as Telly Savalas. It didn't help that she was tall, thick as an oak, had thin eyes that looked like a couple of dashes, and spoke in a slow, halting manner, as though she were programmed and landed here in a spaceship. Julie was peculiar enough to be my kind of friend.

Besides having weekly meetings after school where we'd participate in creating some miscellaneous craft, we lived up to the Campfire Girls' name: we went camping. When we arrived at the campground and unloaded the cars, the other girls were already on the warpath to exclude and ridicule my friend Julie. Luckily, Julie never seemed to have an ounce of self-consciousness or give a rat's ass about other people's judgment of her. Everyone thought she was different, and she knew she was, but it didn't seem to bother her in the least. She liked who she was. I, on the other hand, was self-conscious enough for the both of us and always hyper-aware of what people saw when they peered over at me, or what they thought of my actions, my appearance, my clothing. Their opinion of me was the only one that counted. That was also true of my father's opinion of me. Whatever he thought I was worth, that's how valuable I felt, not only with him, but to the rest of the world. And, unfortunately, to myself. It seemed I was the Incredible Shrinking Woman in his eyes, and on this camping adventure, in everyone else's. The troop went about the ritual of snubbing me because I was with Julie. Shunning by association.

Julie and I made our way down the hill, separate from the rest of the girls huddled together giggling and pointing in our direction. I was suddenly the bodyguard there to protect my friend who had already numbed herself to ridicule. She didn't seem to mind the verbal arrows, but I did. They were targeting my neighbor, my friend-by-proximity, and that snickering meshed with maliciousness was firing in our direction with the cruel intention of offending and wounding. Sadly, I hadn't figured out how to successfully tune out intimidation and teasing. This was bullying, pure and simple, and I was going to stay loyal to my team of two: Julie and myself.

We both laid out our sleeping bags and personal belongings far from the main camp and away from the cackling crowd. Once we rolled out our sleeping bags, we huddled together in a cozy twosome. The sky darkened; the air chilled. Even the leaders of our group didn't seem to involve themselves in this war of words and snickers. It was a long and torturous night—for me. Julie slept like a rock. I was overwhelmed with feelings of separateness and sadness and longed for my soft bed and even softer cat. I hated camping.

All Is Fair

Two years after moving into our U-shaped hub, neighbors began to improvise an impromptu cultural event that ultimately came to be known as the Fairglen Art Festival. The event would feature the artwork and musicianship of blocks of our talented neighbors.

The origin of the Fairglen Art Festival has been macraméd together from oral history passed from neighbor to neighbor and from one generation to the next. Contrary to what its name might suggest, the event did not begin on Fairglen Avenue, or on Fairwood, Fairorchard, Fairoak, or Fairlawn Avenues, or on the only un-fair streets in the neighborhood, Briarwood and

Andalusia Drive. It didn't even begin as the Fairglen Art Festival. Its beginning can be traced to 1962 and my neighbors Maggie Caploe and Les Lambson, and a handful of residents in homes outside our cul-de-sac.

One summer afternoon, Maggie set up an exhibit of her creations on the walls of her Eichler and invited a few of the neighbors into her home to view her works of art. Visitors noshed on dry cookies rolled in confectioners' sugar and emptied a pot of Folger's from the tall percolator. Drawings, tapestries, ceramics, prints, note cards, and paintings were strategically displayed from the kitchen to the tables beside the couch and on the walls of the hallway. She called them "oddments" and managed to sell a sprinkling of pieces to her guests. Maggie was inspired to bring out more and more arts and crafts. She displayed them on her garage door and on the fence that ran along the street outside our cul-de-sac. Sculpture and pottery were staged on rickety card tables in her driveway, and craft demonstrations radiated a spirit that whispered, "Hey, you can do this, too."

Maggie's oddments brought the neighbors out, including other artists and creative hopefuls who wanted to join in the fun. Les Lambson dragged his potter's wheel onto the driveway and showed the neighborhood children how to form a pot and magically shape a vase. He also demonstrated his Asian-inspired painting technique to those who strolled by.

More and more neighbors pulled their artistic creations into the street or hung them on garage doors and wooden fences. Electricity had suddenly charged the atmosphere. The neighbors and passersby studied the details of each display as they strolled the streets, arms folded behind them like ice skaters. They must have known something special was happening. They must have felt it in the air. How could they not? It was a carnival without the Tilt-A-Whirl ride. It was New Year's Eve without confetti. It was the dead of summer, and someone had parked an old jalopy in the middle of the cul-de-sac for neighborhood kids to climb on. A sign draped from its hood read "Art in Our Alley," which was the original name for this eclectic collaboration of artists and craftspeople.

The following summer, even more artists took part in the fair's festivities. The exhibits filled Fairgrove Court and spilled down the street onto the adjacent blocks. Garage doors became open-air galleries. Driveways became exhibit halls. Musicians performed in the front yards. It was no longer an art festival in our "alley," our cul-de-sac. The artists and activities now stretched over to the Fairglen Avenue thoroughfare towards Fairwood Avenue, the neighborhood's longest street.

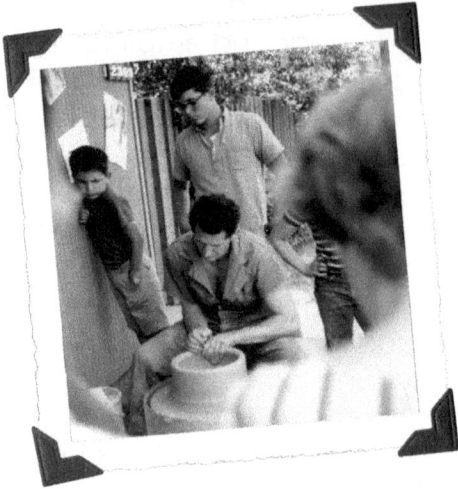

Les Lambson working the potter's wheel in his driveway while neighborhood kids looked on.

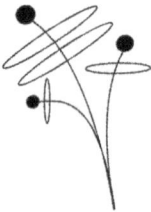

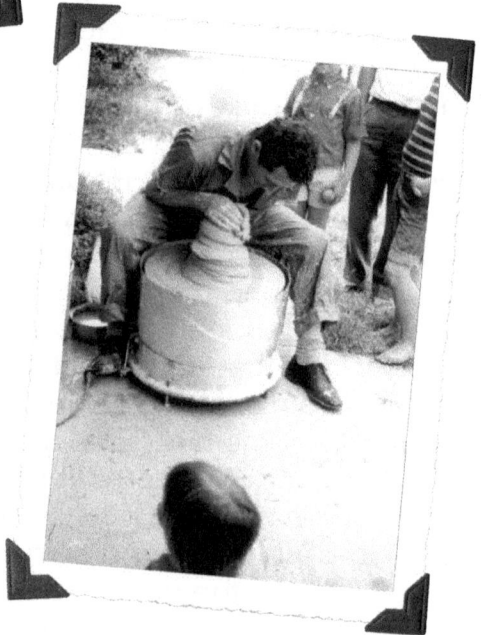

   Soon it was re-christened the Fairglen Art Festival, and from word-of-mouth, with each passing year, the event flourished. Not only did a unique variety of artwork find a home at this show, but neighborhood garage bands performed, folksingers strummed guitars, dancers whirled in the driveways, and local cooks grilled hot dogs and shish-kabobs on well-worn barbeque grills. Resident weavers wove on their looms, and welders spliced metal fragments into abstract shapes. Parades of booths and tables featuring stained glass, clay and stone sculptures, ceramics, quilts, and jewelry ruled the streets. Puppet shows for the younger children, square dancing for restless mothers, and judo demonstrations for active teenagers were featured. According to Elizabeth Giarratana's book *Old Willow Glen,* by 1972 there were more than 200 artists participating, and the art-loving crowds quietly grew to 5,000.

One of our neighbors, James Thatcher, hauled in a truckload of beach sand, dumped it onto his driveway, and fabricated an intricate sandcastle. These masterpieces created from a million little pieces were the Thatcher family's annual signature gift to the Fairglen Art Festival. One of the Thatcher castles even appeared in an article on how to build sandcastles in *Sunset* magazine. Thatcher would spend about twelve hours building his driveway kingdoms. He would begin late Saturday afternoon on the day before the festival, work until midnight, then finish up with two or three hours of work the next morning. Thatcher always built his castles with sixteen doors, sixty-seven windows, and eighty-eight circular staircases. Only he knows the significance of those numbers.

Their intricate walls would require frequent misting to prevent crumbling on hot summer days in the Santa Clara basin. Once the festival was over, the castle sand was offered to neighborhood children to help refill backyard sandboxes. The Thatchers also dumped it in their own backyard. Although most people assumed he was an architect, Thatcher had a desk job as a pension consultant. But he frequently took his five children to nearby Santa Cruz beach, which is where his love of sandcastles was born.

Our next-door neighbor Les Lambson—who was a painter, potter, politician, philosopher, and teacher—would often spend summer afternoons in his driveway tossing clay on his pottery wheels and scratching through layers of paint on Masonite with primitive tools to create huge abstract paintings. His work was soon distributed throughout the world and purchased by prominent statesmen, entertainers, corporations, universities, and museums. More than 1,000 of Les Lambson's paintings soon found their way into private homes and collections, as well as museums and galleries. But in the early Sixties, he would give away his paintings to neighbors—just because. My parents were gifted with quite a number of them. They also purchased a few for pennies on the dollar, or in exchange for a couple of vodka gimlets. Many of our neighbors had similar paintings on their walls, all courtesy of Les Lambson. His fame had not yet struck during those early Art Festival days, but his generosity was already on display. So were his paintings.

Along with a bigger audience and more artists on display came commercial vendors, tax collectors, and other outstretched palms. They were city officials demanding a slice of the profitable pie. By that time, my family had sold the Eichler and moved on. But our memories and Eichler sensibility never faded. Although the Fairglen Art Festival closed down shop in the mid-1990s due to insurance liability concerns, an annual block party continues to be held in the Willow Glen Eichlers. They celebrated their seventeenth year in September 2017. The Fairglen Neighborhood Block Party, an incarnation of the original art festival, includes the selling of baked goods and crafts in a hub of houses that continues to radiate the optimism of the Fifties and Sixties. Approximately 250 attend this annual block party, and they continue to celebrate everything that remains cohesive and charitable about living under the magic dome of the Willow Glen Eichlers. After all, it was never just a neighborhood. The Eichlers were a state of (modern) mind and a creative hub of closeness and celebration. That unfailing unity and sense of fun continues on.

Cafeteria Style

Our elementary school cafeteria always smelled like chicken broth. Even during school assemblies, you could get a whiff of the soup stock and the come-hither scent from some mystery meat baking in the oversized stainless-steel pans. The swing and sway of the elementary school lunch dance was one of the first rituals I studied and became adept in. All the hot lunch kids sat on one side of our grand echoing cafeteria, the bagged lunch crowd on the other. With a single moist quarter in hand, a gourmet meal of fried chicken, lasagna, or loose meatloaf could be had, along with a dinner roll. There was always a corner of the compartmentalized plate for mixed vegetables that we had to consume or hide before we were allowed to go back for seconds. Seconds often included a stick of Velveeta the size of an index finger. It was that horizontal cheese I coveted. I ate string beans so that I could get another mouthful of that cheese-like-food-like product. But did Velveeta qualify as cheese? Or was it something to keep real cheese company in the dairy case? I didn't care that it wasn't "real" cheese. When you're a kid, you go by food texture and taste, not authenticity.

On Fridays, fish sticks were served. Why? As a child, I thought it had something to do with Jesus Christ or another religious mystery. Was it Catholic? Maybe Catholics could only digest fish sticks one day a week the same way Jews and Asians had difficulty digesting milk. I loved those breaded batons, but the cafeteria smelled like rotted fish the day it was plopped on our plate. Better to avoid Fridays altogether and stay home from school and watch game shows like *What's My Line?* or *The Match Game* with Gene Rayburn and his elegant and splendidly skinny super-scope microphones. I'd also watch adult-themed soap operas—or as my grandmother called them, her stories.

The cafeteria served tater tots a few times a week. There was a never-ending supply of these little potato pillows. Our lunchtime beverage was milk in a waxy carton. The school's massive cafeteria also functioned as an assembly room with a stage. When tables were locked away into the walls like Murphy beds, we attended large gatherings or had our classroom photos taken in this room. Sometimes we listened, or pretended to listen, to guest speakers, like when my friend Julie's mother came to talk to us about shrubberies and trees. She projected slides on the wall until our legs became restless. There we sat, rows and rows of jittery jumping beans. I fell asleep somewhere between discussions of succulents and evergreens. We sang "The Star-Spangled Banner" and "America the Beautiful" in unison. I always assumed that *purplemountainmajesties* was one word, but I sang it loud and proud in the cafeteria auditorium.

It was always a deliberate choice: how would you cut your sandwich. On the diagonal or in equal rectangular halves? For years, my mother cut them on the diagonal. Those who had sandwiches cut in oblong halves were the envy of those of us who were provided with triangles. Rectangles seemed more sophisticated. We didn't have a lot of choices to make at such a young age, but one of them involved how to halve the sandwich—and whether or not to like it.

The triangle was easier to shove into my inner cheek, so I suspect that was one of the appeals of the diagonal cut. Since the time of the pyramids, architects have understood the power of the diagonal line. The triangle form was more interesting to the eye. But not to mine. The triangular cut seemed ... pedestrian. I wanted what others were having because I wasn't.

Most days, my mother gave me a quarter to purchase a hot school lunch. She worked full-time and hadn't quite mastered the early morning prep necessary for a peanut butter-and-jelly sandwich. As I fell in line boy-girl-boy-girl and entered the colossal cafeteria, there was always a bustling of activity on the hot lunch side of the room. Indistinguishable sounds ricocheted off one wall and bounded across the hollow space. As I sat there eating my daily meat and roll, I found myself envying the kids in their thermos-and-lunch-pail biosphere populating the other side of the room. I felt jealous of their home-grown meals of bologna and cheese or tuna salad, their one piece of fruit, and a cool thermos filled with God knows what.

Our quarters, given in exchange for a hot lunch, were always sticky and icky by the time we got to the coin collector seated at a card table outside the cafeteria entrance. The quarter felt more like a silver dollar in my small palm. What would I win today? What would be scooped and flung into the separate compartments on the green lunch plate? I was especially pleased when it was lasagna day. But I wasn't happy that I had to sit with the same kids on either side of me. Since we were seated in alphabetical order, and boy-girl-boy-girl, my lunch mate was always Wiley Sweet. He looked like you would imagine a young fellow named Wiley Sweet would look. Thick, oversized black-rimmed glasses; small sideways mouth; dirty yellow hair sticking straight up at the crown on his head. He was the spittin' image of Sherman in the Mister Peabody and Sherman cartoon on *The Rocky and Bullwinkle Show.*

Wiley Sweet would crack his neck from side to side throughout the lunch hour. It was loud, like a branch under a horse hoof. When I cracked my neck, it sounded more like bubble wrap. One day, we finally began to converse over fried chicken and fries. We discovered we had something critical in common: our love for monster movies. For the first time, I looked forward to lunch hour. It was official. I had a dining buddy. I didn't have to sit quietly on a hard bench pushing peas around the plate. Wiley and I would compare notes on this monster and that movie. Time spent with Wiley Sweet became a treat. Finally, someone who spoke my spooky language.

We loved everything from *Frankenstein* to *Creature from the Black Lagoon*. We'd talk about the latest space films where they explored Mars or another planet in the solar system. We wondered if such casual visits would materialize in our lifetime. We'd run home from school, splash down into the living room rug like a space capsule hitting the water, and watch *Chillers of Science Fiction*, which aired late weekday afternoons on KPIX Channel 5. It was later replaced with *Creature Features* on Saturday night, hosted by Bob Wilkins, yet another fellow with oversized, dark-rimmed glasses and a dry sense of humor. Wilkins was the adult version of Wiley Sweet.

Chillers of Science Fiction would generally feature classic films and horror movies of the 1930s to 1950s, including the Japanese "giant monster" movies of the Sixties. But in the mix was my personal favorite: *The Wolf Man*. Even back then I preferred a hairy chest.

These programs focused on science fiction often aired the "nuclear monster" and "space alien" films. Created in the 1950s, these movies were all based on the idea of giant mutants or aliens from outer space terrorizing Earth. They included *Attack of the 50 Foot Woman, The Amazing Colossal Man, Them!, Tarantula, The Thing from Another World, It Came from Outer Space, War of the Worlds,* and the heady film I couldn't watch often enough, *The Incredible Shrinking Man*. I was a particularly pensive third grader.

In elementary school, there was nothing more intriguing than the concept of time travel. I gobbled up the notion of nixing the clock on the wall and taking one step beyond to another time and place. What better thing to do on a school night? It sure beat doing homework. I was drawn to *The Twilight Zone*, *The Time Tunnel*, *The Outer Limits*, *Land of the Giants*, and other timeless tales within the gray cathode scans running horizontally across our television screens.

Harold would struggle with the model kits featuring the most popular monster creatures on the market. He'd put each frightening figure together with sticky glue and a toothpick. Each monster came in a separate box and was broken into a bazillion plastic pieces. Harold had the entire set: The Wolf Man, Dracula, Frankenstein, and the Creature from the Black Lagoon, or "Creature from the Black Legume," as we fondly referred to him.

Harold carefully glued the plastic pieces together so that there wasn't an arm emerging from the head, nor a foot in a mouth. Each completed character was placed in all its plastic glory on top of his polished pinewood five-drawer dresser. Late in the evening, I would sneak into his room, crawl under the covers beside him, and we'd peer across the dark chasm of night at each frightening figure. They might come to life at any moment, or so we feared. Oh, how we loved to be scared in childhood. In adulthood? Not so much.

As I scooted out of Harold's haunted room and back to mine through the darkened hallway, I mumbled, "Good night, Chet." He'd return the only appropriate response: "Good night, David." Harold and I would parrot the Huntley-Brinkley closing on the nightly news until we were well into our teens. But those monstrous figures sitting atop Harold's dresser couldn't rival the terror splashed across our television screen during the six o'clock news. Vietnam and recent body counts were the lead story. We knew war was hell because we heard the numbers and they ricocheted through our own bodies.

"*In South Vietnam Buddhists demonstrate against the government.*"

"*Vietcong score big victory in attacks with massive troop losses (200 killed). China condemns President Johnson's administration policy in Vietnam.*"

"*25,000 protesters protest the war at the White House. Speakers include Dr. Benjamin Spock.*"

News on the Vietnam War was served up at dinnertime. While we ate, we watched a graphic scorecard: how many Americans had died that day, how many South Vietnamese, and how many

Communists. It was a time when everybody, every individual life, mattered. After a steady diet of such reality, those monstrous figures that had taken up residence upon my brother's dresser looked mild-mannered and harmless.

Joseph Eichler used a handful of designs for the Eichler and positioned them all over the Bay Area, from San Francisco and Marin County to Redwood City, Menlo Park, Sunnyvale, Mountain View, and San Jose. The sliding glass doors entering the atrium expanded the home into the garden area. The enormous beams and tongue and groove boards of the ceiling allowed some of the home's structural elements to become visible, another part of the Eichler's appeal and charm. But how did Eichler people make a home in such a transparent space—a space that was never truly dark? Even in the winter, the sunlight bathed our walls. My father placed bamboo blinds over the floor-to-ceiling living room windows, but they were seldom pulled down. We were all slaves to the light. It was our alarm clock each morning, but there was a subtlety to its ring. It was more like a slow and steady purr. Wake up, not WAKE UP!

By the late Sixties, a few Eichler neighbors replaced the cool matte-finished tiles with shag carpeting. Kids today don't know how easy they have it. *Why, when I was a kid, we had to walk eight feet through dense shag carpeting to change the channel on the television set. Then we had to rake it for lost jewelry and bits of dry cereal.* If you attempted to vacuum the long threads of shag, you had to prepare for an ill vacuum cleaner. We often found an assortment of missing items in the vacuum cleaner bag on cleaning day: car keys, hair clips, 45 rpm records. Having shag carpeting installed was an extraordinary event, so unusual that neighbors were invited over to view it. It was like bringing home a new baby.

The siding on the outside of the Eichler home was made of wood incised with vertical pinstripe grooves. The original siding was stained, not painted. Each Eichler was a different shade of beige or green, sometimes taupe or gray, but the accent color on the front beam of the home and the door, which came as a matched set, were bold shades of pumpkin orange, turquoise, paprika red, sunflower yellow, or eucalyptus green. Those accents were confident and courageous. But they radiated fun and teased about what was in store once you made it past the brightly colored door. I never thought a mid-century modern house of glass with ceiling fixtures that looked like moons would be my doing, and undoing.

Behind the Orange Eichler Door

The glue that held our Eichler neighborhood together was a loathing of America's racial inequalities and a rejection of San Jose's "cow town" stigma. If art, music, and sophistication couldn't be found in those early days of Santa Clara Valley, one could easily take a freeway north to San Francisco or a quick drive south to Monterey to the many music venues featured there. Jazz was a favorite, and Monterey had its jazz festivals as well as the famous Monterey Pop Festival. Music. Politics. Loathing. Loving. In the Sixties Eichlerville, we had it all.

Steve Wozniak, co-founder of Apple Inc., and also known as Woz, grew up in an Eichler home. Steve Jobs hung out in Woz's Eichler in those early days of Apple Computer. Jobs called the Eichler "smart, cheap, and good" and that summed it up beautifully. The Eichler's clean design had a profound impact on both Apple co-founders, although Steve Wozniak and Steve Jobs took very different lessons from the home's design. "I was very lucky to grow up in an Eichler," Wozniak has said, referring to his family's home in Sunnyvale, California. "It greatly influenced my liking of simplicity and open style." But Jobs took a different lesson. Eichler's vision for making state-of-the-art housing available to every economic and racial group impacted Jobs' founding premise for Apple, which was the idea that everyone should have access to tools that were previously available only to the very wealthy. Early on, this belief was aimed at personal computers, but later it would include technology like iPods, iPhones, and iPads.

Although Jobs' family residence was not an Eichler (like Wozniak's home), he did come of age in a home designed by two of Eichler's original architects, Bob Anshen and Steve Allen. During this time, the pair also designed homes for a rival developer, Mackay patio homes. The two of them were the Barnum and Bailey of architecture and home development. Together, they created hundreds of stylish houses and were considered a winning team.

Anshen and Allen were very concerned with privacy and decided back in 1949 to create a special structure that would appear as a blank wall to the street. No one thought the concept of such a house would sell, but those homes went like hotcakes, and the duo's visions for the Eichler were an ideal match to Joseph Eichler's ambition to build Modernist-inspired affordable houses for middle-class American families. With their inexpensive and innovative ways of construction, Eichlers and homes like them became affordable for the middle class. Never before were such concepts and designs available to the general public. Their countercultural vision of beautiful products for the mass market stayed with Steve Jobs for the rest of his life.

Anshen was aggressive, loud, and sarcastic, much like my father. His contemporaries described him as so unattractive he looked like a character out of Dickens. He had a small physique and an oversized, oddly angular head. He was a walking caricature. He was a walking Tootsie Roll Pop. But, much like my father, he absolutely commanded attention, so much so that people barely noticed his architectural partner and best friend, Steve Allen, standing by his side. Allen was a sizeable man; Anshen was short and thin, weighing in at roughly 125 pounds. They looked a bit like Mutt and Jeff. Allen was the quiet, unassuming one of the pair, unlike Anshen and my father, whom everyone felt they knew the instant they walked into any room.

Anshen convinced a multi-millionaire to give them their first job, which put them on the map and led to most of the jobs that followed, including the designing of Eichlers. With his outsized personality and head, and seemingly magical powers, Anshen made a name for himself and for the firm. He championed housing for the general population using prefabricated materials, and he worked with Joe Eichler to give the country a considerable collection of modern tract homes.

Although Anshen and Allen were known as a team for building bohemian dwellings like the Eichlers, it was Anshen who secured most of the team's jobs. He demanded attention; he got it. Like my father's, Anshen's face was not particularly pretty, but it was expressive, especially when telling jokes. He too had a gravitational force that drew people to his orbit. And despite his looks, women swooned, just as they did for my father. Apparently, it was common for Anshen to slip behind women at parties and pinch them on their back cheeks. They would turn around in disgust, but he would look at them, with a mouth full of charm and flowery words, and the women would fall on the ground laughing, entranced by his smile and, no doubt, by the power he had as an influential architect. My father had the same magnetic charisma. These two ferocious flirts were cut from the same cloth.

Books and Bouffants at Booksin

My teacher in third grade was Miss Helwig, an off-brand version of Marilyn Monroe. We thought she had an interesting name as it combined two separate adult-type words: hell and wig. We didn't know her first name. Teachers didn't have first names.

Miss Helwig wore tight-fitting pencil skirts, crisp white blouses, cobalt blue dresses, or stylish suit jackets to class. She looked like she should be a stewardess and had no business teaching, what with her overblown bouffant hairstyle like a blonde bubble-cut Barbie doll. But Miss Helwig was no bubble brain. She didn't inspire learning. She inspired napping.

Miss Helwig was low on energy, high on hairdos. If her energy had dipped any lower, she would have been a corpse. But she was a looker. All the boys had a crush on Miss Helwig, and all the girls wanted to look like her. But we all wished she was someone else's teacher, not ours. She wasn't enthusiastic or motivated. Miss Helwig didn't want to be there. She had taken on her teaching career by default, waiting for a husband to pick her up on his white horse and ride off into the sunset and away from the blacktop and tetherball poles of our schoolyard.

We utilized The SRA Reading Laboratory programs under Miss Helwig's regime. It was a bunch of cardboard cards with stories scribbled on them. We had to get up from our desk, go to the card file on the back cabinet of the classroom near the tall windows, pick out a color-coded cardboard sheet (the colors indicated different levels of reading and comprehension), read the story, then answer the questions on the back of the card. I don't know a student who didn't cheat, but I'm sure there were at least one or two. Wiley Sweet, perhaps? For the first time ever, we were on our own, and we were allowed to get up from our desks, read at our own pace, and coordinate our own progress. It made us feel very grown up. Especially the cheatin' part.

Slide 'n' Go Seek

My favorite household event was the ceremonial unfolding and unrolling of the pearly surfaced slide screen. My father would dust off the army green slide projector and prop up a hefty screen in the living room. I was always excited when he decided to drag it out along with the slide trays. "Come on, everybody. Sit down here. Slides!"

We'd all collapse into the squeaky Naugahyde couch and ready ourselves for the show. It always took a while for this rocket to blast off as every fifth or sixth slide was misplaced in the trays and the images appeared upside down on the screen. Some trays were missing slides and would flash bright white light onto the screen. We'd all moan and collectively rub our eyes. A few bent slide frames had the power to jam the machine and halt my father's personal Kodachrome parade.

We were eager and poised for the images to reveal themselves, even though the same images had been projected dozens of times. For a brief moment, we were living the Kodachrome commercial, complete with playground swings, smiles, and superficial glee. There was something about having your past magically appear in an oversized format and in two dimensions on a textured surface that made the moments of your life seem ... historical. And in the case of my father's slide shows, hysterical.

He would always slip in a few slides of the nude studio models he had taken photographs of during his carousing single days in the late Forties. Post-WWII, my father would shuffle around New York City with his Leica camera and his male companions. The sudden appearance of naked torsos and hips immediately after the posed and polite family vacation snapshot smiles were always a surprise, a burst of embarrassment, and a classic Dad maneuver. Those pert, fleshy, pink young women with an oddly alluring language in their limbs and cheesecake poses always livened up the party ... and embarrassed the youngsters. That was especially true when company was scrunched up on the same small couch watching the click-clack of the slide images alongside my brother and me.

We all knew that my father enjoyed underdressed women in *Playboy*, naked women statues, and stark-naked or semi-naked, uncomfortably posed women in his family slideshows. When he was back from WWII, my father and his buddies would go to public photo studios known as camera clubs where young women would pose provocatively for budding photographers. These slideshows offered my first glimpse at female breasts, bulbous tummies, and tubular adult thighs. I had never seen my mother's breasts, so these pictures were like a beginner's class in anatomy. The breasts of the women projected on the screen were often small, their nipples pale pink, the facial expressions filled with surprise or confidence. Perhaps it was the harsh studio lighting, but their areolas seemed like alien beings from another solar system.

The conservative era of the 1940s and 1950s made it challenging for artists and photography geeks like my father to express themselves. Even the daring Bettie Page used camera clubs as a means of self-expression and self-exploration. She began as a glamour model and would often pose half nude or fully nude for these hidden clubs and public shoots. Her lack of inhibition gave Page her own style and popularity as she pushed the boundaries of what was accepted in society.

The raw look of camera club photos threw suburban audiences of the Fifties into a tizzy. In the early Sixties, married couples like my parents sat around their modern living rooms, trying to hold onto 1950's conventions while taking a calculated step into a new decade that celebrated the naked body. Nudity in magazines and in these camera clubs threw societal norms off their game. No one was used to seeing photos exploring various types of sexual behavior, especially in their own living room. Until they saw these types of photos, many people were not aware that sadomasochistic rituals and behavior even existed in the 1950s. The photos from the camera clubs of New York City offered an eye-opening view of the subculture. My father's slides never included any such rituals, only scantily clad young women in uneasy poses. He must have cruised by the camera club corner quite often as his slide presentations were laced with more breasts and thighs than a bucket of Colonel Sanders' Kentucky Fried Chicken.

Dental Devils and Devilish Clowns

Elayna, Joyce's daughter, had bigger teeth than mine, which is saying a lot as my teeth protruded out of my mouth like Mr.

Ed's. I thought Elayna was seriously cool, so I wanted the same type of overhang extending from my own mouth. Everyone had a crush on her, so I assumed that having oversized anterior teeth and incisors was a desirable trait. My ongoing ritual was to chew gum and stick it on top of my teeth to make it look like I had Elayna's mouth. Carly Simon copied me. So did Joni Mitchell. I would also put waxy sweet-smelling Halloween teeth in my mouth and pretend I was Elayna. And because I was her, everyone cherished me. Strangely enough, even after braces, I ended up with massive front teeth that stuck out far enough to make it impossible to close my lips together. I must have manifested my own destiny because I wanted to have Elayna's teeth ... and eventually had them. I willed them into existence and into my mouth. Either that or I inherited my mother's enormous choppers.

All of my teeth emerged mismatched, like some collapsing picket fence. I endured years of torture at the orthodontist's office, and my tormentor and the devil incarnate was Dr. Paxton. Two paintings featuring the faces of circus clowns hung on his office wall. Those sadistic clowns were creepy, and Dr. Paxton was pure evil. His collection of pain-inflicting oral picks and pounding devices were always at the ready. Bang, twist, tighten. Yeow.

The only humane part of these frequent and torturous visits was sitting in the waiting room, where I would thumb through a stack of *Highlights* magazine. The best part was locating the hidden objects on page twelve. After reading his periodicals and enduring Dr. Paxton's chamber of horrors, I would reward myself with a cheeseburger, then go home and try to locate the hidden objects behind the metal and twisted wires strung across my mouth like the grill of our '57 Buick Roadmaster. Trying to dig out yesterday's lunch was no picnic. My smile after a burger and fries looked like the hanging gardens of Babylon.

All four of my back teeth had to be extracted. There were too many swimmers in this pool of saliva. As I lay outstretched on the office gurney like a corpse at a morgue, Dr. Paxton performed the painful procedure right in the hallway next to the check-out desk and receptionist. Two gruesome clowns glared down at me from their frames.

With equal parts dread and detestation, I visited Dr. Paxton's office on a regular schedule. From braces to headgear to retainer, I despised him at every step of the metallurgy. Today, I can't fathom why some rap artists deliberately have gold installed on their front teeth. I never wanted to see my own mouth filled with metal again. This Marquis de Sade of orthodontics held the poison—those terribly painful instruments that mangled, pounded, and eventually tidied my formative years and aforementioned teeth. With his general impatience and harsh oral procedures that bordered on sadism, Dr. Paxton had no business being around children. He had the bedside manner of Freddy Krueger.

All of Dr. Paxton's dental assistants—who seemed to get hired, then rapidly fired and replaced—were the spittin' images of the centerfold bombshells featured on the pages of my father's *Playboy* magazines. This dental office was as surreal as a Russ Meyer film. Blondes with huge masses of hair piled high on their heads, heaving bosoms grazing my paper bib, and pints of mascara that would rival Liz Taylor's Cleopatra were clopping through his hallways on four-inch heels. There wasn't a Plain Jane in sight. Dr. Paxton's band of bodacious hotties would hand him cool steel instruments of anguish, then rush away to reapply lip gloss and readjust their cleavage.

Concrete Jungle

The first time I felt anxiety in my body was when my teacher announced we'd be playing musical chairs. It was raining outside, so we had to remain within the confines of the classroom. Not a bouncing ball or jump rope in sight. The teacher would scratch her head in hopes that ideas for inside recreational pastimes would sprinkle out like dandruff. Then she told us to line up our chairs in two rows, back to back. The heart-pounding pressure of grabbing a seat and tossing a peer across the room in order to secure a chair created inner turmoil and angst. Especially when my classmates weighed twice as much as I did. They all did. I was the stick figure used to play Hangman.

I lived for recess. Whatever project we were working in the classroom didn't seem quite as important as running outside and heading to the tetherball pole or mingling with the gang of girls playing Chinese jump rope. Sometimes we'd get a big rubber ball out of the cardboard box near our classroom door and bounce it back and forth for ten minutes. And maybe those ten minutes would be the best minutes of our lives.

How do certain games, sayings, and notions get started in our collective consciousness? For instance, how did girls know how to play Chinese jump rope on the playground? I was the Chinese jump rope queen in elementary school, but I have no idea when or why someone decided to put a piece of elastic around the ankles and say, "Come on girl, let's play." My foot would tap in, then out of the band without ever touching it. Then the band was moved up behind the knees to make the game more challenging, and then to our waist, as I threw my entire leg up in the air trying not to hit the outer band. Visions of the Radio City Music Hall dancers danced in my head.

I couldn't wait to get out of the classroom and move about with carefree abandon. My classmates would scatter like colorful game pieces on a charcoal gray board of asphalt. Childhood is spent under a brilliant blue sky with puffy cartoon clouds. We were fueled by an endless supply of energy, determination, and elation about every game in the play area.

Besides kickball, tetherball, Red Light/Green Light, softball, Red Rover, and dodgeball (where you found out which kids didn't like you), we also had a few sessions of folk dancing instruction held during recess. The boys tromped about in their high-top Keds, while the girls whirled and twirled like Cinderella at the ball. I felt graceful. I mastered each step. I felt accomplished. I would be a dancer, like the ballerinas splashed across the pink bedroom wallpaper on Long Island. Now in California, I was mastering the steps.

First and Last Position

I was introduced to dance lessons when I was eight years old. Ballet and tap were on the dance menu. It felt natural and was as effortless as breathing. More importantly, I was good at something. My sparkly red sequined belt would be carefully wrapped around the waist of my black sleeveless leotard. I felt like Isadora Duncan, or a princess, or any person bigger and bolder than my puny self.

One day, a young girl with a long blonde ponytail was singled out and pulled aside by the dance teacher. Then I was pulled aside with the two of them. I thought I was in trouble or wasn't doing the steps fast enough, but the teacher simply wanted to ask us to perform in the upcoming recital, just the two of us. What? She told us we were "special" and "the finest dancers in the class." I was certain my red belt would start spinning around and around in excitement. I was thrilled.

I'm the sandwich filling in the middle of two other ballerina wannabes in the Eichler cul-de-sac. Dancing, even in shredded tights, was my dream.

But as soon as my mother heard of this honor, she immediately pulled me out of dance lessons. There would be no dance recital. There would be no spotlight on me and the girl with the ponytail from my dance class. I was dumbfounded. But why? She said I could take lessons in only one area, and she wanted me to have piano lessons. Seemingly out of the blue, she wanted me to learn piano even though I was excelling at dance. I hung my head, knowing I would never be able to change her mind. I felt bewildered and betrayed. Stymied. Pulled away from some beautiful vision of having a capacity and a deep passion for something. The worst part of having my balloon popped? My mother held the long sharp pin that would carry out the action.

We had a blond wood upright player piano in our family room. The player part never worked, but the fabric that covered the scroll area was a chartreuse and beige weave. Since our house décor was bathed in chartreuse, the piano fit right in. But I wanted to dance, not play piano. I detested piano lessons. Let me rephrase that. I detested my piano teacher, Mrs. Pratt. Let me try again. When I was in her presence, I feared for my life.

Mrs. Pratt was my friend's mother. When I was in fourth grade, Ruth Pratt, my Mormon friend, lived in another country beyond my Eichler world. Her country had plastic on the sofa, traditional furnishings, and a mother who would discipline her children with a strong upper hand. I liked Ruth very much. She had a chin like Bob Hope, and her head was covered in messy waves and curls—messier than mine. Perhaps that's why I liked her so. But I didn't like taking lessons from Mrs. Pratt. She was indifferent, icy, and angered much too easily, which was not a good trait to have if you're teaching young children where middle C is located.

I performed in two piano recitals and loathed every minute of both. I would sweat profusely as I sat on Mrs. Pratt's now uncovered living room couch and alongside other nervous children and their proud parents. I would take an enormous breath, play my short piano piece that always seemed too long, then collapse on the couch as I exhaled. That's finally over. There was never a better moment than the one right after you survived your piano performance and could listen to other nervous fingers tickling the ebonies and ivories.

One afternoon, my mother dropped me off for my piano lesson as she always did. "Don't forget to pick me up in an hour," I said to her as she slipped out the sliding door. I was always worried my mother would forget me. As soon as she was out of earshot, Mrs. Pratt sent a look my way that clearly said trouble ahead.

"Never talk to your mother like that. EVER!" I stood motionless in her kitchen with my jaw dropped to my chest. She ran out to my mother, who was walking down the driveway to her car, and told her in a voice loud enough to be heard inside the house, "Don't pick Carol up today. Let her walk home." What? For some reason, my mother obliged. Mrs. Pratt marched back into the house and prattled on about how I was going to be walking home today. "No one is going to pick you up. You're a bad girl. Now scoot!"

"But I don't know how to get home from here. Isn't my house far away?" Mrs. Pratt didn't care. She was like the Wicked Witch of the West on this particular afternoon. She had a bee in her bonnet—or up her butt. Perhaps she was having premenstrual syndrome, or maybe she was like this from time to time and for other reasons. When you're a kid, you don't think too long or too deeply about the why, just the what. And what I knew was that I was going to have a long walk home and had no idea how to get there.

As I left Mrs. Pratt's house, it was close to 5 p.m. and already beginning to turn dark. I didn't look back at the vicious soul hurrying me away, so I looked ahead and kept walking. I walked like I knew where I was going. I didn't. I was at least two miles from home, and I hadn't left bread crumbs. There were no cell phones. There were no familiar houses on the walk. It was growing darker and darker. I couldn't find any familiar windowless Eichler facade, let alone mine. As my bottom lip began to quiver and the chill of the evening was covering my arms with goose bumps, I wondered if I would ever see my room again. Who would give Pushka her Friskies Buffet? Why does Mrs. Pratt dislike me? I walked and walked, looking for something or someone familiar. But everyone was already nestled inside their own homes readying themselves for dinnertime. The sun had already collided with the silhouette of rooftops, and the sky was shifting from a soft blue to jet black. What do I do? Who can I go to for help? I didn't know any of the people in these unfamiliar houses. Had I walked home in the wrong direction? I could have used a GPS. I was terrified and too shy to approach a strange house. They were all strange houses.

Suddenly, in my peripheral vision, I saw a familiar white car pull up alongside me. Relief! "There you are. Get in." It was my mother. I slipped into the passenger's seat, not uttering a word. When we pulled into the driveway, I begged her to stop making me go to piano lessons. Finally, she did, but she didn't let me return to dance class. If I was good at anything, she didn't want me there. That's all I could surmise. I wanted to dance. I still want to dance. That hunger never goes, no matter how many decades pass. We are drawn to what we love.

Sauntering in the Sixties

So much happened during the Sixties, it would be easier to list what didn't happen. The Beatles ushered in the acceptance of rock 'n' roll, new mod fashions, and longer hairstyles that twisted and shouted discontent among the youth. Rejection of "The

Establishment" ranged from hairstyles to drug use, to questioning authority, and ultimately, questioning a questionable war.

The evening of July 20, 1969, a man walked on the moon and planted a flag as I stood in the atrium of our Eichler looking up at a vast black dome of sky sprayed with stars. I meditated on that bright round orb, the centerpiece of that historical night as Walter Cronkite muttered, "Oh, boy" during the broadcast. He removed his glasses and shook his head in disbelief, and we shook ours along with him. "It seems like a dream," he said later. And it did. But it was a collective dream as we all shared that moment of awe. I tried to spot the frolicking footprints of the astronauts, or at least the canister of Tang Drink Mix. I couldn't see a thing. But I trusted the commentators that they were up there blowing all of our minds with their space antics.

On the estrogen-fueled home front, Gloria Steinem and Betty Friedan were leading a charge to shift the landscape of women's traditional roles, not only in the home, but also in the workplace and in every corner of society. At that same time, I was playing Chinese jump rope in the schoolyard and clapping my hands in rhythm against the palms of my classmates, while we sang:

"I had a boyfriend, Tony,
He lived in old Bologna,
With cherries for toes,
And a pickle for his nose,
That's my boyfriend Tony.
One day he gave me peaches,
One day he gave me pears, pears, pears,
One day he gave me fifty cents,
And he kicked me down the stairs, stairs, stairs."

And when we weren't singing that little ditty about domestic violence, it was:

"This old man, he played one,
He played knick-knack on my thumb,
With a knick-knack paddywhack,
Give a dog a bone,
This old man came rolling home."

Between singing nonsensical, non-feminist but catchy ditties and playing kickball, four-square, and tetherball, I had no time for world events. Besides, what did I know about life beyond the fenced schoolyard? Here's what I knew: I wanted to meet a boy named Tony when I was older, even if it meant plummeting down a stairwell.

It was the era of mutually assured nuclear destruction, and we were on guard, or at least our parents were. During the Sixties, the theory of MAD—Mutually Assured Destruction—dominated our consciousness. This meant that if Russia attacked the West, the West would assuredly retaliate. In other words, there would be no winners, just a whole lot of dead and wounded twisted bodies lying on the ground.

The nuclear arms race was a competition for supremacy in nuclear warfare between the United States and the Soviet Union, along with their allies, during the Cold War. During this period of nuclear stockpiles, other countries developed such weaponry, although none engaged in warhead production on the same scale as the two superpowers. It was official. The Nuclear Arms Race was on. Americans were suffering from justified anxiety. It was an "us against them" mentality. We had enemies in other countries, and we had to prepare to be bombed at home or in the classroom at any given moment. Duck and cover.

One of our Eichler neighbors, the Ludnicks, who lived around the corner, famously installed a bomb fallout shelter in their yard. Actually their teenage son, Brian, was instructed by his rageaholic stepfather to dig the hole for the structure, and he did. The duck-and-cover sanctuary sat inside their Eichler courtyard behind the front yard fence. Our little hub of Willow Glen was suddenly a war zone, at least in our collective minds.

One day, my father and his smart-ass friend Fred Coen, who was an attorney, asked if they could be invited into the shelter for a lively game of pinochle once the shelter was completed. Mr. Ludnick must not have fully appreciated my father and his friend's sense of humor, as neither family received an invitation into their completed hole-in-the-ground asylum. Mr. Ludnick paraded his family in and out of that foxhole for drills. While the Ludnicks were preparing for a regional bombing, my parents were preparing the guest list for one of their infamous parties.

Fred Coen would often call our house and ask for my parents. If I answered he'd always say he was Burt Reynolds or Errol Flynn calling. "Tell your dad it's Burt on the line. Carol, when are you going to come visit my Hollywood mansion?"

I was always a little thrilled that Fred played other characters for me by phone. Fred was my father's biggest fan, and he considered Joe Sveilich his brother from another mother. He reminded me often that my father was the Chief of Protocol of the World, whose political rants and blustery sermons were frequent and jam-packed with heady pissed-off goodness.

As I rode my bicycle back and forth in front of the Ludnick house on the way to and from Booksin Elementary School, I would watch mountains of dirt pile up in their yard. The steel and concrete bricks took shape, much to young Brian's chagrin and accompanying sore muscles. Soon the homemade bomb shelter was hollowed out and ready for World War III. There was now a mysterious steel lid on the entry hatch, and no one was allowed to enter the bowels of the newly built shelter.

This strange symbol of war and fear was the talk of the neighborhood. All the kids wanted to see it, but mostly to play in it. We imagined what it must be like inside. Surely there were board games and toys piled to the ceiling and Shasta sodas in a miniature refrigerator. All of the adults wanted to hold parties in it. The reality of enormous bombs and broken soldiers wasn't quite setting in yet. Everything was still a game. Did those who constructed bomb shelters truly think that ten cans of Chef Boyardee and four six-packs of Tab would hold them over through the nuclear holocaust and several half-lives of Uranium 238? Did they think they would emerge from the shelter, destruction everywhere but their shelter, like some *Twilight Zone* episode about the end of civilization? Wait a minute. All *Twilight Zone* episodes were about the end of civilization.

I never fully comprehended duck-and-cover. At Booksin Elementary School, we had to periodically drop to our knees, cover our small heads with even smaller hands, and curl under the wooden desks like bay shrimp. We had frequent drills where we'd take to the sidewalks outside the schoolyard and walk in groups back to our respective neighborhoods under the supervision of an adult. The school administrators were preparing for The Big One, the war to end all wars. Hadn't we already had one of those?

It was a peculiar schoolroom game we were playing at but didn't quite grasp: the preparation for battle. While we were curled in a tight ball under our desks, my classmates and I would make believe bombs were rattling the classroom walls and windows. But would my desktop actually save me? Would it protect me from the collapsing windows in our room and its shattering glass or the air jam-packed with radiation? Not bloody likely. So, we crouched down, giggled nervously, and tossed pencil erasers at the person closest to us.

In the midst of the political upheaval, bomb threats, confusion, and hatred for other countries and races, the Eichler development was flourishing. San Jose was a bit of a farm town when we moved there. Santa Clara Valley was a bowl of cherry and apricot trees, dried fruit plants, bread factories, and pockets of newly sprouting suburban tracts. The builder, Joe Eichler, was one of the first to aggressively promote an open housing policy. Anyone who qualified financially was able to live in his neighborhood.

In 1960 through 1966, it was a very big deal and transition. People of all races and ethnic backgrounds were being encouraged by Mr. Eichler to purchase homes at a modest price and live side-by-side. The Eichlers of Willow Glen was one of the first integrated neighborhoods; but as kids of six, eight, ten, or twelve years old, we didn't have any awareness of such matters. Our friends were our friends. Black, white, and sometimes black-and-blue, especially when they fell off their bikes. Unlike adults, kids didn't care about race.

Up to the age of thirteen or so, I had no awareness of race. Our friends were our friends because of how we felt around and about them. We didn't care about complexion. We cared about the connection we felt and all the fun we had with them. We counted on intuition to direct us to the members of our tribe. It all depended upon how our heartstrings and interests intertwined. Darker skin was something to be envied. My dark-complexioned friends must have spent more time in the sun. They looked healthier than I did with my plentiful collection of pasty body parts. I envied them and their perpetual tan.

In The Eichlers, parents didn't divide by color either. Families partied with neighbors of every race, creed, color, and cocktail preference and got sloshed together.

The Wish Book

During the last week of November, with Christmas around the bend, the Sears Wish Book would show up. It was thicker than a telephone book and had plenty of enticing photos in living color. The cover design was often red with a towheaded young girl surrounded by gifts from her smiling storybook, picture-perfect parents. They stood somewhere in the background or near the decorated fireplace draped with stockings. My Christmases never looked like this blonde kid's elaborate holiday shindigs. We never celebrated Christmas. We never celebrated Chanukah either. My father despised holidays and steered clear of sentimentality like a test driver in a car trying not to hit the orange cones. No birthday cards or anniversary flowers for my mother; no acknowledgement of whatever the Hallmark calendar was counseling us to celebrate. Dad was an obstinate child when it came to special occasions.

Christmas, to me, was a time when other families decorated with lights, sprayed their windows with faux snow, and propped up a dead tree in the window. They experienced that glorious moment while wrapping gifts when the scissors hugged the colorful paper and began to glide, seemingly on their own, as if they had their own destination in mind and a separate power source other than a hurried hand. It was what I silently labeled *The Scissor Effect*.

I adored Christmas. When my father wasn't looking, my mother, the compulsive shopper, would slip us a package of socks or underwear, or some clearance-priced pajamas that were too long, too hot, and too scratchy. One holiday I received day-of-the-week panties with the words Monday, Tuesday, Wednesday, Thursday, Friday, and Saturday embroidered on the front. Sunday was missing from the package. Why? As Meg Ryan explained in *When Harry Met Sally*, it's "because of God." But despite perky Meg Ryan's explanation, I never fully understood. Were Christians not supposed to wear underwear to church? I can hear my mother say, "Too drafty."

Every year, I'd thumb through the catalog where Sears was dangling the most dazzling dolls, toys, and games in front of our collective noses. The item that most children coveted was a bicycle, and if you were lucky, a Stingray bicycle. It was my true obsession, second only to Elvis. I thought about a Stingray bike day and night, for weeks that turned into months. I knew if I had one under my rear end, everything in my life would be better. It had to be. So I willed it to happen. I have been willing things to happen my entire life. I don't quite know how that works, but I know it does. I was the fastest runner at my school, at least in short distances. When I had to run the 50-yard dash, I would picture myself already crossing the end of the finish line. I wouldn't run to the end; I would fly, at least in my mind. I don't know what happened between the START and FINISH lines, but I knew how to propel myself to win. I saw myself winning. It seemed to work every time.

We had one of those Shoot the Moon games on our coffee table at home. Before Neil Armstrong and Buzz Aldrin landed on the moon in 1969, my family displayed this 1940's game in the house. It featured two metal rods and a metal ball with a wooden base. You were supposed to move the two metal rods farther apart or closer together to create enough motion for the ball to move upward. Then you'd attempt to drop the ball into designated holes in the wooden base, with the last one being the best. I was able to will it to the top hole every time I put my mind to it.

I was raised without religion, but I often wondered if willing was the same as praying. So I willed myself a ruby red Stingray. After weeks of begging and pleading for a banana seat on two wide wheels, one landed in my atrium. I rode it back and forth to school every day. But after a few days, I was ashamed to be seen with such a unique machine. I would have preferred my old beat-up bike, or even a homemade skateboard with roller skate wheels and a two-by-four. For several months, it took me to school and mingled with my friends. Like me, it stood out, but not in a good way. The bike was apple red. Soon I realized that most of the other kids at school didn't have one. Not yet. Suddenly, I wanted to fit in more than I wanted to ride a bike that stood out like a red apple in a bin of oranges. I didn't want to stand out. I wanted to blend in. I wanted to know how to pray. I wanted to wear a cross or a star around my neck. I didn't want to be a loner. I wanted to belong.

I rode the Stingray to school, lowering my head in senseless shame and embarrassment that I had something so radically different from my peers. When you're ten years old, you must fit in or perish. I wanted a bicycle with "regular" handlebars and a small padded seat. But I was already tainted. It was already labeled as being different and by association, so was I.

Schwinn Stingrays eventually wound up in more kid's hands and garages. Those trendy bikes glided over sidewalks, flew down neighborhood streets, then collapsed sideways on driveways and lawns. Eventually, a number of those chopper-styled bicycles pulled wheelies in my own cul-de-sac, on the streets around The Eichlers, in schoolyards, and on dusty open lots. Finally, there were a bunch of banana seats and a lot of kids other than me hanging ape-like on the high handlebars. We parked our bikes on grass to let them graze. We grazed too, but with our fingers and the palm of our hands, running them across the peak of each blade like we were the wind.

Horseplay

What little girl doesn't love horses? I did, although I thought about them more often than I rode them. The first time I rode a horse was with my friend Donna Hansen from elementary school. She lived around the corner from me in The Eichlers. Donna's best friend in elementary school was Linda Hagstrom, a girl who had the identical white-blonde hair and cappuccino freckles. I thought they were members of some secret Scandinavian club that only accepted blondes with fair skin.

Donna regularly rode horses at the stables in the hills surrounding Santa Clara Valley. One afternoon, I was invited to her riding ranch. Propped up on my assigned horse and straddling the saddle, I felt like I was situated in some equestrian form of penthouse, and I could see the entire world from there, or at least a quarter mile of open field. Lady Godiva had nothing on me. I was royalty, at least for those forty-five minutes on the mount. When my horse trotted, my heart galloped.

The second time we went riding I was saddled up on a horse who was much more spirited. My previous horse was nearly comatose by comparison. While Donna galloped up the pathway, my noble stallion and I stayed behind. I assumed he was a gentle fellow and would treat me kindly. No such luck. He began to trot, then gallop. The beast must have thought I was

Annie Oakley. Faster and faster we flew as I began losing control of my equine nemesis, a creature that refused to respond to my tugs on the reins. Suddenly, he floored the brakes like he had just seen Charlton Heston standing in the road with a whip and clad in *Ben-Hur* attire. I was flung into the brush.

"Help!" I yelled.

There was no one within earshot. Shaken, I was not certain what to do next other than untangle myself from the thorny branches and check my pulse to see if I still had one. I quickly concluded that it was safer to play with model horses in the confines of my bedroom or on the front lawn than to take another stab at riding them.

Although this particular horse didn't seem to like me, and my fondness for him was quickly beginning to fade, I remained in a constant state of daydreams about horses. I marveled at their beauty and placed them in my fantasies. Soon I was collecting plastic models of varying breeds and placing them on my bedroom shelf. Dapple Gray. Palomino. Clydesdales. Shetland ponies. But when they sat on my shelf, I referred to them as the black one, the white one, the gray one with spots, the pony. I did have one favorite. It was Fury, a black model horse that I had put together myself with a tiny tube of glue and one confounding instruction sheet. He still had a little dried glue oozing out of the seams of his hindquarters, but no matter. He was Fury, and he was grand. I didn't pretend I was riding him. I pretended I *was* Fury as I ran him through the blades of grass in the front yard. Around this same time when I had such enthusiasm for steeds, I found Mr. Ed to be very erudite and sensitive. If he had been a boy in my class, I'd have dated him—or at least passed him a love note.

The first book I ever wrote or illustrated was a petite booklet titled *I Love Horses*. It was two inches by two inches, illustrated and written in pencil, and stapled with one long staple on the side. It was so small that you could have used a soapy Sen-Sen breath mint as a bookmark. I was nine when I completed this literary gem. All of the breeds of horses that I had studied about and longed to ride were in there, but the book itself was not much bigger than the staple that held it together. "I love palominos" one page read. I would draw different breeds of equine to accompany the in-depth text. "I love Shetland ponies." The same pencil scrawl would illustrate each horse, which looked oddly the same as the last horse, although some had spots, some were darkened in with lead, and some were left white on the page with a mere outline suggesting their form. The booklet contained no drawings of the bucking bronco that had tossed me into the bushes like Jacqueline Kennedy had tossed out the previous White House furnishings.

The Shots Heard Around the World

In 1961, when President Kennedy announced his goal to put a man on the moon before the end of the decade, the adults around me laughed at the thought of this impossibility. But my eyes widened at the prospect of science fiction becoming real life. I had seen enough science fiction films to think it was possible. Anything was possible. Childhood was full of hopes and dreams—and so was our youthful and handsome president.

It was 1963, and I was entering the fourth grade. The day President John Kennedy was shot I happened to be home from school with a sore throat. I was watching television that afternoon, but I couldn't figure out what was going on because my programs were continually being interrupted with news flashes and frantic fuzzy figures operating in panic mode. News reporters were scurrying. Cameras were out of focus, and images were tilting all over the screen. Everyone was rushing, shrieking, and weeping on the small black-and-white screen.

I decided I was too sick to figure it out. I turned off the television, crawled back to bed, sipped hot Lipton tea, and munched on some saltine crackers. An hour later, Harold came home early from school. "What are you doing home?" With his usual youthful exaggeration, Harold explained that the entire school had been dismissed because the president was shot, and "all the teachers were crying and couldn't teach." Huh? I didn't have a clear idea of who our president was and what was in his job description, but Harold was jumping up and down like a jumping bean with even more spastic movements than usual, so I tried to pay attention. It seemed ... significant.

"They told us that the president was killed. A television was rolled into the room so that we could watch the news. Wow. You missed it all, Carol. Watching television at school? It was bitchin'. Then they let us go home early. Cool!"

He was overjoyed, and not because the president was dead. Like most kids, he was kicking up his heels because the entire student body had been released early from school. Now he could head outside to play. But I didn't feel like playing. I was sick, and I was worried sick about John-John and Caroline.

It's hard to imagine, but there was a time when the political parties worked together, when the future was full of exciting possibilities, and optimism filled the air. President Kennedy wasn't a perfect man, but he seemed perfect for the job of bringing people together to work for common causes that would better every person in the country. If you're too young to remember November 22, 1963, and have only experienced the shock of the events of 9/11, it was the same stunned horror show, but different.

I was too young to grasp what had truly happened on that day, but the tears of the teachers at school and of my parents and their friends were something I had never witnessed before. It worried me. There was so much my mother and father wouldn't or couldn't discuss with me or even with each other as they sat in silence. They remained hunched forward with hands clasped, unable to speak or explain. Their eyes seemed a million miles away. Our neighbors moved through each other's Eichlers like magnets that couldn't do more than join together in stillness. They sat quietly on our couch, shoulder to shoulder, numb and silent. That was not like my mother or her friends. They watched the shaky images on our black-and-white screen. We were shaky too. The entire country was shaking like autumn leaves in the fall of 1963.

The funeral was shown on television. I saw Jacqueline Kennedy float by like a ghost, concealed in a black veil and dress, but my eyes were focused on the Kennedy children. Caroline was two years my junior and John-John five years younger. He stood in his miniature four-button coat that looked more like a dress scarcely covering his bare legs and saluted a goodbye to the era of hope along with the rest of us. Harold and I knew the world had shifted in some significant way. We were too young to know why or how much.

It was the start of distrust, violence, anger, and protests. It was 1963. We had lost our president. The country had lost a substantial piece of its shared dream for the future—a better future. Innocence had left the building. And much as Americans did after the events of 9/11, the adults bonded together in grief in a way that would never quite leave their collective psyche. Faith in ideals was falling away from our suburban utopia. No one seemed to trust anything or anyone in that moment.

I came to know the Kennedy family through my father's comedy record *The First Family.* It featured stand-up comedian and impersonator Vaughn Meader as Kennedy and Naomi Brossart as the First Lady. John-John, Caroline, and other Kennedys were also imbedded in the grooves of that record. My father kept quite a few comedy albums in his collection—mostly recorded by Allan Sherman, Jackie Mason, and other Jewish comedians—but *The First Family* album, released at the end of 1962, was something bold for the time. Meader's delivery and imitation of John Kennedy was spot-on. The timely skits featured on the album were hilarious, smart, controversial, and daring. I listened to it nonstop for an entire year. Thanks to that album, I felt like I knew the entire Kennedy family and the political goons and cast of characters that surrounded them.

Meader later revealed, "A lot of people don't know this, but we recorded *The First Family* on the night of October 22, 1962, the same night as John F. Kennedy's Cuban Missile Crisis Speech. The audience was in the studio and had no idea of the drama that was taking place. But the cast had heard the speech, and our throats almost dropped to our toes because if the [live] audience had heard the Cuban Missile Speech, we would not have received the reaction we did." *The First Family* won the Grammy for Album of the Year in 1963, the same year Kennedy was shot. I still have my father's well-worn copy of the record.

After Kennedy was shot, Lenny Bruce opened his act that night with something akin to, "Boy, is Vaughn Meader fucked." And it was true. Suddenly, *The First Family* album was pulled from stores, along with its sequel as the publisher, Cadence Records, didn't want to appear to be "cashing in" on the assassination. Quickly, Meader's scheduled gigs were canceled, his career over. In a single moment he became a living reminder of the nation's trauma and the tragic death of our young president.

By the late Sixties, I had graduated to comedy recordings by the Smothers Brothers and George Carlin. During my college years, while I was working at a medical clinic, I would experience Dick Smothers in my own way. He was living in Santa Cruz County where I was going to college. One afternoon, he popped his head in to see Dr. Campbell, one of our general practitioners. I was elated. It was as if he had jumped off the album cover or television screen right into our small reception window. His skin was flawless, as if a fine powdery mist was covering every flaw, filling every pore, and camouflaging the lines on his face. He was perfect. His teeth were so brilliant and white, they looked as though they had been treated with 20 Mule Team Borax. He looked as he had on *The Smothers Brothers Comedy Hour* in 1967. I felt giddy. I felt nervous. I felt like a blithering idiot.

In a low voice to deflect attention, he muttered, "Checking in to see Dr. Campbell. Two o'clock appointment." I looked him square in the eye, this television hero of mine, and without thinking about what might jump out of my overanxious mouth, I muttered, "Mom always liked you best." As soon as it left my lips, I had unsolicited speech regret. Why did I say THAT? He looked at me with a well-deserved sneer, sat down in the waiting room, and raised a *National Geographic* magazine to hide his face. No one recognized him that day. Dick Smothers didn't seem funny that day. He could have been anyone with sniffles as far as the rest of the waiting room residents were concerned. I stared a hole in the back of that magazine as I studied his well-manicured nails. It's a wonder the Gawk Police didn't carry me away.

Other records in my father's wire bin, beyond the assortment of cool jazz and Big Band recordings, included The Limeliters, a folk trio who used comedy bits between songs, and Mitch Miller, a guy who wanted everyone to sing along with him even though he looked like the guy who cashiered at a cigar store, or worked in a Mafia ring, or perhaps was the guy who tossed a pepperoni pizza high in the air. He never seemed like a songster, but he is solely responsible for getting the lyrics to "By the Beautiful Sea" stuck in my head for decades. An earworm atrocity.

While I was in elementary school and unaware of politics or the power of the new political climate, so much history was taking place. Besides the first Catholic president being elected, and then assassinated, Reverend Martin Luther King Jr. had "a dream" and brought the Civil Rights Movement to a crescendo at Washington, D.C.'s Lincoln Memorial. He was also silenced with a gunshot, and the waves of grief rolled over the entire country like a tidal wave. Shortly after the shooting of King, Robert (Bobby)

Kennedy picked up his brother's torch and ran with it, only to be gunned down. They were all gone. Abraham, Martin, and John ... and Bobby.

* ❄ *

Fourth grade was a very different animal from the rest of my experiences at the elementary school zoo. It was defined by Kennedy's assassination and another singular event: being tripped by my teacher in front of the class. Mrs. Stelling embodied the character and charisma of an old biddy like no other. I was walking back to my school desk, and she was seated in front of the class ready to read *Charlotte's Web* and *Stuart Little* to my fellow classmates. With forethought and malice, out came her leg, wrapped in a stocking indistinguishable from a thick sausage casing, and—ka-boom!—I landed face down on the cold classroom linoleum. My classmates laughed as Mrs. Stelling shook a scolding finger at me.

"Don't you dare walk in front of me again. Now go to your seat."

I could feel the flush of embarrassment in my cheeks as my classmates giggled and pointed. Gathering myself to my feet with bruised knees and a wounded ego, my breath gummed up in my throat. Suddenly, I was the poster child for classroom humiliation. There was a bit of the devil behind Mrs. Stelling's spectacles.

For half of the school year, I was seated next to Joe Sharino, a boy of Italian descent who came from a land far, far away: Massachusetts. I couldn't spell it, but I tried to imagine what it was like there. Endless rows of trees in full bloom came to mind. Joe had a 100-watt smile and dark flirty mile-long lashes like Paul McCartney's, and shared my father's first name. His smile and good looks knocked me off my feet faster than a swift, perfectly aimed dodge ball. We'd joke around in class and often get scolded for doing so.

One day, Joe started waving his hand at me, motioning me to give him my arm. My arm? I did. He slowly removed his ID bracelet and fastened it around my wrist. Me. The little Russian girl with unruly hair and a crooked smile in every class picture. He never spoke a word about this primitive ritual or what it meant. I never asked. It was understood: I like you; you like me. Here, take this. As I ran my fingertips back and forth over each engraved letter spelling J-O-S-E-P-H, a thought bubble popped over my head: "Carol Sharino. Sigh." I repeatedly scrawled the name on the inside cover of my peach-colored Pee-Chee folder, always accompanied by a splattering of hearts. I heard bells, and not the recess bell. I was smitten. My love affair with boys had officially begun.

But our cavorting was quickly punished by—you guessed it!—the Wicked Witch of the West Coast, Mrs. Stelling. She scolded us for talking to one another, then separated Joe from my corner of the classroom. She relocated him and his dazzling smile to the furthest distance away from me. Joe and I never spoke again.

A few years later, we would share small smiles in the hallways in junior high and high school, but I wasn't convinced he recognized me. I barely recognized him. Joe had shot up about two feet and was now towering over a mob of swooning classmates. By that time he was popular and dashing and on the yearbook committee, and I was the peasant-bloused hippie chick who was too-cool-for-school. But apparently not cool enough for Joe Sharino.

Hair Come the Beatles!

In 1964, I was sitting at the kitchen table struggling with fractions and long division when I heard something that made me sit straight up in my wonky kitchen chair. What the hell was that sound, why was my heart beating faster and faster, and why did I feel so energized and excited? What was happening to me was The Beatles. Their music was spilling out of my brother's room at full throttle from down the hallway. It grabbed me and never let go. My attention was now and forever focused on the four lads from Liverpool.

"Love Me Do." "Please Please Me." "I Wanna Hold Your Hand." Beatlemania was in full throttle, and we were captivated by everything The Beatles had to offer. Madison Avenue was busy promoting a wide array of Fab Four products including: bobble-head Beatles for the back of your car, the Fab Four bedside lamp or thermos, The Beatles Magnetic Hair Game that featured a drawing of each Beatle's face and a magnet wand to move small iron filings onto their heads, Beatles lunch pails, salt and pepper shakers, Beatles boots, bubble gum trading cards, Beatles hair spray, and Beatles bath salts. The first few notes of each song from the four mop-topped boys turned otherwise composed girls into a shrieking mess. They pleased, pleased us.

The Beatles arrived on American soil in February 1964. That same month, the United Kingdom flew in half a ton of Beatles wigs to the United States to try to meet the increasing demand. Every kid with Clearasil smeared on their chin and cheeks wanted one. Those glossy synthetic wigs looked like dead rats wrapped in plastic bags ... but there was a bit of magic in those man-made strands. Beatlemania was alive and well, and one day one of those wigs appeared on the head of my fourth-grade classmate Aaron Allison.

Aaron was a good-looking surfer dude with seaweed-scented blond hair. His father owned a successful car dealership in Santa Clara: Allison Pontiac. When Aaron placed that Beatles wig on his head during our lunch hour, every girl in class started chasing him around the school field, including me. We screamed, we chortled; we were possessed by the charmed headpiece sitting on Aaron's head that could only be attributed to the phenomenon known as John, Paul, George, and Ringo.

I was a comic book kid. Slowly but surely I became obsessed with everything to do with Superman, Batman, and Archie. In addition to the DC Adventure series, I was also drawn to comic books with titles that began with "LITTLE." Harvey was an American comic book publisher. Some of Harvey Comics' biggest stars were three little girls with big dreams: Little Audrey, Little Dot, and Little Lotta. Audrey was a Paramount Pictures animated cartoon movie star who became a major comic book headliner in 1948. Her comic book stories were packed with her lively proto-feminist antics and rivaled those of her forerunner, Little Lulu.

Little Dot was my favorite. This particular comic character was more than a little obsessive, but who wasn't when it came to dots? If she were around today, she'd likely have her own design show on HGTV. Little Dot went dotty over dots. Her trademark dress was brightly colored in red with black polka dots and her hair was neatly pulled back with a polka-dotted bow. Her bedroom was full of polka-dot objects, and she constantly dragged home anything and everything circular or dot shaped. Little Dot, her love of dots, and her unique family of eccentric uncles and aunts became the basis for some of the best tales in comic book history. One of Little Dot's best friends, and another favorite comic book character of mine, was the poor little rich boy, Richie Rich—the ultra-wealthy, gentler, and kinder alternative to Donald J. Trump.

Last, but hardly least, was Little Lotta, and there was an awful lot of her. She was an oversized young girl bursting at the seams. Little Lotta could have easily been a contestant on *The Biggest Loser.* She defied the "big" girl stereotype with energetic activity showcasing the incredible strength that equaled her insatiable appetite for life, even if that life was in the confines of a cartoon frame.

I loved my LITTLE friends, whether they were rich, poor, big, polka-dotted, or small. I was surprised by how many of my friends' parents didn't allow them to read comic books. I had dozens of them stuffed under my bed for easy access. They offered me valuable exposure to creative thinking and storytelling. They were all friends, even Richie Rich, the poor little rich kid. I didn't identify with his riches, but I certainly did with his desperate desire for companionship. I couldn't find it in my household. I looked for it among my friends, but they were often called home for dinner, and I was left curled on the bed in my comic book world.

My reading material eventually shifted to *Tiger-Beat, Teen* magazine, *16* magazine, and *Seventeen* magazine, which inspired young girls to look like Stepford teens, an astronaut's wife, or Barbie. When I was twelve or thirteen, I read *16* magazine, which focused on recording artists and groups. When I was fifteen, I read *Seventeen* magazine, a publication spotlighting fashions and relationship advice. I was always one step ahead of my age group. I wanted to be with it and hip. I wanted to know all about boys and make-up and dating before there was even the slightest possibility of such happenings. Everything and everyone was airbrushed, pleasant looking, well adjusted. Who were these people and what neighborhood did they live in? And more importantly, how did they get their hair so perfectly coiffed? I was still trying to get mine to poof on the top of my head like Gidget and to fall into a perfect flip. Slick idealized images. What chaos they created in young lives.

The back of comic books featured an array of colorful eye-catching ads. ANY OF THESE PRIZES CAN BE YOURS WITHOUT COST! I was in like Flynn. I simply had to palm off packets of flower seeds door-to-door and send the company every penny. It sounded easy enough, except for the fact that I was dreadfully shy and had never sold a thing in my life except at a card table lemonade stand on the corner of the Eichler cul-de-sac. Neighbors felt obligated to give us a few pennies for our paper cups filled with a warm beverage that looked like urine. I also sold bags of cherries to our neighbors who all had the identical cherry trees in their backyards. They bought them anyway.

In preparation for my new sales career, I followed the instructions for how to conduct winning dialog at the front door. "Hello, my name is Carol. Would you like to buy some colorful seeds to plant in your garden?" I was a terrible salesperson, and Les Lambson, our next-door neighbor, told me so. After opening his front door to me, he gave me a watery handshake, the sort an adult offers a child as they loosely hold their small hand, afraid a squeeze might crush the delicate, soft bones.

"Why would I want to buy anything from you? You're not selling hard enough. Lift your head, Carol. Win me over with your personality! Sell it, dammit. Okay, try it again."

Les Lambson, who was built like a tall brick building in Brooklyn, towered over the small girl standing before him on the front step of his Eichler. He continued to scold me. My head and shoulders collapsed and closed like the petals of a California poppy when night falls. I wasn't pushing my wares hard enough. Lambson scolded me again.

"You're selling the wrong types of seeds and flowers for San Jose! They will never grow." I looked up at him with my giant Keane painting eyes, speechless and shivering in my now sweaty plastic zoris. He must have taken pity on me, as he ended up buying out my entire supply of outdated marigold and petunia seed packets. I was overjoyed. I ran home, ordered my choice of prize from the one-page catalog—a black plastic camera— shoved my coins and paper into a poorly sealed envelope, and waited for this enchanting gift to arrive in our mailbox. My father had a camera and was continually taking pictures. Now I would do the same.

I checked the mail every day for two weeks. Did they get it yet? Did the money fall out? Did I remember to put a stamp on the envelope? The camera arrived fourteen days later. I tore into the brown wrapper, grabbed the child-sized device inside, and in my excitement I dropped it on the floor where the camera broke into several shattered non-fixable, non-functional pieces. That was my last experience with the wonderful world of sales, but not with plastic cameras. I would own many of them, beginning with a Kodak Instamatic. But I would never list *salesgirl* on my resume.

Cameras and photography have been ever-present in my life. I dated two professional photographers while I was in college and learned my craft in their darkrooms while learning other crafts of intimacy in their dark rooms. Composition, balance, and subject matter all came easily to me. I was convinced my father's eye on the world had become my eye as well. He was always carrying a camera and documenting our outings, his friends, and slice-of-life scenes of signs and strangers. He recorded the ironies and the juxtaposition he saw in the world around him and transferred that view to Kodachrome film. He snapped while those around him conducted their lives without awareness of his lens.

But my father never seemed to be infused in the moments of his life. He was too busy capturing it in pictures. He took a constant stream of photographs. I inherited the same practice. That's not to say that I have any regrets about catching the photo bug. I truly believe that without my photographs, and certainly his, most of my memories of certain time periods, people, and events would be washed away. A camera is a diary without a key, and photographs are the words on the page telling us a story about a moment in time. I took photographs of my friends, my cat, my foot. Photography captivated me and gave me a sense of control that I was lacking at home and at school. I could capture and manipulate the scene. I was in command of the vertical and the horizontal.

The Sunday comics were vital. I looked forward to reading the thought bubbles and checking out the ink-outlined cast of colorful characters every Sunday morning as I sprawled out on the living room floor. These simple images spread out in front of me looked like a complicated, colorful rug.

There was the always-perplexing "Pogo," a strange collection of characters doing and saying God knows what. At the time, I had no idea that the title character in Pogo, America's longest-running comic strip, was a possum. None. I didn't know what it was, and frankly, I didn't care. I found the cartoon strip a bit ...

disturbing. And I couldn't figure out how Dagwood could eat so many sandwiches and still be thin as a piece of onion skin. And what was with his multiple hair-sticks?

Meanwhile, *Mary Worth* was moving at a snail's pace and solving everyone's problems, while having no life of her own. But for some reason I centered on Ms. Worth, the wise Ann Landers of the Sunday comic strips. Mary Worth was a mature woman in her 50s or 60s who distributed advice like Halloween candy. She seemed extraordinarily wise and much too sage for a cartoon strip. She was the great Buddha of my Sunday morning and generally made only brief appearances to react and give her matronly and prudent advice. Although I couldn't seek her counsel because, after all, she lived in a comic strip, I read her advice and admired her calm demeanor. The panels of her comic strip were like a soap opera where things unfolded at a painfully slow tempo and precious little transpired from week to week. She was the comic section's grande dame with white hair and world-weary wisdom, but not a lick of wit.

That particular strip had an eight-decade run beginning in 1938 under the title *Mary Worth's Family.* One night, on the *Carol Burnett Show,* I was thrilled to see Burnett presented a satire, *Mary Worthless,* in which the Mary character helped people "whether they liked it or not." But the Sunday comics and comic books weren't my only early passion. The other infatuation? Elvis Presley.

"The King" and I

Elvis was my king ... and The King. He was my first crush, my first unraveling as I approached the male galaxy. My earliest memory of this legend is lying in bed in San Jose listening to my treasured pink radio on the nightstand. I worshipped at the temple that was my AM radio. As I scrutinized and celebrated every new song that poured out of the speaker, each artist and tune painted a picture with detailed nuance. The first songs through that crackling speaker were Elvis' "Return to Sender," which I thought was "Return, Tasenda" where he was singing about someone with an unusual name, and "Crying in the Chapel." I had no idea what a chapel was or why my beloved Elvis was crying, but I wanted to comfort him and dry his tears with my flannel pajama sleeve.

I was stunned by Elvis' appearance, his movements, his chiseled cheekbones and sideways smile. I would pretend he was the pillow I held close at night before I drifted off to sleep in my pink pajamas. After a few minutes, I'd grab the pillow, shove it behind my back, and pretend Elvis was lying beside me, his caring arms snug around my waist. In my pre-adolescent mind, we cuddled close in the wilderness in our two-person pup tent. The King was whispering in my ear and filling it with his deepest secrets, and I was the one-girl-show who would save his soul. Before entering dreamland, I would slip my fingers down to my thighs and imagine they were Elvis' fingers trying to figure something out, but I didn't quite know what yet. Not yet.

The two of us—Elvis and me—were madly in love. Sorry, Priscilla. My apologies, Ann-Margret. Too bad, all of you screaming fans. Fat, thin, pale, tan, old, young, bloated or bony thin, awkward or charming, with sideburns the size of Texas, the big "E" was mine, all mine. He should still be here. Damn those fried banana and peanut butter sandwiches and those vats of prescription pills. Every last one of them.

When Elvis performed on *The Ed Sullivan Show* for his third and final appearance, he shared the stage with a rising comedienne named Carol Burnett. By this time, Elvis' spicy gyrations had stirred up quite a bit of controversy across the country. As a result, CBS censors demanded he be filmed only from the waist up during his performance. He sang several songs that night, including "Hound Dog" and "Don't Be Cruel," as well as his gospel favorite "Peace in the Valley." At the end of the show, Ed Sullivan himself went out of his way to compliment Elvis.

"I wanted to say to Elvis Presley and the country that this is a real decent, fine boy, and wherever you go, Elvis, we want to say we've never had a pleasanter experience on our show with a big name than we've had with you. So now ... let's have a tremendous hand for a very nice person." Sullivan certainly had a way with down-home declarations. It was not a sophisticated endorsement, but one that everyone could understand and appreciate. Elvis bowed, appearing clearly grateful, and exited the Sullivan stage for the last time. He went on to become one of the most adored and well-known artists in the history of entertainment. In the same way Walter Cronkite represented a trusted father or grandfather figure for the masses, when Ed Sullivan said someone was okay in his morality book, he was clearly okay for all of us to enjoy. Walter and Ed would never lie to us, right?

I Want My Mummy

On school field trips, we felt like prisoners forging an escape route from the school grounds as we climbed the three tall steps to our bus seats. We didn't care where we were going. We were happy to be going somewhere—anywhere—and leaving our dull classroom and familiar playground. We wanted to see a new sort of playground, even if it was only through the smudged glass window of a school bus. We wanted to see a slice of the real world, not chalkboards and wall maps.

Our field trips in San Jose included jaunts to Langendorf Bakery, which was owned and operated by the Langendorf sons. Our classes were also dragged through the dried fruit plants in Santa Clara Valley. The air reeked of sulfur dioxide, which smells like rotten eggs. We had to cover our noses and mouths in order to survive that particular excursion. The California Prune and Apricot Growers (also known as Sunsweet) was a co-operative for prune and apricot growers in Santa Clara Valley and handled all types of prune- and apricot-related products. Naturally, the second-best part of any field trip, beyond the anticipated break from the classroom, was going home with free samples provided by the facilities we toured. I brought my mother two bags of hotdog buns from Langendorf and bags of apricots and prunes from the dried fruit plant. She was thrilled. And over the next few weeks, and after all that dried fruit, we became much more regular.

Another class field trip took place at the Rosicrucian Egyptian Museum, a building that was non-flamboyant and sat quietly in the heart of Santa Clara Valley like an obedient child in the back of the classroom. It didn't make a big fuss, raise its hand, or holler that it was there. The buildings were inspired by Egyptian and Moorish architecture, and the grounds contained beautiful gardens on the outside with ancient artifacts on the inside. It was the Valley's own Hostess Cupcake with a surprise interior coupled with an appealing exterior.

The museum housed a considerable collection of Egyptian artifacts, including mummies and ancient relics, and kids love mummies and dead stuff. The displays detailed information on burial practices, the afterlife (according to the Egyptians), tombs, kings, and pharaohs. The ancient Egyptians believed that the *ka* or life force of a person would leave the body at the time of death. They also believed that, even after death, the ka required nourishment from food and assorted beverages just as the person had during their lifetime. It was a real all-you-can-eat-and-drink buffet type of religion. Therefore, relatives of the dead would place offerings of food items for the deceased to nibble on. These practices were unlike our current belief system where you die, ascend to the clouds, ring the doorbell at St. Peter's Gate, and play a harp. Apparently, all of these exhausting activities follow on the heels of your last breath.

One of the museum's most memorable features was the enormous Foucault pendulum that greeted us when we walked in the front entrance. This magnificent beast of swinging metal was two stories tall, which seemed monstrous at the time. Apparently, the form of this particular pendulum provided visual proof of the Earth's rotation. The one in the museum had been designed in 1851. A few years later, I noticed ads appearing for the "Rosicrucian Order" in the back of magazines. I couldn't imagine what they were advertising. Did people want to be mummified again? Did they go to services and hypnotically stare at the to-and-fro movement of the lobby's pendulum? Was it a religion that included hypnosis? I was in the dark. And the museum itself was dark, cool, and mysterious.

I enjoyed wandering the hallways and viewing the exhibits behind glass. There was something familiar about the Egyptian side-view scrawls on the walls, the relics and ornate jewelry. When I doodled in class, it was always of facial side views. Now I was seeing them splashed all over museum walls, and there was something strangely comforting in that. The darkened halls of the museum felt cave-like and calming. The mummies seemed content. I wanted to curl up and sleep in the corner surrounded by these quiet and shadowy figures. I thought I could sleep better there than at home in the Eichler. The little mummy children and adults seemed more like family members than my own parents and sibling.

Assault with a Deadly Weapon

When I was a pre-teen, I kept a diary. It was my first experience expressing myself … my true self. I always found it interesting that girls kept diaries, but boys did not. How did Hemingway get his start?

As I cracked open the book with the flimsy skeleton key, words filled up the pages. I poured everything into those vinyl-bound volumes. The cover was pink, with the words DIARY embossed in black with a gold fleck border around each letter and a drawing of a prototypical teenage girl in silhouette. Every daily event, every hope and every dream found its way onto the blue-lined pages. I finally had something I could commune with on a daily basis.

"Dear Diary … today Julie and I went to Woolworth's and stole a candy bar. It was a good day." Then the cover would close, and it would be locked with the "yes, it's included!" metal key. The thoughts scrawled on the pages inside this special book were mine and mine alone. That is until the small metal lock was broken in two by Harold and his friend Brad from across the cul-de-sac. My father affectionately referred to him as Bad Brad. It probably took them a couple of seconds to break the flimsy lock. They read every word I had written. They teased me in some horrifyingly endless ritual. Now someone knew about my crush on John, how I envied Jane's boobs, which days I got my period, and what I ate for lunch. My buried treasure of inner thoughts and fears had been uncovered, its contents now fodder for ridicule. The boys tormented me with their chuckles and teasing until my bottom lip gave me away. It was vibrating like Elvis' pelvis. Then the tears came. My private thoughts put to paper were no longer sacred, no longer a club of one, no longer mine. I never wrote in a diary again, so I began keeping one in my noisy head.

In my senior year of high school I began to keep a detailed journal. I wrote about classes, teachers, boyfriends, kisses, friends, films, parents—all through the filter of teenage angst. But the journal writing was different from the diary kept years earlier. I also wrote about isolation, the mystery of life, wanting to love, not knowing how, wanting to leave home, wanting to stay, wanting to get laid, wanting a Prince Charming to enter stage left and save me from my miserable adolescence. I wondered through scribbly scrawl what the hell we were all doing here.

When I was happy and things were going smoothly, I didn't write a word. Only when things at home were plummeting into a deep abyss and my emotions were bottoming out did I open that journal and pick up my pen. I wrote when I was consumed with fear about a relationship or mistakes I perceived were the worst missteps ever made in the history of womankind. I wrote to release the demons, but they stuck around.

Some days, nights, and weeks, I felt as though I were moving through a storm, an ongoing losing streak. My father was gnawing at me with his words or rattling me by ignoring my very existence; Harold was sucker-punching me with his glare or ridicule when he wasn't pummeling a clenched fist into my stomach for no apparent reason; the popular kids looked right through me like I was vapor. It was adolescence, and everything seemed to be hitting the fan at once and getting cut up into little, painful, jagged pieces. Boom!

But in another day or week, I would feel like a different person perched in a completely different seat with a new set of eyes staring out at a brighter view. I told myself to remember, when you're in the midst of a storm, there is an endpoint where everything will become unruffled and seem right again. I never remembered. I always forgot. Selective amnesia. What I wanted to remember was that luck, good or bad, seemed to move like water. It kept rolling and changing. There was no such thing as steadily treading trouble in one place forever. I strained to remember but failed and sank again. Sometimes I sank rather deeply. Sometimes, when Bad Brad was around, I sank deeper than ever. He was the thorn in my side, and at my side. He didn't have a kind word to say to anyone, certainly not to me.

Bad Brad, with his elongated Bob Hope chin and appalling cackle, terrorized all the young girls in the cul-de-sac. He had a wicked nature. This unsavory sadist repeatedly tickled me to tears. There was no joy in being touched by this boy. I wanted to be released from his evil laugh, digging fingernails, and cruel and sardonic smile. When Bad Brad announced that he wanted to play hide and seek, he'd disappear for the rest of the afternoon leaving me to look for him everywhere, until I was finally on to his dodgy tricks.

One summer afternoon when boredom was running high, Brad crawled into my bedroom window, tossed me on top of the bed, tickled me in his usual rambunctious and nefarious fashion, then shoved my head between his legs, but not before daring me to take my pants off. "Go down on me." I wouldn't. Then he dared me to touch him "down there"—but I shouted an emphatic "No!" I was naïve. I didn't yet understand what he was doing or wanted me to do.

Before I knew it, his zipper was unzipped, and he was pressing my head onto a massive bone-like appendage, a towering obelisk the likes of which I had never seen or could imagine. He wasn't asking me to shuck his cob of corn; he was telling me to. I was twelve or thirteen, and he was sixteen or seventeen, but that didn't stop him from turning his ramrod into a massive sticky kielbasa and forcing me to consume it. My small mouth had no idea what to do or not do with this Cape Canaveral rocket buried and banging into my inner cheek. It tasted like sour sweat and salt swirled together. After he left, I ran to rinse my mouth out with Lavoris … for about an hour.

Much later, I discovered that he tried to force the same maneuver on the young girl who lived across the street. It only took us fifty years to compare notes and make this discovery. Bad Brad had no problem whatsoever living up to his moniker.

It never occurred to either one of us girls to tell anyone about being force-fed by Brad. We blamed ourselves. After all, we had a window with a flimsy screen in our bedroom so … it must have been our fault, not his. In the Sixties, silence was golden, and sexual encounters, foisted upon us or otherwise, were never discussed, certainly not with an adult. Sex was a forbidden mystery that produced giggles and bewilderment.

The Boob Tube

In the early Sixties, Santa Clara Valley offered a small spattering of television channels. ABC, CBS, and NBC were the major broadcast stations, but we also had Channel 2 from San Francisco and eventually Channel 36. Carol Doda, a topless dancer in San Francisco, became the spokesmodel for Channel 36. In fact, Ms. Doda was one of the first modern topless dancers in the United States. In 1964, she made international news, first by dancing topless at the city's Condor Club, then by enhancing her bust from size thirty-four to forty-four through silicone injections. Her boobs became known as Doda's twin forty-fours and the new Twin Peaks of San Francisco. When I first saw her, I looked at the peaks on her mountain range, then mine, and decided we were two entirely different species.

In the Channel 36 studio, filmed from the waist up and wearing clothing that amplified her prominent physical attributes, we'd watch her coo, "You're watching the Perfect Thirty-Six in San Jose." Occasionally, Doda would even present editorial commentary on the issues of the day. She was a Bay Area celebrity of sorts, this young gal who, at age fourteen, dropped out of school and became a cocktail waitress.

The Republican Convention was held in San Francisco during the summer of 1964, and many of the delegates went to see Carol Doda. She was the brightest star on the streets of San Francisco and was later profiled in Tom Wolfe's 1968 book *The Pump House Gang.* She also appeared that same year as Sally Silicone in the film *Head,* a 1968 film created by Jack Nicholson and Bob Rafelson and featuring The Monkees. Yes, stars were colliding in the Sixties.

$$* \quad \maltese \quad *$$

Whether it was Channel 2, 36, or 7, television was always playing in the background. Throughout the Sixties and early Seventies, it was our friend, our babysitter, and offered several channels of prototypes featuring unattainable relationships and family dynamics.

Hollywood wasn't a few hundred miles south of our Eichler. It was around the corner when we stepped down the hallway and into the living room. We all wanted to look like the teenagers on the sit-coms and dramas that appeared on our home television screens. Throughout the Sixties, many of the shows began with "the" and many of those were my favorite programs. I never missed *The Dick Van Dyke Show, The Patty Duke Show, That Girl, The Andy Griffith Show, I Dream of Jeannie, The Beverly Hillbillies, The Man from U.N.C.L.E., The Twilight Zone, Land of the Giants, Bonanza, Get Smart, Father Knows Best,* and of course, *The Ed Sullivan Show.* My heart would race a bit faster when I read the upcoming program descriptions in *TV Guide:*

In answer to popular demand, Sullivan will show again the animated fantasy "A Short Vision," which depicts abstractly the effects of the H-bomb. On the guest list tonight: singer Nat "King" Cole; dancer Carol Haney; comedian Jack Carter; ventriloquist Ricky Layne and his dummy, Velvel.

Now, that's entertainment.

Up on the Roof

My father was always active on our Eichler roof. The Eichler roof was flat as an excuse and constantly in a state of leakage. Water collected up there after rainstorms to create Olympic-sized swimming pools.

Often, he'd urge me to jump onto the top of the fence on the side of the yard and walk to the edge of the rooftop. Naturally, my mother wasn't watching this dangerous deed. I'd hoist myself up to the top of the fence, walk to the roofline edge, pull myself up to the rooftop with every ounce of strength I could gather, stand tall once on top, and marvel at the view from the high vantage point: rows and rows of identical roofs, homes, yards, and cherry trees. I felt like a little god up there, surveying the land and assessing my place in the neighborhood—and in the universe.

But getting down from the roof and back onto the top of the fence with wiggling feet was another story. Panic would wash over me like mighty waves as I lowered my feet from the roof to the fence top that always seemed miles away from the toes of my sneakers. As I was suspended from the roofline, there were moments of terror when my toes couldn't locate the fence top. I begged my father to catch or guide me down. I wanted to be brave, but I wasn't confident enough to maneuver the landing. As I dangled from the ledge with floppy marionette puppet legs, he offered no rescue or reassurances. "The next time I won't be here. Get down yourself." Then he would walk away to fill a hole on the roof. I would try. Finally, and reluctantly, he would grab my upper arms and lower me to the fence, this Raggedy Ann doll. I was safe!

✳ ⚛ ✳

While other kids were seeing circus animals or inanimate objects in the billowy clouds over Santa Clara Valley, I was seeing faces in the fences. The knots became noses and expressive eyes. The wood grain morphed into a knowing smile. In the summertime, I would water our side yard fence with a garden hose and watch the wooden planks turn from light to dark. I imagined I was a famous painter creating a new image onto an old canvas. After concluding my sprayed artwork, I would wander to the backyard and shave the large rocks with the end of a Popsicle stick or small tree branch. The ground in the yard was bursting with such toys. I named the rock Hercules and visited him daily to complete this grooming ritual.

San Jose saw some mighty rainstorms, and the Eichler roof had a distinctive sound when it rained or was blustery. All the loose pebbles were like tiny ballerinas, tapping their toes on the rooftop and producing the most wondrous symphony. I cherished the evenings I would fall asleep to that soothing sound.

Sometimes the gusty winds would pick up debris and move rocks around the cement walkway or bang or blow furniture against the fence. Is someone building a ship out there? It was a noisy wrestling match without a referee. Sometimes those sounds would make their way into my dream world. I'd be riding a rocky stagecoach or perhaps I was being tossed around on a rickety boat at sea. In the morning, when all had quieted and calmed, the trees stood straight against the sky with no evidence of the evening's wicked weather. The wind chimes had stopped dancing. Did I hallucinate the gale winds and wet winter nights of youth? At times, childhood seemed like a dream.

The first dishwasher we owned sat unused in our Eichler kitchen. We utilized it only for storage. My father insisted that the appliance used too much water and therefore no one was to use it. The few times it did run, I was always surprised by how much activity was going on in there. All that churning, whirling, and splashing sounded ferocious. It was a choreography of sophisticated scrubbing and scouring. Either that or there was a crew of little men in bright white jumpsuits cleaning the melamine dinnerware behind the sealed door.

Not everything about growing up in an Eichler was a bowl of Bing cherries. Our roof had to be patched every year, and always by the man of the house, who went into this suburban paradise knowing it was going to require unending maintenance. During the winter, when mornings were chilled from the night air that burrowed right through the single-paned walls of glass, my father refused to turn the thermostat on. The floors would have warmed the bottoms of our feet, but he left the furnace on the OFF position year 'round. Childhood often felt like frigid winter months.

My father and brother in Eichler backyard, doing what fathers and brothers do.

An old neighbor of ours who lived across the street from our Eichler home recently told me that my father was outside mowing in a T-shirt and shorts one cold December afternoon. "I yelled to him, 'What are you doing in shorts, Joe? It's freezing out here.' He came over, collapsed on the lawn next to me, pulled his knees to his chest, and told me that he just got off the phone with his mother in Brooklyn. She had told him that the snow was four feet deep in New York City." San Jose was like summertime, even in the dead of winter, at least to my father. "It's very mild and beautiful out today," he explained to our neighbor. My father didn't feel the elements. Sometimes I wondered if he ever noticed the world around him. He then went back to the business of mowing the lawn in his summer wear.

"Your father!" she said, with a smile strung across her face. "He was so funny. Such a funny little man." To onlookers, my father's offbeat behavior was nothing short of endearing.

On the rare occasion the Eichler thermostat was utilized, the radiant heater buried under the linoleum tile floor made a sad attempt at keeping our shivering bodies warm. The heat never seemed to reach anywhere above knee level. We were as cold and immovable as the frozen orange juice concentrate in our freezer door. But I enjoyed the changes in weather patterns: the balmy nights, ferocious storms, wild winds, and spring showers. The drizzly gray days, when pavement smelled like rain, were keepers. The charcoal thunderheads, the lacy gold and peach morning sky, and feathery cirrus clouds were welcome. I celebrated all the moods of the Bay Area sky, usually with a warm glass of Ovaltine. A few dry pieces of malty powder always floated in the liquid. I'd crunched down on them with my back teeth. It was so satisfying to grind them down with my molars, this sugary breakfast.

Throughout grade school and well into junior high school, I felt ill every time I left the domain of the Eichler to go to school. It was my version of morning sickness. I didn't tell my parents. I didn't confide to my friends. I didn't know if there was something wrong with my gastrointestinal tract, but I didn't want to know. I had learned, quite successfully, how to ignore problems. My mother, the queen of denial, was my teacher. When an uncomfortable moment demanded her attention or life became too complicated, my mother would go numb and fill with apathy like an overflowing bathtub, then exit the scene of the crime, the crime of emotions. I witnessed it over and over, in subtle and not-so-subtle ways. Then I went about the business of emulating her.

I fought the morning queasiness long enough to stir up my mint chocolate-, French vanilla-, or eggnog-flavored Instant Breakfast in one of our tall orange-striped kitchen glasses. The strawberry variety made me want to barf. Carnation introduced this kindly liquid breakfast in time for my ninth birthday and fourth grade. That thick concoction of sugar and flavoring would line the twisted knots in my tummy like Pepto Bismol. There were no other breakfast options available in our Eichler kitchen. That was okay with me since I could barely manage to swallow liquid, let alone gobble down eggs or pancakes. I shivered from the cold Eichler morning until I dashed into the toasty classroom where our teacher told us what to do, when to do it, and how.

＊ ✳ ＊

Every Willow Glen Eichler backyard came equipped with two cherry trees, orphans left behind from the vast orchards that were sacrificed to make way for our homes. In the summer there was an overpopulation of "For Sale" and "Get your fresh cherries here!" signs, at stands where neighborhood kids would peddle countless bags of tart yellow and pink cherries, or the deep dark red variety, carefully wrapped in Saran Wrap. Why would neighbors want to buy more cherries from children when they already had a crop sitting in their backyard? But they bought bags and bags of them. It was the Eichler way. Some cherries made their way into pies. Most rotted on kitchen countertops. Others were tossed at the heads of neighborhood kids. Too many were eaten. Everyone had diarrhea. We learned the hard way that guzzling down bag after bag of fruit was not always something to celebrate.

Sticky Fingers

My friends and I spent hours in the local strip mall stores perusing toys, books, candy bars, and comics. We soon had our eye on stacks of items so tall there was no way we could afford to buy any of them, let alone all of them. *Mary Poppins* and *My Fair Lady* were released in 1964; *Dr. Zhivago* and *Help!* in 1965, which to me became known as "The Summer of Thievery." How it got started is murky, but it seemed to begin with a matter-of-fact pact made with my friend Julie, who seemed to already know the ins and outs of thievery. "It's easy," she said as she nudged my shoulder with hers. "What is?" I asked. "Shoplifting," she replied.

Our target? The shops at Willow Glen's Hacienda Gardens strip mall. We were around nine years old, incredibly bored, and terrifically hungry for all that "stuff" that our parents wouldn't buy us. Perhaps it had to do with a lack of allowance and too much time to flounder and fantasize. It all seemed a bit too easy. We looked like innocent kids roaming the aisles, poring over candy bars, thumbing through comics, then meandering out the door with our pixie-faced expressions. Who would suspect us?

Our usual targets were Rexall Drugstore, the grocery store, and a few other small shops. Our master plan included an initial stop at the Safeway grocery store where each of us girls would grab a paper bag from the stack near each checkout counter.

Then we'd make our way to each shop and nonchalantly drop items into a Safeway bag. No one seemed to notice or care. Not the employees nor the shoppers browsing around us. We felt like contestants on the game show *Supermarket Sweep*. We could win whatever items we wanted, and no one was going to take it away from us. Not the store manager, not our parents, not God. We were kids in a candy store, metaphorically and literally, and the sugary treats and plastic toys were ours for the taking.

The first object I reached for was a box of Crayola Crayons, the sixty-four pack. Score! Next it was candy bars. You could not have butter fingers while pocketing Butterfingers, Mounds, Mars, and Milky Way. I could gather as much and as many as I wanted. It was like dying and going to junk food heaven.

The practice seemed effortless with seemingly no downside. I was finally good at something. We eventually moved on to shoplifting books. Lots and lots of books. Donna Parker books were my target. I never cared for Nancy Drew, nor her mysteries and shenanigans. Then there were coloring books, books on nature, and the "How To" books that helped kids learn math and science.

Julie already had a Barbie, a Barbie Dream House, and a Barbie car at home. There was nothing I wanted more than a Ponytail Barbie doll. I didn't know too many things with great certainty at this time of my life, but I knew my life would be complete if I had that plastic bendable-limbed companion in my room. My mother wouldn't buy me Barbie, Ken, or Skipper. "Too expensive. Here, get this one. Babette." Babette was a bargain basement version of Barbie, with larger limbs and no other clothing or shoes other than the swimsuit she wore and her two large bare feet. If Barbie was a sleek and sophisticated Ford Mustang, Babette was an oversized Edsel.

Soon I was stuffing Barbie and friends in my brown paper bag and taking them home while I pressed my red transistor radio against the right side of my head. "Wooly Bully," "My Girl," "Help Me, Rhonda," "King of the Road," "The In Crowd," and "Mrs. Brown, You've Got a Lovely Daughter" were playing in my ear. But I wasn't Mrs. Sveilich's lovely daughter. I was an immoral, unlawful hooligan who developed a winning technique for swiping desirable items and carting them home.

Yet I could not take Barbie or any of her mates or family members out of their plastic cases. I looked at them for less than a minute, felt flooded with guilt and undeserved status, then shoved everything—the books, dolls, a vast assortment of candy—under my bed. I didn't allow myself to enjoy any of it, play with it, consume it, or even look at it for very long. It was like I was cast in *The Tell-Tale Heart*, and my heart wouldn't let me venture under the bed no matter how much I fantasized about playing with each toy or about munching down those chocolaty treats. I finally decided it was futile. In my mind, I wasn't worthy enough to have them. I took everything I had stolen and placed it all in our garbage can outside. I wanted the entire lot of goods to disappear. They didn't belong here. Harold found Barbie and Skipper and Hershey bars sitting inside the side yard garbage can and told my mother I was a criminal. I was horrified. My misdeeds had been discovered. Would I go to jail? Would I get grounded, even though I had never been grounded? But my mother was taking a nap. She barely woke up enough long enough to mutter, "Don't do that again," and went back to sleep. That was the extent of my punishment.

Shoplifting started with Julie, then my friend Denise got in on the act and reignited this unwanted habit. We'd go to the only dress shop in Hacienda Gardens, slip into the dressing room with several selections, layer the most desirable and hip clothing in the store, ones that would never be affordable to us, and causally walk out as if we had an appointment or were going to catch lunch. We could have won the Best Supporting Actress and Best Actress Award that year. We couldn't believe our ease, our skills, our luck.

One day, Denise and I hitchhiked to downtown San Jose. A man in a beige business suit picked us up. He had a cauliflower nose that spread in various directions and a buzz cut. He didn't look like one of us, but he got us to our destination. An unbearable Bay Area heat wave was in progress, but Denise wore her heavy suede fringed jacket. I wore my black velvet jacket. We walked into the trendy clothing stores we would never dream of entering without a large sum of money stashed in our purses. Inside the dressing rooms we began layering up the most desirable blouses with lacey fronts and cool snap closures, then moseyed outside like a couple of thespians. Pedestrians on the street were wearing their summer shorts and halter tops, but we looked like overweight brown bears shuffling down the sidewalk. How long would our luck hold out? I suspected it wouldn't be much longer, so I stopped. I mean ... I just stopped. I had my ruffled white blouse with the three snaps down the front. I had my lacey lightweight top with the long sleeves that looked like something out of *Gone with the Wind.* I had everything I had ever dreamed of ... and I felt like crap. I stopped one day, likely one day short of turning into a known felon. Or Winona Ryder.

Book 'Em

David T.W. McCord once said, "Books fall open, you fall in." My salvation and safe habitat in fourth grade was between the covers of various volumes stitched together in all their hardbound glory. My teacher read us E.B. White's classic stories, *Charlotte's Web* and *Stuart Little* during our in-class reading hour. But Madeleine L'Engle's *A Wrinkle in Time*, a borrowed book from my friend and neighbor Marvin Reedy, took me to another place and dimension and made me think profound thoughts about life and tempus fugit, perhaps for the first time in my young life.

In the meantime, mystery novels remained a mystery to me. Personally, I never understood why the Hardy Boys never hooked up with Nancy Drew and her girlfriends. I didn't explore either series. I stuck with Donna Parker books in their big-print format with full-color images splashed across the book jacket. That kooky coquette was always off on a madcap, romantic, seemingly implausible escapade. Donna Parker's adventures couldn't rival those of the promiscuous starry-eyed Carrie on *Sex and the City,* but for my age group they came pretty close. There were exotic destinations, romance, devastations, and quick resolves. Fade in—it's a normal sunny day. Then catastrophe and suspense followed by happily ever after. Fade to black. Where will Donna's next adventure occur? Likely between the pages of her next two books: *Donna Parker: A Spring to Remember* or *Donna Parker Takes a Giant Step.* Who will she fall in love with, and what country will house her adventure? What toppings will she choose for her pizza in Venice or Milan? What unexpected delights will stuff her crepes in Versailles?

The Donna Parker books were literary soap operas. Unfortunately, the most exciting thing that ever happened to Donna Parker was a snowball fight. Therefore, I grew up with extraordinarily low expectations of the early stage of amorousness and conflict resolution based on these well-packaged stories. Donna Parker's tales reflected an idealized vision of post-WWII life in small-town America. Her life was radically different from mine, but I was at an age where I clung to the high ideals, coveted plaid skirts, and crisp white blouses, and longed for the lifestyles of others.

In elementary school I became fanatical for biographies and autobiographies. I was a misplaced child reading tales about misplaced or misunderstood boys, girls, men, and women. Their stories soothed me. Their tales of being ostracized and atypical allowed me to feel much less lonely and less of a misfit. Furthermore, reading provided a protective bubble to keep myself from the chaos of family dynamics in my Eichler. This fleeting escapism put me smack-dab in the middle of someone else's life and ordeal.

But even in elementary school, I felt driven to read about factual people living actual lives. Who gave a rat's ass about the Bobbsey Twins? At age ten, I read the simplistic child-friendly biographies of Helen Keller, Madame Curie, Mark Twain, and John Adams, and learned about life on the Oregon Trail. *It's a miracle they survived!* I thought. Strangely, someone would say that about me years later when they ran into me at a twenty-year high school reunion.

Getting Schooled

Every time mid-September rolled around, you could catch a whiff of the tips of freshly sharpened pencils and the ink of mimeograph machines, both heralding the start of school. My new blue vinyl three-ring binder could have doubled as a bear trap as it tried to demolish my fingers with a sudden and always surprising … SNAP! It was accompanied by a package of three-hole-punch lined paper, new pencils and pens, and that single clear plastic binder page that held pink erasers, paper clips, and a Butterfinger chocolate bar left over from the previous school year.

The forest green alphabet in cursive upper- and lowercase letters bordered the top of the classroom blackboard. We memorized the letters by singing A, B, C, D, E, F, G, H, I, J, K,

ELEMENO, P.... " Penmanship was vital. We even received a grade on such a skill, or lack thereof. My penmanship mark was always my lowest grade. I was left-handed, and that imparted some awkwardness and special challenges to my young wrist.

Desks in elementary school were designed for right-handed classmates. So were spiral notebooks, scissors, and binders with their hefty life-threatening rings. I had a perpetual messy ink blob on the outside of my left hand from reaching over to write lefty in a righty world. In childhood and adulthood, southpaws would stare at can openers for hours because "it" was backwards ... not us. Lefties are not only different, they die sooner because they're left-handed. Studies have shown lefties will die up to nine years before righties. As if that weren't bad enough, my cursive writing looked like a physician's scrawl. I started writing upside down to avoid hitting the rings of my binder with the outer edge of my hand and to keep my elbow from falling off the desk. The curve of each letter as it fell above and below the line had to be just so. Such things don't matter today. You type your homework, text, emails, and ideas for manuscripts in the NOTES section on a tiny phone or laptop computer. But in the Sixties, we had to write—and to write legibly.

The night before each new school year began, I would simmer in a stew of nerves and grapple with a staggering litany of "what ifs" that was longer than Santa's shopping list. My sleep was always unsettled and filled with the worries and ordeals lurking around the corner. What if my teacher was mean? What if I couldn't locate the assigned classroom? What if no one wanted to talk to me or play with me? What if I was nauseous and couldn't keep my breakfast down before I made it out the orange Eichler door? Now they call it social anxiety. I don't know what it was called in the Sixties. I just knew I was sautéed in dread.

"Monitor" assignments created copious feelings of pride in fourth-graders just learning the ropes of responsibility. One week you were window monitor, the next door monitor or coat monitor. We already discussed milk monitor and promised never to speak of it again. But whether you were eraser monitor beating gray chalky squares against the outside classroom wall or traffic monitor taking your life in one hand and a STOP sign in the other in the crosswalk, nothing compared to assisting with audiovisual equipment when filmstrips were wheeled into the classroom. Once threaded, the projectors cast a dusty tunnel of light through the dark and through images upon the film screen positioned in front of the class. Most of these dated films revolved around personal hygiene and historical events. Walter Cronkite informed us that "that's the way it is," and we all daydreamed out our classroom's wall of windows or studied the clock's second hand until the presentation ended.

I fancied the freedom from math assignments that blackboard monitor presented. Not only could you be outside rather than inside the classroom, but you were able to release all that pent-up ten-year-old restlessness and anger for a few precious minutes. Everyone wanted to be blackboard monitor. We were all weary of trying to figure out math problems that involved buying forty melons for eleven cents a pound, as if that was ever going to happen, or calculating the arrival of a train at the station if you left at nine in the morning and were traveling at forty mph.

✳ ⚛ ✳

What was more terrifying than being assigned an oral report in elementary school? Vaccination needles? The dentist? Wearing mismatched socks to school? No. Nothing compared with the horror of having to deliver a report in front of your fellow classmates with the teacher looking on, masked in a scowl like the judge on Perry Mason.

When I was in fourth grade, we had to prepare a speech to deliver in front of the class, and it had to be on the topic of one particular country. I was assigned Sweden. What did a descendent of a maiden from Minsk and other Eastern European regions know about Scandinavia? *Zilch. Nada. Nästan ingenting!* I didn't even fully realize there were other countries in the world. In 1964, I barely got out of the Eichler neighborhood.

Consumed in angst as zero hour approached, fate, normally recalcitrant, arranged for me to accompany my mother to the local Safeway store. It was there, on a small shelf on aisle 3, that I found stacked boxes of Ry-Krisp crackers. Growing more and more excited about their doormat-like texture and shape,

I pulled a box from the shelf. Written in small print on the side of the box: CRACKER OF CHOICE IN SWEDEN. An idea hit me like a bag of frozen Swedish meatballs. Jackpot! I had found a winning visual aid.

The next week, sweating like in a *shvitz* and covered in a blanket of stress pimples that ran across my forehead, I spoke a total of sixteen words on the topic of Sweden in front of my squirmy classmates. The response? A collective blank stare. I began trembling. It was already late afternoon and eyes and heads were drooping from the post-lunch insulin crash. I knew I had to give my visual aid a try. Before their brain waves collapsed in flat line, I began handing out squares of parched crackers to each row of classmates. I had learned how to engage an audience. I had put the scam in Scamdinavia. FREE SAMPLES! The distribution of crackers was an enormous hit, and I learned a valuable lesson: When in doubt, fill a mouth.

P.S. I got an "A" on Sweden.

* ✳ *

In each elementary school class, there were three distinct levels. Somehow, we all knew which level and classroom we had been assigned: slow, average, or above average. Additionally, within each class, there were also three separate levels for reading and math. We only had to look around our circle of classmates to realize to which group we had been assigned. Instead of referring to the groups as smart, average, and slow, the educational system referred to them as the red, blue, and yellow groups. I was in the advanced group. Then, suddenly, I wasn't.

On the first day of what was to be my fifth year at Booksin Elementary, I scouted out the classroom with my name listed on a piece of paper taped to the classroom door. I quickly found a seat inside. As I peered around the room, I saw unfamiliar faces. My usual classmates—my comrades—had taken their seats in a different classroom a few doors down. I spent a few miserable weeks in that class, usually irked and bored.

One morning, the school principal came into our classroom and asked me and another female student, a girl with golden braided hair, to join him in his office. I was shaking as he walked behind us down the walkway to his office. What did I do? No one went to the principal's office without being guilty of something horrendous … like leaving the desktop up or spilling milk. I had done that a few years earlier. Was that why he was calling me in?

As the principal sat us down in his office that smelled like a fine mix of leather, wet industrial carpeting, and Hai Karate cologne, he morphed into a stern authoritarian figure right before our eyes. Blondie looked like she was going to pee her pants. "You two are in a class that is not right for your abilities. I'm going to move both of you to a different classroom. Congratulations."

Huh? As we were walking out of the principal's office, he pulled me back in and told me something that sounded odd in my ear. "We had received a call from Mrs. Prole, Julie's mother. She didn't want her daughter in the same class with you. We have decided to overrule that request."

My friend Julie? What? Why? Was it because my family was Jewish and noisy, or because we ate TV dinners? Julie had always marveled at my diet at home. The fact that we ate frozen dinners at mealtime was radically dissimilar to her own mother's home-cooked meals. The one time Julie did eat over, she was so impressed with our selection of TV dinners that she insisted to her mother she should get Swanson's fried chicken TV dinner for her special birthday meal. Julie always got to pick her favorite food on her birthday. Her mother, a great cook, would whip them up in their Eichler kitchen. I couldn't imagine anyone choosing TV dinners over carefully crafted meatloaf. But after a short while, Julie couldn't quite stomach the eating habits of my family. My father would shovel an overabundance of food into his mouth at a rapid pace and chew with his mouth open. I hadn't yet realize that was a misdemeanor in the court of public opinion and public eating habits. Not until Julie pointed it out.

But why did Julie's mother want us in separate classes? Did Julie's mom disapprove of the way I dressed? Was I a bad friend? Was I "wrong" in some other way? I found out years later that Julie had thrown me under the bus (her words) when she was caught shoplifting long after I stopped. "Ma, Carol told me to." Little did Julie's mom know that Julie was the one who had helped fine-tune my criminal behavior. But now I was home again among my classroom peers. It was the happiest day of my fifth year at Booksin Elementary. I was back with my smarty-pants classmates. The teacher in this new classroom was Mrs. Lewis. I don't remember one thing about her or the class, just that I was in it. But I remember everything about Mr. Laird's sixth grade class in 1966 and my final year at Booksin Elementary School.

Blood, Sweat, and Tears

I was still a year or two away from beginning my period when my mother gave me a pale pink Kotex starter kit that had everything in it but the Midol. She had ordered it from the back of a magazine. It was her way of telling me about menstruation. "Here, read this." She was now off to her phone friends to discuss the weather.

I thumbed through the literature and came to a page that warned, "Do not take hot baths during your menstruation flow, as it will check it." Check it? What? I had never heard that term before. My mind was whirling. How will it check it? The bath will know I have a period because it will check to see if I do?

After sifting through the small, rather horrifying booklet, I scrutinized each contraption in the tall feminine box of female gear. The package housed one pink and white sanitary belt, several narrow boxes stuffed with varying sizes of sample pads, and some other alarming information on menstruation. I was mortified. This can't be. This is going to happen ... to me? To everyone? Stop the world, I want to get off ... and take this sordid tale, this leaflet filled with gothic horror, and these harrowing narrow boxes of cotton fluff with you!

The day after my mother gave me this mystery box of nightmares, I rode my Stingray bike to school beside Julie. I could carry one lightweight classmate on that elongated seat, but usually rode solo. It was like having my own palomino pony. Julie wouldn't have been an easy passenger on my banana seat. She was too tall and thick with tight blonde curls, like a cross between Julia Child and Shirley Temple. Julie always stood out in class pictures and was made to stand in the back row with the tall boys and a scattering of towering females.

With great hesitancy, I reported to Julie about the information in the Kotex booklet and what was going to happen to us, not once, but every four weeks. "We're going to bleed. We're going to BLEED! And it's going to happen every twenty-eight days."

The whole ordeal sounded like a bizarre fact in *Ripley's Believe It or Not!*

Julie's jaw dropped to the pavement. She nearly toppled off her bike when I reported this disastrous news. She looked at me as if she had just seen a ghost ... or heard a ghost story. Her full head of soft curls shook back and forth in disbelief. She wasn't buying it. "Blood? What? From where? Huh? No!"

We were both shocked to learn a monthly and unwanted visitor was coming to call on us all. Julie thought I was making it up—a wicked bedtime story, or in this case, a saga perched atop a Stingray bike. A part of me didn't believe it either. Little did I know that the curse of womanhood that would come knocking at the door of my girlhood would be unlike my friends. When it did arrive, it came in like a lion, not a lamb. And it roared like a son of a bitch.

But back in fourth grade, Julie and I were ten years old, and I still had another year to be period free. I would get my period early, at eleven years old. Julie would get hers at fifteen. From age ten through fifteen Julie no longer believed anything I had to say ... about anything. She saw me as a fraud. A liar. A carrier of bloody fables. A weaver of yarns. But she finally learned the ugly truth. We were all going to cramp. We were all going to change the bulky, bloody, multilayered Modess Sanitary Pads and eventually shove a stick of cotton up our innards and hope we could locate the string later when it came time to yank it out. We were all going to embrace our changing young bodies. We were going to experience premenstrual syndrome and want to murder our siblings more than we could even imagine. We were going to cry at sentimental commercials. We were going to waddle around with a saddle of bulky cotton layered between our loins. We were all in the same soggy boat. Our stomachs sank. Our minds scrambled. Then we picked ourselves up, gathered ourselves together, and marched into the unknown— and the sanitary napkin aisle.

From the beginning, my periods didn't seem to be like other girl's periods. When I bled, which was every two or three weeks, it was an unstoppable flow that soaked a giant-sized pad every fifteen to twenty minutes. The cramps were fierce and caused me to sweat and sometimes vomit. My tummy blew up like puffed pastry. Even my thighs and back would cramp and spasm for days. I sat in class not knowing how I was going to make it through another few minutes. Surely the liquid would escape the pad and run down my legs, stain my skirt, and embarrass me beyond measure. The cramps were persistent and brutal, causing me to double over in pain like John Wayne's fist had pummeled into my tummy. This was womanhood? This was normal? It turned out not to be. Only years later did I discover that I had a case of severe endometriosis. My quickly sloughing uterus lining was flowing like the Russian River, which made perfect sense. I was half Russian.

I'd often sit motionless in class watching each minute tick away on the oversized classroom clock. I didn't know if I'd make it to the restroom in time to change the soppy mess. I was changing out pads between every class, stacking them up, one on top of the other, like a Big Mac. Womanhood was for the birds.

Around this same time period that revolved around periods, my brother's friend-by-proximity, Bad Brad, who lived across the street, came into my bedroom when I wasn't home and proceeded to toss three full boxes of Kotex pads around my once private space. I was mortified by the remodeling he had managed to accomplish in such a short time. Private feminine objects were tossed hither and yon. Mostly yon. I entered and saw napkins flung over lamps and bookcases and hanging from the ceiling's light fixture. I shoved them back into their pink boxes and thought about hiding under the bed for the rest of my life.

Brad's antics continued. A couple of years later, he was arrested at school. As they were dragging him out to the patrol car, he leaned over to Harold and whispered, "Get the smoke bombs out of the sock drawer in my room!" Yes, he was building some sort of explosive device in his house—a haphazard concoction of celluloid material (found in ping-pong balls) sealed inside aluminum wrap or a canister. Then he would ignite them. This practice was widely recognized to be a health hazard, and Brad was widely recognized to be a hazardous jerk, at least in our cul-de-sac. It's a wonder the entire neighborhood didn't combust and disappear in a plume of black smoke.

Some of Bad Brad's behavior rubbed off on Harold, or perhaps all boys push their parents' vehicle down the driveway in the evening while the adults are entertaining neighbors and friends inside of the house. Harold would quietly push our Dodge Dart down to the street and start the engine once he was well out of earshot of the adult partygoers. He was not old enough to drive, but old enough to get into plenty of mischief. One night, Harold urged me to accompany him on this regular ritual. Once the car was successfully pushed down the driveway and was sitting quietly in the middle of the cul-de-sac, I hopped into the passenger's seat. He slipped the key into the slot, pushed a few buttons—reverse, neutral, drive, second, oops, and back to drive, and we were off and driving down the road. Where would our parents not want us to go? Wherever that was, that's where we wanted to be. For us, it was the El Rancho Drive-In Movie Theater on the corner of Almaden and Alma Road in San Jose, where we proceeded to watch grainy triple-X films, one after the other, until we both felt nauseated—a stomachache caused in equal parts by the movie dialogue and the stale pepperoni and mozzarella on the snack bar pizza. I had seen many films at this drive-in, including *The Day the Earth Stood Still* and Haley Mills' *The Parent Trap*. My father had dragged the whole family to see *The Bridge on the River Kwai*, but I fell asleep in the back seat while the bombs exploded.

The outstanding element at the El Rancho Drive-In was the backside of the screen, which faced the intersection of Alma Avenue and Vine Street. It had an enormous depiction of a cowboy on a bucking horse, all outlined in glowing white neon to give a backlit effect. But watching the movie while bathed in anxiety about the stolen car was not my idea of fun. We headed home again to quietly push the car back up the driveway and put the emergency brake on. Unfortunately, my parents had come out to wave goodbye to their friends and noticed there was something missing: their white Dodge Dart. Before calling the police, they called us to come out of our rooms. Silence. The jig was up.

The Breast Is Yet to Come

In 1966, there was Twiggy, Vietnam, and *The Monkees* television show. It was the year *Batman* debuted on ABC. Lyndon Johnson was president, unemployment was at 4.5 percent, life expectancy was 70.2 years, and the family median income was $7,400. *The Sound of Music* won Best Picture at the Oscars, and the Uniform Time Act was decreed, which rolled in Daylight Savings Time standards for the country. We've been complaining about it ever since. The Beatles gave their last public performance at Candlestick Park in San Francisco that year. It was also the year John Lennon stated that The Beatles were more popular than Jesus Christ. But I thought my new teacher, Mr. Laird, was more popular than John Lennon, or should be.

It was the first day of sixth grade as I took my seat behind Kathy Christy, one of the most popular girls at the school. She had a sing-songy name and two perfect syllables in each one that seemed to go together like peanut butter and jelly. But her high-pitched voice was like a drill against a back molar.

Kathy's brother, who was one year older, had the buckteeth of a zebra. Kathy had the same unfortunate overbite, but the most alluring long blonde hair that seemed to cancel out her dental misfortune. She also had some peculiar, newfangled, horizontal apparatus running left to right under the back of her crisp white blouse. The contraption was a bra, known to twelve-year-old boys everywhere as an "over the shoulder boulder holder." We're supposed to wear bras now? I certainly didn't require one. Not yet. Kathy was the first in our class to sport this undergarment, and she took every advantage of her early blooms.

Her small breasts sat like molded Jell-O inside the stylish duplex of her brassiere. The light fabric of her blouse and the dart lines of her garment gently landed on top of each smooth cup. She had the bodice of a goddess as she paraded around the classroom and playground in her sheer top. Kathy's garments easily revealed the mysterious mechanism housed underneath the fabrics, much to the delight of every salivating boy in class. Their eyes would dart back and forth, forth and back, nearly burning a hole in the back of her blouse, while mentally unhooking the two clasped loops. The boys noticed the bra. The other girls in class noticed they didn't have one. Not yet.

Breasts, bosoms, boobs, bazongas, bazooms, boobies, sweater puppies, feeders, hooters, jugs, mammaries, melons, mosquito bites, ta-tas, the girls, and the twins. They were a soft-as-pudding part of the female landscape. But my mother never spoke to me of bras or any female equipment, except the thing I needed the least: a girdle.

When I was in sixth grade, she announced in that knowing voice that only mothers possess, "Your stomach sticks out. We have to get you a girdle." And she did. There was no arguing with latex—or my mother. The girdle was extraordinarily tight. It felt as though it was several sizes too small, even for my undersized frame. What purpose did it serve other than making me gasp for a full breath of air? I didn't know the answer, or the purpose, but I wore it each school day because I was supposed to and because she told me I needed it.

But what I genuinely coveted was a Maidenform bra like Kathy Christy. It attracted boys glances like honey pots attracted bees. I wanted the boys to stare at me, from the front, the back, and the side too. I scouted out bras for young girls in the Sears catalog. They had stitching that circled 'round and 'round the cup and always seemed to crunch at the top. They looked uncomfortable, but sort of sexy in a Jane Russell sort of way. It was a better choice than the flat, elastic, stretch-as-you-grow beginner's bra. But I was not only razor thin, I was flat-chested. When I turned sideways, I was marked absent.

As the school year went on and I started to experience growing pains in the upper body region, my mother never mentioned female undergarments. She didn't speak about bras, deodorant, or boys so I started to hunt down information on my own. After a few more female classmates began to sport bras under their outfits, I began to feel ostracized from this mysterious club. Back to the pages of the Sears catalog I went, then on to pages of the Montgomery Ward's catalog to choose a junior bra. I wanted to look like the pre-teen in the catalog—well proportioned, pert, and impeccable—and it wouldn't hurt if my hair was in a perfect Gidget-styled flip.

In the mid-Sixties, you had no other protocol than to send cash through the mail in a plain white envelope if you desired a product. I ran to my mother's drawer, pocketed some pocket change, and dropped the coins in the envelope addressed to the catalog company. Then I licked it closed. I wasn't sure if I filled out the form properly or enclosed the right coins and paper. Whatever I did, I did correctly because a small package showed up weeks later.

Inside the plain brown wrapper was a cotton circular-stitched bra with petite cups, seemingly made for two soft-boiled eggs. As I hooked the latches in the back of the bra and turned it around to my front, I shimmied the garment up my torso. My barely budding buds were swimming in the size AA teen cups and cotton crunched fabric. It looked wrinkly under my dresses and blouses, like I had shunted some misshapen handful of wadded up newspaper under my dress and it didn't belong there.

There was only one dress hanging in my closet that I could wear the bra under with any success at all. It was a blue-green cotton empire dress my grandmother had sent from the Bronx. I determined I would wear only dresses and blouses with embellishment along the top bodice when I went to school. If my empire dress had buttons or stitching in front, I could successfully hide the new crunchy chest fashion: my cotton bra. But in my other dresses without surface adornments, I looked like I had two handfuls of aluminum foil crumbled into edgy balls where each breast should be. The search for the perfect containers of concealment would continue throughout the teen years and well into adulthood.

Fashions were changing quickly, including hemlines. The length of my dresses started out above the knee. Suddenly I was sashaying around in a granny gown with hems sweeping the sidewalk like prairie brooms on a porch. From there I went to miniskirts, where I remained uneasy in a seated position. Then the lengths dropped again to below the knee and were called maxi dresses. My sixth-grade class was also stricken with girly Laura Ashley fashions, dresses with spaghetti straps, and the aforementioned floor-length granny gown. It was as though a contagious virus of petite lace and small flowery prints had invaded the student population. Both the popular and the unpopular girls wore these delicate but dreadfully dated floor sweepers. Even I had such a puffed sleeve prairie concoction that teased the floor and looked like something my grandmother would wear if she were living on the plains. But my grandparents reigned from Brooklyn and the Bronx, so what was I thinking? I wasn't. I was trending.

Granny gowns were initially embraced by the Bay Area's flower children. These old-fashioned gowns with a yesteryear vibe offered a romantic illusion transported from another time. A few years later, the same young girls would be wearing hot pants and miniskirts. Some would even dress in micro-miniskirts, garments that were barely visible to the human eye.

But in sixth grade, lace and calico prints in floor-length garments with conservative necklines reminiscent of Victorian times were happening. This nostalgic trend, complete with high-necked Edwardian or Peter Pan collars, transported us back to the days of chivalry. We were buttoned up and busy covering everything but our head and hands like a troop of pioneer women bucking the Machine Age. Julie began wearing granny gowns every day, not only to class, but after school. Her classmates, sprinkled with mean girls, called out "Hey, Granny!" behind her back despite my power-packed glares of disdain for such name-calling. If looks could kill, those bullies would have been toast.

I looked around the room at my sixth-grade classmates, then at the laid-back Mr. Laird seated at his desk thumbing through our answers on the last class exam. The papers were stacked behind a large, uneaten, and rather flawless apple. I felt safe and content. Everything was as it should be. I knew every students' first and last names, which borough of San Jose they lived in, and if they were the outgoing type like Marlo Thomas in *That Girl* or an Eddie Haskell type bully. I knew if they were a class doofus, like *The Beverly Hillbillies'* Jethro Bodine, A *Batman*-type Joker, a Laura Petrie sweetheart, or a Davy Jones heartthrob.

In 1966, there were no mushroom clouds outside our classroom door and no air raid drills to rattle the windows. There was no more mention of the Bay of Pigs, only a bridge where Captain Kirk and Commander Spock watched over the controls of the Enterprise. They led us towards an optimistic future where women held command positions, and kisses were shared between every race, creed, and color. We were being teased with a blended, bright, and better tomorrow. We told ourselves we were secure and protected. In my mind, not one of the kids in my class would become ill, or divorced, or suffer drug addiction or homelessness beyond the confines of our sheltered classroom. No one would suffer. No one in this room would become mangled in a war zone. Life would be as neat and tidy as the books stacked under the lid of our pinewood and steel desks.

It was unusual for men to teach elementary school in the Sixties. Teaching was thought of as a woman's profession, an extension of nurturing or mothering. Mr. Laird was the only male teacher in our school. His Adam's apple sprung from the middle of his throat, protruding like a ping-pong ball stuck in his esophagus. He was mature, mischievous, shipshape, and manly. In short, Mr. Laird was the Paul Newman of Booksin Elementary. He was our tall, tan, lean, and lovely instructor. He was our *Man from Ipanema.* As one of my classmates put it, he was put together. More importantly, he was casual and playful. He made learning fun and didn't seem to take himself or the business of learning too seriously. My kind of man. Decades later, I discovered he was gay, but in 1966, there was another word for homosexual. An ugly word. Fag. But we didn't care if he swung this way or that. At ages eleven and twelve, we only knew that he was our favorite teacher ever.

Jews Don't Camp

During that last school year at Booksin Elementary, the entire class was bussed away for a week to a campground high in the mountains outside San Jose. Initially the preparation for the trip was exciting, fueled by unrealistic expectation, joyousness, frantic last-minute packing, inevitably forgetting to take this or that. My family had never gone camping—real camping—so I was anxious to see what this experience was all about.

Young students catapulted up the steep stairs of the school bus that would take us to an unknown destination for five days and four nights. The ride itself was exciting. The scenery out the window quickly shifted from suburban orderliness to urban sprawl, and finally to dark forest pines. The strain of the engine signaled we were climbing, up, up, up.

My classmates were beginning to look different. Now they were people on a long caterpillar-shaped vehicle. They were no longer my familiar chums sitting at woody desks. They were soldiers on the battleground known as the campground, and their expressions were those of strangers. My best friend Jill gradually blended in with the crowds of other kids from various local schools. Her eyes darted this way and that, never at me. Although we were inseparable in and out of the classroom, she was suddenly distancing herself. She was becoming one of THEM. I was left alone, at least in my own mind's eye.

When we arrived at our high and rugged destination, we found it scattered with small cabins and a spacious mess hall. My mind and heart rate were already nose-diving into panic mode. I had all the signs of a full-blown panic attack, but I didn't know what a panic attack was. I knew I had to escape ... everything, or I would surely die. My breaths were brief and shallow, my pores were oozing sweat, and my heart was beating faster than Ringo's drumbeat in "Twist and Shout." What was this foreign land where we had been dumped? And why did it smell like rain even though it wasn't raining? My new temporary home and playground were carpeted in mossy damp soil and wallpapered with oversized evergreens. But I was a suburban kid who didn't know a pine tree from a bottle of Pine-Sol.

Nothing appeared familiar. My mother and father weren't there, but that's not what was bothering me. Even when they were there, they weren't there. I wasn't longing for them. I was longing for my neighborhood. My Eichler. The safe haven of my bedroom with the dark mahogany walls and record player. That was my safety net. It wasn't just home. The Eichler was a part of me, and in the acres of tall scented pines, I had lost my footing and was beginning to shiver from the cold indifference of this new wilderness. That boxy structure with gray floors and wood paneled walls had always provided the illusion of safety and identity. That was what I missed. Not my family. They weren't my shelter in times of fear. The security of the Eichler fortress was my warm poncho of protection. My beloved indoor/outdoor home had vanished and was now replaced with only outdoors—and acres of it. No atrium, just a damp woodland. Not an illusion of indoor/outdoor living, but the real deal. I wasn't trying to draw a red squirrel inside the bold black outline anymore; I was spotting the real life fuzzy-tailed creature in some nearby brush.

As the sun began to sink into the distant outline of a mountaintop, the shadows grew, and the temperature dropped. It felt as though a pit had opened up in front of me, or rather inside of my stomach. I was as lost as an Easter egg on Passover. I felt out of sorts—a 78 rpm record on a 33⅓ rpm turntable. There was nothing to grab onto to break my fall or soothe my panic. Each second felt as painful as stepping barefooted on a Lego brick. The tears began to sting my eyes, and my knees weakened. Here I was, far from the Eichler; far from anything familiar. No warmth. No bulbous lighting dangling from the ceiling of sky. No neighbors, just bright stars and dim classmates who suddenly seemed like random strangers.

As the sky shifted from sapphire blue to gray, we were corralled and dragged to an assembly-like presentation. Welcome to Hell, kiddos. My friend Jill was seated several rows away from mine. I tried to grab her glance with mine, but her eyes turned away. Her body language was one of openness with the others seated in her sector. Weren't we best friends? She looked right through me. I was invisible. It felt familiar—a well-worn but comfortable feeling that fit me like a soft glove. I was shrinking among the pines and smoke-filled night air. I didn't know any of the hundreds of other students around me. Furthermore, I didn't want to. The kids from other schools were mashed in with our own classmates from Booksin Elementary. It was a mess hall full of messy emotions. I wanted to lean my shoulder against my friend Jill's shoulder, like we always did. But announcements were made, songs were sung, and my stomach twisted up like a Girl Scout knot, even though I was a Campfire Girl. Dread turned to fear, and fear turned to nausea as my tummy began to rumble like a California earthquake. Take me home. Somebody, please ... take me home!

I was dragged to the nurse's office by a camp counselor. I had tugged on her sleeve to tell her I needed to go home ... NOW, as if that could be easily accomplished. "I'm sick. I need to be at home." As I lay on a cot inside the brightly lighted but claustrophobic medical tent, they called my mother. Surely, she would want me to come home. I breathed a sigh of relief and told myself to hang on. It shouldn't be long now.

The nurse came back to my cot with a scowl on her face. "Your mother said you're not sick. She said you're staying here for a week." What? "They have plans for the evening." WHAT? Parties? Happy hours? Lawrence Welk?

I was assigned to a multi-bed cabin with no heat and ten strangers. After I brushed my teeth, I crawled into the upper bunk that had been assigned. I slipped on my socks and lay under that heavy blanket. Minutes turned to hours. Crawling down from my bed, I rushed in and out of the bathroom, then entered the camp counselor quarters.

"I can't sleep." I felt ashamed, weak, beaten.

They gave me an aspirin and told me to go back to bed. I crawled under the covers and listened to the counselors gossiping before they took to their own beds and went to sleep. As I lay on the top bunk, I watched 1:59 a.m. roll into 2 a.m. on the small clock radio near the bathroom. "I still can't sleep! I tried. " I went back into the counselor's quarters. She told me to lie there until I fell asleep or until morning. *Aye aye, sir. I mean, madam.*

It took me several days and nights to adjust. I went through the motions of saluting the flag and singing the national anthem first thing each morning, eating at long tables beside kids from other schools, taking walks with counselors, and learning about pine cones, trees, and birds. No one talked to me, and I didn't talk to anyone. It was as if I weren't there. I counted the hours until I could crawl back on that giant yellow and black caterpillar with wheels and head home. In those five days, I managed to meander through at least three or four circles of Dante's nine Circles of Hell.

On the last day at camp, and much to my surprise, I awoke happy and refreshed. I was ecstatic, not because I would soon be leaving, but to be at camp. The panic switch had mysteriously been clicked off. For the first time since I had arrived, I breathed in the cool mountain air with ease and noticed all the wondrous greenery and wildlife around me. I looked closely at the veins in the leaves and watched for squirrels in the forest. I was salivating at the thought of eating in the mess hall with my classmates—a hall where I had previously been unable to keep my breakfast, lunch, or dinner down.

Jill sat next to me for the first time since we had arrived at this enchanted forest. As she leaned her shoulder into mine, Jill whispered in my ear, "I'm feeling sick and homesick. I can't wait to get out of here." She bounced hard against my shoulder, as if she was trying to open me from the side and slither into my sweatshirt to hide. "I'm gonna throw up! Come with me."

Hand in hand, we shuffled off to the restroom. As I held her head over the basin, I noticed that her emotions and stomach were unsettled, but mine weren't. For the first time, I was at home here in the wilderness without Eichler walls, parents, or ringing phones. I was happy to walk the wet trails and learn about the evergreens and insects. I even enjoyed the raising of the flag and the patriotic crap we sang in unison. I raised my voice higher than the other campers when I hit the line "purple mountain majesties" as I finally knew what that meant. They were all around me.

I wanted to remain in camp now. No one was more astounded than I was. But it was time to pile into the school bus where Jill recognized me again. It was time to head back to our familiar classroom with the hard chairs; the textbooks leaning against one another in the corner bookcase; the cubbies for galoshes; umbrellas, and coats; the large windows opened to release daydreams; the weeks-old wad of chewing gum under my desk; and the familiar ticking of the lone clock on the wall of Mr. Laird's classroom alerting us about when to stay and when to dash out the door.

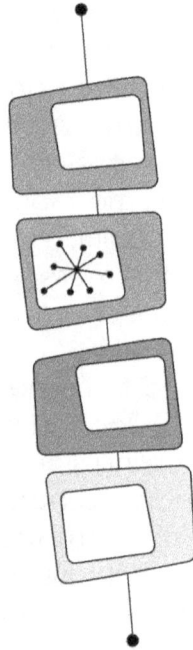

California Funhouse
Zit's a Wonderful Life

When the Sternfelds moved out of their Eichler, another Jewish physician moved in: Dr. Levin and his young family of four. It seemed the house was destined to be occupied by a Jew, two small children, and a medical degree hanging crookedly on the den wall.

Dr. Levin had married Candy, a petite nurse with short, dirty blonde hair and colorless skin with a subtle splash of rosy blush. She was in her early twenties and looked like a child herself. Dr. Levin was at least a decade older, with a heavy bear-like stroll and tight black curls streaked with gray. He was one of those men you were certain was hiding acres of dark curly chest and back hair under his starched white shirt and navy blue suit.

The couple seemed ill-suited for sexual activity, but they popped out a couple of babies and entered the Eichler cul-de-sac with a son and daughter, both under the age of six. I later learned that Candy was just shy of twenty years old when she had her first child. If the Pill had been readily available to her, she likely wouldn't have gotten pregnant or married—certainly not at nineteen. There was no scarcity of unenthusiastic parenting in our cul-de-sac.

Both Harold and I experienced extreme outbreaks of pimples, but when it turned into acne on our cheeks and ravaged our chests and backs, my parents took us to see Dr. Levin, dermatologist by day, Marlboro chain-smoker by night. Physicians in the Sixties smoked like a fleet of Peterbilt 18-wheelers. I would often spot him sluggishly ambling around the cul-de-sac, head lowered, tobacco stick in one hand and his other arm swinging ever so slightly to advance his pace. There was a lot of sauntering going on in that neighborhood.

Dr. Levin was the Sixties version of Tony Soprano, if Tony Soprano had been a dermatologist. He certainly wasn't Troy Donahue. Dr. Levin was a tall, big-boned man with a substantial gut that hung over his neatly belted slacks. He seemed to be a world removed from his new young family, but Harold and I liked him fine. He got right to work as we lay on the examination table in his office, first one of us, then the other. Initially, the good doctor would go about the business of attacking ripe pimples and blackheads, squeezing the living daylights, pus, and slime right out of them. It hurt, but it was a pain we were willing to endure. Anything but acne!

Following the instrument that popped and scraped our most glaring imperfections came the dreaded and painful dry ice treatment that would burn off layers of our skin. My brother and I would emerge from Dr. Levin's office with bright red cheeks, chins, and foreheads that would last for days, and the redness was not only from embarrassment. We were burn victims. In the Sixties, dry ice and burning off multiple layers of skin seemed to be the treatment for an acne-ridden youth. I don't recall that it helped, but it was my first and only chemical peel and might have kept my skin more youthful over time. At least, that's what I keep telling myself.

Clearasil was a flesh-toned lotion that came in a tube. Ads had youngsters convinced it would camouflage even the most glaring pimple, like the one that broke out on the side of your nose before you had to give a book report or go on a date. The main ingredients in this product were benzoyl peroxide, sulfur, resorcinol, triclosan, salicylic acid, and other substances that, with enough applications, would melt your face right off. Clearasil was a regular sponsor of American Bandstand, which was a brilliant marketing ploy because the viewing audience suffered frequent breakouts. Even the dancers and audience on the show were blanketed with pink bumps and a ripe grove of blackheads.

Clearasil was also marketed through magazine ads that were designed to emphasize popularity and mimicked the look of an advice column. One ad was even called "Clearasil Personality of the Month." The ads appeared in girls' magazines like Seventeen and in the male equivalent, Boy's Life. The early Clearasil campaigns in Seventeen demonstrated how marketers spoke directly to girls, as it was first advertised as a "revolutionary new skin-colored miracle medication." It was both a medicine and a cosmetic? Genius! And it hid pimples while it worked? Insert circular yellow happy face here.

Back in the Sixties, the Noxzema ad promised that I'd look like a stunning blonde teenager if I used their goopy white cream. Even though my Semitic *schnozzola* couldn't have differed more from the Noxzema model's upturned nose, and my hazel-colored eyes paled in comparison to her striking baby blue peepers, I believed the ad. My eye color looked like it was created in some tie-dye machine, with whirls and twirls of green, brown, and gray spun together and whipped into a frenzy. They looked like a swirled flavor-of-the-month at Baskin Robbins.

"What color are your eyes, Carol?"

"I dunno. Take your pick."

Perky teen models could be seen everywhere. They included glamorous Jean Shrimpton and the girl-next-door Colleen Corby. She modeled everything from teen bras to go-go boots. Corby looked cool like Linda Ronstadt before we knew who Linda Ronstadt was. She wore the blouse I longed for and the culottes I coveted. She modeled the first bra I owned, was featured in the pages of the Sears catalog, and was poised and posed on Simplicity and Butterick sewing pattern envelopes. Corby had the hair, the eyes, the look that we all longed for and didn't know how to achieve.

Then Cybill Shepherd came along and appeared in ads for face cream and makeup. Shepherd was the perfect girl nobody looked like except the high school cheerleader who went steady with the football captain. Why did those girls exist except to cast shadows on the ordinary?

Those of us with perpetually pimply skin and acne had a collection of helpful products on the bathroom counter. They included Stridex Pads; Noxzema face cream; pHisoHex Cleanser in the cheery bright green bottle; and Clearasil. Their target? Pimples, blackheads, whiteheads, and everything that made boys go "eww." As a pre-teen and teenager, I studied my cheeks, chin, forehead, and the sides of my nose like they were my own personal planet, a planet covered in plugged craters, blackheads, and pus. No matter how many pounds of Clearasil I slathered on my face, it would make my screaming red blobs looked unnaturally caked with flesh-toned ointment. Some of those skin protrusions felt like they had a root system that went miles deep. How could I be expected to camouflage such monstrosities? I tried, but it was futile.

Throughout the pre-teen and teen years, I used Noxzema face cream. It smelled like mint and came in a cobalt blue jar with yellow label that assured us it was "greaseless" and that we would soon "feel the heal" from that medicinal goop. With all the stinging it produced, it felt like it was doing something. Nobody knew what. Noxzema's success was all about marketing, including a name that sounded scientific. N-o-x-z?

The consistency of Noxzema was like a cold cream: white, cool to the touch, with a strong scent. The scented camphor and menthol ingredients caused a tingling sensation as it disappeared into my skin. I would scoop a couple of fingers full and rub it all over my face in a circular motion, just like in the commercials. The voiceover in my head would be telling me how clean my skin would be once I patted it dry. It was opening every pore on my face while the menthol scent stung my eyes.

* ⚛ *

Although my father always called Dr. Sternfeld by his first name, David, he was a bit more formal with Dr. Levin, who was not as approachable. He seemed to pull along a gray cloud, unlike his youthful bride, Candy, who always wore a crooked smile like she was hiding a devilish secret. Eventually, Dr. Levin shocked all the residents in our cul-de-sac by committing suicide shortly after he and Candy separated. She was left to raise their two small children on her own in Fairgrove Court.

One night, in the middle of our cul-de-sac, after a Fourth of July picnic and annual Red Devil firework show, I watched my father flirt ferociously with Candy, nonchalantly charming her with his clever observations and jokes, hoping she'd take the bait. After all, everyone bit.

Candy moved her pink fingertips to her lips as she giggled at my father's antics. After all, he was the Fairgrove Court jester. He casually followed her back to her Eichler. I stood there frozen like a July Popsicle, watching them slither away from the boxes of sidewalk snakes, cones, and sparklers. They didn't seem to notice the cardboard standup figure called Smoky Joe and his filthy cigar pouring out thick smoke on the sidewalk or the wobbly log cabin with the brick-like paper chimney whose thick black smoldering remnants reddened our eyes. Nobody looked as they zigzagged up her driveway and were suddenly out of view. I finally peeled my eyes away from Candy's house. I didn't want to know what I already knew. I felt as though I had been watching a movie starring my father as Kirk Douglas and Candy as his lusty paramour. I was the onlooker watching this play out, but I didn't dare tell my brother and certainly not my mother. It was my father's little secret. I was in on the sordid affair, but I wanted out.

Relation-Ships: Sink or Swim

The Robbins family occupied the house on the other side of ours. They had a daughter, who became my friend-by-proximity. Her name even sounded sing-songy, like a bird: Roberta Robbins. Her bedroom window faced mine, and we made full use of that convenience, often making faces at one another and hollering across the fence through our window screens.

"Rooooberta! Are you theeeerrrre?"

"I'm here, Carrrrrooool!"

The Robbins' nest was filled with dark antiques and traditional pottery pieces with white and deep blue designs. There was not one modern trinket or furniture piece in their home. What were they doing in a mid-century Eichler?

Janey, Roberta's mother, was a stout woman with acres of freckles and close-cropped black hair laced with a few strands of early gray. She reminded me of perky Debbie Reynolds. Janey's husband was an animated, nervous fellow named Lenny. He looked like a Lenny. He'd often massage Janey's back with his hand as she told a story. A long glance of tenderness and reverence would fall over his face as he gazed in her direction. She would softly brush his face as though her fingers were five thin watercolor brushes. They adored each other. I studied carefully and took mental notes. Hugs and squeezes. Check. Hand kisses. Check. I didn't see that in my house, but it was conveniently located next door at Roberta's house.

Even as a kid, I decided which couple or individual I wanted to be like, and as soon as I could, I went about the business of seeking them out or emulating them. I wanted a watercolor brushstroke to my cheek. I never saw my mother brush my father's cheek in such a fashion. Not with the front of her graceful hand, the back of her long fingers, or her orange-lipsticked lips.

My parents were not big on affection. There were no words of endearment offered from either direction. They called each other "Blos" or "Joe" as long as I can remember. Not one dear, darling, honey, or sweetheart was uttered. Their marriage was a boxed cake mix missing that one crucial ingredient: adoration. They fought, they ignored, they barely tolerated, but they didn't touch tenderly with watercolor brush affection. For a long time, neither did I. I didn't know how. In fact, when I turned eighteen, my new boyfriend informed me that I didn't seem happy to see him whenever he entered my apartment door. "You ignore my existence!" is how he put it. Accused of not expressing pleasure when he came by, even though I was filled with joy, was sobering. I quickly realized where I had acquired this learned behavior early on, so I went about making a diligent effort to modify it.

Harold's hell-raising birthday bash in the Eichler kitchen featuring party of three.

My parents reveled in their Space Age marriage, mainly because there was a lot of space between them and little intimacy. They would often go for hours in each other's presence without uttering a word to each other, or touching an arm or a cheek. They only needed to know the other person was close. No interaction required. No unnecessary intermingling or communication expected.

I believe that distance, an unspoken contract that they both required, was the glue that held my parents in the bond of not-so-holy matrimony. They needed one another, but there was no sentimentality in my father's vocabulary. His own father was enormously affectionate, his mother was overprotective and overbearing, yet my father couldn't buy a gift, give a card, utter "Happy Birthday" or "Happy Chanukah" or even "Merry Christmas" to anyone in our immediate family. If it hadn't been for my mother and her need to coordinate and control social functions, including birthday parties, I wouldn't have known it was my birthday. My father was missing the Hallmark card gene.

My viewpoint on marriage has shifted over the years, many times. My generation had one foot in the Fifties and traditional unions and one in the Sixties where "anything goes"—and sometimes goes right out the window. When I was much younger, I didn't agree with the institution of marriage. It seemed like a forced financial union and one that held some couples together longer than they should be or wanted to be. It was a business agreement. But then I got married, and it was good for a long while—twenty-eight years. Then, it wasn't. When I divorced I thought I would never consider marriage again. And again, I find my viewpoint shifting like fashion trends or the weather.

Do all relationships have an end date, like a carton of eggs? Or can love survive the many challenges life presents and grow stronger, not weaker, with time? My parents fought for the entire span of their marriage but remained together and married. They also danced together and occasionally there was a quick smile between them. They held hands and took walks, first on the streets of New York and later in our San Jose suburb. They downed shots of tequila and clinked tall Tom Collins glasses. They felt despair, then ordered another round. They endured, they survived, but did they thrive? Is it necessary to thrive? Many couples in the Sixties just got by.

Duck and Cover

One afternoon, Roberta from across the fence floated over to my house, as friends often do. Sadly, my father was alone in the house and was in one of his agitated states that seemed to come out of nowhere. The stack of explosives that was Joe was ready to go off at any minute. But I was oblivious to potential danger, not at all cautious of where I stepped. I was too busy talking and playing games with Roberta in my room. She was barefoot, and I decided to go barefoot too, even though it was discouraged by my parents. In their eyes, the ground was a danger zone and going without shoes was a federal offense of considerable proportions.

"No bare feet in the house!" both parents barked in unison. "You'll step on something. Put your shoes on. Now!"

On that particular day, my father was fully loaded with ammunition and in need of a target. As Roberta and I walked into my Eichler living room barefoot, giggling and telling knock-knock jokes, the dynamite exploded. I knew there was going to be trouble as soon as my eyes met my dad's furious stare. Our Eichler was like a minefield at times. Small things became triggers for massive explosions. Like small feet without shoes.

I don't recall any of the words used after "What the hell ..." but the storm clouds were enough to blow Roberta right out of my family's living room. With a look of dread, her smile turned to a frown, then fear washed over her face. Roberta quietly slipped out our sliding glass door and ran through our atrium to the front door, directly to her front lawn and into her room. My father plowed towards me, his own version of Dr. Frankenstein's monster out for revenge. I ran down the hallway for safety as fast as my bare feet could move, but there was no safe haven in my home, not even in my bedroom. His howls, accompanied by clomping footsteps, followed too closely. Before I knew it, I was in my bedroom, head covered with both hands, curled on the floor like a lone shrimp on a platter. *Duck and cover, Carol.*

The steel toe of his work shoes plowed into my back as I floated out of my physical body and into my worries about Roberta. What was she thinking? How scared is she? Is Roberta sitting in her room and—oh no!—listening to the rage gusting out of my father's mouth like a fire-breathing Godzilla targeting his enemy? I tried to stop the tears that were welling up with each blow. I didn't want my father to know I was crying. I wanted him to be proud of me for taking what he was dishing and kicking out. Most of all, I didn't want Roberta to hear me whimpering. In that moment, and in my mind, the worst thing in the world would have been for the evidence of my father's fury to surface in front of a friend or to have them witness his unpredictability. Rage-fueled kicks into my lower back and side continued. *Please stop, please stop, Dad. I'll never take my shoes off again. Not ever!* I was certain I would perish right then and there in a pool of pain, blood, and humiliation. I would surely die, either of bodily injuries or of embarrassment. Certainly of shame. For a house filled with light, the Eichler held a lot of dark shadows.

Roberta and I had always shouted, giggled, and played games back and forth between our bedroom windows. That day, I heard her voice call to me a few minutes after my father left the room. I heard her say my name in the loudest whisper she could manage. She wanted to know if I was okay, but I wasn't able to respond. I couldn't crawl to the bed and hoist myself up to the window. I was mortified. Humiliated. I don't know if I was more ashamed to be me, or more embarrassed by my father's behavior, which by that time seemed normal to me.

I disconnected from the ache now settled in my lower back. I couldn't move. I wanted to be a Fizzies tablet dissolving in mid-air or a Bromo-Seltzer disappearing in a glass of water. I didn't want to feel fragile, but in that moment I was a broken toy on the cold gray tile. My flushed cheeks and back matched the pink rug as I lingered there in a ball on the floor—a floor I wished would open and let me fall through to another time and place, another set of circumstances, another family. Where was my perfect magic trick now? *Houdini, come free me!*

I quickly became gifted at hiding things from others. Like one of those FIND THE HIDDEN OBJECT puzzles in magazines, I kept my emotions well hidden, kept the secrets of family outbursts to myself. After all, that wasn't the person my friends or my father's friends knew. I must have done something to bring out "the beast" because he seemed well behaved in the company of friends and strangers. *It has to be my fault. It just has to be.* I had so many secrets by this time, I was running out of places to store them. I couldn't let my peers find out about my nocturnal terrors, my reluctant parents, the random brotherly fist to the stomach, my self-image getting shoved, slapped down, and pinned to the ground on a continual basis. I couldn't reveal the shivering attacks of morning anxiety soothed by French Vanilla Instant Breakfast and Barnum's Animals Crackers, my ability to absorb other people's feelings in moments, the unintentional skill to feel the distinct personalities and history of rooms and homes, and a hyperawareness in sensing events before they happened. Childhood became synonymous with secrets, and I had a Pandora's box bulging at the seams.

At the end of the block lived a family that seldom joined in the cul-de-sac activities. They were a smart-looking young couple with no children. The young man worked for Johnson & Johnson. One afternoon, when I was peddling seeds, greeting cards, or warm glasses of lemonade door-to-door, he opened the front door wide enough to reveal boxes and boxes of sanitary napkins covering the living room floor. I thought that was odd, but what wasn't odd in the Eichlers?

There was never a more attractive couple. She, a slender blonde from Sweden with long wavy hair, and he a male model from the Sears Christmas Catalog. All he needed was a pipe and a pair of slippers. The Barbie and Ken of the cul-de-sac were seldom seen in the front yard. When they moved into their Eichler, they were newly married. Even though there was a house located between our Eichler and theirs, I often heard the sounds of their ferocious lovemaking pounding against the glass of my bedroom window. Pushka's ears would perk up in horror. Then she would go back to her nap in the sun spot on my rug.

Soon they had their first child, a little girl with white hair and peachy perfect cheeks. Her face could have been on the label of any variety of baby food. They tried for a second child, but there were problems.

Fertility drugs weren't new, but they were radically different than today's smorgasbord of treatments. There were two major types of fertility drugs. The first was a drug called clomiphene citrate, which came in pill form and was approved for clinical use in 1967. The second type was derived from the urine of menopausal women and was therefore called human menopausal gonadotropins.

Twins, triplets, or higher-order pregnancies were an important consequence of treatment with these fertility drugs. The multiple pregnancy rate with clomiphene was approximately ten percent, nearly all twins. Barbie and Ken finally conceived and had twin boys with an overabundance of health problems.

The father quit his good-paying day job at Johnson & Johnson to stay home with the three kids. The lanky Swedish blonde went to work every day in her trendy red convertible MG. Soon they announced their divorce and put up a FOR SALE sign on the front lawn. As I stood at my bedroom window, silence hitting the glass, no passionate moans coming from the house two doors down, I found myself wondering, *Do attractive people cheat and divorce more often than average-looking people?*

*   *

Every few years, families moved out of the cul-de-sac and a new crop of kids and set of parents moved in. After the Shoensteins moved out from next door, an unlikely duo moved in: Les Lambson and his petite young wife, Marge. There seemed to be no shortage of petite young wife material with close-cropped hairstyles in the Sixties and in our cul-de-sac.

Lambson had been removed from his position as a university professor for having an affair with his young student. That student would become his wife, Marge. After losing his career, Lambson had to reinvent himself, and he did. He became a well-known artist, sculptor, and potter extraordinaire. Celebrities—including Frank Sinatra, Winston Churchill, Andy Williams, and The Osmond Brothers—collected his work, and his paintings brought in hundreds and thousands of dollars. In the Sixties, that was akin to millions of dollars. From the late Sixties through the early Eighties, you couldn't walk into a gallery without seeing one of his distinctive paintings. Lambson's artwork continued to be exhibited in galleries in the United States and abroad for several decades.

These paintings were characterized by understated lines and colors scratched into multiple layers of paint. Landscape was his main subject, but the unique technique used to create his work was his own. He acquired his formal training primarily from two strong personalities: the great European teacher, Paul Bonifas, in whose home Lambson lived for two years, and Shoji Hamada, on whom the Japanese Government bestowed the title of National Living Treasure. Before establishing himself as a full-time artist, Lambson was a member of several prestigious universities. He married Marge in 1960 and went about creating the thousands of oil paintings that found their way to private homes and collections as well as museums and galleries throughout the world. But on Fairgrove Court in Willow Glen, San Jose, he was just another Eichler resident.

The Great Escape

It is 9:35 in the evening. A school night. My parents are watching The Fugitive *in the living room. Harold is sequestered in his bedroom doing homework. Scratch that. "Reading"* Playboy. *The soles of my feet are padded with cotton gym socks to muffle my escape. With both tennis shoes in one hand, I inch down the hallway towards the bathroom between my bedroom and my brother's room. One of my shoes drops with a clop. Crap! I stop dead in my tracks, as I wait to see if the sound will draw attention from my family. My mind flashes on the 1962 film* Escape from Alcatraz, *in which three inmates fashioned papier-mâché replicas of their faces and placed them in their prison cots before making the first and only successful escape from the desolate island. I, too, fashion such a deception. My bed covers are stuffed with clothes to simulate a figure and head so that my getaway won't be discovered. I look up one side of the darkened hallway, then the other. The coast is clear. As I make my way through the bathroom door, it squeaks softly and only once. I move quietly past the sink and tub, then reach for the brass knob on the escape hatch in my bathroom that leads to the Eichler's side yard. With one counter-clockwise turn, I am free. I tiptoe down the walkway towards the gate, lifting the latch so quietly that not even a neighboring moth can sense it. I take one lengthy deep breath of night air. I am free at last, free at last!*

Where did I run off to on these calculated escapades? Most of my destinations were the curb or neighborhood sidewalks, where I would sit or walk beside my friends and try to make sense of our small world. When I grew into my teens, the side bathroom door was an escape hatch to forbidden boys with their fidgety hands, waiting laps, and klutzy lip-locks. There was always somewhere to be, often where I wasn't supposed to be. But sometimes anywhere was better than a cage with kinfolk.

After supper, I sauntered out the front entrance, slithered out my bedroom window, or snuck through the external bathroom door—my own personal escape hatch—to join my cul-de-sac comrades. Everything was an escapade at night. I was always where I shouldn't have been. More times than not, the kids from the ten homes would congregate under the streetlight, its bright beam flickering across the twilight sky, turning trees to skeletons.

While tapping the toes of our tennis shoes to the beat of a popular song, we would scatter the pebbles about and talk about our favorite singer or television show or have a detailed discourse on how much we disliked our current teacher. But what I really wanted to do was perform. I'd often start humming, then begin singing the chorus of a song from *The Pajama Game* or *West Side Story*. Sometimes it was *Gypsy*. I knew all the words by heart. My friends knew none of them. I listened to each Broadway musical album for hours. While my friends were doing their homework or playing four-square, I was Ethel Merman

I foisted an introductory lesson on my friend Heather, who lived across the cul-de-sac. It featured some simple steps I had choreographed on the spot so that she could accompany me under our stage-light, the streetlamp above. Lyrics from *Hernando's Hideaway* would pour from my diaphragm as my feet shuffled this way and that.

Heather cocked her head until her ear rested on her shoulder, eyes in a squinted confused stare. *Huh?* Soon she would struggle to learn the lyrics, then mangle the steps. "No, not that foot. This one!" After losing interest, she'd go back to the four-square game still in progress on her own driveway.

That streetlight attracted neighborhood kids like moths to a porch lamp. We'd gossip, play games, and later struggle out vocal harmonies with a six-string guitar. Jane—Heather's older, wiser, buxom sister, who often attracted moths to her own headlights—would bring out her acoustic guitar and play Beatles songs or folk tunes. We'd all sing along as if we knew how to harmonize like John and Paul, or Simon and Garfunkel.

I looked up to Jane, not because she was a foot taller, but because she had vocal talent, poise, and waist-length hair that was straight, shiny, and parted in the middle—a look and 'do most young girls in that decade coveted. Oh, and she could make barre chords with her long fingers, toss her long hair back and forth, and had much bouncier breasts. Those two pillow-globes beckoned the full attention of all the boys in the neighborhood, but she remained unaware of their superpowers. We'd gather on the lawn cross-legged, or on the curb, or under the streetlight, and harmonize to The Beatles' "You've Got to Hide Your Love Away" or The Stones' "As Tears Go By," but I preferred the Marianne Faithfull version. On the nights we weren't singing, we'd use the streetlight as home base and play hour-long games of hide-and-seek. We'd hide behind cars, dodge into thick ivy or the widest bushes, and lie still, frozen lizards in the night shadows. These were our glory days. We just didn't know it.

The tenants of the ten house Eichler universe would celebrate Fourth of July by pooling backyard picnic tables, dragging them to the middle of the cul-de-sac, and contributing assigned potluck dishes. We played badminton in the middle of the street while sweating through the dog days of summer. Santa Clara was a basin that held heat in its tight fist and wouldn't loosen its grip until mid-September.

Not one moment was misspent in youth. There was joy in simply running up and down the street or kicking stones with sandaled feet under a star-bathed sky. There was pleasure in running away or running towards something—anything. Every moment was filled to the brim. We roller-skated with recklessness as if there were no speed limits imposed on my friends and me. Laws were enforced on everyone, but not us. We flirted with precarious outcomes. And although our young lives didn't come with warranties, our youth-fueled vitality sang and sometimes screamed like a strained engine. Nothing could touch us, slow us down, or dissolve us into the ether. We were too young to die.

The kids in the cul-de-sac kicked the leaves off of each other's lawns and knocked the front yard rocks down the sidewalk and into the street, but we never kicked each other out of our peripheral vision. We were there for one another. Our lives and lawns overlapped. We shared the air-space and parked our cars in our small U-shaped suburban harbor. We knew, tolerated, and supported each other. Eventually, when adolescence made its entrance, we screwed each other. There was a lot of flirting and foreplay going on in that curvaceous cul-de-sac. After all, it was the Sixties. Sex, drugs, rock 'n' roll.

The Times, They Are A-Changin'

Many of my friends were black. We lived within blocks of one another, fidgeted in the same classrooms, became followers of the same trends in fashions, used the same slang words, and listened to the same songs, dictated to us by the few radio stations we picked up in Santa Clara Valley: KEWB, KLIV from

San Jose, and KYA and KFRC from San Francisco. They provided the soundtrack of our youth, and we were happy to have it. Motown, underground hard rock, poetic folk tunes, ballads from Glen Campbell, and, of course, The Beatles, Gerry and The Pacemakers, and The Dave Clark Five.

But in the latter part of the Sixties, our musical influences would be the product of underground radio stations such as KSJO and KOME. These two stations were on the FM dial and played little-known or progressive artists and what some refer to today as alternative music. Our alternative music looked and sounded much different back then. Late night FM radio would take on the full versions of particular songs, while AM radio would play only the shortened "radio-lite" versions of The Chambers' Brothers song "Time Has Come Today," CCR's "Suzy Q," The Doors' "Light My Fire," and Iron Butterfly's "In-A-Gadda-Da-Vida." I was exposed to many songs, artists, and bands on these stations, including Laura Nyro, Fred Neil, and Bob Dylan with his rambling free verse wisdom.

Some music seemed perfectly wired for FM's underground approach. LP-length songs by Moby Grape, The Moody Blues, Cream, Tim Hardin, Jefferson Airplane, Big Brother and the Holding Company, Blue Cheer, Santana, The Youngbloods, Melanie, and Country Joe and the Fish filled our ears. Local Bay Area bands and artists such as The Chocolate Watch Band, Count Five, Syndicate of Sound, The Loading Zone, People!, Tower of Power and Cold Blood could finally be heard on radio. I listened to them all through massive headphones while I sprawled out on my bedroom rug. These artists weren't getting pop radio play or gaining on the Top 40 chart, but I knew them well. They became part of the late nights when I tuned out, then turned up the music.

At this same time, a band calling itself Mother Earth hit the underground airways and their haunting song "Down So Low" penetrated my ears. The female lead singer, who would later become a solo artist, had a delivery that resonated with me like no other songstress. Her voice was rich and lush, her lyrics dark and moody, while both picked at the pieces of a broken heart and spit them out to the audience. I was convinced she was singing directly to me, coughing up heartbreak with each line. Her name was Tracy Nelson, and she accessed the blues like no other and ricocheted them back to her listeners. She opened for Janis, Jimi, and Jefferson Airplane, but as far as I was concerned, she soared high above them all.

As freeform rock was growing in popularity, KOME radio followed KSJO in format, dropping their jazz focus and moving into the longer versions of songs featuring local, emerging, and cutting-edge rock artists. For much of its history, KSJO was locked in a bitter rivalry with KOME, which also flipped to rock in 1971. I gave both stations equal time.

In 1967, it was easy to become lost in the late night FM radio ramblings of Arlo Guthrie's song "Alice's Restaurant." It had a protracted spoken monologue, repetitive finger-style ragtime guitar, and short chorus about getting anything you want at this particular dining establishment. It had all the ingredients for a successful hit record, and at nearly nineteen minutes long, it was a true commitment for restless teens everywhere. The song was his own first-hand account of a true episode from Guthrie's life beginning on Thanksgiving Day in 1965. The tale began with a citation for littering and ended with the refusal of the U.S. Army to draft him because of his conviction for that crime. The final part of the song encouraged the listeners to sing along, to resist the draft, and to end war. My friend and I were more than happy to oblige by giving the peace sign to strangers and basically adopting the mindset of "Make Love, Not War" even though many of us were still virgins to lovemaking and military service.

The clean lines and bold colors of 1966 were radically different from the fashions of previous years. The clothes reflected the pop culture of the time and rebelled against the prevailing grain. *Batman* brought in a campy kaleidoscope of fun images. Rock 'n' roll bands ditched their crisp suits for wild patterned clothing as psychedelia crept in. We sat at the intersection of the more formal Fifties and the hip freedom of the Sixties. Our parents still had their influences on us. We held one foot on the platform of traditional sensibility, fashions, and our roles in society, and one foot on the vibrating new vehicle that was loading curious passengers and asking them to think for themselves and see things in a fresh way. Be innovative, take a leap of faith into the great unknown, and drive a VW Bug.

✳ ⚛ ✳

Every life has its own soundtrack. There is a tune that makes me think of the summer I spent rubbing baby oil on my limbs in pursuit of the deepest coffee-colored tan, a song that reminds me of tagging along with my father on Sundays to the local Thrifty Drug Store to pick up a canister of Revelation Pipe Tobacco, another that reminds me of shuffling my feet at the first Teen Dance while I wondered why all the boys were leaning like ladders against one wall and all the girls were super-glued to each other's hunched shoulders, and the song that brings me back to my thirteenth year, where I played spin-the-bottle with a boy whose breath smelled like grilled cheese.

Iconic songs remain with us on classic rock stations, and iconic images became indelible memories. Take, for instance, the early and uncomfortable pose of The Beatles on the sleeve of one of my first 45 records. Those Fab Four stances are forever recognizable, along with their signatures scribbled on the image. Whether they were the actual signatures of the boys in the band, who knows? I still memorized the curve of every letter and meditated on the facial features of John, Paul, George, and Ringo. They were my gods, and each one of their tunes was tied to my own elations, my heartbreaks, and eventually, my politics. They marked special occasions, such as falling in love; wanting someone I couldn't have; heading back to school in autumn; drugs, sex, rock 'n' roll; and the excitement of wanting to hold someone's hand.

My favorite Beatles album was *Rubber Soul.* The songs were catchy, sincere, and powerful, and many were played in minor keys. There was so much heart and soul in that record. "I'm Looking Through You" and "You Won't See Me" were favorites. Each song was an unexplainable thrill provided in a special language that only a fellow teen could understand. It was vinyl magic. I would stand in front of my full-length door mirror in the Eichler and play the album from start to finish, my reflection swaying and twirling wildly. In my imagination, I was a go-go–booted babe standing high on a boxy pedestal, a love interest of Paul's, or a famous model like Jean Shrimpton or Twiggy wearing a paper minidress. Wild abandon had found me, and The Beatles had provided the release. In my mind, I was a gainfully employed Hullabaloo dancer.

My favorite Beatle kept changing with each year. Initially, it was Ringo who caught my eye. He was not only clever, but also adorable. After a year or two, when I started to notice boys, Paul became the target for my arrow. He was the cute charming Beatle no one could resist. In my final year of high school, John moved to the top of my list. His depth and intelligence won out above cute and adorable. Besides, he was the co-writer on most of the group's songs, and I preferred his lyrics and insights to the light and airy Paul-penned numbers. Last, but not least, was the quiet Beatle, George. He was so quiet that he disappeared, at least from my sight. Initially I wasn't drawn to him. I didn't understand him or appreciate him until much later when spirituality became a more important piece of my jigsaw puzzle. Only then did he snap into a top-tiered spot on my list.

The Beatles were ever-present throughout the Sixties era. Their faces wallpapered my bedroom walls. I dreamily stared at their features for hours, days, months, years. Beatles poses featured on cardboard were packaged with bubblegum. Their heads bobbed up and down in the back of our car. The hum of their melodies sat in my throat. They still do. Now there are quizzes online asking: What does your favorite Beatle say about you? What's your favorite Beatles song or album? John or Paul? George or Ringo? As if they would be anything without the other, or anything without producer George Martin. My favorite Beatle was The Beatles.

Kevin Sent

Why does every class photo in elementary school look like it has the same kids in it? As a result of my sometimes woolly and wavy hair, I wore a hairband or bow in my hair throughout elementary school—and always for our class picture. My higgledy-piggledy hairdo was sometimes pulled back in a last-minute ponytail, with a few fugitive strands creeping down each cheek. In most of those four framed photos, I could pass for some scruffy refugee or Anne Frank's twin sister. A tiny bow came in for a landing on the top of my head and appeared in my sixth-grade class photo. I wore it to lasso in one of my male classmates: Kevin Carroll.

We never actually spoke except to mutter "hi" or nod when we were heading in or out of the classroom. We never kissed. Kevin never even held my hand. But we did stand at opposite ends of my small bedroom closet at the urging of our two best friends, Jill and John. Both of our jailers held the two doors closed in hopes Kevin and I would fall into one another's arms and lock lips like Liz and Dick. I was drenched in shyness. So was he.

I couldn't see even a hint or outline of Kevin in the dark. But in the light, Kevin was a beautiful boy. His dark eyes had long eyelashes against freckled skin. They didn't seem to go with the reddish highlights in his hair or pale skin. He combed his auburn hair to the side and shoved his hands in his pant pockets. He had a bent smile that rode up one side of his mouth and sleepy eyelids that drooped in a youthful sexy manner. In this dark, small space, however, he was quiet with an occasional shuffle of feet. I couldn't see him, but I tried to imagine his posture and thoughts. I was hoping we would get tangled like the wire hangers in my closet, but we never came close.

Shy Kevin and I spent an awkward five minutes that felt like five days as we stood in that dark space saying and doing nothing until our disappointed friends released us. When we fell out of that dark chasm, embarrassed and awkward, I noticed the freckled wallpaper of skin on his arms and face. It's as if those freckles just jumped off the pages of an Archie comic.

Freckles are a curious phenomenon. When you have them, you want them to disappear. When you don't have them, you long for them. I never had them, but I marveled at friends who did, and I marveled at everything about Kevin Carroll. The curious constellation splattered across his cheeks and nose made him look childlike. I wanted this complicated skin art for myself. My own skin was freckle free and olive toned. We all want what we don't have. We're too thin or too fat, too tall or short. We want what's over there. The grass is always greener. But beyond freckles, Kevin Carroll was sexy before I knew what sexy was. In sixth grade, I was a smitten kitten.

All my classmates saw it. Everyone knew. They teased us. They sang embarrassing ditties. "Kevin and Carol sitting in a tree ... K-I-S-S-I-N-G." In the classroom, Kevin and I glanced longingly at one another at regular intervals or on the blacktop during recess as we stood in the tetherball line, but that was where it began and ended. Nothing ever happened between the two eleven-year-olds.

At the end of the sixth-grade term Mr. Laird went around the room and asked each classmate what their classmates would be doing in ten years or so. Everyone giggled when they came to me. One annoying classmate read from her lined paper: "Carol will be married to Kevin and have seven children. Her married name will be Carol Carroll." Everyone laughed as if those were the wittiest two words ever mushed together. What the rest of my peers didn't know was that Kevin and I had already been secretly "crushing" on each other. Mr. Laird chimed in and broke up the teasing. "Okay class, that's enough. What else will Carol be doing?"

I never heard the other answers. I was too crippled by embarrassment to notice as my cheeks turned the shade of a ripe Braeburn apple. I was in love. If that was wrong, I didn't want to be right. So what if my name was Carol Carroll in ten years? It would have been a welcome relief from my unpronounceable surname.

The Wonderful World of Color ... and Black-and-White

Do you ever catch yourself looking at a couple or a face in the crowd and find yourself wondering, *How can we be the same species?* I felt that way about Heather's parents. I actually felt that way about every family in the Eichler cul-de-sac. My own family of four was unique. We were odd. We didn't function like other families, where children threw their arms around their parents' necks with great glee. No one touched in my household. No one offered up the word *love* in their exchanges. No one called one another honey, sweetheart, or darling, although my father called the female half of every couples he knew by the term *dear.* He called his own mother *dear.* I wanted to be dear to him too, in one way or another.

I didn't relate to any of the members of the *Father Knows Best* family, but I watched the show religiously, along with other close-knit family models on television programs such as *Leave It to Beaver* and *The Donna Reed Show*. Dick Van Dyke was my hero. I would have been his Laura Petrie in capris any day of the week. In fact, my goal by age ten was to grow up and write catchy sketch comedy bits for television shows, copy for advertising products, or captivating Valentine's Day puns, the sort that appeared on flimsy single-paged cards slipped into transparent envelopes. Naturally, my writing partners would be Sally Rogers and Buddy Sorrell.

But not one of those television families looked or behaved like my own family. Their homes were pristine and adorned with traditional furnishings, more along the lines of my friend Heather's and Julie's conventional living rooms. There was no sign of the Eichler pizzazz, no shelves of tchotchkes, and no sign of impractical design on our black-and-white Zenith screen.

The faces and foibles of each television show cast member became as familiar as a family member. I knew the way Rob Petrie's funny face would scrunch, his head would jerk to one side, and his chin would fall forward, just like I knew the idiosyncrasies of my restless brother. I knew how Rob's legs would cross and uncross when he was nervous the same way Harold would jump his thigh up and down off the chair when he couldn't sit still and how he'd use the eating utensils as drumsticks on the various bottles and glasses at the Sveilich kitchen table.

I knew when Patty Duke was being Cathy and when she was being Patty with her masterful shifts in energy and nuance in speech the same way I knew when my father was getting angry and when my mother was sad and lost in daydreams.

But our family doctor didn't look or act like the calm, cool, collected Dr. Kildare or fine-looking Dr. Ben Casey, and our neighborhood didn't look like the Cleavers' or the street on *My Three Sons* with multileveled houses and mischievous boys. While Wally and Beaver were politely asking to be excused from the table, one by one the members of my family unit would quietly lift their rumps from the comfortable curve of the Eames kitchen chairs and vacate the premises like fading ghosts. No one at my table kept their mouth shut while chewing or kept their elbows off the table. No one asked about my day. There was no free-for-all conversation, just loud open-mouthed chomping and departures.

Robert Young, the father who knew best in his perfectly jolly *Father Knows Best* series, lived across the street from me at my friend Heather's house. Her father not only looked like Young, but also he cooked his daughter a full breakfast of bacon, eggs, and pancakes before we walked to school each day. I would unlatch the gate and walk through the front door of Heather's house to meet up for our bike ride or slow stroll to school.

Beyond the front gate, I often found her finishing her breakfast buffet. I had guzzled down my imitation eggnog-flavored Carnation Instant Breakfast and was foaming at the mouth for some chewable food. Bacon! I would take a chair in the adjacent family room surrounded by old-style walnut furnishings, hold my school books close to my training bra chest buried under my sweater, and inhale the freshly fried bacon, real maple syrup, and love. It was the best aroma of my childhood, but it lived across the street in someone else's childhood—Heather's. She might as well have been living in a different solar system. Heather had a fatherly father. A caring dad. An adoring parent. He was, for all intents and purposes, Robert Young. The only thing he and my father had in common was an ever-present pipe. Heather's father, Jim Kirby, wore poorly knitted sweaters and carried a pipe with a stem straight as an ear of corn. It rarely touched his lips and served more like a stage prop. And, so, I began the lengthy and in-depth study of my friend's sitcom parents.

Carl Jung once asked, "What myth are you living?" My myth was that my parents wanted to be parents. In truth, they were ambivalent about having children and even more reluctant to contend with their own. In my own home, I was unseen and felt loathed. I had a bad case of *Father Knows Best* envy. I would have settled for Father Knows Second Best. I wanted at least one parent who desired a daughter, listened to her, laughed with her, asked about her, and looked forward to hearing about her day; told her about why people believed in G-d, or God; or the meaning of menorahs.

If someone had given me a pop quiz in *TV Guide* wisdom, I would have aced it. Like the kids today who stare at their iPhones and other electronic devices for hours on end, my eyes were forever affixed on the jumpy and grainy visions from the living room television set. *Leave It to Beaver, Burke's Law, Bachelor Father, The Andy Griffith Show, The Patty Duke Show.* Let's not forget *Bewitched,* a show I didn't really enjoy, but it was in front of me, so I watched it. I favored *Bonanza* and the Cartwright boys: Adam, Hoss, and Little Joe. I preferred the shenanigans of *Hogan's Heroes,* the antics of *The Addams Family,* and *The Munsters* (although in my eyes, the Addams family was far superior to the Munster bunch), and the hilarity of *Green Acres, The Dick Van Dyke Show, The Mary Tyler Moore Show,* and *Get Smart.* The excitement of *Star Trek, The Invaders, The Outer Limits, The Jetsons, The Time Tunnel,* and *The Land of the Giants* nearly made my head explode. And then there was *The Man from U.N.C.L.E.* I always assumed that U.N.C.L.E was the name of some city in the United States.

In 1963, I was fixated on Gene Barry, the star of *Burke's Law,* and his fetching assistant, Detective Tim Tilson (Gary Conway). Both men were strikingly handsome, idealized males who filled my girlhood fantasies and managed to solve every case in sixty minutes or less. In a word, they were dreamy. I went back and forth on which man was the most desirable. The show's main character, Amos Burke, was like Bruce Wayne combined with Columbo. The Burke character was a millionaire captain of the LAPD who, for some unknown reason, cruised around in a chauffeur-driven 1962 Rolls-Royce Silver Cloud II. It was a dazzling but completely unrealistic concept.

※ ⚛ ※

I inherited my father's love for *Your Show of Shows.* I had a youthful crush on Sid Caesar. How could I not? He was a mountain of a man, like one of those tall and mile-wide brick buildings in New York City. Caesar was funny as hell. But in real life, he was imperfect. He drank to excess and popped pills like they were M&Ms. But he beat those addictions. It wasn't easy. But neither was comedy.

Your Show of Shows was reality television before *Keeping Up with the Kardashians.* Everything was live, brilliantly flubbed, then recovered. Caesar was one of television's original comic stars and a member of my parents' generation, but his comedy spoke to all generations, and it certainly made me howl. Despite his battles with the bottle and an assortment of candy-colored pills, Caesar lived to age ninety-one. That's a good long life of ups and downs. And enough drama and comedy to fill any stage. He left behind a body of timeless work and a bellyful of laughs. My father was our home's Sid Caesar, with his quick wit, improvised approach to life, and dinner table shenanigans. No, my father was funnier.

In many ways, I took after my father. He was a lunatic. He also had a bold and uncommon sense of humor, coupled with the prurient interests of Hugh Hefner and Larry Flynt. During the first decade of my life, and without design, I managed to pick up his skewed vision of the world. It came in particularly handy at the end of sixth grade when everyone decided to buy Mr. Laird separate parting gifts. I had to pick out something exceptional, because Mr. Laird was exceptional.

Ah ha! I had an idea. I believed, beyond a shadow of a doubt, that my gift was not only ingenious and inimitable, but was one Mr. Laird would fully appreciate. Since there were so many *Playboy* magazines scattered around the Eichler, I decided to gift-wrap a few of them in cheerful gold and silver paper and present them to the tender Mr. Laird. It was a farewell present and a multi-paged gift of gratitude for being the best teacher ever.

Anchored at my desk, I watched Mr. Laird open each chaotically wrapped gift from my fellow classmates. As my favorite teacher began to rip off the cockeyed tape and ribbons from each gift, the carefully chosen tokens of appreciation began to emerge. Pens. Books. Poems. Even flowers. As he made his way through the practical and sentimental offerings, his fingers found their way to the last parting gift—mine.

"This one is from Carol," Mr. Laird chirped as he met my gaze. I always felt Mr. Laird and I had a special bond and shared sense of the absurd. Perhaps I assumed too much, especially on this particular day.

I held my breath in anticipation and hoped he would revel in my selection. He turned the decorative paper over once or twice in his hands and scrunched his brows in a curious pose of suspense. As his fingers carefully separated the layers of paper and sticky tape and Mr. Laird caught his first glimpse of its contents, his expression quickly shifted from curious to confused. His jaw dropped and positioned itself above the floor. Mr. Laird slid the periodical under his stack of graded exams and away from the eager meddlesome eyes of my fellow classmates ... but not before shooting me a grin he was trying desperately to suppress. A chuckle escaped from under his breath.

"Okay. Well, thank you, Carol."

Up until that moment, it never occurred to me that such a periodical wasn't an appropriate parting gift. After all, what states more affectionately and appreciatively "thanks for a great year" more effectively than 36DD cups on an airbrushed female physique?

As he slipped the pages of images under his paperwork, Mr. Laird muttered a polite "Thank you, Miss Svee-leech."

For once, I was happy to have my last name mangled like a piece of bratwurst destined for the grinder, but I felt a warm rush of red reach my cheeks.

What had I done? I buried my head inside my open desk. I was more than ready to escape Booksin Elementary School. Today, as on most days, no one pronounced my last name right. And today, I didn't get it right either. I gave a gay man a magazine filled with images of naked women in front of my classmates. In retrospect, he would have preferred layouts of cowboys in chaps. Now it was official. It was time for me to move on to a bold new adventure: junior high.

One-Armed Bandit

A Bay Area summer in the boiled-out Santa Clara basin was what my mother termed a "scorcher." Residents were sticky and drippy and the valley filled with perspiration like the water in Lexington Reservoir outside of Los Gatos. But we were kids. We moved through the warm waves of June to September like sharks, never suffering from the oppressive heat like our parents. Adults required the constant application of Mum Deodorant Cream or a cool, wet cloth around the neck. But we were skilled at ignoring the elements while the sun raised a fresh generation of freckles on our bare shoulders. In those blistering summer days, we passed the time with our friends. We skinned our knees, burned our noses until they peeled, and fell off bikes—all temporary intrusions.

By age twelve, my summer months seemed miles long. I had a buffet of Popsicle flavors and colors at my disposal, all held in my sticky grasp. There was time to do and be everything. There was no end date, no rush, no worries. I was being given too much too often, with too many idle hours to play and no burdens to carry other than occasional chores around the house. I slummed it through the summers, with little attention to nutrition or hygiene, and occasionally waved down the ice cream truck.

We had a one-armed ice cream man named Everett who regularly cruised our Eichler neighborhood. His right hand and arm were missing from the elbow down, but that didn't stop him from driving and dispensing cool treats on summer afternoons. As he zigzagged up and down the tree-lined streets, Everett seemed to own the neighborhood as much as we did. He would bounce up and down in the driver's seat, a menu of chilled treats printed on the back door of his truck. Gathering all the necessary ice cream bars and cartons with one hand, he never dropped a treat or change on the ground. Instead, Everett manipulated his heavy coin-belt in a gracefully orchestrated one-limb movement. It was beautiful to behold his single-appendage ballet.

The kids in the neighborhood were a little afraid of him. Okay, I was a little afraid of him. Perhaps I watched too many after school science fiction movies featuring characters with missing limbs, not to mention the one-armed man on *The Fugitive.* But after a while I looked forward to the distant sounds of scratchy tunes filtering through his vehicle's sad speakers: "Turkey in the Straw," "Do Your Ears Hang Low?" "Pop Goes the Weasel," and a few other repetitive refrains that caused ringing in the ears. The Murphy's Oil Soap jingle featured on their television commercial sounded identical to Everett's ice cream truck melody as he drove down our street. Whenever I heard those tunes in the distance, my anticipation grew. My friends and I would frantically wave down Everett as he turned his white truck around the corner and onto our block. We waved like we were landing a plane. He'd hop out of the truck with a spirited bounce and greet us with sweaty armpits in his beige shirt and a quick grin. Suddenly, I was no longer afraid of Everett. We never asked what happened to his other arm. We thanked him, gobbled up our Fudgsicles, marveled at the Strawberry Shortcake on a stick, sucked on the Missile sherbet pops, broke apart and shared our root beer Popsicles, struggled with our chocolate and nut-topped Drumsticks as the nuts fell to the ground with the sun's heat, pulled apart our ice cream sandwiches, pushed up our frozen Push-Up treats, and chipped away at the old standby Eskimo Pies.

Still, as I lay in my bed late at night, I wondered and worried about Everett and what happened to his other arm. We gossiped and guessed about it among ourselves. I also wondered what Everett did in the winter months. San Jose had cold seasons, when no one wanted ice cream. Did he work in another field? Did he spend his days in a small apartment watching mind-numbing game shows on a portable television set? Did he read books, solve jigsaw puzzles, mow lawns with his one arm? I never found out. But Everett and his worn white truck brought us the sounds of sunny seasons with a string of jingly-jangly notes cutting through the summer swelter. In midsummer throughout the Sixties, there was no Häagen-Dazs. No Ben and Jerry's. No Rice Cream, Almond Milk Bars, or Coconut Milk treats. There was something better: Everett.

Summer months in our cul-de-sac consisted of hanging out curbside, making idle chitchat about nothing and everything, and quietly joking while sucking down Creamsicles and Dreamsicles. My cul-de-sac buddies and I paraded back and forth to Hacienda Gardens, a nearby strip mall. This small but welcoming line of stores, which sat a mile away from our cul-de-sac hub, was nothing like a hacienda, nor were there any gardens to be found, just a Safeway grocery, a Rexall Drugstore, a Woolworth's, a fabric store, a candy shop, a small record store, a toy store called Pixie Palace, and a Chinese take-out. All contained essentials of suburban life. This was the place to hang out. Harold and I didn't receive a weekly allowance, but my other friends had twenty-five or fifty cents per week for doing chores—or for simply being born. Sometimes I raided my mother's purse when she wasn't looking, or I'd pace back and forth at the mall, a window-shopping—not shoplifting—an exercise in unsatisfied longing. We'd mosey around the stores, then head back to the cul-de-sac, talk, and play four-square for a while, then head back to Hacienda Gardens yet again. Killing time was the name of the game, and as long as we were with our friends, it was time well spent. During those summer months we all could have earned an A grade in accomplishing as little as possible other than enjoying each moment of summer vacation.

The first McDonald's hamburger joint in Willow Glen sprouted up a few blocks away from Hacienda Gardens. Hamburgers were only twelve cents. We could easily find enough coins lying around the house to pocket for this squishy concoction of mustard, ketchup, and a meat patty that looked like it had been run over by an eighteen-wheeler truck. Mere blocks away, a Marie Callender's Restaurant & Bakery opened with pie selections as far as the eye could see and the nose could smell. I would wander or bike over to the restaurant with Heather or Julie and instruct them on how to save money when ordering a pie and beverage. "If you get a glass of water rather than a Pepsi or root beer, you can drop a packet or two of sugar in, and it tastes like soda pop. Close your eyes, and presto! You can make it be whatever you want it to be." They tried it. They liked it. Hey, Mikey! This became a common practice among my friends. Julie would always get the triple-layered chocolate pie with three different consistencies of chocolate. I went for an apple pie and ate half of Julie's when she wasn't looking. We both drank sugar water. In our minds, it was a deliciously sweet soft drink.

I once saw my gym teacher behind the counter of a local record store. I thought all my teachers only had last names, but customers in the music store called Miss Labrash *Maxine.* A smaller strip mall we patronized was located in the other direction on Foxworthy Drive. Jolly 5 & 10 Cent Store was a favorite, as was Georgio's Pizza, and later in the Sixties, the Pop Shop, where we'd finger through the top selling 45 records in the wooden bins. The sunbaked, masculine, muscular, and youthful Miss Labrash owned the Pop Shop and dated one of The Beach Boys, at least when he was in town. That was the rumor in the girl's locker room. But when The Beach Boys came along, they weren't considered cool by any of my friends who preferred a harder rock sound. None of us would be caught dead in surf-striped T-shirts. Away from my friends, I secretly enjoyed their harmonies and especially liked their more somber songs like "Warmth of the Sun" and "Caroline, No." I never owned a Beach Boy's album, but when their songs came on the radio, I turned them up.

There really weren't too many other places to hang out in the early days of Santa Clara Valley. There were a couple of giant malls—Westgate and Valley Fair—situated in our bedroom community, as well as a tourist trap for those who required one:

the Winchester Mystery House. The landmark was the massive haunted house of Santa Clara Valley. Tours began there in 1938 allowing paying customers to walk "the famous stairs to nowhere," but the interesting history of the sprawling mansion seemed like baloney to me. I was too itchy to listen to dull stories delivered by a white-haired docent. All I was interested in was seeing the ghosts that supposedly lived there. I craved mysterious creatures, and I didn't see one spooky shadow. What a disappointment not to find Casper among the many rooms, especially when I was an avid reader of Casper comic books. But the house had some dangerous aspects to it since some of the doorways led to a drop off to the next floor and some floors were left unfinished. It was like a funky remodel job taken on by some drunken construction crew.

Be-In, Sit-In, Laugh-In

During the Fifties, with the Cold War and anti-communism in full swing, and with Americans settling comfortably into a middle-class existence, it was clear that everyone was expected to live like the middle-class lived. We saw it on our television screens. A home life and status like the families portrayed on *The Adventures of Ozzie and Harriet* and *Leave it to Beaver* was the ultimate goal. With family dynamics like theirs, we'd all be content and feel loved.

Black people were left out of this middle-class dream. They were supposed to remain invisible. There was no *Good Times* or *The Cosby Show.* Not yet. But such ideas were beginning to shift in the Sixties, and cracks in the armor of the past began to appear. People wanted to live within their means, but they also wanted a nice house, good car, steady job, a pet, and two kids. Blacks, Asian Americans, and Mexican Americans all had the same dreams, but no one talked about that or showed it on television. Not until *The Jeffersons* moved into the neighborhood via television screens across the country. But in The Eichlers, we were already integrated and peacefully so. It may have been one of the few peaceful havens in the country.

By the mid-to-late Sixties, the country was grappling with segregation and discrimination issues. Young people questioned the morality of the Vietnam War and the entire middle-class value system was being held to the fire, questioned, and condemned. Protesters marched in the streets; flags, joints, and bras were burned; equal rights were demanded—along with the right to be ourselves. To be called out for middle-class values and be called a "square" were the ultimate insults. Above everything else, we wanted to be hip, righteous, right-on. We wanted to fit in beside our fellow rebels.

Ironically, we all wore the same uniform of rebellion: bell-bottoms, suede jackets with fringe, colorful beads, and strung puka shells and peace signs around our necks. Headbands and leather ropes wrapped across our foreheads. Bell sleeves on corduroy blouses were accented with paisley and bright patterns. Navy blue pea coats with large brass buttons were a Bay Area uniform of choice for eveningwear. Our army was marching to the beat of a different drum, but we didn't want to stand out from our own cool crowd. We were rebelling and resisting, but in armies sporting similar apparel.

With the civil rights movement came sit-ins; human be-ins, like the sizeable organized event in San Francisco's Golden Gate Park in 1967; and plenty of *Laugh-In* on television. Sit-ins protested such conventionally accepted practices as restricted housing, or boycotting the Elks Club, which at that time excluded blacks.

My friend Yolanda was black before I knew what black was. So were Cicely, May, and Adrian. We had all grown up in the same cohesive neighborhood during this otherwise turbulent era, but the hurly-burly didn't touch us. It was a time of change, yet as kids, we didn't notice much of the racial hoopla happening all around us. Our friends came in a rainbow of colors. We didn't care. It was not on our radar. We cared only which board games they had at home, if they were free for a game of hopscotch on the sidewalk, or whether they were available to fill out a game of four-square.

Although Cicely's skin color was different from mine, I recognized her immediately as one of my comrades. We sported the same haircut, wore the same types of dresses to school, and shared eye rolls at the same humdrum moments during summer school class. We were inseparable. Summer school during the Sixties in San Jose wasn't full of discord or pulsing with racial violence. None of my teachers were as handsome, astute, or inspiring as Sidney Poitier in *To Sir, with Love*. Oh, how I wished they had been. Black, brown, and white kids sat side by side, passing notes, cheating off one another's pop quiz papers, giggling about a classmate's untied shoe, and melted together like the flavors in a box of Neapolitan ice cream. We all worked together in perfect harmony ... to make our summer school teacher miserable.

＊ ⚛ ＊

When my family moved to San Jose in 1960, "The Twist" was the move for the dance floor, as well as in the living room, the kitchen, and almost any other room in the house. It became popular because it was so simple. Just ... twist. Even rhythmically challenged boys and girls could do the Twist. As Chubby Checker explained, it was like putting out a cigarette with both feet or coming out of a shower and wiping your bottom with a towel to the beat. But the Twist managed to bridge the generation gap, since both kids and adults could learn and do it easily. It was a dance where the participants didn't touch each other, which became a new trend—dancing apart. But that trend didn't help to keep birth rates down.

My birthday Twist Party. How low can you go?

My mother was the queen of birthday bashes and parties in general. I am not a party person, but I'm glad I had themed birthday parties when I was a kid. We'd rub inflated balloons on our pant legs and place them on the walls with our own electricity. And we had plenty of electricity in our bodies. One by one the balloons would fall from the wall, but not before the last guest went home.

I had a different theme party each year. Peppermint Twist party, Roller-Skating party, Miniature Golf party, Dress-as-Your-Favorite-Television-Star party. That was the theme of my tenth birthday. I dressed as Morticia from *The Addams Family*. Julie came as Andy Griffith of *Mayberry R.F.D.* Donna Hanson dressed in pigtails and looked a bit like Mary Ann from *Gilligan's Island*, if Mary Ann had been blonde and nine years old. My school friend Carlin came in some sort of geisha girl gown that had nothing to do with television sitcoms and everything to do with the fact that her father was in the Navy and her family had lived in Japan for several years. It was the closest thing to a costume in her closet. No one seemed to care that it had nothing to do with the party theme.

We went to the Elks Club swimming pool for my twelfth birthday in my mother's Dodge Dart. As we strolled by the pool, our giggling group of girls couldn't wait to slip our suits on and jump into the blue, heavily chlorinated water. We laughed louder when we read the sign: "We don't swim in your toilet. Don't pee in our pool." As my friends and I snickered and sprung into one another's shoulders like pinballs against flippers, we piled through the doorway of the club's locker room. One by one, we pulled our swimsuits up and on. Suddenly, my mother reappeared and announced we had to find some other way to celebrate. "What? Why? We're ready to swim. Look! Everyone is already suited up."

My mother had a blank expression on her face as she hurried us to get dressed and go. We un-suited ourselves, dashed out of the girl's locker room, and piled back into the Dodge Dart. A carload of pouts. My mother instructed me that our group had to find something else to do, but no reason was offered up to my friends and me. At twelve years old we didn't qualify for an explanation. The Dart moved down the street to the miniature golf course with the giant windmill. I didn't have any idea why we were rushed out, but I was easily distracted by the child-sized architecture, smooth hills, and this new game with friends on a picture-perfect summer afternoon.

Years later, I learned why we were dismissed from the Elks Club. Six out of the eight friends who were helping me celebrate, including my good friend Yolanda, were black. At that time, the Elks Club didn't allow blacks to swim in their pool, nor to use any of their other facilities. Apparently, the Elks were not like The Eichlers, even though they both began with a capital E. In the Elks universe, my friends weren't allowed to splash in the same waters with white folk. If my mother had told me the reason at that time, I would have screwed up my face in disbelief.

For years, my mother never mentioned the incident and didn't tell me why we had to leave the premises that day. But the very next week after the swimming pool–golf club switch-a-roo, my parents quit the Elks Club forever. They never looked back.

Years later, Cicely's younger sister, Dawn, told me that her parents moved to our neighborhood from Chicago when she was of school age because the vibe in that city was becoming heated and the streets were filled with racial violence. Her parents didn't want to raise Cicely and her two sisters with the same anxieties and pain caused by racial divide as they had had to endure. During the Kennedy era, The Eichlers, now fully immersed in fondue parties, was a genuine melting pot. Integration was cracking the mold of America. And many in the country were ready for a change and hoped it was gonna come.

Home Sweet Homeroom

The transition from elementary school to junior high school was a colossal leap. Failing grades. Brain tumors. Death. They all paled in comparison to the weight of freshman and sophomore year of junior high. As I merged into this brave new world, it was like entering a freeway after driving only side streets. Teachers and classmates shifted with each hour. Thank goodness for homeroom, where familiar faces ruled. For thirty minutes a day, we were seated alphabetically. I was seated beside Smith, Stollman, and Swartz, and some Thompsons and Thomases. We listened to school announcements over the scratchy speaker on the wall, then we were released to survive the rest of our day and a full schedule of classes in Social Studies, Math, and English. The bells sounded, and we had to be seated. The bells rang again, and we were released to the next subject, room, or laboratory, our feet moving faster than Sammy Davis Jr.'s tap shoes at Caesar's Palace. Kick-ball-change. Kick-ball-change. The dancer in me would shuffle to class in rhythm with my classmates. We were twelve years old and moving quicker than the Matterhorn at Disneyland, faster than Elvis' pelvis, and we would soon be higher than the budget for Cleopatra. Everybody must get stoned.

In the Thin of Things

The rudest awakening during seventh grade was having to locate the gymnasium locker room and strip myself bare in front of perfect strangers who had bodies that didn't quite look like mine. I'd shyly slip on my gym uniform hoping no one was watching. On went the white short-sleeved shirt with snap closures and navy clownish shorts, my limbs emerging from their openings like wiry pipe cleaners.

I was thin as a bedsheet throughout my childhood, even though I ate as often as I could. I loved food. In fact, I inhaled everything edible. This Sveilich's svelteness was genetics, plain and simple. My father had always been lanky and thin-boned in his youth, and I took after his side of the family. On the other end of the spectrum, and the kitchen table, was my mother who was what my father would call "a good eater." She was a husky, big-boned daughter of an obese mother. My mother's calves were thick, not fragile. Blossom's breasts were several numbers and alphabet letters bigger than my barely budding blossoms. Her waist featured cascading rolls of flesh. Mine had ribs sticking out the side like a standing rib roast.

I longed to have meat on my bones, but no matter how much or how often I ate, it didn't happen. I was self-conscious about my reedy limbs. So much so that I would layer two or three pairs of knit stockings over my legs to make them look fuller. Only then did I feel substantial. Only then did I feel acceptable enough to blend in. Before leaving for school each day, whether I was wearing a dress or pants, I would bulk up my legs with stockings in this top-secret layered fashion. White, loose-knit stockings held up with a garter belt became my go-to wear under dresses, even in the hottest months of summer.

When I looked in the mirror I despised what I saw. In 1967 and 1968, my nose outsized my face, my forehead was wallpapered with pimples, and my hair was too short, ragged, and riddled with waves that didn't lie down or match the other side of my head. My clothing hung on me as if looped on a pole. I was a lollipop, a stick figure with a spherical head. Nothing matched, and nothing meshed. I was a big fucking mess.

It Feels So Write

I never learned to compose stories or poems, but I was compelled to write. At the start of junior high school, the locker room repairs were not quite complete. Instead of holding gym classes, we were forced to sit for two miserable weeks in an echoing gymnasium and kill time until our next class began. I didn't know anyone in the class. They left me alone, and I left them alone.

In elementary school we had built-in playground friends. But junior high school was more like real life. You had to rub shoulders with diverse populations from different sections of the city to see if you could find common ground. In junior high school, I wasn't sure where my tribe was or if I still had one. In each class, I wanted someone to see me, befriend me, and connect. I wanted my peers to consider me as a worthy contender, mainly so that I could see myself in that same light. Every day, I hoped they'd want to be around me despite my own misgivings about being around them. I collapsed into myself, folding like a piece of Jewish origami. I strained to locate my place in the classroom— and in the world.

Soon I began to write short poems constructed out of secret rumblings. I never stopped this ritual that began in the hollow gymnasium during that two-week break from activities in gym class. I wrote about the sounds emanating out of my napping cat at home. I mused over the Eichler and my bedroom haven. I scripted short lines of prose about my fears and fumbles, my parents, the world and my place in it, if there was one. At that time, I had my doubts. Inner life became vastly more compelling to explore than my outer life, and written thoughts became much more significant pouring from the tip of a Bic rather than expressed in my butterfingered verbal skills. It all started with a golden-key diary, but graduated to a lined notebook of verses, limericks, and ornamental prose. I wrote because I felt deserted. I wrote to escape from the groups of classmates clustered around me that didn't invite me in. I wrote to beat down anxiety and to appear otherwise occupied when I wasn't. I wrote to save myself.

In junior high school, we entered the rousing world of teen dances. Garage bands would unpack their small amps and thin Fender guitars and entertain a not-so-surefooted crowd. Our toes tapped, but we seldom danced as often as we wanted to dance. Most of us swayed in place.

The boys would line up on one side of the gymnasium, the girls on the other, huddled in bunches of threes and fours, bright colorful bouquets. Beautiful wallflowers. Most of the night was spent running in and out of restrooms to apply and reapply frosty white Yardley Slicker to our chapped lips. It was such a subtle shade that it appeared to vanish entirely within ten minutes. We layered our lips in glossy white until we looked pale and sickly ... or at worst, deceased. I hadn't started wearing lipstick yet and never wore very much, but frosted Slicker lip- polish was a decent launch pad for pre-teens to experiment with, seeking that Cleopatra-like exterior while dragging around a wobbly interior. Besides, it came in a cool metal orange and hot pink striped tube. In the Sixties, you were allowed to have orange and pink sitting side by side. Pearly White was the look for our gently parted lips in 1967 and 1968. It made us appear so pale that I'm surprised no one closed the coffin. This magnificent stick of nothingness made you feel like a hip English chick. You could almost taste it. But more importantly you could smell it. Yardley had a way of making lip cosmetics hit all the senses. My first stick of Yardley was a milestone; much like a first kiss or the first time a boy attempted second base.

I had a collection of Yardley Slicker "Dollys" that were tiny samples of different frosted non-color lipstick. They looked like little fingertips in the shocking pink packaging. I enjoyed hours of fun pretending I was some English fashion model running down the cobblestone path hailing a cab or running after The Dave Clark Five with "Catch Us if You Can" playing in the background.

The stores didn't carry much in the way of cosmetics and girly girl things, but they had Yardley Love's Lemon Scent Cologne, Love's Baby Scent Splash, and Heaven's Scent toilet water, which for a long while I thought was siphoned from someone's bathroom. It was our first step into womanhood, or at least our first step towards the cosmetic counter. When we splashed drugstore toilet water or cologne on the fuzzy patch at the nape of our necks, an entirely new world was revealed. The velvet curtains parted, the soundtrack started to soar, and boys who would never know our names noticed us because we stank, and our lips were white. We were young ladies. We could smell like jasmine and springtime, fresh lemons, cotton candy, and musk. Why was that good? We'd find out soon enough.

It never occurred to us to wear or buy the colors, cosmetics, and colognes our mothers wore. Channel No. 5, White Shoulders, My Sin, Tabu, Interlude. Did perfume lead directly to sex? The names of perfumes seemed to allude to that. There were few options for purchasing beauty items in the Sixties. There were no department store counters with eighteen thousand colors and glosses and products aimed at teen consumers. You got one gloss or lipstick tube and made it go up and down until the stick of color fell off in your lap or you used the very last dose dug out of the case with your fingertip. You didn't realize you'd remember that brand for the rest of your life, but you did.

As I took the massive leap from junior high to high school, my uniform became my home-sewn black jacket. My methodical makeup was a soft pink or white lip color and a bold pencil line inside my eye and above the lower lashes. It probably wasn't sanitary for the eye, but at that age, youthful body parts could fight off everything but poison oak and the common cold. Finally, of course, a thick coat of light blue eye shadow was dragged over my sleepy lids. Donna Bednarski showed me how to apply everything. She was well versed in Max Factor liners, mascaras, and other eye irritants. I left my upper lashes alone. They were already dark, thick, and long, and they outlined the top line of my eyes without applying products. Even without an upper line outlining my eyes, my mother informed me I looked like a whore with makeup.

One late afternoon when I was playing a benign game of hide 'n' seek with Heather at Bad Brad's house, there was a loud knock at the door. Heather came out from hiding and swung open the front door to find my mother standing there, fuming like someone had rear-ended her car … or her daughter.

Before I realized what was happening, the palm of her hand flew across my cheek in a mighty slap, and a word crawled up from the bowels of her anger as she hollered:

"Slut!"

Huh? I stood there mortified and speechless.

She then proceeded to drag me by the shirt sleeve across the cul-de-sac muttering "Slut!" with every few steps. Then the word whore came flying out of her mouth like flames, although when she said it, it was with a guttural Bronx flare. "Whoor!" It was at this point I gathered that being called a whore or slut was not a good thing. I was stooped over in humiliation. What had I done? Why was she so angry? Was it menopause, or me? I ran to my room and shut the door, listening like a spy for any clue that might come from the living room.

By this time, my father didn't look my way long enough to call me anything. "Do you know where your daughter was?" she shrieked into his ear as he remained transfixed by the television screen.

"Keep it down, Blos. I'm trying to watch."

My mother continued, rage filling her throat like water in the tub.

"Across the street at that bad boy's house, that's where! Can you imagine what was going on there? Can you imagine?"

"Pipe down," my father muttered in a rare calming voice. "Leave her alone. I'm watching *Combat!*"

My mother stormed off, still fuming about something I didn't do. She was rather wild in her young days. Perhaps she was projecting her past onto my present. I could still feel the sting to my right cheek, but what was worse was the sting of embarrassment and of being howled at in front of my friends. I felt ashamed. Humiliated. I wanted to crawl under a rock. Or be one. I am a rock, I am an island.

* ⚛ *

Luckily, both Marvin Reedy and Blaine Carpenter resurrected my self-confidence and sense of self-worth. Both boys had a crush on me in a "friend" sort of fashion, so I had two built-in dance partners at the Teen Club dances. I would dance with one, then the other. If we danced too close, the chaperone would separate us. The necks of teenage boys smelled like soap and their father's Hai Karate. I buried my nose in both collars and never wanted to come up for air. It was soothing to cuddle up to someone. It was new. Jefferson Airplane's "Somebody to Love" was playing over the modest speaker system as the new local band Anthony and the Barons set up their equipment on stage. For that evening, I had not one partner to fall into, but two. Between the feedback from the sound system and the pitchy harmonies, life was good. Once dance at a time …

In seventh grade, as *Star Trek* was first airing on television, Marvin and Blaine would take turns walking me around our own spaceship: the Eichler cul-de-sac. Since I couldn't decide which one of the two had won my heart, or had gained hand-holding privileges, and wanting to be fair and just, I would initially hold Marvin's hand while we walked around the ten house radius, then take Blaine's hand and walk around our U-shaped block in the other direction. Strangely enough, they tolerated each other as they both felt that this was a proper, nonviolent approach to a duel. No swords, simply strolls. Each boy would kiss me once, but they were closed-lip, quick smooches. They didn't serve up anything that would make my knees wobbly or require a fainting couch. If this was chemistry, I preferred to be making a bologna sandwich in the kitchen. Marvin and I fell in "like" for five months, Blaine and me for five weeks. Marvin gave me a ring to wear on a string around my neck. I gave it back when Blaine moved up a few notches and looked acutely cute in a particular light. When you're twelve years old, all's fair in love and war and walks around the block.

Stephen Sondheim wrote the lyrics to "Something's Coming" in one day. He was only twenty-seven at the time. He went on to write the lyrics for all the tunes in *West Side Story.* It remains one of my favorite musicals and films. More importantly, the actor who played Tony was the embodiment of everything I thought I wanted in a boyfriend. His soft full lips, warm skin, passion, sincerity, and the heart he wore on his sleeve were my ideal. I wanted all of that. Marvin and Blaine didn't provide any of it.

✳ ⚛ ✳

My "first time" was not when a boy pulled out a condom or unhooked my bra. I consider my first time the day love arrived. Not necessarily lust, but a tenderness of immeasurable potency for another person. It was like someone had flicked on a switch. My switch.

My first deep kisses were from my first boyfriend, Ricky. His mother, Dawn, worked with my mother at the Santa Clara Valley Welfare Department. Although Ricky lived in San Francisco with his father and went to school there, our relationship bloomed quickly through the ancient art of letter writing. We wrote to each other months before we ever met. He always sent his letters on lavender-colored stationary with a floral design scrolled down one side of the page. Some may say that was a terribly feminine paper for a boy to be using to write to his girl, but I saw it as dreamily romantic. Whenever I saw one of those pastel envelopes mixed with our regular mail, my heart skipped a beat. I still remember his penmanship and the way he signed his name. It was scrunched down like someone had stepped on the "R" and the "Y" and everything in between. Although it was barely legible, I found it precious. I found everything Ricky said or did endearing.

One day, Ricky slipped a photo inside the floral envelope. Up until that time, I had no idea what he looked like. In the picture, he was seated near a fireplace, wearing a suede shirt opened with leather crisscross ties at his neck. His electric guitar sat next to him, and I could have sworn he was Glen Campbell's younger brother. They were twins! His head and jaw were square-shaped, and his mouth was small, like Campbell's. That photo sealed the deal. This boy who had a wonderful way with words and who wrote indescribable letters, would soon be wallpapering my neck with love bites.

Ricky was fifteen, and I was fourteen. I was sitting in the living room waiting for Ricky and his stepfather, Vance, to pick me up. It would be the first time Ricky and I would meet after weeks and weeks of heartfelt letters crossing in the mail. But I was dressed like someone else as I sat wrapped in our dark brown Naugahyde lounge chair. I had borrowed Donna Bednarski's fluorescent pink minidress. But it didn't help the look of the atrocious short haircut my mother had insisted upon, the one that made my nose appear even more prominent on my face that had yet to grow into it. My pimply face was covered, unsuccessfully, with dabs of Clearasil as I awkwardly crossed and uncrossed my unsteady legs and their magenta shoes with two-inch heels and white stockings, both borrowed from Donna's closet. I had never worn heels before, so I was even more wobbly than usual. My fishnet stockings were hooked with a garter belt because there was no such thing as pantyhose yet. The nervous twitches, the yearning in my pre-adolescent body—for what? I wasn't yet sure. I soon found out. It was Ricky's smile.

When Ricky and I finally met in person after weeks and months of letters cuddled up in mailbags, we fell even more deeply for each other, because when you're young, you fall hard and feel everything tenfold. We did, even while sporting my bad hairdo. Jim Morrison once said, "Some of the worst mistakes of my life were haircuts." I wish I could say the same. I've made some bad choices and more significant missteps than bad hair. Falling for Ricky wasn't one of them. However, I was uneasy about our first meeting, and the bad haircut wasn't helping matters.

My mother had taken me to a beauty parlor thick with hair spray, the aroma of Tonette, Toni, Lilt, and other hair permanent chemicals, Prince Matchabelli Windsong, and Avon's kerosene-based colognes such as Charisma and Topaze were radiating off the women seated under space helmets. They were reading *Woman's Day* and *Harper's Bazaar* until their hair was fully baked. My own tresses fell well over my shoulders at this time, and the woman assigned to do the scissory deed looked like the Wicked Witch of the West.

"Cut it all off. I want it short for summer," my mother sternly instructed.

Suddenly it was my own mother who was the Wicked Witch of the West. When I saw inches of hair falling to the floor, I was mortified. No! Too late. Another security blanket bites the dust. I came home and was afraid to go out of the house, let alone the cul-de-sac. My hair was shorter than a boy's haircut, my face was covered with pimples, my nose felt like the Empire State Building. What an ideal time to meet my first boyfriend.

Ricky's stepfather, Vance, drove Ricky to our Eichler to fetch me and my borrowed pink dress and magenta shoes. One man and one boy pulled into our driveway in a Chevy El Camino. I can still hear the hum of the motor. It sounded more like a freight train. When our eyes met, I wanted to dive into a deep hole, face and botched haircut first, or put a paper bag on my head. But Ricky smiled. He seemed to see something beyond my clumsy adolescent exterior. He saw *me*. His eyes said *Yes*. I was relieved. As we huddled close together in the front seat of Vance's El Camino station wagon, me seated in the middle between Vance and my new love, Ricky took my hand as Paul Mauriat's instrumental "Love Is Blue" came pouring out of the car's AM radio. It was official. That was our song.

We arrived at Ricky's mother's house in a section of San Jose called Blossom Hill, where there were few blossoms and only distant foothills in sight. I was introduced to his mother, Dawn, but quickly became distracted when I started counting the number of Siamese cats catapulting back and forth on the furniture and sitting on appliances and tables. Had I died and gone to Cat Heaven? The house was filled with wall-to-wall cats. One sat on top of the refrigerator, three were on the couch, one was on the kitchen counter as Dawn attended to dinner. Several others were scattered around each room. Something smelled like pot roast. Suddenly, I felt more at home than at home. Can I stay here? Forever?

I should have connected Dawn with the Four Seasons' song of the same name, but I didn't. There was a popular, moderately sappy song released the year I met Ricky. It was sung by Bobby Goldsboro and entitled "Honey." The lyrics revolved around the age-old story: A young and hypersensitive woman plants a tree in the yard, nurses it, and dies. The end. Whenever this sentimental song came on the radio, Honey was replaced in my mind with this fiercely independent mother figure named Dawn.

"You kids go for a walk or something. Be back in twenty minutes. Dinner will be ready."

After Ricky smiled a small smile and winked in my direction, he took my hand and walked me around the neighborhood. No one had ever winked at me. He seemed so adult.

The late afternoon sky was darkening, and there were few other houses and even fewer streetlights on the block. There wasn't much to see nor sidewalks to stroll on. Dawn's neighborhood was being built, and there was nothing but one block of finished structures, one of them Dawn and Vance's home. The rest were in various stages of preparation. With his soft hands resting on my shoulders, Ricky guided me around and through the newly framed homes.

"We will have a home like this someday," he whispered.

Sigh.

"Here is our living room."

I was suddenly living out Tony and Maria's wedding shop scene in *West Side Story* as we pretended how perfect our future would be as husband and wife. And, yes, for the first time ever, I felt pretty, oh so pretty. Ricky pulled me to his firm fifteen-year-old chest in our imaginary new home and kissed me in a way I hadn't been kissed by Marvin or Blaine and certainly not by my first kiss distributor, Danny Fowler. My knees buckled. My flesh started to moisten, even though there was a fall chill in the air. Something was stirring inside of me that couldn't be measured or contained. Love? Lust? Or maybe the hope of fitting in here, or somewhere.

When we returned to his mother's house, we were seated in their formal dining room for dinner. I couldn't taste anything, but I remember it smelled heavenly, and I felt surprisingly calm and at home. Their home. Dawn talked to me like an equal. Ricky treated me like a lady. Vance ignored me and everyone else as he grabbed for seconds, then thirds. I was terribly distracted throughout dinner as Ricky and I exchanged glances. I saw a twinkle in his eye that made me beam. I was drawn to him like some sweet pastry in the dessert case. We played footsie under the dining table throughout the meal. He seemed mature with his charming, talkative, caring way. I had never seen those qualities in boys my age or in family members, certainly not around our dinner table. Dawn and Vance treated me like I was already accepted as one of them. I liked it. I was not a kid in this household. I was not being discounted or ignored. I was being asked for my opinions. They seemed interested in what I had to say, who I was, what I thought. This was a new world, and although it felt foreign, it suited me just fine.

While Dawn cleared the table and did the dishes, Ricky walked me down the hallway to his parents' bedroom. We sprawled out on his parents' queen-sized bed, turned on the television, and proceeded to watch, but mostly not watch, Alfred Hitchcock's *The Birds,* which happened to be playing on television that night. We made out like a couple of desperate lovers who fell together after a lifetime of being separated. He held me. He kissed me. He gently breathed in my ear. I never wanted to leave that room in that house. I never wanted to leave his embrace. I had found a home—a new sort of home. It was a person, not an Eichler

Fifty Shades of Suede

Why did we think wearing suede during the Sixties, specifically fringed suede, was the height of cool? Was it the raw and fragrant scent of the soft leather? Was it the sound of the fringe rustling as we strolled? Denise was my best friend in the later years of junior high and throughout high school. She had a bedroom painted in the saddest color blue and a suede jacket that weighed about forty-two pounds. It registered nine out of ten on the Richter cool scale. When I borrowed it for special occasions, I felt hipper than when I was without it. I even wore it to the beach on a hot summer day to meet cool guys. I felt empowered. I felt like a completely different person. I felt seen, but in a subtle and bitchin' sort of way. I also felt heavier, a positive thing at a time when I was as light as a sugar wafer.

Clothing empowered me and an entire generation of Baby Boomers. Our uniform spoke volumes, even if we were eventually too damn stoned to speak for ourselves. If I wore something that assisted me in fitting in, I suddenly felt trendier and hipper than I actually was. Clothes bolstered the confidence of most teenage girls, and I was no exception. It helped me feel sophisticated and stylish, when I was neither of those things. Whenever I'd wear something new, I'd assume everyone noticed that it was fresh and more unique. When I strutted around in brightly colored fabrics, I felt particularly visible. When I wore black, I felt mysterious and spicy. When I wore a lacy garment, I felt feminine and demure. Granny gowns, miniskirts, maxiskirts, Nehru collars, bell-bottomed pants and sleeves, peasant blouses, tie-dyed T-shirts, headbands, corduroy pants, embroidered trim wrapped around wrists and stitched at the bottom of our jeans—all were designed to help us fit into a counterculture parade of fashions.

I screamed for ice cream four out of four seasons. My father and I would roll down the jarring road in his colossal navy blue '57 Roadmaster convertible with its plush bucket seats and removable white canvas top. We called this particular impulse buy *The Boat.* It was not a car, it was a vessel—an ocean liner on four Firestones. Our destination? Thrifty Drug Store. Why? They had ice cream at five cents a scoop. That meant that for fifteen cents I could choose both Mint-Chip and Jamoca Almond Fudge, and perhaps top it with a little Rocky Road. It was summer melting in a sugar cone.

One afternoon, while I was sitting in the Thrifty Drug Store parking lot waiting for my father, who had run into the store for his Revelation Tobacco tin, I spotted someone I recognized from the hallways of junior high school: Denise Patterson. She was leaning against a mustard yellow Mustang two parking rows away from our vehicle. As she raised her hand in recognition, I raised mine back, as if we were foreigners who had spotted someone from the homeland. We decided to make a courageous attempt to get past our awkward fifteen-year-old selves and greet one another.

Could Denise be someone from my tribe? She didn't look like me. Her hair was long and russet brown like mine, but it was law-abiding, straight, and glossy as it fell over her shoulders with sun-kissed threads. Denise was also much prettier than I was, with her straight sharp nose, rosy cheeks, and blue eyes. Her closet was full of current high-end fashions that put my discount threads to shame. Shortly after that brief exchange, we found ourselves in the same sewing class where we worked together, shared the same Singer machine, our budding friendship sutured into tight unbreakable stitches from that moment forward.

Sewing class opened up an entirely new world. Colorful fabric on bolts and rolls, cutting shears, seam rippers, and funky fashions printed on Simplicity and Butterick pattern envelopes. There was something celebratory about the moment your anxious electric scissors began to glide across the fabric and around the corners of the flimsy papery pattern pieces, careful not to catch a pin—a cutting device powered by some hidden source in the ether. It was as if the light of God was fueling those stainless-steel blades. I loved this new universe and found my first sewing machine in the same modest Thrifty Drug Store where I purchased my first two-piece bathing suit. Thrifty was an eclectic mix of unrelated items—aisles filled with everything from flip-flops to Planters Peanuts, sewing machines to Alka-Seltzer, to the left of the store's ice cream counter. It was our own personal Shangri-La.

The scent that seeped out of the fibers as I ironed certain fabrics was intoxicating. One brightly colored orange-and-yellow flowery cloth released a sweet floral smell under the heat and weight of the iron. I had never smelled anything quite like it. It was an organic scent with floral notes, but it didn't smell like any flower I had ever sniffed. It was as if an entire bouquet had been magically embedded in the fibers. The variety of materials—jersey, cotton-poly blend, and corduroy or paisley prints in reds, blues, oranges, pinks—were oddly inebriating and strangely invigorating.

Dotted Swiss fabric always radiated Easter, its colorful raised dots mimicking the little colored dot candies that came on paper. I would fall into a hypnotic right-brain trance as I sewed each garment in my bedroom on my Thrifty Drug Store sewing table. I had always operated in the left-brain mode where logic, analysis, and linear thinking ruled. Now I was hovering in a zone where time didn't exist. Creativity and intuition were at the wheel, and the hours would fly by as I lost myself in the up and down motion of the sewing machine needle and marveled at the colorful bobbins and their ballet movements. While I was lost in the spaces between the stitches, Harold was building model airplanes and ships using model glue in an enclosed small room. Childhood hobbies were intoxicating, in one way or another.

One of my first seamstress projects was a red corduroy bell-sleeved top with colorful two-inch trim pieces stitched onto the end of each sleeve. I wore that top at least three times a week. Simplicity and Butterick were the guides. With my new skills I could make any garment, including culottes, empire-waisted frocks, A-line shifts, minidresses, maxidresses, modified Nehru collars, and bell-bottomed everything, from pants to sleeves.

Another one of my first home sewing projects was more than a bit ambitious: the aforementioned black velvet jacket. It wasn't velveteen, but velvet, a more precious and slightly more pricey fabric. Unfortunately, I had forgotten to line the jacket as I focused a bit too closely on the collar and sleeves. It was my first attempt at sewing a full collar, and one side of the lapel emerged slightly wider than the other. Oops. But I wore that beloved jacket every day—to school, to play, in the midst of a boiling summer and the chilly days of winter. I refused to remove it. It was my security blanket. I felt hip, mysterious, confident, Elvis-like when it was wrapped around my shoulders and covered my narrow arms. But my mother reviled that jacket. She called it "ratty" and thought it made me look like a tramp. My mother loved calling me a tramp. She also loved singing "That's Why the Lady Is a Tramp," but I don't think it reminded her of me. It reminded her of Sinatra.

One day I came out of the shower, and my black velvet jacket had vanished along with my cardboard box of comic books and plastic container of 45 records. Poof! I knew she had secretly tossed it all out even when she insisted she hadn't. I felt like I had lost a beloved pet or a part of my own anatomy. It took months to adjust. We all need security blankets, especially in adolescence. That ratty, cockeyed collared black velvet jacket was mine.

If that jacket was my number one security blanket, the runner-up had to be the well-worn faded red bandana that I used to manage my unmanageable waist-length hair. I would place it on my head and tie it at the back of my neck because that was cooler than tying it under the chin like a babushka.

The red bandana was usually paired with a couple of gold-finished hoops that were clip-on earrings scrounged from the bottom of the bargain bin at Woolworth's. My mother wouldn't allow me to pierce my ears.

"Why would you want to get a hole punched in perfectly good earlobes? You'll get an infection!"

Naturally, that was the first rebellious baby step I took when I moved out of my parents' home.

"I'll show them. I'll poke holes in my ears."

It was my way of saying, this is my life ... and these are my earlobes. It was my defiance and my early stab at independence. I thought the combination of gold hoops and a shabby red bandana made me look like Linda Ronstadt. Of course, it didn't do anything of the kind. It made me look like I had a red rag on my head. My Russian relatives would have been proud.

In junior high school, I "pegged" my pants at the inseam so that they held tighter to my sorry thighs that were the same circumference as my lower legs. At that time, I didn't have a sewing machine, so I would grab a needle and thread. It usually took twenty minutes to close up the seams by hand in long, uneven stitches. They looked terrible. But when my pants pressed against my thighs, I knew I was in business. I pegged all of my pants. I was determined to be fashionable, even if could only accomplished it with mismatched stitches.

In gym class, I always had to grab the XS (extra small–sized) bathing suit at the "cage" where they handed out thin black nylon suits to each girl. I swam in them, literally and figuratively. The leg holes never closed around my thigh. The bodice of the suit hung on me like excess skin hung on an elephant. Nothing clung to my frame. My legs swam in the standard issue cobalt blue gym shorts. I felt foolish, and my body felt as if it would never curve or bloom.

Our seventh-grade locker room was like having a peephole into a wide variety of female forms. Most girls were still undeveloped, but some were fully formed, with mama-sized teardrop breasts. A few girls had the sort of pert breasts that were propped up perfectly like upside-down cereal bowls.

My new best friend, Laura Mothrup, with her velvety peach cheeks and unblemished skin, had breasts that emerged from her Playtex Cross-Your-Heart Junior Bra like two perfect Hostess Snoballs. Others had lengthy oblong-shaped water balloons attached to their chest. Most of us were barely ripe with our early pink buds, but the comparison game was off and running. She's bigger. She's smaller. She's fuller. She's darker. She's lighter. She's taller. I'm too short. She's just right. I'm all wrong. She's cool, and I'm … invisible.

Seeing the kinky curls and new crops of pubic hair popping up like Chia Pets on the crotches of others was a relief. I wasn't the only one suddenly sporting fur. Suddenly hair was everywhere. On boy's chins, under girl's arms, and … down there. Breasts were sprouting up all over campus like muffins in tins rising in the oven, almost as noticeable as the frequency of zits. Getting naked in front of perfect strangers was a new venture. I had never been naked in front of anyone. Even my mother looked away when I undressed. Now I was naked in front of the entire world. Thank goodness for those little white towels and our twelve-year-old hands that tried to cover every body part as we changed our clothes.

Heather's sister Jane, who lived across the street and was three years my senior, had thick and curvy muscular thighs like a palomino pony and showed a distinct tan line where her shorts ended. Jane paraded around proudly. She was bigger where

I was smaller. She was curved where I was a bundle of Pick-Up Sticks. She kept a small jar of Mum Deodorant in her room. She actually needed to use it. I didn't. She was already shaving her underarms and legs and had adult-like stubble on her thighs sprouting out of tiny pink dots. I wanted that. But I had dark hairs running down both legs that I tried to hide in gym class. I could have run a piece of onion paper over the front of my shins and sliced and diced those fine hairs. Jane's razor-sharp sophistication and skills were right on target; I wasn't anywhere near the bull's eye.

I never understood women who wanted to appear rail thin or those who celebrated celebrities who were. Classmates and certainly the boys thought my body looked "wrong" or sickly. They made fun of my weight. Carol Swizzlesticks! That was my nickname. They were spot-on. My legs did look like sticks. My arms too. I may have been thinner than oxygen, but I wanted to be as tough, weighty, and muscular as a biker chick.

In my mind, I was unnoticed by people at home and elsewhere, in part due to my weight. I turned sideways and disappeared, just as the kids on the schoolyard said with a snicker. I wanted my parents or someone—anyone—to see my worth so that I could see it. But my body was unformed and my face, un-pretty. My mind wandered too often, and I daydreamed too much. I was a card-carrying member of the Sit-Down-Shut-Up party at home, and now at school.

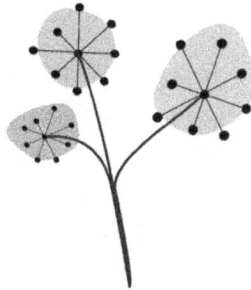

Sax, Drugs, and Rock 'n' Roll

Assume the Crash Position

Our Eichler neighborhood was the original *Knots Landing* (for those of you who remember the Eighties) or *Desperate Housewives* (for those who don't). My parents would hold frequent cocktail parties—the sort of gatherings that the Sixties were famous, or infamous, for. Modern jazz saturated the air, and alcohol filled the lowball glassware. Everyone and everything was merry and bright in the spotlight of the Eichler tract.

Mom and Eichler neighbors Chuck Elkind and Don Mathias jamming at a party.

In this integrated bohemian hub known as the Fairglen Eichlers, bossa nova, cool jazz, and early Beatles music played in equal measure. As Harold and I would lean against the glass wall in the hallway and gaze through the atrium at the grown-ups huddled in small groups, deep in political discussions and existential debates, jamming on the piano, bass, and saxophone, guzzling too much bourbon and scotch, laughing too loud, and too late, we felt like the lone adults looking in on a teenage party. We couldn't wait to grow up and be more childlike—more like our parents and their network of beboppin' friends.

One of many adult parties in our Eichler home.

All was not well after midnight. Our Eichler rattled, roared, and rocked even after those frequent cocktail parties ended. That's when the late night kitchen fights began. Even before the start of any given party, Harold and I absorbed the rise and fall of my parents' voices as they argued across the open atrium and across the kitchen table. They didn't cook in the kitchen; they quarreled. Since the kitchen was the most distant location from our bedroom, they assumed we couldn't or wouldn't hear a word. They assumed wrong.

My father puffed harder on his pipe when he was pissed off, blowing into the rooms of our Eichler like a steamship run off-course. On this occasion, he had uncovered the numerous bags of clearance dresses and sale pajamas and socks my mother had squirreled away in various closets. She was always hiding her purchases like nuts for another season, mostly in the corner pouches of our house. My parents had an unwritten agreement: he earned, she spent. As she stood at the counter emptying the powder for her diet drink into a tall orange-striped glass, she ignored the man with the smoke pouring out of his ears. "Blossom!" She looked up at him, smiled with closed lips and deepening dimples, looked away, then went on to tell me about the clearance sale at the local J.C. Penney department store. I wish I hadn't wandered into the room at that moment. "I'm not made out of money, ya know," Dad fumed. Mom walked over to the blond upright piano in the family room, her long fingers reaching for a couple of chords while still standing, and started singing "Misty" in her lowest register. *"Look at me, I'm as helpless as a kitten up a tree...."* But in that moment, there was nothing helpless about my mother. Cunning, yes. Helpless? Fat chance.

"That won't work this time. You can't spend more than we have coming in."

As my mother turned to face me again, she was oblivious to every smoke signal my father was sending. Her grace and the sound of triad chords permeated the air around us in a way my father's smoke never could.

When my brother and I would hunker down in our section of the house where the bedrooms, washer/dryer, and kids' bathroom were clustered, our parents' arguments were like a distant train, fast approaching, gaining speed, rumbling the closet doors as the bickering turned to hollers. At this point, Harold and I were porous sponges, so bickering penetrated easily. Waves of anger and the resulting wounds from emotional injury filtered through the air, curling and resting in tender ears. We detested these frequent battles. Even with hands placed over the sides of our heads, the noise of these disputes always trickled in against our will as the canals of our small ears became saturated with furious noise. Hearts would speed. Stomachs would knot, and nausea would ensue. Here they go again. Assume the crash position.

My father's bark was worse than his bite, and my mother's bite was drowned out by his bark. Although their heated arguments would echo down the hallways, they were partially muffled by the walls and distance. We listened closer for further indications. Who was irritated? Who was about to sob? Who was frustrated … fed up? Who would eventually collapse and accept whatever demands were up for auction as they quarreled across the kitchen table? We didn't need to distinguish a single word. The sea of sound would quickly reveal who was angrier, who was about to give in, and who would eventually console the other.

The distant whimpers coming from my mother broke my heart. I wanted to run to her and throw my arms around her quivering shoulders, but no one touched in my home. In those moments I despised my father. Whatever the mighty war of words was about, my mother's bawling turned him into a monster in my mind and, for a time, my enemy. I wanted to shelter her in a protective blanket and shield her from the loud barks and verbal bites. Her tears became my own as I soaked my pillowcase at night, feeling in my bones what she was feeling, reeling in what she was reeling in, her misery invading my own body. I was a trapped, wounded bird with wings beating against the cage—a cage that was my father's domain. We were the temporary tenants in his castle of wood and glass.

My bond with my father began to wobble. No more plane rides over the orange circular living room rug. I spent many minutes, hours, and years fearing his unpredictable outbursts and fits of anger. In solitude, I raged against him under the bed covers, safe and sad in the protected quarters of my bedroom. I fumed about his dissatisfaction with my mother, his worry and frustrations released like cannons and targeted in the wrong direction. With eyes squeezed tight and the side of my head propped up on a soft pillow, every muscle tensed. I lay in bed until midnight in an uneasy fight-or-flight mode and wondered why this man who loomed so large, a gargantuan personal deity and devil, was making a god-awful mess of our modish home.

What did they fight about? Everything. Anything. Often, these quarrels revolved around my mother's management of their recurring party schedule. She adored social get-togethers and orchestrated frequent and often epic gatherings in our Eichler. Neighbors and neighbors' friends were invited. Come one, come all. We have assorted nuts, stuffed celery sticks, and Lipton onion soup dip. Having people over always involved the same buffet of treats: two wooden bowls of pretzels; Fritos Corn Chips; assorted licorice pastels stuck together in oddball shapes and colors, some even rolled in tiny sugary dots; painfully dull Chex Mix; and lukewarm Sanka. Why the Chex Mix was so dry remains a mystery, as it was usually whipped up with a full stick of butter or tub of margarine and a pinch of Worcestershire sauce. There was always a wide array of greasy crackers in dominos formation and a block of cheese the size of a car battery.

There were lowball glasses for high party guests; plastic ice buckets; colorful frilly toothpicks; cocktail swords; a globe-sized cheese ball rolled in nuts; fondue pots filled with warm, salty Gruyere cheese with a sprinkling of nutmeg; plenty of party-themed paper napkins from the clearance bin that always had an odd smell to them; and a suburban husband ruminating in the master bedroom. As long as their party guests didn't rifle through our kitchen cabinets and drink the Tang or take boxes of my Screaming Yellow Zonkers or foil-wrapped Space Food Sticks, I was fine with my parents' parties.

These shindigs were thrown too frequently to bother with written invitations. "We're having some people over Saturday around 7:30. Come by, won't you?" My mother would spend a couple of hours on the phone calling the entire neighborhood. She was always on the phone, her twisty-turny umbilical cord. At that time, there was a cartoon in *MAD Magazine* of a man who was on the phone too long. His phone ear was enormous. I would often study my mother's ears to see if one was enlarging.

Since my parents were named Joe and Blossom, I always thought J&B on the green Scotch whisky bottle with the red-and-yellow label was created especially for them. Was it some wild coincidence that J&B bottles were littered all over our Eichler?

A stock of hard liquor was always in the cabinets and stored on top of our refrigerator. Liquid courage was a big part of every adult party in the Swingin' Sixties, and supplying enough liquor to sink the Titanic is what my folks did best. Drunkenness was the measure of a party's success. The more it moved the inebriation needle, the better.

By midnight, party guests were staggering down the hallway to use the bathroom that my brother and I shared. The Eichler had two bathrooms: one in the master bedroom and one that was sandwiched between my brother's room and mine. Without fail, my parents' party guests would end up in our bathroom, not theirs. We would listen with ears pressed to the wall as they riffled through our medicine cabinet at warp speed, pulled out drawers, and opened cabinet doors under the sink.

Mom and neighbor dancing at an Eichler shindig.

"What are they looking for, Harold?"

He didn't know either. At times, they were trying to locate my mother's prescription for Valium. Once in a while, a couple would moan and groan behind the bathroom door and end up playing hide the cocktail frank near the sink where we kept our Gleem.

My father often chose party time to put his foot down and to try on the alpha male hat. The protest over hosting parties continued for years.

"Enough with the parties. We just had one! Who are these strangers in my house? No! I don't want people in my house. Get out!"

Like clockwork, he would threaten to lock himself in the master bedroom and not come out until every guest left our Eichler.

"You have your party. I'm going to watch television."

And just like clockwork, he would stay locked in the bedroom until the third guest arrived. Then he would emerge from his coop like a jutting peacock, strut around the living room and family room, and greet all of his guests with a bold off-color joke and a lengthy, hilarious, sometimes fictional account of an ironic or amusing situation from the previous week. His charisma filled every corner of every room. Party guests would orbit around him, while rooms would fill with drunken gaiety. Their parties sounded like a law firm. The Offices of Obnoxious, Chortle, and Cackle.

These verbal boxing matches before every social gathering became frequent. She was the partygoer and party thrower. He hated superficial social gatherings but always ended up the life of the party. But in the middle of all the arguing sat a decorative, divided wooden bowl filled with pistachio nuts on one side and Planters Peanuts on the other. My mother would put a bowl of my father's favorite treats out, a sort of peace offering, or more accurately a trap with the temptation of salty bait, to encourage him over to her side. My dad hated parties, but he loved nuts.

Although he despised parties, my father loved being the center of everyone's universe. His perfectly delivered fables would attract party guests like groupies to Elvis. He knew how to tell a story, giving it the right rhythm and cadence and always including a cliffhanger. My dad could also be endlessly charming. He was the master of "Do you know what happened to me last week?" and like E.F. Hutton, when Joe spoke, people listened.

✳ ⚛ ✳

My brother kept a fun box of ridiculous "novelty" items at the ready whenever my parents' parties were about to start. He would carefully place a Whoopee Cushion under one of our living room chair cushions. Hilarity—and a spanking—would quickly ensue. The hot cinnamon toothpicks were always a hit just before my brother got hit. And then there was the fake vomit, always placed near the bathroom sink for amusement.

Novelty items appeared in comic book ads. Most appeared near the "Amazing Live Sea Monkeys" and "Magic Rocks," a colorful collection that would grow in a kitchen juice glass right in front of your eyes. And, of course, there were the X-Ray Specs, a "hilarious optical illusion" that assisted you in seeing through walls, viewing the bones in your hand, for only a buck.

My brother's favorite party pranks included faux ice cubes with dead flies in the center of them, and a plastic—but realistic—pile of doggy doody that he enjoyed placing on our orange living room rug before party guests arrived and while my mother was busy scooping the onion dip into a bowl. My brother the party pooper.

Soon, the music would grow louder from the hi-fi, or the party guests would gather at the piano to sing and play instruments, and the chatter and laughter elevated a few decibels. The mood would lighten and liven, and the live music would begin. Party guests who happened to be musicians would gather around my mother when she lowered herself onto the piano bench. She was one of the key players during each jamboree.

Mom could play any and every jazz standard by ear, but only in the key of C. Partygoers with their horns, string bass, saxophones, and castanets would join in. It was a regular hootenanny fueled by phenomenally talented musicians, Jim Beam whiskey, and Smirnoff vodka. Even the father of modern jazz and piano great Earl "Fatha" Hines was in attendance.

Hines often sat deep in conversation with my father at these gatherings. Since Dad was a lifelong lover of jazz, he and Hines had a lot of musical notes to compare. Hines had a world-renowned keyboard technique. In his work with Louis Armstrong in the late 1920s, he virtually redefined jazz piano. With what he called *trumpet style*, Hines played horn-like solo lines in octaves with his right hand and drove them with chords from his left. He carved out a place for the piano as a solo instrument outside the rhythm section and defined the role of both hands for the upcoming generations of jazz pianists.

At the time he was attending our Eichler shindigs, Hines was still in the process of giving triumphant concerts and maintaining his recording activity. This gifted pianist was elected a member of *Downbeat* magazine's Jazz Hall of Fame in 1965. In 1966, the United States sponsored his group on a tour of the Soviet Union, where he played for 92,000 people.

In the early to mid-Sixties, Hines and his family lived in a sizable house in the Oakland Hills, where he too gave many legendary parties. But he especially enjoyed attending the Eichler gatherings as they were filled with wall-to-wall jazz lovers and were fully integrated, much more so than most neighborhoods.

Dad in deep discussion with jazz
great Earl "Fatha" Hines and neighbor
Maggie Caploe at an Eichler
party. Maggie founded the annual
Fairglen Art Festival.

The debris left behind on the party battlefield included empty plastic tumblers, a half-eaten cheese ball, crumpled napkins, walnut shells littering the floor, leftover onion dip, and lipsticky cigarette butts in every known brand. Just another Eichler party—always the same, but different. Always an event. Always the place to be. Always the cleanup on Sunday morning and the reliving of prized party moments at the dinner table.

The Eyes Have It

"You can never go home again"
"Home is where you find it."
"Home sweet home."
"Toto, there's no place like home."
"Home is where the heart is."

The Eichler was not only a structure, a shoebox, four walls, and a flat roof that leaked like a sieve on an annual basis, although every father in the neighborhood could be found in the early days of autumn tromping around the pebbly surface and placing roof patches here and there. The rainy season brought with it an annual guessing game. Where will it leak this year? No one took bets. Everyone knew it would always appear in a new and unexpected location.

The Four Tops had a hit record in 1967 titled *7 Rooms of Gloom.* But our Eichler provided seven rooms of comfort and protection from the gloom. I would go to it when there wasn't anyone or anything to turn to, and it would be my security, my identity, my friend. Those mahogany walls would offer a warm hug and cushion me from my parents' fights, from peers who wouldn't acknowledge me, from teachers who took me to task for my blank stares as I daydreamed out the classroom window. I was at ease in my bedroom. It was home. Out in the world I felt like a stranger in a strange land, much like the character in a favored book assigned by my teacher Miss Dibble. Her high school literature class, Fantasy in Fiction, focused on science fiction novels while her students focused on her otherworldly disheveled appearance and oddly shaped limbs. Miss Dibble's chubby arms were two packages of poppin' fresh dinner rolls that exploded out of her dress sleeves. Her legs and neck had the same doughy appearance. She looked positively eatable, as if you could slather her with whipped butter and have her for lunch.

* ⚛ *

I had one of those pathetic wide-eyed Keane paintings hanging on my bedroom wall. My mother found the monstrosity in a drugstore bin as she was thumbing through the "Wall Art" that was drastically reduced. Keane paintings were first thought to be created by Walter Keane, but were later revealed as the work of his wife, Margaret Keane. The artwork featured children with dilated eye issues who often had a strategically placed tear rolling down one cheek. I always imagined those tears were a result of a childhood disorder such as conjunctivitis. These enormous, seemingly possessed eyes appeared in every dental office and on many bedroom walls in Sixties suburbia. Their eyes followed you around the room, begging and pleading with you to do something—anything—to help them. Many of these enormous-eyed urchins held dogs or cats in their arms, the furry beasts showing the same wide-eye misery. Sad, sadder, saddest. Please, someone ... help the children!

Some people loved them, and others were deeply offended by the gloom and poverty they depicted. They were like an ever-present *Feed the Hungry Children* magazine ad. Those kids would never close those massive and dilated eyes. The perpetually awake doll-like images sat in corners and stared at us as we went about the business of being kids. The Keane kids never went to sleep, and neither did I when I gazed at those distressing peepers from across my bedroom. They were anything but keen.

Dad

"Don't put holes in my walls!"

My father would not allow posters or pictures on the walls of my bedroom, so my brother and I took Scotch tape, turned it in on itself, and placed it in the corners of our room posters. This technique caused no damage the walls, but the posters never remained up for very long. They would curl off and drop to the floor on a recurring basis.

Posters wallpapered the ramparts of the Sixties and Seventies. Now you rarely see a poster tacked up with thumbtacks. Everything has to be framed, sophisticated, exact ... and the frame has to match the flooring or furniture. Feh! We wallpapered our rooms with psychedelic posters, ripped pages or foldouts from magazines of our favorite bands, prints of black-light fantasies, kittens draping their paws over the end of a rope connected by a single claw. "Hang in there, baby!"

But it was growing increasingly more difficult to hang in with my family. I needed a soft place to stumble into, like a board game token finally making it to the last square on the game board—a place to rest and recover. I couldn't find it with the people who lived under the same Eichler roof as I did. My family members were like soldiers from an entirely different branch of the service, seemingly dropped into my unit—or I was dropped into theirs—and without the proper paperwork and clearance. How did I land here?

My room became a decent substitute for all things tender and welcoming. Those four walls allowed me to feel sheltered, safe from the world, protected from my father's rage and my brother's taunts and teasing. There was no lap or shoulder to lean my head upon, just a single bed with a pastel bouquet of security blankets; a couple of mismatched white dressers with pink knobs; a candle to offer a solitary flame of comfort and contentedness; a right-handed lefty guitar with strings strung backwards, although to me they were properly positioned; posters of The Beatles taped against the wood grain of the wall; a lock at the door, which I used frequently; and one well-worn record player with a dull needle. The tender warmth of the walls would wrap around me like a fort. A small pink rug teased my toes and told me I was a girl, or that I would feel like one someday. Right now, I felt like a tomboy and a refugee in my own home. But my room was my base camp. My safe and sacred Shangri-La.

I would search for a feeling of home my entire life. I would look for it in structures because I couldn't find it in people. My room nestled me from age six to seventeen. Then it kicked me out. I went in search of the arms of men to shelter me, the castle of home to shield me, and a secured gate to keep me safe from harm. My destiny wasn't so much a place as much as it was a feeling, a sense of security. When I listened to Sammy Davis Jr.

singing the lyrics to his first hit record, *Shelter of Your Arms*, I was given a glimmer of hope that I might be able to find it in a person rather than a place. But what I really needed to do was to find it within myself.

One weekend afternoon, my mother drove my brother and me in her white Dodge Dart to a small Chinese café called Chop Sticks Kitchen. My father wasn't included in such outings. I'm not sure what he was up to, but it wasn't lunch. As my mother sat us down at a small table, she ordered a plate of chicken chow mein and proceeded to throw a grenade into our tender noodle lunch. It was more like an H-bomb.

"Your father and I will be living apart. We're not getting divorced right now, but we probably will eventually. We are not getting along, so … we're going to take a break for a while." Most children would be upset at such news. I was thrilled, although I quietly held my joy close to the vest, hidden in my clenched jaw. "You are?"

It never happened, though. They decided to go back to their regularly scheduled bickering and verbal brawling in and out of the kitchen. Oh, sure, my father would disappear on phantom business trips for days, sometimes weeks. I later learned he was living with coworkers when he grew tired of quarreling.

A year before the discussion of divorce over wonton soup and those crunchy bits you drop on top, I was playing two-square with a neighborhood friend on the driveway of the Eichler. We heard loud wails and howls, like some injured animal. I couldn't make out what was being said, but there was a lot of shouting and bawling coming from the direction of my living room. I felt the blush of embarrassment pounce to my cheeks. My friends were not supposed to know what went on behind our orange front door. What had been heard by my playmate? Nothing? Everything?

"I've got to go home for dinner," my friend said with a quiver in her voice.

The ball bounced away as my friend quickly ran down the block to her quiet parents and home. I was left on the downslope of the driveway trying to summon up nerve. I knew I had to open the front door and discover what nightmare was inside. That door acted as a security door between my family and me. I didn't want to enter, but I didn't know how to play two-square with one person, so I slowly turned the knob. As the door opened far enough for me to peek my head inside, I peered across the atrium to the living room and witnessed an unusual sight, I saw my brother seated on the floor, holding onto my father's pant leg. Harold was sobbing, his words undistinguishable. I had never seen him cry before. It didn't fit his brash nature. My father tried to shake him off his leg using hard, jerky moments.

"Don't go, Dad! Please! Don't leave us."

It was clear that my father was at a boiling point. He hollered the phrase I grew up listening to again and again, like a repetitious nursery rhyme.

"I can't take it anymore! That's it. I'm going!"

I spotted his two blue canvas suitcases on the floor, seemingly packed and ready for takeoff. By this time, it was clear my father was eager to walk out. Mom was nowhere to be seen. As I cautiously moved into the house, I spotted her sprawled out on her bed in the master bedroom through the left corner of my eye. Was she napping? Was she dead? I ran down the hallway to the safety of my room. Had she passed out from too many glasses of Martini & Rossi? For my mother, social drinking was an escape from her suburban jail. She didn't drink often, but at parties and after work she would get properly plastered and do outlandish things, like dance on top of the picnic table in our atrium or sing at the top of her lungs as if she had won an Ethel Merman singing competition. Apparently, her drinking at parties had embarrassed my father. That's what I surmised, but I didn't know if that was the whole story. I only knew my mother was lying half-conscious in the bedroom. My father was not having any of it, whatever "it" was.

I had heard his threats about leaving many times before, but I had never seen a pair of fraying suitcases accompany his fury. I ran to my bedroom, smashed my head into the pillow, and did something that was surprising, even to myself. I pressed my palms together, looked to the sky, which was the ceiling of my bedroom, and whispered to nothing and no one in particular. "Go, please go! Make him go. If there's a God up there or wherever, please have him leave our home. Leave me and my mother alone!"

I was my mother's silent and sole protector. I couldn't make my father leave, but I believed I could will him to leave. I was certain that would work. But it certainly didn't. As much as I believed my will could move mountains or win relay races, or even move steel balls up a wobbly double track to win points, it couldn't move my father out of our house. He unpacked his bags, my brother's voice dropped a few decibels and calmed to a low whimper, I crossed my arms and optimistically muttered to myself. "Next time. Maybe he'll walk out the orange door—next time."

Soundtrack

If popular rock music was the soundtrack of my youth, my parents' music was even more deeply ingrained. It made an impression on me as deep as the marks on an ancient fossil. I cannot hear "My Funny Valentine," "Misty," "Fly Me to the Moon," "Sentimental Journey," or countless other standards without hearing the tinkling of my mother's fingers on the keyboard or my father's attempts at blaring out a few correct notes among many incorrect ones on his soprano sax or clarinet. My parents played music together nearly every evening. Those songs were my bedtime lullabies. At some point, my brother joined in with a washtub string bass. But I didn't play anything well enough to join in with their playroom jamborees. I felt as useless as the G in lasagna.

Even when I felt abandoned and separate from my family or from my classmates, I believed that someone, often a deceased singer-songwriter, knew me better than my own family or any of my friends. Those songs became my buddies. Whether it was a haunting melody and the aching lyrics delivered by Jimmy Ruffin in "What Becomes of the Brokenhearted," or the head-over-heels exhilaration about falling in love expressed in Al Green's "Love and Happiness," or the isolation of "Sitting on the Dock of the Bay" with Otis Redding, these artists provided a reason to feel less alone. As I sat cross-legged on my bed, the room illuminated by one candle on the floor, I tried to pluck out the appropriate chords to Judy Collins' "Who Knows Where the Time Goes?" and Bob Dylan's "Mr. Tambourine Man." When I played guitar and sang, it felt as though someone in the ether had my number and was sending down a lifeline—and just a little tenderness.

Lights, Camera, Joe!

I come from a gene pool of fast swimmers. We didn't linger; we leapt. My father couldn't sit peacefully or patiently. If we went to a restaurant and the waitress was taking more than a few minutes to get to our table, he'd bounce from the booth and was off in another direction to a new destination.

"Let's get going."

I must have heard him say that same three-word phrase a thousand times.

I was always fast, but not in any sort of long-distance run. I was the fastest in the fifty-yard dash. If I had to run one and a half times around the track, forget it. I came in close to last. I was the first to finish with my drawing, but I never stayed inside the lines. I was quick, but the quality didn't stick. Like my father, I needed to get through things at a rapid pace and move on to the next.

Not only did I inherit my father's restless nature, but also his over-excitement for objects with flashing lights, his intolerance for this and mostly for that, I too was born with a curious and busy brain. I also possessed his quick, slightly cockeyed wit, his photographer's eye for composition and design, his adoration of whimsical products, and his objective observances and rants about life as an absurd circus where we all have a front-row seat. I love the things that people love about me, because they are the things that I loved about my father. He never ran away from controversy. He ran towards it and the absurdity of life, then turned it into a five-star tale with perfect timing, riotous delivery, and panache.

My father impulsively bought the oddest, most delightfully useless items. Anything with a lot of colors or blinking lights, or a statue with massive breasts, a picture with something askew—those were some of the items found in my father's shopping cart. One afternoon he came home with a painting featuring skyscrapers with holes drilled in the canvas to reveal the actual flashing lights lodged behind the picture. He would turn it on and the entire painting would light up the room. My father's smile would light up the entire Eichler.

"No, Joe! Get that damn thing off of the wall. Now!"

My mother hated this kitschy artwork, but my father's delight always vetoed my mother's preferences. In San Jose there was a curious import store named Akron where all of these miserable items sat and gathered dust until my father went on one of his shopping binges and brought them home to rot in our garage. He knew how to have fun with such intriguing and absurd items. He became childlike with each new purchase and whimsical device.

In addition to the flashing wall print, my entire childhood was illuminated by miles and miles of fluorescent tubing. Thin horizontal bulbs appear on the walls, not ceilings, in every photograph of my parents' Queens apartment. Those tubes would reappear in every one of my parents' homes. Long tubes were installed throughout our San Jose Eichler home. The living room. The kitchen. The hallways. Even bedrooms. Our house was so illuminated you could spot it from Pluto.

* ⚛ *

At holiday time, the colorful Swiss Colony catalog featured fifteen-layer chocolate tortes along with assorted cheeses and nut mixes. My father would order not one, not two, but a dozen of these multilayered high-calorie slabs. The sugary bricks would sit in our freezer for decades. We'd graze on one for about three months and forget about the rest taking up space in the Frigidaire. The Pyramids of Giza could have been constructed with our annual leftover confections. Nothing said Christmastime like one of those bricks and a multilayered box of chocolate-covered cherries. Dad would sit with an opened box of cherry cordials on his lap and devour their dark chocolate coating and sweet syrupy interior in record time. Within a half hour the box was empty. His love for bitter dark chocolate was contagious, and I caught it.

* ⚛ *

Peanuts are an essential part of my childhood, and the memories I have of my father. Not just any peanuts, but the Planters brand. Dad took innumerable photographs, slides, and stereo-slides of Times Square in the late 1940s and early 1950s. He managed to capture the magic of that time period, especially the razzle-dazzle of downtown. There was a massive Mr. Peanut sign located in Times Square. Mr. Peanut would move his top hat on … off … on … off … in neon-infused animation. Dad managed to capture every movement of that magic with his camera lens. It was at a time when extreme advertising would appear in bright lights and signage with moving parts. The late 1940s-era slides of Mr. Peanut, as well as the comic book character Little Lulu pulling a Kleenex out of a king-sized box, were my favorite slides in the collection. They were my entertainment. So were my father and his larks. Despite being difficult, with dark moods and nonsensical rages, and my prayers to some vague image of God that I prayed to make my father pack his bags and leave our Eichler, my father remained high on my pedestal, his approval always the unreachable ring.

Dad always had an open can of Planters Peanuts in the house and ate them round the clock, always with an opened mouth so that we could see all the pieces of peanut skins and nut meat. His fingers were coated with salt. Once he switched to dry roasted, but quickly switched back, missing that oily feeling on his fingertips. When the *Peanuts* television specials aired, I couldn't figure out what they had to do with my father's favorite snack. Why was it called *Peanuts*?

Dad was continually purchasing multiples of useless items. It was a theme that ran throughout his lifetime. Maybe it had something to do with the Depression. Perhaps he liked the sense of having this great find in his hand and wanted to share it with everyone he knew. But he seldom did. If he spotted some useless trinket that fascinated him, he'd buy not one of them, but ten of them. Strange statues. Flashing devices. Silly hats.

"It'll make a great gift."

That's what he'd always say. But most would sit in closets or corners and gather dust-bunnies for years. My father never gave gifts. Not at holiday time or on birthdays or anniversaries. His way was to boycott Hallmark holidays and anything and everything sentimental. For all the bickering about my mother's impulse shopping, my father had a similar affliction.

One evening, my father grabbed my mother's arm, and they both drove southward to Tijuana from San Jose on a whim, a non-denominational prayer, and a full tank of gas. It was the middle of the night. Yet another impulsive, unplanned trip. When they returned home, his arms were loaded with statues of black, brown, gold, and white armless creatures. I referred to them as THE MANIC MULTIPLES. Thanks to his buying sprees, our home became furnished in wall-to-wall perky breasts with the tease of cloth draping around womanly hips. As my father positioned what we referred to as "the naked lady statues" all over our Eichler, I started to dislike Venus de Milo with a vengeance. One white statue—as white as Pushka—sat proudly with her heaving bust on our living room fireplace mantel. It caused enormous embarrassment to the rest of us, but he didn't give it a thought. He was not only shameless, but also Dad was his own headliner and audience.

Mom and Dad with a couple of friends from work—posing with one of a dozen "naked lady statues" situated around our Eichler home.

No Tell Motel Soaps

My parents never went to movies on weekends. Instead, their entertainment consisted of a trek to the rather small San Jose Airport, where they would sit in the terminal and watch people tumble off planes, greet one another at the gate, and fall into the arms of loved ones. In the early Sixties, San Jose did not yet have an International Airport. It was a small user-friendly travel hub that didn't require a map app to get from one end of the airport to the other, or to find your parked car, or locate the car rental building. My mother and father would sit for hours with a bagged lunch and watch the show. There was no admission fee and no time limit. It was their own unorthodox staycation ritual.

But when we did travel out of San Jose, my family of four took road trips. After a long day of driving, we'd stop at Motel 6 or the EZ-8. Those were the days when Motel 6 was actually six dollars and EZ-8 was eight bucks and came with a vibrating mattress. It shook you senseless for five minutes after you slid a coin in the slot. Motel 6 meant minimal accommodations with plenty of road noise, bed bugs, and parking spaces that allowed cars to shimmy right up to the room's entrance. My job, because I wanted one, was to remove the crunchy paper that covered the drinking glasses. Then I slipped the little motel soaps into my small suitcase. The soapy chips seemed custom-made for pint-sized hands.

✳ ⚛ ✳

Every time we were scheduled to go out of town, I found myself getting sick to my stomach the night before as I mentally wrung my hands and let every scenario that could possibly go wrong spin through my mind in heavy rotation. Certainly nothing could possibly go right. By morning, I was exhausted, as I had only managed a few hours of sleep with a travel trove of bad dreams. I didn't care about how the trip would be. I was too busy with the dry heaves.

Our road trips were not much different from the Griswold family's vacations with Chevy Chase. We hopped into our four-wheeled clunker and embarked on long, hot drives through miles of monotonous landscape in record-breaking heat with inoperative window cranks. The roadside was peppered with billboards featuring grown-ups doing all the things we thought grown-ups did and we would someday do: smoking, gambling, wearing sparkling evening gowns, and drinking martinis. Then we'd pull into the service-with-a-smile gas station where an attendant pumped our gas and cleaned our windows until they squeaked. A quick visit to the grungiest, most wretched restroom this side of Route 66, and we were on the road again.

Vacations always involved car rides. There were no planes to here or there, just four heavy doors that swung open so that we could park ourselves on the upholstery. We'd stick to the seat while we strained our eyes on the roadside scenery to keep the boredom at bay. One of the places we visited was Palm Springs. There was a downpour of biblical proportions on that particular road trip through the desert. The open landscape was unseasonably drenched as we drove all day, droplets on the windows the size of marbles. My father wouldn't stop the car for anything or anyone. When he had a destination in mind, he was determined to meet his goal in record time, come hell or the high water surrounding our four tires. When we finally arrived at this sunshine city lined with tropical trees and fallen palm leaves, we ran into our motel room and hoped for a long nap or a room with a television set. We sat in our motel room for three days, unwrapping bathroom glasses, glaring out the window at the oil splatters on the parking lot asphalt, now rainbows, and running back and forth to the vending machines with a plastic bag over our heads.

On another car trip, we went to Disneyland and Knott's Berry Farm, but my mother insisted we stay grounded. She prattled on and on about the hazards of each ride. We weren't allowed to board anything that went up 'n' down or 'round and 'round.

"Much too dangerous," she recited repeatedly as she dragged us off to tiresome Tom Sawyer's Island and the Swiss Family Treehouse where nothing spun or moved, even the branches of the tree.

Despite the restricted activities, Disneyland was pure magic in the form of pancake-battered mouse ears and PeopleMovers. We moved through the rotating entrance and every attraction and moment became a familiar filmstrip of fun that still ratchets forward and plays repeatedly in my memory. We covered our ears in "It's A Small World," then stood shoulder to shoulder in a generous-sized room to watch "America the Beautiful" splashed on circular screens that followed you wherever you turned. We took the Skyway to Fantasyland and climbed down into the Submarine Voyage with an assortment of faux seaweed and colorful plastic fish swimming in the water outside the faux-submerged window. I was astonished my mother allowed me to go on that ride without a HAZMAT suit. Once in a while a plastic sea creature would attach itself to the glass and the uniformed Disneyland employee would have to stop the ride to pop it off the window. I liked the bottom of the ocean. It was cool, quiet, blue, and crowded with mermaids and synthetic sea life. I could have remained submerged for several months, certainly through my teen years. My parents would have appreciated that too.

One of my favorite rides was Rocket to the Moon, where the seats would inflate and deflate to provide the sensation of taking off and landing, as well as flying through space. It was like a slowly deflating Whoopee cushion, minus the sound effects. Rocket to the Moon was exhilarating, as was Adventure Thru Inner Space, where a booming voice piped in through the loudspeakers informed you "You're getting smaller now!" The voice supposedly belonged to a scientist (okay, a voice-over actor) who informed you in his knowing tone that you were turning into the most minuscule formation of a snowflake. An eyeball peered down at you through the lens of a mighty microscope and watched your gaping mouth fall to the floor of your seating compartment.

In order to take this daring journey, guests had to ride the Atom-mobile and "shrink" to the size of a molecule or atom. According to the voice-over actor, you continued to shrink as you entered the crystalline structure only to find yourself in a sea of massive H_2O molecules. Electrons were now spinning all around your head as you penetrated the wall of an oxygen atom and contemplated what you were going to have for lunch at the Mickey and Minnie Café. Now you were facing directly into the glowing red nucleus of the atom. *Incredible!* As the snowflakes melted, you started getting larger again, and suddenly you're back in the moving vehicle and readying yourself to reluctantly crawl out of your seat. As the ride came to an end, the bouncy theme song "Miracles from Molecules" by Robert and Richard Sherman—the team responsible for the industrial-strength earworm "It's a Small World"—played on. The fantastical concept of passengers shrinking to the size of atomic particles became the hallmark of this attraction. And as we witnessed spinning atoms and molecules around us, we eventually spotted the tourists in the gift-store downstairs below us. Suddenly the jig was up. We were catapulted back to reality. There was a strange juxtaposition between losing yourself in the ride and at the same time enjoying the tops of people's heads as they purchased Donald Duck and Goofy hats and mugs below the tracks of the passenger carriages. You were inside and outside the ride at the same time, just as you were inside and outside the Eichler when in the atrium.

Our car trip to Las Vegas was memorable, and not because we stopped at Hoover Dam on a day when the thermometer read a thousand degrees. And not because the streets were lined with hotels that featured exciting names like Sahara, Dunes, Golden Nugget, Aladdin, and Tropicana. In the early Sixties, Vegas wasn't the destination it is now. Today, there are child-friendly attractions and hotels. In 1962, it was a city for "adults only," providing adult mischief. Once we arrived at some side-street motel situated off the main Vegas Strip, my mother managed to find a babysitting service where parents could drop the kids off in a small, stuffy room while the parents gambled their kids' college funds away. Harold and I sat in the back of the minuscule room on metal folding chairs and watched the jumpy images of wild animals roaming free for several hours. But we weren't free. We were glued to uncomfortable seating. I was certain my parents would never return to scoop us up. They were too busy eating free shrimp cocktails and playing the nickel machines. We sat and sat in this stifling room, our buttocks sore from the metal chairs, until we were the last kids waiting around for pickup.

Finally, my father poked his head in the door and said, "Come on. It's time to eat."

I had never before felt such an overwhelming wave of relief move through me. No more lions, tigers, and bears. No more movies of dry desert terrain and needle-covered cacti with a shaky soundtrack and unintelligible narrative. We were off to the all-you-can-eat buffet line for a dry and crumbly dessert.

The only place we would travel to on a recurring basis was a campground located in the Sierra Nevada Mountains outside Lake Tahoe. This high-in-the-sky campground situated at 7,114 feet in elevation was called Echo Lake. The grounds featured funky residences that had a half-tent upper portion and a cabin body for a base. It wasn't really camping; it was like half-camping, or top-half camping. And Echo Lake contained swarms of regulation pests. The campgrounds were eighty percent mosquitos, ten percent poison oak, and ten percent wildlife. There were no in-cabin toilets or showers, but there were copious amounts of pine cones and squirrels. A community restroom and shower required a lengthy jaunt for middle-of-the-night trips to the bathroom, so we made certain we did our business—all of it—before we headed to bed.

Unfortunately, the air was too cold to relax our urethra and sphincter muscles, so we'd sit there visualizing waterfalls and other means of surrender. Youngsters and adults lined up at the sink, shivering in the icy community restrooms and brushing chattering teeth. We'd often fake the brushing ritual long enough to excuse ourselves, run back to our half-tent/half-cabin shelter, and hop into our warm and cozy flannel-lined sleeping bags.

Harold and I rarely saw my parents when we vacationed at Echo Lake. As soon as we piled our suitcases onto the springs of the single bed base and threw our sleeping bags, radios, pillows, and other miscellaneous doohickeys onto its shaky coils, Joe and Blossom were off to meet their Eichler neighbors and new friends for Happy Hour with assorted beverages. The boisterous bunch quickly took over the entire campground, with their collection of hard liquor and domestic beers for this seemingly undomesticated crowd. The soundtrack of their alcohol-infused hours of cackles, whoops, and hollers was loud and legendary. An occasional caterwaul would escape the boozy deck and echo off the canyons and nearby lake. No wonder they called it Echo Lake.

Happy Hour didn't last an hour or two. It was an all day, all night affair. This gin and vodka love-fest was the magnet that pulled parents to Echo Lake for a celebration of fresh air, gin, whiskey, and freedom, mostly from the kids. Left in the cabin/tents to fend for ourselves, we quickly learned to do just that. There was plenty of mischief to be had in those wooded acres, not the least of which was hanging out at the arts and crafts tent, developing crushes on fellow campmates, and collecting and exchanging Bazooka Bubble Gum wrappers from the on-site general store. We managed to chew acres of gum.

One night after the tooth-brushing ritual, I returned to my tent, curled up in my undersized sleeping bag, and hugged my knees to my chest in a shivering ball. I shared a cabin/tent with my brother. My parents were God-knows-where. Our sleeping bags, sitting on the noisy coiled single bed frames, would have been much more comfortable placed directly on the hard ground. The beds squeaked and squawked every time I moved a muscle or appendage. Why were there no mattresses in the wilderness? Even a mattress the density of a sliver of paper would have been appreciated.

*Adult Happy Hour
at Echo Lake Camp
near Tahoe.*

I was deep in my sleeping bag and even deeper in sleep when the sound of rustling inside the cabin/tent woke me. I didn't see anything as I peered out into pitch-black night, but the noise was loud enough to speed my heart rate. The scent of evergreens was heavy in the night air as I tried to quiet my nerves and fall back asleep. I had no idea what time it was, but morning couldn't come soon enough.

I went back to sleep hoping that the next time I was awakened by a noise, it would be the mess hall bell calling the campground to community breakfast. The sun would be rising, and my mother would be staggering into our shelter to rustle around in her suitcase, scouting out her red lipstick case and a circular cardboard container of foundation by Coty. She never strayed from this drugstore brand of loose face powder and used it for over four decades. I couldn't wait to grow up and dust myself in the same loose powder. What it did for or to her, I had no idea. Her porcelain skin appeared the same with or without it.

But what was that noise in my cabin late at night? Did I imagine it? The great reveal didn't happen at the Echo Lake Campground. When we got home from the trip, my parents began the ritual of shaking out our sleeping bags in the living room. Much to our surprise, an assortment of the tiniest baby chipmunks dropped out of the bag. They were alive! Apparently, the mother had managed to crawl into my sleeping bag, give birth, and run out for food. No wonder there was rustling around in the cabin that night. The babies were napping in the bottom of my sleeping bag, but their mother was not. After the shrieking stopped—mostly mine—we moved into a collective panic. What were we going to do with all these infant orphans?

My father called the local veterinary hospital to ask for advice, but their advice was to let them croak. Without their mother, they weren't going to survive. I cried for a week. I thought it was my fault. After all, it was my sleeping bag that had attracted the mother who gave birth. We pulled away from Echo Lake before she had a chance to return to her young brood. Despite my empathy for the babies, I cringed at the thought of sleeping with so many creatures near my toes at the foot of my bag. Had their lives not been tragically cut short, those chipmunks could have gone on to become the next Simon, Theodore, and Alvin.

There's an old Hebrew saying, "When one cries, the other tastes salt." I was burdened with excessive compassion and being highly attuned to the suffering of others. I was what some would term an *empath*—a person who could not only sense, but also take on another person's sadness or happiness in their own body. Without effort or design, I managed to feel what they were feeling, even baby critters in sleeping bags. The curse of empathy would follow me my entire life. If there was distress hovering about, I pulled it in and wrapped a blanket of concern around its wobbly shoulders. And when my own mother or a baby chipmunk cried, I cried too, right down to the depth of my soul.

* ⚛ *

During another trip to Echo Lake, a massive thunderstorm came rolling into the campgrounds in the middle of the night. At two in the morning, my mother shook our sleeping, hypothermic bodies as we tried to hold steady to our warm dream state. The rain pounded relentlessly on the cabin's tent top while my mother primed us. My father had decided to leave and head home because of the weather. Now?

"Yes, and let's go. You know your father."

If I had a nickel for every time my mother said, "You know your father," I'd be in the top one percent of the wealthiest citizens in this country.

With our wool coats swollen with rain and pajamas drenched, as if they had taken a swim in the washer, we piled into the car. My father turned the key, but it took five or six attempts to wake the motor. It must have been in dreamland too. We backed out of our parking space very carefully so as not to rouse the remaining residents of the campground who were fast asleep and not at all troubled by the rain. Why were we?

My father maneuvered the sharp twists and turns of that precipitous mountain road with the skills of Magellan moving through the straits. The rain was a mad fist pounding on the hood of our car. I couldn't determine whatever was in front of the nose of our hood. I couldn't even see the hood. It was not only pouring rain, but the fog was as thick as a French Vanilla shake. It remained soupy and blinding down that endless spiraling road.

At any other time, I would have been frightened by such a colossal storm. But on this particular moonless night, as I lay in the back of the car and gazed at the profile of the godlike navigator spinning the car wheel, I felt profoundly shielded and serene. Did you ever have someone in your life holding steady and being resilient through every twist and turn in the obstacle course? That person was my father, and I was nothing like him. I was a wobbly presence, always unsure of my footing. But my father was another breed altogether. He plowed through the night, maneuvered the barely visible road and ferocious storm, and pierced the darkness with his X-ray vision as we sailed around one blind curve after another. The dense fog was no match for my father's superpowers. I believed he could accomplish anything. In that moment, he was superhuman, slashing through the elements like a seasoned bushman through the undergrowth. He knew what he had to do. He was a soldier of the dark sky, master of our family, and commander-in-chief of our vehicle. Adrenaline fueled his decision-making, and he never wavered; he never flinched.

That night, and throughout my childhood, despite our differences and difficulties, my father was the almighty savior. In my home, we were raised without a God, a Lord, or Jesus Christ. But in my mind and heart, my father was a god of sorts, especially that night. His commanding grasp on that wheel, his vision in a four-hour staring contest with the highway's broken white line as he moved his nuclear family through the arduous elements and merciless darkness, cut through the depth of night like a man with a cool steel machete shaped like a Dodge Dart.

Lady and the Camp

I took one vacation without my family. My friend Heather invited me to go camping with her family. Genuine camping. My mother couldn't understand such craziness, but off I went without her blessing.

Heather and her parents, John and Betty, names right out of the *Dick and Jane* book series, took frequent trips to Big Sur. This was the first place I went camping—real camping. Not Jewish camping, with half cabins/half tents, a mess hall, a country store with Bazooka Bubble Gum, and craft classes, but raw camping complete with a Coleman stove, s'mores, spiders, and wild boars. Sleeping outside under the stars with the perfume of evergreens and coolness of dawn and dusk that permeated even the densest winter coat. So ... this was the great outdoors, eh?

Although I was filled with the usual angst and hesitation about trying something new, I agreed to join them on this adventure. Heather became carsick on the steep climb and the curvy Highway 1, but I barely noticed the clutched barf bag. I was too enamored with the scenery, as waves of lush greenery rushed by my window. I also felt a sense of relief that, for once, I wasn't the one throwing up. I was entering a new world and one that my parents, the New Yorkers, would never know. That in itself was exciting, and more than a little terrifying. As I cranked the handle downward, a gush of freedom blew in from my car window. I closed my eyes, smiled, and inhaled this new sea-kissed oxygen. I could nearly taste the pine needles on my tongue.

Once we arrived at our designated campground, Heather and I scooted away from her parents as they set up tents, camp chairs, and cooking equipment. That was their job. Our job was to get in as much trouble as possible in the shortest amount of time. As we ventured up a nearly vertical path and came upon a waterfall and stream, we witnessed an exhibit of naked bodies draped across the boulders like flesh-colored towels on a bathroom floor. Other fleshy men and women were showering beneath the cascading water. A heavy scent of dope saturated the air. We thought we were in a dream. We never wanted to wake up.

The nudists were a few years older than we were, so we didn't join them in disrobing. We watched from our distant rock as they washed their long hair in the falling water. Curious and enchanted, we observed their inhibitions as they washed away in the waterfall. Men's erections sporadically popped out. It was a classic Sixties landscape and included a panorama of pubic hair, coarse as steel wool scrubbers, male wood on parade and steady as hat racks, and breasts from pert to swaying melons. We wanted to be them, but we weren't quite comfortable with our prepubescent bodies. Our breasts were barely visible, our hips were narrow, and our pubic hair had not yet multiplied. But they were all so free, so beautiful. We wanted to be beautiful too.

* ⚛ *

At night, Heather and I lay outside while her parents housed themselves in an adult-sized tent. We were determined to sleep under the stars instead of in a shelter, even though her parents had provided a two-person tent for us in the shape of a hot dog bun.

As we lay under the redwood trees and the night sky, nestled in our sleeping bags and drinking in the dampness saturated with the sound of crickets, Heather whispered, "Wait! I see something. Don't move."

Sure enough, there were several vicious-looking piglike creatures discharging otherworldly sounds. The curious four-legged grunting hunters moved in closer as they circled our campsite, scaring the hell out of two young girls.

"Wild boars! If you talk, they'll attack!" Heather warned.

We hushed. We stayed hushed. Heather fell asleep under her heavy-weighted blanket, and I stayed on hyper-vigilant patrol to make sure we didn't perish in the night. I finally dozed off and awoke to the scent of bacon suspended above our campsite like some salty 'n' scrumptious perfume. Heather's father, whom I had spun into the textbook-perfect parent, was making the most flawless pancakes. The wild boars had raided our breakfast cereal, but left us enough for a tantalizing outdoor-style breakfast. Decent fellows.

After Heather's parents had visited the campground store to replenish our food supply, the two of us girls grabbed our own individual cardboard boxes from the Kellogg's Cereal Jumbo Variety Pack. We carefully punched the top of the box and the perforated line with our fingernails, pounded open the entrance with the end of our spoons, and poured milk into the small cardboard vessel of deliciousness suffused with sugar. Before our breakfast became too soggy, we devoured every cinnamon-coated Apple Jack bit and Sugar Pop morsel. Meanwhile, Heather's parents broke their two gigantic rectangles of Shredded Wheat apart in the deep blue and white speckled camping bowls and let them float in two percent low-fat milk until they were a perfect mixture of moisture and dry hay. The sensual bliss of the great outdoors, courtesy of Battle Creek.

The next night Heather and I took a short hike and ran across a couple of teenage boys around our age. I was coupled with the charming blond kid who looked like he knew a thing or two about girls. Once the sun began to set, we wandered down the campground service road. He took my hand. I didn't know where Heather had wandered off to, but I figured she was in good hands. The blond boy and I stood at the side of the road kissing like you kiss outdoors, feeling every gentle breeze and pine tree waving in your direction, cheering you on.

Suddenly, a park ranger drove up to us in his service truck, nearly toppling two kissing fools.

"You kids are not supposed to be out here. I'm taking you back to camp. There are some people worried about you. Get in!"

We jumped into the vehicle, and the driver dropped me at our campsite where I proceeded to get a verbal lickin' from Heather's parents. Heather was already snug in her sleeping bag with brushed teeth and brushed flannel pajamas.

"You can't just wander off. We didn't know where you were or if you were safe! How could you do such a thing?"

I was in trouble. I knew what it felt like to get in trouble at home, but here with different parents it was not half bad. These people seemed genuinely concerned about my safety. They didn't want me in danger. I felt strangely relieved and pleased, as if someone had given me a precious gift. That is, until they separated Heather and me, and we had to sleep in separate quarters—the campground version of grounding. I never saw the boy with the skillful mouth again. As his image faded, I silently uttered a non-denominational prayer and hoped a bear didn't eat him.

Pour More J and B

My father scoffed at doctors and their warnings. He scoffed as he inhaled the smoke he insisted he wasn't inhaling. Years later, I concluded that smoking that damn pipe probably did him more good than harm. It calmed him, and he needed calming at regular intervals because we had a great amount of restlessness and anxious foliage quivering in my family tree.

Smoke from my father's pipe was absorbed in the mahogany walls of our Eichler. It sat in loveseat and chair fabrics and meshed itself into our household rugs and the various paintings on the wall. I loathed tobacco smoke and the stink of it. I loathed the headaches and eye irritation it caused me and my family. I dreaded being locked in our car with it. But I loved that it pacified Dad. I loved the ritual of going to the drugstore with him to pick up a can of his favorite tobacco—Revelation—in the yellow, black, and red canister. I loved that it became his signature look; a curvilinear pipe draped from his mustached mouth. I didn't like what it did to his lungs, the furniture, and his family. On a daily basis, my mom would inform anyone who would listen that the second-hand smoke from his omnipresent pipe would kill her. She muttered it until she was 85.

✳ ⚛ ✳

Stoically, my mom sat on our tweed chartreuse couch like Queen for a Day. Unfortunately the set for this scene includes other chartreuse furnishings, such as matching lamps, tables, and bookcases, all in that disturbing shade of green that seemed to glow in the dark. During the Sixties era, my mother looked like Mary Tyler Moore on *The Dick Van Dyke Show*. Her hair was piled in a mile-high bouffant using a gallon of Aqua Net, which turned it into a solid mass; her Revlon red-lipsticked mouth was wide and toothy, and her pale skin contrasted with raven black hair. Her beauty? Undeniable. She had a soft round face, Jewish nose, saucer-like brown eyes, and tubular limbs, unlike mine that were reedy and fat-free. My mother was bulky and would fight her weight issues with suffocating girdles and every fab fad diet that emerged in the Sixties and Seventies. But her mouth showed no trace of calamity or struggle, unlike the chartreuse tragedy/comedy masks nailed on the wall in our hallway. Every smile on my mother's face was the same. Deceptive and overly pleasant.

Mom in our living room.

But my mother was not the only restless housewife in our Eichler neighborhood who rejected an apron and abhorred the vacuum cleaner and wash day. Many young mothers in the Sixties seemed to want to throw up their hands and walk out to see if there was another way to live. Yet the housewife role was thoroughly ingrained. They were told that they were born to borrow sugar and fold laundry. They were bored but had found themselves in a life surrounded by gingham tablecloths, recipe exchanges, babysitting pools, and gossipy neighbors. Isn't that what they had always wanted? Such a role had been drummed into them until they started to believe it.

Yet, some young mothers in the Eichlers started to question a role that had been expected. A few ran away from home and from their families, returning to a single life, leaving children in their father's care to fend for themselves without a mother. Several of my friends had mothers like that who were suddenly MIA. Mommy had packed a bag and run off in the middle of the night. They went back to old goals or ex-lovers, or charted a brand-new life sans housework.

For the mothers who remained in this suburban Eichler oasis, many of them found other ways to entertain themselves. They went back to school, opened card tables and held happy hours with neighbors in their family room. Sometimes those hours went on for days.

A good number of women in the neighborhood postponed their educations until their kids were old enough to go to school. Simultaneous with the feminist movement, my mother and many of our neighbors enrolled at community colleges or San Jose State University and left their kids at home with the babysitter, commonly known as the boob-tube or, in our household, the idiot box. My brother and I had a new babysitter every night. Sometimes it was Gidget, other times it was Lucy.

Hear Us Roar

There were a lot of alcoholic parents in our neighborhood and a lot of moms on Valium. Even with the appearance of serene suburbia, there were still stressors in the Sixties that pills were needed to soothe and comfort. It seemed The Rolling Stones were singing about our neighborhood in "Mother's Little Helper."

My mother kept a bottle of those little yellow pills in our bathroom cabinet. I don't know why, other than it was trendy. It certainly wasn't because of nerves. My mother was calm as a tranquilized elephant. If she had any worries, they never revealed themselves. She already took life in slow motion, unless she was doing battle with my father. That was the only time I saw the hair on her head expand like a porcupine and her face contort like some flabbergasted cartoon character. On more than one occasion I would pop one or two of her curious yellow pills. I thought they were powerful aspirin coated with a promise to keep all types of pain at bay. In some ways, they were.

Some of the parents in The Eichlers had psychic pain they were trying to manage. Why did they have it in the first place? Was it the raising of kids? Was it their spouse's infidelity, which seemed to be an epidemic in the Eichlers of Willow Glen? Was it the shifting of women's roles and aspirations from Fifties to Sixties sensibility that was causing confusion? What was all the adult drinking and pill-popping about?

Women's Lib was alive and well, and so was the use of the birth control pill. My mother was taking them. She didn't want another rug-rat when she was launching her new life in night school, working at various department stores during the day, or juggling my father's many moods in the air like some circus act on a variety show.

Many of the mothers and wives in our neighborhood had a sudden thirst for a college degree and a cigarette called Virginia Slims. One of the most famous advertising campaigns in U.S. history had its launch in 1968. "You've come a long way, baby" was the provocative tagline for a new, thinner cigarette produced by the Phillip Morris Company and marketed specifically to women. "You've come a long way, baby" became an instant national catchphrase. The campaign meshed well with the budding feminist consciousness and the rise of "The New Woman," a woman who was independent, self-sufficient, and eager to demonstrate her confidence.

The first test market was San Francisco, a few miles north of Santa Clara County, but Virginia Slim ads were plastered on billboards nationwide. Television ads featured women of the early twentieth century being punished for smoking cigarettes. Suddenly smoking was being connected with a set of traits in this era of equality: independence, slimness, glamour, and liberation. The ads featured attractive and fashionable actresses, and women were buying it. Young mothers everywhere demanded their own chronic respiratory condition. Sock it to me! As it happened, the only equality this campaign ended up supporting was lung cancer. Today, women and men die at similar rates from that disease.

A few years later came the embellished Eve cigarettes, which in contrast to the empowering Virginia Slim ad campaign were marketed to those who wanted to look feminine while smoking. Eve used feminine artwork and marketing, even with the cigarette itself, which was long and slim, originally 100mm and lengthened to 120mm within two years. Tobacco giant Liggett & Myers intended for Eve to be identified with the feminine ideals of Twiggy-type slimness. The cigarettes were decorated with flowers, signifying that this was a ladies' brand. They were even marketed in association with a fashion line, featuring colors and floral prints that matched the Eve cigarette pack design. Eve offered an equal opportunity smoker's cough.

Is Anything Okay?

Some of the neighbors under the Eichler dome were Jewish, but they were not like my nuclear family of non-practicing Jews. They went to temple for high holidays, studied the Torah, and sent their kids to Hebrew school. In my family, we practiced Judaism by eating deli food on a regular basis and remaining in a constant state of agitation. Although he was raised in the Jewish faith, attended Hebrew school, and had a bar mitzvah, my father was a self-proclaimed atheist. He remained skeptical of organized thought, distrustful of religious leaders, and non-spiritual in the traditional religious sense. Yet he was generous to his friends and family and cared about politics, applauding those who did right and good. What he did or didn't do, he did out of ethics rather than religious rules. My father's religion was sarcasm, skepticism, and sound advice.

My mother, on the other hand, considered herself agnostic. Maybe there was a God. Maybe there wasn't. "Why is that my business?" she'd ask, not requiring or requesting a response. Neither of my parents believed in God, but my mother always held the door ajar just in case there was something—or someone—hovering about. She frequently asked out loud, "How could a good God allow such bad things to happen?" She had a point.

Dad's own reckless rants involved everything else. Politicians (whom he referred to as "a bunch of lying thieves"), the IRS, ungrateful and undeserving celebrities, dogs making piles on our front lawn, and the foolishness of the unwinnable wars we watched on the nightly news with Chet Huntley and David Brinkley. The only leaders my father followed were The Three Wise Men—Larry, Moe, and Curly—and his gurus Laurel and Hardy. He didn't ask too many questions about existence nor ponder the big questions. But I did.

I believed there was a non-examined life and a too-examined life. There were two kinds of people in the world: detectives and non-detectives. Detectives were always trying to figure out why things happened, how they happened, and why they didn't happen when they were supposed to. The non-detectives were oblivious to such matters and shopped at Kmart, or spent weekends watching someone hit a little white ball into a hole on the golf channel. The members of the second group got on with the business of living their lives, but not necessarily examining them. I preferred to be a member of the golf group, but alas, the die had been cast. You are assigned one side, and you play on that team from birth to death.

Like many other members of my tribe, I mentally turned worries over and over until I was distracted or exhausted or I simply didn't care any longer. Nearly every Jew I've ever met suffers from terminal anxiety. With a history filled with distress (or in Yiddish terms, *tsuris*), we likely developed a DNA mutation in our genes known as: If anything can go wrong, it will. It's a motto that flows through our veins and travels throughout the bloodline.

All my relatives were like Goldilocks. Forget porridge. We were either too cold or too hot. We needed a sweater, or we needed the air conditioning turned on, then off. The pastrami was either terribly tough or much too lean. Soup? Too cold. No, too hot. Nothing was right. Furthermore, we weren't happy unless we were discussing food and how extraordinarily delicious or horrifically inedible it was. We could hardly wait for supper, and we could barely contain ourselves when it came to complaining about it. It's too salty, too fatty, too generous a portion, as if too large a portion were such a thing among the Jewish people. It's like the age-old joke where the waiter comes over to the table and asks a group of Jewish women, not "Is everything okay?" but rather, "Is *anything* okay?"

Our tribal mutterings around the house consisted of deep sighs, exclamations of *feh!*, melodies of moaning, wails, and laments, and a lot of *oy veys*. My father coined the expression "Oy mush!" and used it frequently. I don't think it was a genuine phrase from Yiddish or anything that appeared in Hebrew. It was his creation and he used it often. It was every sound of disgust rolled into one neatly wrapped package.

Jews owned worry and anxiety. We were the champions of angst, the kings and queens of pain. Our collective goal in life was to stop worrying about worrying so much. Sure, we kept therapists in practice with our examinations and reexaminations of past actions or inactions. We not only didn't know peace in Israel, we didn't know it in our own psyches.

Unfortunately, anxiety and worry are not seen as virtues, but as unpleasant weaknesses. They are 6,000 years of collective discomfort about survival and thriving coursing through the body of every Jew on the planet. For centuries, being Jewish has also meant a curiosity and an enthusiasm about questions, discussing, scrutinizing, dissecting, and arguing over every aspect of human existence. Such questioning and examination is the heart of being Jewish, and despite being kept at a discernible distance from temples, Judaic rituals, holiday practices, and any form of religious training, I inherited this trait along with the cockeyed hair wave on the right side of my head and my prominent schnoz.

I eventually convinced myself that anxiety, uneasiness, and unquenchable thirst for answers and knowledge were desirable traits. Even existential philosopher Søren Kierkegaard managed to make the argument for anxiety. There's a history of claiming that anxiety is a sign that the people doing the worrying are in a higher intellectual state than those who don't worry as much. They are more alert and alive to life's absurdities and contradictions. They have a sharper focus, and their sensitive skin serves them well in fields that involve creativity. In short, my people are conscious as hell and questioning to the point of annoyance. Is that so wrong? I convinced myself that it wasn't. I had to. What else could I do with a boatload of anguish?

In some ways, the Jewish people are bipolar, with excruciating highs and euphoria when it comes to certain matters (e.g., food) and devastating lows when it comes to every other thing in existence. We are depressed and despondent about all things, then suddenly and miraculously, we are carried to the mountaintop of exuberance. Jews have no middle ground. No baseline of normalcy. It's all or nothing with my people. We have no appreciation for fifty shades of gray. Give us chocolate or vanilla and let my people go … eat!

Fairgroover

The real trouble began in adolescence when my mom's shoes matched our bright orange shag living room rug and I didn't match anyone in my family. I started to look outside our Eichler home and into our cul-de-sac for affirmation and affection.

I was inquisitive about people and wanted to discover who they truly were. I wasn't interested in the facade presented to the world, like my own mother on the phone, twisting the cord around her fingers while she discussed the weather or the latest gossip about the party guests, chatted about the happenings at the last Democratic Club meeting, and announced the sale on cotton balls at the Rexall Drugstore, among other tiresome trivialities. I was after the authentic story that sat beneath the surface; the psychological manifestations of discontent and joy. I wanted to write articles and conduct interviews on important matters. I wanted to probe into the lives of others to find similarities and differences. Hell, I was after just one person who might be more like me than my immediate family.

This quest to find the truth behind the mask budded early. At age ten, I decided it would be a decent idea to create a neighborhood newsletter. It would focus on the ten houses in our cul-de-sac and the neighbors and strangers behind those colorful Eichler doors. What really went on behind the windowless frontage of each home? I was on a mission to find out, or at least to find out more.

The Fairgroover newsletter contained all the news on our cul-de-sac families. With pad and pencil in hand, I ran around the radius of our short block and interviewed the adults about their grownup lives. In other words, I asked about things that were none of my damn business. Although I was terribly shy, I relished the interview process. It gave me a welcome sense of control, and the reporter's instruments felt as natural in my hand as a butterfly net. Candid questions were fired at Mr. Churchfield and Mrs. Reedy to uncover their interior landscape. I was a nervous wreck in front of a class of elementary school students, *shvitzing* like I was in a warehouse with no air-conditioning. I repeatedly lost my place during my oral book report, but speaking with people one-on-one was in my comfort zone. This intimate form of communication would manifest repeatedly throughout my life.

I even purchased a compact green reel-to-reel tape recorder at the Safeway grocery store. It was my prized possession for many years until the tape twirled off the reel and all over the floor. The brand name of the tape recorder was even Safeway, which seemed odd at the time and still does. I thought they specialized in produce and breakfast cereal. I have no idea why Safeway was selling small tape recorders, but you don't ask such questions when you're ten years old. I'd slide this new technology under my bed, invite friends to my room, simultaneously press the ON and RECORD buttons, and begin to ask penetrating and ridiculous questions. It's a good thing I wasn't sued for secretly recordings unsuspecting friends. Nixon could have learned a thing or two from me.

A Brazen in the Sun

I clearly recall the day sexual desire arrived. It was like someone turning on the switch near my pelvis, and it involved—you guessed it—Elvis. Images of him and some of the other "teen idols" in my *Tiger Beat* and *16* magazines would curl my toes and rock my world. I wanted to experience something with them. I just didn't know what.

The initial teen stars were androgynous. Bobby Sherman, Paul Anka, Fabian, Dion, Bobby Rydell, and Frankie Avalon. Gray, soft-focus pictures of them torn from magazines wallpapered my bedroom walls. In my imagination, each boy was polite, neatly dressed, gentle, and asexual. But now I was ready for a boy who was not necessarily a fold-out with a staple in his ear. I was ready for adolescence. I was ready for actual contact. I was ready to be kissed.

* ⚛ *

Spin the Bottle was a reliable Eichler neighborhood activity that took place in various venues. Often it was in Marvin Reedy's yard behind his side fence or in his garage on the cold concrete floor with a group of kids huddled around one another like they were staring at a campfire, not a bottle. In fifth or sixth grade, we were not well versed in kissing—or sex. To us, kissing *was* sex. As the bottle twirled, I hoped it would land on Blaine or Marvin, the only two boys around my age whom I wanted to kiss. If it didn't land where we wanted it to land, one of us would force the bottle in the direction of the most desirable lips. Whenever the bottle would spin to Heather, the boys would bark and holler and refuse to pucker up.

At this time, Heather was a flat-chested tomboy and not particularly keen on becoming an alluring female or sexual being quite yet. Oddly enough, she would become pregnant at age fifteen, long before any of the other girls in our group had even had intercourse or figured out how all the equipment on either side worked. Heather would receive the first abortion of the group, and long before the end of high school. At fifteen, she was chock-full of urges for boys and sexual favors that would rival even the most hormonally fueled teenager. But for now, in this cold garage with the taunts of chortling boys, she was the neighborhood tomboy. And even though I wasn't developing at a rapid pace either, I was the shiny apple of both Marvin's and Blaine's eye.

Boys began to take up more of my brain-space and hours in the day. I went from Elvis to teen idols to gazing at the four Beatles. I still hadn't been intimate with anyone yet, but something was stirring. The sexual tourist was beginning to squirm.

I frequently read through my father's paperback books on sex. He kept quite a few on the nightstand next to his side of the bed. Most of them had to do with chambermaids and feather dusters. I couldn't put those books down. The man does what? The woman has to … where? It made no sense. For the longest time I thought a man put his penis in a woman's vagina and left it there napping like a thick stick of dynamite until it started to quiver and quake out of seemingly nowhere. Then ... KA-BOOM! I didn't realize it required movement to ignite. I didn't realize a lot of things.

A Swell Soup

Campbell's Alphabet Soup was in a lot of mid-century kitchens. Childhood dreams were spelled out in broth, then immediately digested. We always had alphabet soup in our kitchen pantry, and it was always problematic because once the letters swelled, no one could tell a B from a D ... or an E from an F. How could we be expected to spell out or digest anything of substance with such a significantly flawed noodle? But we drank it because it was like white bread, bologna, or peanut butter. Soup was a childhood staple.

Whenever I was home from school with a cold or flu bug, my mother would do a disappearing act. She didn't want to catch what I had, but she managed to bring in cold toast and hot Lipton tea a couple of times a day. To this day, when I smell black tea leaves brewing, I immediately feel a rush of nostalgia for home. The tea was always too hot to drink, so she'd leave it on my nightstand. "Here, drink this when it cools." She would hold her breath, quickly scoot out of the room, and disappear for the rest of the day. On rare occasions, she would bring me crackers and tomato soup, my least favorite. As it burned a hole in my throat, I could feel it coating my esophagus with acid and harsh spices.

When I became terrifically ill with a 101-degree fever and some achy, sweaty, card-carrying bug, I hid under my covers and tried with all my might to will my body to heal before my father arrived home from work. By this time I was terrified of my father. When he got home from work, he'd raise his voice in angry tones and disgust about me staying out of school, then inform me that I wasn't sick. I could hear the hollers from the kitchen across the Eichler. "What do you mean she stayed home from school? No one stays home from school!" I slipped further under my blanket and covered my head with a pillow to muffle his next words. "Feh! She's going to school tomorrow. That's it! That's the end of it." I crawled deeper under my cotton shelter of blankets and started to whimper. I cried so hard one evening, my body went entirely numb. I couldn't feel my limbs or even sense them attached to my body. Every time his voice scratched the air, I fell deeper into dread and distress. I felt weak. Disgusting. Worthless. My feet were gone. My fingers wouldn't move. The sobbing had washed them away and into a sea of paralysis.

The times when my fever would spike dangerously high, Mom would arrive with one hand covering her mouth and a washcloth in the other hand to rub me down, being very careful not to touch my skin with her fingers. Germs! It felt like love, but it was a washcloth.

I came to hate being sick. I'd hide it as long as I could, and when I couldn't put on a false front any longer, I'd stay home from school buried under blankets, dreading the moment my dad pulled into the carport after work hours. Someone from my class would always bring over a binder with the day's homework, courtesy of my teacher. They seemed understanding at school, but at home it seemed I had the plague. No one wanted to get near me. Even to this day: sick = guilt = weakness. My father would have none of it.

"Get up! You're not sick. You're going to school tomorrow. Enough of this nonsense!" Most everything with my father was nonsense.

Strangely enough, I still yearned to be home in my room. I felt safe there. Not cared for, just safe. I sensed my household wasn't "normal" when I saw classmates bring their parents to Parent's Day and father-daughter dances. Unlike my classmates, it felt as though my brother and I were afterthoughts. My parents had bigger fish to fry and most of them had to do with adult activities: working, going out for Happy Hour, weekend adventures, parties, jam sessions. My brother and I were passengers on the back of their bus. We may have been a household of four people, but we were all coexisting in very separate worlds. My father could effortlessly spin a quiet gathering into a blazing hootenanny, my mother could play most tunes by ear, and my brother could do paradiddles on his Ludwig drum set 'til the cows or my folks came home, but I rattled around in their world like an observant alien, recording the nuances around me and turning them into whimsical poetry or short ditties. My only superpower was provided through a leaky pen.

Friends-4-Ever

Every year of my childhood brought me at least one buddy, sometimes two or three. A handful of those pals became lifelong friends because their reliability and commitment would stand the test of time. There were others who were what I would term seasonal friends, who came into my life for a time, perhaps for a school year or the span of a particular class. It was vital to not have lofty expectations of seasonal friends, as this could only lead to disappointment.

At the start of each school year, I scouted out new buddies seated at desks near mine. But I tended to hold on too tightly to my comrades, usually with both hands and with my heart planted firmly on my sleeve. Sometimes that heart became tattered when they were assigned a different classroom, transferred to another school, or—God forbid—moved to another community. They might as well have been in a spaceship headed to the moon.

Most of us had friends-by-proximity. Sometimes it was the closeness of two desks randomly placed in one classroom. The person kicking your chair behind you in Social Studies class became your friend. The person you were paired up with in sewing class became your best pal. The new kid you met in a summer school class when summer felt as endless as the drum solo in "In-A-Gadda-Da-Vida" became your best buddy. That is, until the new school year began. Then they shuffled off to parochial school while you went back to public school. The two kids who lived across the street were friends because, well, they were there and so were you. You had nothing in common with one another other than the fact that you avoided the same cracks in the sidewalk on the way to school. Nobody wanted to break their mother's back.

Two of my friends-via-classroom-proximity couldn't have been at further ends of the faith spectrum. Jill sat next to me in sixth grade. In this case, it was the only job requirement for being best friends. She wore her cottony white hair in a short 'do and sported dark blue glasses with the corners turned upward like someone in the secretarial pool. Jill appeared scholarly, and I looked like a Russian refugee. We had less in common than most, but we were fast friends. Her family was Christian. I soon felt out of place in their home and at their kitchen table, where grace was unintelligibly muttered before each meal and cloth mouth-dabbers were used in lieu of Safeway paper napkins. Several crosses hung in the hallways, where Jesus appeared to be having a bad day. I didn't understand her world, but I sidled up next to it and peeked inside.

Two years later, in eighth grade, while Apollo 8 was being launched, Donna Bednarski became my new best friend. She was from an Orthodox Jewish home where two sets of dishes were housed in a blue-and-white kitchen the size of a football field. Even in Donna's house, I felt like a gefilte fish out of water. I didn't understand the two sets of dishes. I wasn't that kind of Jew. I'm not sure what kind of Jew I was, but we never ate from two sets of dishes. We ate from floral melamine plates, aluminum trays brought to us by Swanson, and pie tins courtesy of Banquet.

The dietary needs of my family differed from most of my friends who were black or Christian. My father liked marbled meat, marbled rye, and marbled halvah, and ate a raw onion like it was an apple. The entire family consumed a variety of Jewish foodstuffs, but we considered it New York fare. *Blintzes*, bagels, matzo crackers, potato knishes, salty bites of pastrami on cornmeal dusted rye, and *kishka*, which was stuffed derma, made from … well, you don't want to know.

In Poland and Lithuania, *kornbroyt* or corn rye, was a tasty regional specialty. It was my father's favorite bread and through osmosis or genetics, became my favorite as well. Those little pieces of caraway seeds would stick between my teeth for days, but I didn't care. That was the price paid for a respectable pastrami sandwich on rye.

We also consumed our fair share of liver and onions, as well as chopped liver. My favorite, however, was *kreplach*, a delicacy that sounded much worse than it tasted. This ravioli-like dumpling stuffed with seasoned minced chicken perched in chicken stock with coarse sliced carrot was a soothing meal. There is a rabbinical debate on its origins. One rabbi claims it began when a fortune cookie fell into the soup stock. Another says it started in an Italian restaurant, and the owner yelled at the chef, "Dis-a pasta testes like krep!" At least that's the story my brother made up, and I believed it. I believed everything Harold told me.

Our freezer was stocked with boxes and boxes of blintzes, a part savory, part sweet treat. Blintzes are basically the Jewish answer to Crêpes Suzette. They were even offered on the menu at the local International House of Pancakes, where gentile customers never knew what the hell they were eating. In ignorant bliss, they served them half-frozen and told customers they were stuffed with cream. They weren't. They were stuffed with cold ricotta cheese doing its best vanilla ice cream impression.

My favorite Jewish delicacy by far was noodle *kugel,* which was the Jewish version of mac and cheese dish. It was akin to a sweet bread pudding but with noodles instead of bread. And it was fun to say. KOO gul!

My favorite snack cracker, *matzoh* (or *matzah* or *matzo* or *matza* or dry cracker), was spelled in an odd way, like everything else my family ate. Matzo crackers consisted of a mix of flour and water. No eggs or flavor in sight. When made especially well, it tastes like the side of a cardboard box recycled from the Tel Aviv city dump. That's why I favored the egg-and-onion-flavored variety. That particular flavor profile wasn't kosher, but neither were we. My taste buds eventually followed the flavor trail to snacks like Daisys, Whistles, and Bugles, crunchy cornmeal concoctions produced in whimsical shapes, some of which we stuck on our fingertips or played with before we ate them. For some reason we like to eat things that look like other things, like these General Mills snacks … and Barnum's Animal Crackers.

Wonder Bread was not kosher, but that colorful wrapper of red, blue, and yellow dots surrounding the word *WONDER* was a part of every sandwich prepared in our Eichler kitchen. The best thing about Wonder Bread was that you could roll the entire loaf into a ping-pong ball–sized doughy treat and fling it across the table at the sibling of your choice. I never did buy the hype that "Wonder Bread builds strong bodies twelve ways" unless, of course, they were referring to pitching the loaf across the room like a football.

Spaghetti and meatballs seldom appeared in my house, although we did have Swedish meatballs, which my mother made in the pressure cooker for parties and social gatherings. Think meatballs swimming in a can of sweet-and-sour sauce. On those occasions when I was invited to dinner at a friend's house and I was served spaghetti and meatballs, I was drawn to that garlicky tomato sauce. I thought I had found a golden tureen of enchanting red sauce at the end of the rainbow … and it was filled with pasta noodles.

Go Greyhound

At a young age, I became well acquainted with bus travel, be it Greyhound or the San Jose City bus system. Plunk went the coins into the metal slot. I took a seat, sat back, and watched the carnival of performers and pedestrians unfold. Prior to taking my daily jaunts from school to home, my mother would often take my brother and me for daylong excursions on weekends to San Francisco via Greyhound bus. In downtown San Jose's Greyhound bus station, we purchased our tickets beside the disheveled and forgotten. The station's waiting area was always littered with homeless souls, the intoxicated, and screaming babies bundled close to their mothers. Paper sacks were suitcases stuffed with clothing and bottles of vodka. Shopping carts piled high with possessions decorated the station. I always thought that's why it was called Greyhound: everything inside and outside the station felt gray, decaying, and dismal. The pavement around the station was always perfumed with a fine mixture of urine and gin.

My father never accompanied us on these day trips. He wasn't a doer like my mother; he was a stay-at-homer. We hopped up the stairs to our bus seats as the driver moved our sleepy metal caterpillar on wheels through the broken corners of downtown San Jose. We crept towards the City by the Bay. The grand maneuvers of our vehicle, the gentle roar as the engine accelerated, and the magical way the big banana slug managed sharp corners fascinated me as we plowed through the graffiti and garbage of downtown. Our bus filled with lookie-loos peered into the backyards of East San Jose residents. We gawked downward at the worn furniture, dead strollers, and black metal barbeques from our high perch. Someone had torn the skirt off of the lives of the poorest residents. We ogled their personal spaces, fragmented belongings, browning lawns, and back views of their dwelling from our Trojan high horse on wheels. This was a part of the city that often went unseen. To Willow Glen residents, regions of downtown San Jose were like a Third World country. To my brother and me, it was a rude awakening and felt more like the neighborhoods of my grandparents in Brooklyn and the Bronx than Santa Clara Valley. Through a smudged bus window, we learned about homelessness, alcoholism, broken fences with trash-lined backyards, and the slow decay of poverty shoved into those forgotten corners of the Bay Area.

We pulled into the station in San Francisco, hopped down the steps, and wandered around the city streets. The three of us shared a five dollar bowl of warm wonton soup in a basement-level café, then made our way to Chinatown and purchased boxes of rice candies bound in edible wrappers. Occasionally I'd get a colorful plastic hand fan that would fold and unfold for the entire duration of the bus ride home.

Every shop in Chinatown carried identical merchandise; it was just arranged differently on the shelves. We'd ride the cable car up and back to Ghirardelli Square, make our way on foot to the bus terminal, puffing up one long vertical block after the other. I was sure we'd eventually reach the top of the sky. Once in the station, I was allowed to purchase a tuna salad sandwich wrapped in plastic from the vending machine. That feast would accompany me on our ride home. There was something about the way they mixed the relish with the tuna and mayonnaise that dazzled my taste buds every time I took a bite. I had no idea how to recreate the recipe, but I vowed to try. It seemed to be mixed with a little magic.

We took our bus seats. The engine revved up and jolted forward through the dark and dimly lit parking lot to the streets peppered with hookers, addicts, and couples with their arms wrapped around each other like mink stoles to ward off the cold. We were on our journey homeward while they were out for a night on the town. But San Francisco wasn't our town. We were just visiting, and we felt like tourists. The sky was now black except for a few blinks of headlights and store signs. I wondered about the lives of those silhouetted in the apartment buildings above, where they watched *The Ed Sullivan Show* on television. What did they eat? Who did they eat with?

I'll never forget that street scene of pedestrians and the divine tuna salad sandwiched between two pieces of white sticky bread as we exited town on a gassy Greyhound as the sun was dropping in the sky like a raw egg into a massive bowl of egg drop soup.

Tilt-a-Girl

Every year when the Santa Clara County fair opened, Tilt-A-Whirl was the ride I ran to first. I'd be thrown side to side and spin on its precarious frame of twisted metal. Harold wouldn't accompany me as he always became sick and dizzy while whirling and twirling. Motion didn't agree with him, but it was my favorite sensation. When I was spinning or being lifted on a ride, it was like being caught in the middle of a tornado where I was helpless to the forces around me. I liked the sensation of throwing my arms in the air and letting go. I seldom let go at home. I always had a protective force around me to ward off harm and hurt. Here, I had permission to fall back and fly through the air. It was freeing.

When I was fourteen, my friend Donna Bednarski and I took a city bus to the Santa Clara County Fair. First on our agenda was checking out the cutest boys. We would survey the landscape with the detective eyes of Honey West or Columbo. Rides, exhibits, boys, animals … food! Visiting the food booths had to be first on the menu.

One day, we quickly gobbled up a hotdog-on-a-stick coated in corn meal and smothered in gobs of mustard, then headed to the entrance gate of Tilt-A-Whirl. A minute or two into the ride, my friend Donna's face began turning pale, then green. She covered her mouth with her hand, but a small dab of cornmeal began to seep out of each corner. A mere preview of things to come. I could plainly see that this twisty ride was not going to turn out well. I had never seen or heard about projectile vomit, but I witnessed it that day, and it readied me for my first viewing of *The Exorcist* a few years later.

Both of us turned with begging eyes to the acne-cheeked ride operator, pleading with him to halt the ride early. He looked back at us for a moment, chuckled under his breath, and ignored my plea and Donna's scrunched face. She looked like she just ate an entire lemon. As soon as the ride came to a halt, Donna quickly unlatched her seatbelt, bolted out of our seating compartment, and hightailed it towards the ladies' room like the Roadrunner. *Beep Beep!* Get out of her way! I'm sorry to report that Donna didn't quite make it to Destination: Toilet Bowl. It's a very good thing there was sawdust on the ground, as she covered several square feet of it with a mixture of chewed hot dog, cornmeal, relish, and ketchup as it soared in a horizontal line. I wasn't sure what I was seeing, but I was quite certain it wasn't good.

I dragged Donna to the nurse's station, conveniently located inside the rides section, and sat quietly while they gave her something to soothe her tummy. Within minutes she seemed to recover and was good to go. Suffering some form of carnival amnesia, we ran off to stuff our faces. Cotton candy, candy apples, more corndogs, and bananas dipped in hard chocolate. "Let's go on Tilt-A-Whirl a second time!" Life was yummy again.

Soon our focus turned to meeting and making out with boys. They could be any boys. Boys from other schools, boys a bit older, boys with blue T-shirts. We weren't fussy. As we headed to the *4-Photos-for-a-Quarter* booth with the scent of farm animals in the air, we scouted out the dusty prairie of the fairgrounds for male victims. Within an hour, one or both of us were buried under some stranger's sweatshirt on the grass, deep in cuddling with cute boys we'd never see again. But for now, our hearts were tilting and whirling in the summer sun.

Mom's the Word

My mother felt she was destined for a different sort of life. Like her own mother, who was always berating her husband because she didn't have the life she deserved, my mother regretted and resented her own lot in life: two kids, a distracted husband, and an emerald green front lawn.

While still in her early twenties, my mother had fallen in love with a blond gentleman before she met my dark-haired father. I found a photo of her at Jones Beach standing next to him. He was handsome, and my mother looked quite fashionable with her jet black hair and 1940s bathing suit. But I learned her mother, my grandma Mae, forbade her from marrying this man.

"He's blond! What are you thinking?"

Mom didn't know what she was thinking. She only knew what she was feeling. But she obeyed her mother and kept searching for a mate, often at the post-WWII dances in downtown New York.

She would tell us this story, perhaps because she wanted us to know she had settled, not only for my father, but for a suburban life she had no need or desire for. After all, she was a city girl and loved the hustle and bustle of downtown—any downtown.

She imagined herself a showgirl, or playing music on stage to thunderous applause, performing plays, or whatever would throw her into the limelight. Motherhood was a thankless job and provided no spotlight or fanfare, only dirty dishes and extra loads of laundry. Besides, she couldn't relate to children. It was the world of adults and adult beverages that Mom thrived in.

She always wanted to get out of wherever she was at that moment. Out of the house, out of the role of mother, out of my father's domain. But she remained, at least in a physical sense. All the while, she daydreamed of other times, other possibilities. She appeared unhappy in her marriage and seemed disappointed in us. She would lose herself in novel after trashy novel. Her bedside in the Eichler was stacked with books by Jacqueline Susann, such as *Valley of the Dolls* and *The Love Machine,* and Harold Robbins' *The Adventurers* and *The Carpetbaggers.* She had Truman Capote's *In Cold Blood* open at all times. She was always juggling several books at one time. I'm not sure she ever finished one of them. There would be one sitting open on the coffee table, another by her bedside, and one was always left damp with morning dew on the backyard lounger. Surely the adventures in those books seemed more exciting than her tepid existence in Fairgrove Court.

✳ ⚛ ✳

Musical theater was my mother's passion. She would take me to the Circle Star Theatre to watch plays, vocal performances, and musicals. At one point, she gave me two LP records from her collection of musicals to play on my record player. One was of the original Broadway cast recording of *Gypsy* featuring Ethel Merman and Jack Klugman, and the other *The Pajama Game* featuring Bonnie Raitt's father, John Raitt, one of the great leading men of Broadway's golden age, with his robust baritone vocals and rugged good looks. I'd spin both records on my portable record player until the grooves wore out.

In *Gypsy* the overbearing stage mother tries to reach for fame through her daughter's dancing and singing career because she never had the opportunity or talent to get there herself. I always saw my mother in that role. She hungered for recognition and wanted desperately to perform, but grudgingly settled for family. Yet when I began to succeed at dance, she dragged me out of the spotlight, away from the crowds and applause. If she couldn't have the accolades and limelight, why should I?

The Hot Lick Sveilich *at a local pizza joint gig. Mom on piano with Eichler neighbors.*

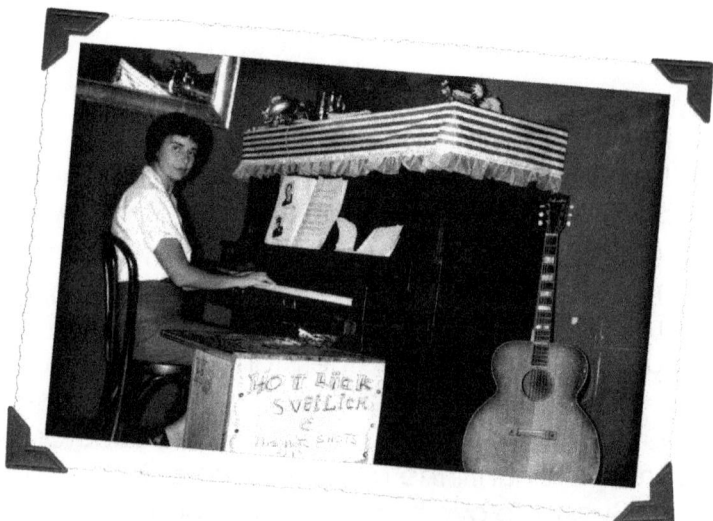

Mom wanted to perform and was always seeking out venues to do so, which is likely why so many parties at our house concluded with a performance featuring her on our piano, singing jazz standards and belting out requests. For a while, my parents performed music with a few neighbors. They called their combo *Hot Lick Sveilich and Her Hot Shots* and would play jazz tunes in a small pizza and beer joint near our neighborhood. Naturally, no one could properly pronounce the name of the group. One evening, my brother and I were able to tag along and see them perform. With pepperoni spilling into our nostrils and pizzas rising in the ovens, we danced around the checkered picnic tables set up in the main room for pizza consumption. It was the closest my mother ever got to the spotlight, as she sat close to the noisy clanks of the kitchen and belted out the song "Blue Skies" with occasional hums here and there to fill in forgotten lyrics.

Years later, Mom would develop a considerable crush on a coworker who was also a musician, specifically a horn player. The two of them, with another employee from work, would play jazz standards after hours. My mother was in heaven … and late for dinner. I had no idea about these desires and secrets of hers until I was an adult. The year after her death, I read a few lines of her journal from that time. They included starry-eyed fantasies of running off with this trumpeter from the office. Never mind that he was two decades younger than my mother and had a new baby and a young wife. My mother's daydreams ran deep and lasted a long time. A lifetime.

Mom resented her parents, my father, and her children, but she couldn't bring herself to actually leave us. Instead she seemed perpetually grumpy and dissatisfied. Her escape from the mundane came in the form of work, school, parties—anything that would give her mind something to focus on other than cleaning or fixing something for dinner. If she had followed her fantasies and left, the Jewish guilt would have gobbled her up, leaving nothing but bare bones and black mascara. She was miserable, but she remained in the Eichler.

Instead of seeking out stage work or piano gigs, my mother would take me to all the latest movies, many not appropriate for children. She had a strong interest in music, stage production, and escapism, and that enthusiasm was passed on to me.

But Dad couldn't get through a 30-minute TV show, let alone a movie, without flying out of his chair. He was antsy and had no interest in watching images dancing and prancing across a large screen. So my mother would take me to matinees at the Garden Theater in our San Jose neighborhood. Her afternoon guilty-pleasure ritual became my own.

Most of the films we watched had adult themes, and every man on the screen looked like William Holden or Glenn Ford. Martinis, long couches, Pall Malls, and low lighting were always involved. I never knew what the hell was going on in the soapy storylines on screen. Some guy was sleeping with another guy's wife, everyone was hollering and heated, or they were philosophizing and drinking martinis in stilettos. Still, it was fun to be there in a bouncy, plush, cushioned seat with the smooth red velvet curtain opening and closing in a darkened space. I didn't care what was playing. I wanted to stay seated for the rest of the afternoon in that cool dark room with my leaky Drumstick cone and a double feature. I wanted to hear my mother laugh out loud and breathe quietly during the dramatic scenes. I had no idea what was going on with Liz and Dick in *Who's Afraid of Virginia Woolf,* or Steve McQueen and Lee Remick in *Baby The Rain Must Fall,* but I'm certain it wasn't appropriate for a ten-year-old. It certainly wasn't compelling to see McQueen, a tempestuous prisoner out on parole, fumbling around a dusty Texas town for two hours. The film was much too understated for a restless pre-teen, as were all of her other selections. I would have preferred Jerry Lewis' *The Disorderly Orderly, The Nutty Professor,* or *Cinderfella* to my mother's black-and-white smoochy dark dramas. But just being there with her superseded what was moving on the screen. At least I was sitting next to Mom with a movie-sized box of Milk Duds, Junior Mints, or molar-cracking Jordan Almonds. It was one of the few times I spent one-on-one time with her, and even though we were silently staring at a shimmering screen most of the time, I felt the brush of her sweater on my shoulder and that was enough. That was everything.

Mom would also take me to stage productions and concerts. Our favorite musicals included *Finian's Rainbow, Man of La Mancha, A Funny Thing Happened on the Way to the Forum, Oklahoma!, My Fair Lady, The King and I, Guys and Dolls, Carousel, West Side Story*—anything with good melodies or a mighty chorus. In addition to musicals and movies, my mother often got tickets to see some of the popular performers of the day. One of those performers was singer Tom Jones.

In the late Sixties, it was not cool to be seen at a Tom Jones concert. But my mother had season tickets for the Circle Star Theatre in San Carlos, and my father was too antsy to accompany her. She needed a partner in concert crime. I fit the bill. I was hoping none of my classmates would show up and see me. It was not acceptable to be diggin' this particular performer's tunes. But when Tom Jones came out from behind the curtain and onto the stage he … uh … really came out. It was impossible not to notice the anaconda that had somehow managed to slither into the crotch of his pants. Was it a sock? Was it a dozen socks? Was it a water balloon? Was it really … him? I didn't know. All I knew was the performance I was dreading quickly turned to droolin'. I was in a trance, and Tom was my master. Let's go on with the show.

It's not unusual that Jones opened his performance by howling out his latest hit song. I continued to study his polyester slacks. Applause. On most occasions, Jones' voice was deep and bold as a rich cup of java. His voice could move mountains or make you shout "Hallelujah!" and raise your hands in the air, even if you were Jewish. He started a second tune but stopped a few notes in and began speaking in a hoarse voice. "I'm so sorry, folks," he said in a charming Welsh-tinged apology. When he said "folks" we felt as though he was in our small living room chatting directly with us over General Foods International Coffee, not up on stage in a ginormous domed theater. "I don't have much of a voice as I'm struggling with a blasted flu right now. I don't think I feel well enough to continue. Please accept my heartfelt apologies, ladies and gentlemen."

After all that charm sputtered out, he was off and running. Literally. He ran off stage, much to the disappointment of his old fans and this new one. Off went Tom Jones and that bag of rice in his trousers. I was disappointed, but it actually endeared him to me even more. I wanted to run backstage with a couple of Bayer aspirins and Vicks VapoRub and take care for him.

Jones had his own TV show in the late Sixties with musical guests such as Janis Joplin, Sammy Davis Jr., Joe Cocker, Lou Rawls, The Who, Aretha, Little Richard, and The Moody Blues. The show's vibe was hip—that is, until he introduced "What's New Pussycat?" Uh, not so cool. "The Green, Green Grass of Home?" Corny, but the sort of sentimental, hackneyed tale I secretly enjoyed at the time. I gave him a pass on "Delilah" and "It's Not Unusual" mainly because his voice soared. "Help Yourself" and "She's a Lady?" Not so cool. "I Who Have Nothing"? Vocally splendid. Tom had something special. There was no arguing that.

We took in many musicals and plays as well as more solo performers at the Circle Star. Its stage had the ability to rotate in either direction without limit. It was a theater that swiveled. That in itself was a novelty.

From the start, I relished the thrill of live theater, and I appreciated any sort of musical performance. The songs and raw emotions displayed on stage gave me goose bumps every time. I would imagine myself standing on stage left or right with the children's chorus or townspeople—somewhere that I wouldn't stand out. I would have loved to blend into the crowd and the painted scenery and sing at the top of my lungs. I would feel chills from my head to my toes when something dramatic, romantic, or chilling occurred on stage. Without effort, I meshed with the performers. I felt everything they were pretending to feel.

Musical Memories and Melodies

"A Lover's Concerto," by the girl group The Toys, was a favorite of mine. I sang it in front of my mirror and talked about it with my good friend Yolanda Zesati, whom I called Yo. Her skin was the color of the darkest coffee beans and her tight beehive 'do, mimicking the Eiffel Tower, was worn high on her head. Yo's early, over-developed, torpedo-shaped breasts would swing and sway and occasionally poke out of her shirt as if they wanted to escape. She seemed unaware of their magnetic powers, but every boy in the neighborhood stood at attention when she walked by.

Yo was tall, and even taller when her hair was piled high. Taller than her mother who was thick and squat and always outfitted in an apron and the brightest whitest smile. Like other black families, Yo's had moved out from the Chicago area in hopes of finding a gentler environment to raise their kids. One day, a neighbor kid who lived on Yo's block made the mistake of calling her the "N" word. She nearly pounded him down like white pizza dough. Other than that one incident, Yo told me she felt comfortable and safe in the Eichler bubble of tolerance and integration.

On sweltering summer afternoons in the mid-Sixties, Yo and I would harmonize to the popular Chiffons' tune "Sweet Talkin Guy." We'd toss the record back and forth between us like a Frisbee. Those were the days when you shared everything, especially music. Tightly rolled joints would come later.

When she'd head home for supper, I'd keep the records spinning while standing in front of my bedroom door mirror, hairbrush in hand, the perfect stand-in for a microphone. Mouthing the words to my collection of 45 rpm records, I'd move to the beat like some crazed go-go dancer. The beat in every Motown tune was infectious. The first time I heard The Supremes or Martha Reeves belt out a song to the hook and beat of The Funk Brothers, who backed up nearly every classic Motown tune, I was hopelessly addicted. Listen to that music!

Although rock music pounded through the miniscule speaker of my transistor radio on a regular basis, Motown connected to something deeper inside of me. The songwriters for Motown had the knack of writing lyrics and catchy melodies that appealed to all audiences. Stevie Wonder, Diana Ross, Marvin Gaye, Mary Wells, and Smokey Robinson were at the top of the charts, but there was no mistaking that Motown sound, no matter who the artist happened to be. Those songs moved my feet and penetrated the velvety roped entrance to my soul like no other. They made me want to throw up both my hands. They made me want to shimmy. In my empire dress and white go-go boots, knee-deep in my geekiest stage, I'd pretend to be someone else. Anyone else. Often it was a Motown singer, but being a *Shindig!* dancer was another popular fantasy.

On summer afternoons, Yo and I would dance on her front lawn and pretend we had our own girl group. Sometimes it was Diana Ross and The Supremes, and others Martha and the Vandellas. But what my friends didn't know was, hidden deep in my imagination and in the confines of my room, I would pretend to be black. Black like my friends; black like Yo, Cicely, and Dawn. I thought Yo was beautiful. I would have traded both dimples and muddy hazel eyes for her generous lips, smooth dark skin, and ebony eyes. I wanted to be in one of those girl groups, and

I wanted to be the same color as many of my friends. I wanted to sing out in those rich rhythmic tones when I mouthed "Don't Mess with Bill," "Be My Baby," and "Stop! In the Name of Love." I wanted to fit in with my friends and their world. I was unaware that their parents were fighting hard for their children to have the right to exist without having cruel boundaries drawn between us and them. While I was busy envying them, they were busy trying to fit in.

In addition to Yo, another Eichler friend was Patrice O'Hara, who was doll-like, delicate as an eggshell, and akin to a pint-sized version of Olive Oyl. Patrice and I would pedal around the Eichler turf on our bicycles. One afternoon, as were pedaling down Fairlawn Drive, Patrice told me she was born with a hole in her heart. Oh no! I pictured a hole shaped like a Valentine in my fragile friend's chest. I began to worry about her all the time. Would she die on our bike rides from her home to mine? Would her waif-like body collapse during a game of basketball? Would she be able to graduate from junior high? Patrice's constant need for medical attention would inspire her to become a surgeon, but decades earlier, in a land far, far away called Eichlerville, I would often stop at her house right before dinnertime to check on her, make sure she was okay, and see if we could manage to fit in a few more minutes of benign playtime.

When I rang the doorbell to see if Patrice was available, I would often be greeted by her mother outfitted in massive rollers, ill-fitted undergarments, and a menthol cigarette drooping from the corner of her mouth. So many of the mothers in the Eichlers appeared disheveled at all hours of the afternoon. They rambled around the house in knee-length slips or bras and panties. Everyone smoked in The Eichlers, including my mother, although she pulled out a pack only at parties or during cocktail hour. It was an accessory used in social settings to appear groovy.

Patrice's home was radically different from mine, and not because their family lived in the "other" style Eichler without an atrium. Her home felt claustrophobic. The television at Patrice's house was always blaring in the background at top volume. Her mother, who was now parading around in a shabby chenille bathrobe that looked like it was sewn from an old bedspread, looked haggard, as if she had been up all night. Her robe would often fall open to expose much too much information. Her neck was perfumed with coffee, cigarettes, and apathy. With bathrobe open, revealing her nylon slip, she'd stare off into space as she prepared dinner at the stove. Then the entire family—Patrice, her two tiny sisters, and her petite parents—would seat themselves at the built-in Eichler kitchen table. Like a family of robots, they'd stare at the small television set propped up at the end of the table as they ate and watched, ate and watched. Not a word was spoken. That's when I knew it was time for me to head home. There was no dinner prepared at home, but it felt familiar and strangely comfortable. Our Eichler felt like home. My home. Their Eichler felt like it was occupied by several stray Martians.

Next door to the O'Haras lived the Eaglestons. One afternoon, I went over to their house with Patrice and found the entire family of five walking around buck naked. Robert, the man of the house, was so tall I thought his head would clunk on the bulbous light fixture hanging from the ceiling. With his John Wayne build and rugged good looks, he appeared every inch the scientist he was. At the time, he held a doctorate in psychology. He went on to work as a clinical nutritionist for twenty-five years and received a prestigious Swedish award in alternative medicine. But back in the Sixties, and in his very private Eichler, he was walking around naked with his wife and three children, all parts dangling. I had never seen some of those body parts before, certainly not on adults. I quickly scuttled out the front door and onto my trusty bicycle with images of breasts and testicles swaying to-and-fro like the pendulums of grandfather clocks.

Directly behind our Eichler were the four depraved Fowler boys: Dan, Dana, Dick, and Doug. Yo had her eye on Dick Fowler, the oldest boy with the often-ridiculed first name. Dick was two or three years older than Yo and myself. I was drawn to Danny, the brother closer to my age. Danny gave me my first kiss as we awkwardly squatted in the bushes near my house so that we could hide our daring deed from our friends. It was his first kiss too. As thorns of the brush scratched my arm, he put one hand on each of my shoulders and came in for the kill. His lips were bulbous, but dry as matzo meal. As he planted an uninspiring kiss on my waiting lips, five seconds felt like fifteen hours. Neither one of us puckered or took a breath. I quickly realized that he had no idea what to do with his mouth. Then he lifted his face from mine. Did I just smooch a stucco wall? That's a kiss? A wave of disappointment sunk my spirits. Perhaps there were more gifted practitioners in the art of smooching on the horizon.

Leave It to the Idiot Box

Leave It to Beaver was the first TV show to feature a toilet, which wasn't their only claim to fame, but it was an impressive one. In this historic episode, Wally and The Beave had a baby alligator that was given a home in their toilet. It did not seem far-fetched to me at the time. My brother had gotten a baby alligator when he was around nine years old and I was seven. As he was putting it in a cage in his bedroom, he suddenly became frightened that it would bite him, so he threw the spinning reptile up in the air. It looked like the propellers of one of those balsa wood airplanes as it spun 'round and 'round. Not straight up, but off to the side. I was standing in his doorway at the time—and bam!—the whirling beast hit me smack in the face. Startled, I ran screaming at the top of my lungs for at least six blocks before I felt safe enough to stop. It took quite a distance to convince myself that there wasn't a baby alligator attached to my left cheek. The poor critter was likely traumatized by my ear-piercing cries. As for my brother, I still haven't forgiven him.

The Beave and Wally had an alligator, but that's all my brother and I had in common with their household. In the early Sixties, a slew of shows were missing a mother who was present. I was too. Perhaps that's why I was drawn to the *Bonanza* boys of the Ponderosa, *My Three Sons*, *The Courtship of Eddie's Father*, *Sky King*, and *Bachelor Father*. There was no mother figure in sight donning a kitchen apron. No one except Hop Sing.

Make Love, Not War

It was just Dad seated beside me and the broken line on Hwy 17 as we headed towards Seacliff Beach near Santa Cruz. I wanted to get down to the water while my father attended to some real estate business. I had to get my toes covered in sand and seaweed. After weeks and months in San Jose's suburban mecca, Santa Cruz was a wonderland only 45 miles away on a road that was like a twisty-turny pretzel.

As I shuffled down the hill towards Seacliff Beach, the sun felt like golden butter melting on my cheeks and the bridge of my nose. My father yelled out, "Be back in an hour. That's when I'm leaving." Would he leave without me? Probably. My father didn't have two words to say to me on the drive over. I was his invisible passenger on a ride that would last an entire childhood.

Why couldn't I live at the beach all the time? Little did I know that in a few short years I would reside there. But for now, I was inhaling the salt air and letting every teenage care blow away. The briny breeze was my sanctuary—my happy place.

On this particular day, I could hear the sounds of a guitar player between the crash of waves. I spotted a boy a few years older. He was seated on a rock between the parking lot and the sandy beach, and he was playing some tasty blues licks on his well-worn guitar. I gathered up my confidence, what little I had, and walked over to listen to him play. I recognized the tune right away. It was "Let It Bleed" by The Rolling Stones.

I edged up next to him in my peasant blouse and corduroy pants, and listened more intently. My eyes grew wider as the words of the song played in my ear. It sounded sexy, earthy, direct. The groovy boy in cool shorts was straddling the rock and strumming with eyes closed. He broke into the chorus as I broke into a sweat. I never understood the lyrics when The Stones sang them, but I understood every word from the young man rockin' out on the rock. Was he singing directly to me? Did he even see me standing nearby with my wild beach hair, tapping my sandaled foot? When he was done, I walked up to him. It wasn't like me to be so bold, but I had to seize this moment.

"You sounded great. I really enjoy your playing." Now we were off and running into a deep conversation about guitar licks and beach waves. But it was getting late, and my father would be tapping his toes. Not to the music. To my delay in getting back to him.

"I have to go. I'm heading back to the Valley now." To my surprise he took my hand in his as we walked to the top of the hill. I was even more surprised when he pulled me close and kissed me. Was he falling in love with me? Me? A clueless 15-year-old girl with beach hair?

"Why don't I call you sometime?" I gave him my number, but I was too young to go out with him. I knew that. Unless I snuck out, there was no possibility of every feeling his salty lips on mine again or his fingers knitted into my hand.

He did call me, just once. He was a student at the University of Santa Clara.

"Can you come out to a frat party tonight?" I had to tell him no. The scene at the university seemed light-years away.

I never heard from him again—the boy with the salty lips and blues licks. I was a young caged animal. I wasn't ready for the world quite yet, or perhaps it wasn't ready for me.

A small cluster of us teenage girls would march down to Seacliff Beach on a regular basis, spread ourselves out on multicolored beach towels, and toast our youthful skin to copper with a few seared edges. If there were three of us gallivanting together and my friend Denise was among us, the remaining two would feel like bookends holding up Cinderella. She was the great beauty of the bunch, with her long, straight brunette hair sporting highlights from Sun-In hair lightener. When I sprayed the same product on my head, it turned my hair orange. It was like QT Tanning Lotion for hair. QT was a quick-tanning product that turned our skin the color of tangelos until it ran its three-day course. When we got fed up with the unnatural tanning qualities of QT, we would drench our shoulders, lower backs, and legs in Johnson & Johnson Baby Oil. The ritual included rotating ourselves tummy up, then tummy down on a sandy beach blanket while collecting a pound of sand on our sticky limbs. Then, like chickens baking on a rotisserie, we slipped onto our backs in unison until we were a crisp shade of russet brown or rooster red.

Denise, Heather, and I would hold hands with bronzed boys named Chuck and Tim and gobble up cheeseburgers at the Sno-White Drive-In where they were generous with their watery mustard sauce. When evening approached, we'd lie awake for hours and talk about the many vast mysteries of the universe, the existence or non-existence of God, the best and cutest pop singers, and the glories of kissing boys. Clearly, we had too much time on our hands.

✳ ⚛ ✳

During my junior high school years, weekends were often spent baking in the sun at Seacliff Beach in Aptos, a sleepy beach town located south of Santa Cruz. I often brought Denise or Heather along for the weekend, but always one at a time. Denise wasn't crazy about Heather, and Heather didn't really relate to Denise. Julie didn't care for either one of them, but since I was the straw in this cocktail of friends, we all hung together except on these weekend jaunts to the beach.

My friends' parents were always reassured that there would be a chaperone with us on these weekend beach excursions, but there never was. We stayed in what we called "the little room" located in a garage converted to a closet-sized sleeping space on the first level of a four-plex apartment building. My father purchased it as an investment. There was no shower. We'd splash cold water under our armpits and grit our teeth during the process. There were no windows in the room, and the toilet was outside the room in the back of the apartment complex near the community washer and dryer. It was pitch dark when night fell and even darker when morning broke. The room had a couch, a queen bed, and a television set, and we didn't need one thing more.

On one escapade to the beach, Denise sat on the curb beside me as we were trying to decide when to go to dinner. "Don't your parents care about you?" she muttered, as if she was thinking out loud but it seeped out from between her lips. "Why would they let you go to the beach alone? My parents would never do that!" As soon as she saw my eyes well up, she apologized for the next half hour. But the reality of being an Eichler orphan was beginning to set in. Was it my fault they didn't give a damn where I was or what I did? It must have been. Was I not lovable? Didn't they care if I got bitten by a bear—or a boy? My parents didn't seem to have an issue with leaving underage girls to fend for themselves on a pleasant stretch of beach. But when Denise's parents discovered that it was the two of us staying there alone, or Heather's parents made the same discovery, they prohibited each of them from accompanying me on these seashore weekends. "No chaperone, no beach!" That was their rule. I would go it alone, and go Greyhound, after that.

✳ ⚛ ✳

The best part of my teen years was spent during those ephemeral sun and sand days with friends at Seacliff Beach. We always managed to meet boys around our age, or slightly older. John, Mark, Jim, and assorted other toasted beach bums. We'd fall in love, or lust, tumble hard and quickly into their arms, and wrestle with their tongues. Then the weekend would end, and the memories would wash away like struggling sand crabs being pulled back to sea.

The radio was always blaring, reflecting all the romantic feelings that we couldn't put into words. From dawn to dusk, we'd listen to our small transistor radios as the beach sand filled the holes of the speaker. Neil Diamond's "Sweet Caroline" was in heavy rotation that year. I was Carol, not Caroline, yet the song always felt personal to me.

My friends and I were in junior high school and a year and a half away from Sweet Sixteen. We hadn't learned to drive or to parallel park. For me, parallel parking always meant parking somewhere else. Anywhere else. We weren't doing our own laundry when there was schmutz on it. We threw it in a basket, and it magically became clean. Our parents still tended to some of our housekeeping needs, but in our minds, we were on our own, dressed in the proper late Sixties uniform: puffy-sleeved peasant blouses, oversized ponchos, rumpled corduroy pants, and sticky, tousled beach hair that looked unruly, but appropriate for any teenage venue.

It was a late afternoon, and the sun was barely gracing the sky. Denise and I began our routine walk down Searidge Road towards the shoreline. But first, a quick stop at our usual burger haunt, Sno-White Drive-In. It was neither a drive-in nor drive-through, just six card tables inside a decaying hamburger joint. Two male figures walking in the opposite direction on the pathway greeted and engaged us with their openness and boyish charms. Their faces were barely visible as the sun had already dropped from the sky. Although we could barely see the faces of these strangers, we were drawn to them in the same way a sightless monarch butterfly senses milkweed. The two young men, still boys, were oddly polite, strangely formal, thoroughly engaging, and surprisingly respectful. Both boys were going into the Army the next morning at Fort Ord, located down the road towards Monterey. This night was their last precious stretch of freedom. We felt honored that they chose to spend it chatting with two strangers who were kicking rocks down the road in the direction of the coastline and eating some cheeseburgers.

After gobbling down a few fries and some overcooked meat, we continued a slow stroll to the beach, moving along the sidewalk as a foursome. The cold began to penetrate our sweatshirts. The two boys invited us back up the hill and into their car to warm ourselves with the heater. I crawled into the back seat with the soldier boy I had my eye on. He jumped in beside me and threw his arm around my shoulders as I leaned into him. Denise got into the front seat with the other boy, but they didn't seem to be chatting or hitting it off. Their communication only included changing radio stations from this one to that. On the other hand, my back seat boy was sidling up next to me on squeaky upholstery. Our arms now wrapped around each other like a fortune cookie, windows fogging, kissing like every contact was our last. I felt as though I was in one of those romantic movies my mother had dragged me into at the Garden Theatre, and he was my Glenn Ford. But the Vietnam War was in full swing, and soldier boy was marching in that direction come morning. His future was as opaque as the steamy windows. I no longer recall his name, but I remember every detail of his slow, deep kisses and the way he gently breathed into the hollow of my ear. It sent tingles to places I didn't know could tingle. The car windows fogged and remained fogged for hours that felt like minutes. We had been transported without a moving vehicle. The only things moving were lips.

Every sixth or seventh song played on the radio that evening was "Sweet Caroline," so it must have been the year the song was first released: 1969. Neil Diamond's voice was in our ears. This nameless, faceless soldier made an awkward ugly-duckling adolescent feel like she was his Sweet Caroline. Good times never felt so good.

Around 0400 military time, we sprang out of the car and into the waiting apartment that Denise and I would call home for the next twenty-four hours. We were all weary. It was too cold to stay in the car, and too tempting to get a few hours of shut-eye. The perfect stranger crawled into bed next to me, holding me, kissing me, but never fondling or going further than a cavalcade of deep kisses. He took me in his arms and placed a bouquet of whispered words in my ear every few seconds. It surprised me. It felt different. I felt different. Cherished. We drifted off to sleep, fingers entwined and fully clothed. The air in the room was chilly, but the blankets and the soft breathing of the soldier warmed something inside of me that had been shivering until now.

I worried about the pimple on my cheek that was going to become as visible as cinnamon-flavored Red Hots candy in the light of day. The darkness of dusk had hidden it until now, but in an unforgiving dawn, my small pimple had turned into a raging blistery mess. I checked it in the mirror before he awoke, moaned to myself, and crawled back to bed. He slept beside me for a few hours, then kissed me goodbye when the sun sobered us up to what the day had in store. And just like that, he was gone. No scribbled address. No future plans. He didn't have any. After all, he was going off to war. It was his last night of freedom, and for one moment in adolescence, I felt treasured and extraordinarily worthy.

After the boys left, Denise and I conducted a brief verbal wrap-up of the evening's events. She had little to offer as she had not made a connection with his friend. They didn't share any physical tangles, conversation, or saliva. I slipped into a white peasant blouse with colorful embroidered short sleeves and my corduroy bell-bottoms and went through the motions of caring about what I looked like, what I was going to do with the rest of the day, and who I was going to do it with. All I could manage to accomplish was replay flashes of moments with the boy who took my breath away with his dancing tongue as it gently tapped in and out of my ear. He had burrowed his way into my heart, but he didn't burrow his hand into my pants. He had valued me. He was virtuous, but like a flash, he was gone.

* ⚛ *

In a short while, my brother popped over, and we all walked to a strip mall that housed a small breakfast café. I couldn't taste my eggs and sausage. I was inconsolable. I missed the nameless, virtually faceless soul who passed through my life like a friendly ghost through a wall, leaving a small trace of his essence. *I'll never see him again,* I thought. How can that be? I felt dejected. Miserable. *Heartsick*—the perfect word for this imperfect moment.

I missed him so much. My heart ached. I could still feel him in my bones. I was lovesick. They haven't come up with more telling words than lovesick and heartsick.

But he couldn't hear. I no longer had him beside me. The U.S. military had him now.

As we returned from breakfast, I stood on the second-story balcony looking out at the tall pines and distant ocean. But I was the one lost at sea. I missed someone I had only known for a few short hours, and yet I felt the loss in every part of my body.

Suddenly, like some made-for-TV romantic movie, a car pulled into the driveway, and my soldier boy came barreling out from the side door. I thought I was imagining his image as he moved closer to the stairs. Was this a hallucination? Was I dreaming? Am I delirious from being up all night? No. It was the soldier boy I never thought I'd see again. He took two steps at a time coming up the stairs to the balcony where I was hung over the rail like a wet sock. I thought about the massive red dot on my cheek that had no chance of being hidden now, not with all the cake-batter Clearasil in the county. Oh well. This is me, take it or leave it. Please take it.

"I couldn't bear to leave like that," he chortled with a beaming smile. "I may never see you again. I still have a few hours before I have to report to base. Can we spend some time together?"

If I was dreaming, he was my fantasy man, my Elvis, my knight in shining armor ... and I had a massive zit on my cheek.

"Of course! I'm so glad you came back."

I threw on Denise's russet suede jacket with the mile-long fringe and found it weighed more than I did. I didn't care. It made me feel tough. It made me feel cool, even in the blistering heat. It empowered me and raised my hipness factor several degrees. I had a pimple the size of Russia, but the cool jacket in the hot sun cancelled it out. All was well.

My solider boy and I walked down to the beach, arm in arm. My precious new love. All of the love songs I had ever heard on the radio were written about this moment. We were two lovesick puppies, one dressed in a T-shirt and jeans, the other buried under forty pounds of fringed suede in the peak of summer. I was trying to look cool, but it was ninety-two degrees and I was anything but cool. We threw a beach towel onto the sand near the pier, then cuddled and kissed under the warm sun. I was sweating from the cool, hot, hip suede jacket. I finally slipped it off. We kissed, we nuzzled, and like a wish from genie's lamp, he softly blew in my ear with his warm breath in some beguiling way that no one had ever done before, or since.

For that afternoon on the beach, I was his, and he—this near-perfect stranger—was mine. Then he was off again to fight, but who was going to fight for us? We never connected again, even after he scrawled his mailing address at Fort Ord on a piece of paper and placed it in my lined pocket. Well, Denise's lined pocket. I wrote to him almost immediately, but I never heard back. He was gone. Bombs away. I could still smell the sea on the back of his neck. I could still feel the gentle wind of his breath in my ear from his warm mouth. His transitory kindness warmed me. We didn't need desperately romantic letters or rushed telephone calls. We had moments strung together and latched into a chain of permanent memories.

✳ ⚛ ✳

I spent the rest of the summer making brief trips to the beach, standing on the freeway overpass with Denise or Heather, making the peace sign with our fingers and waving them at the cars below. A good number of drivers flashed the two-finger symbol back, which made us feel as though we had done our part to inspire world peace, to end the war, to bring our boys home. *Please bring my boy home!* In truth, we hadn't done diddly-squat. I desperately wanted peace for our country. I wanted peace of mind for myself. Most of all, I wanted a peaceful tour of duty for a valued soldier boy who was likely being shaken and stirred like a messy cocktail in a land far, far away called Vietnam.

Billiards and Billie

My father's frantic temperament required soothing projects. Without a mission or assignment to distract him and focus his restless energy, he was at odds with the world like a three-year-old child in need of a nap.

A draftsman by trade, he was gifted at design work and liked to create new projects or fix things around the house. There were often more problems with execution than there were in the theories scrawled onto a piece of paper with a number two pencil. He threw up paneling in the garage, which bowed outward like they had gained water weight; he constructed a patio cover in the backyard that swayed when the wind blew; he impulsively sawed a rectangular opening in our dining room wall and shoved a room air-conditioner in its gaping mouth, which shook and shuddered whenever it was turned to the ON position.

One afternoon, Dad decided to attack our one-car garage and turn it into a pool hall. He nailed vertically grooved paneling to the walls, tiled the floors, punched out a rectangular opening in the garage door for a window, and inserted glass and a frame. He nailed a pool stick and chalk holder onto the paneling, which always made a loud creaking noise when leaned against. Then he sunk a sweet sound system into the mix.

Our Voice of the Theater speakers were meant for massive concert halls and had the capacity to rock out the entire neighborhood. But instead of situating them in some large venue, my father played his jazz albums through this massive sound system in our garage. Dave Brubeck's *Time Out* or *Time Further Out*, Cal Tjader's *In a Latin Bag*, Stan Getz and Charlie Byrd's *Jazz Samba*, Anita O'Day's *Anita Sings the Winners*, Vince Guaraldi's *Cast Your Fate to the Wind*, Sergio Mendes' *Look Around*, and, strangely enough, Big Brother and The Holding Company's *Cheap Thrills*, featuring Janis Joplin. He thought Janis was "the bomb" and the best of all vocal powerhouses. He often said he could hear Billie Holiday's spirit pour through Joplin's interpretations. *Cheap Thrills* was played at full throttle. The paneled walls would shiver and shake. So would our neighbors' eardrums.

One of the first recordings I recall hearing was my father's copy of Billie Holiday's 1959 release *Memorial*. He played that particular album every weekend. The cover design made Miss Holiday appear otherworldly. I would stare at her facial features and study them closely. I thought she was from Hawaii or some other tropical paradise as she often wore a flower behind one ear. Her lips were crimson red. So was the moon that appeared in the sky behind her. Who was she, this woman who charmed my father and made such an impression? The songs began to grow on me: "Yesterdays," "Lover, Come Back to Me," "Strange Fruit," and "I'll Be Seeing You."

I always wondered who Tom Collins was and what he did with my parents after work hours. Frequenting cocktail bars was a clandestine activity to me, but those beverages always made my parents late in coming home from work. The coast was clear until 7 or 8 p.m., so my friends and I would perfect our game of eight-ball after making up our own game rules. We became skilled at pool, while Tom Collins soothed my parents' workday nerves.

I wasn't allowed in the garage/pool palace. It was a sacred space for my father and brother or my parents' party guests. However, during the long summer months that felt as endless as a filibuster, my friend Heather and I would head to this holiest of places. We came alive in our garage's pool room. Sometimes we would drag a boyfriend into our eight-ball game, but most of the time it was the two of us battling it out on the green felt, chalking our cue stick and bumbling bank shots. And sometimes it was without clothing. After all, it was hot as green curry in that garage pool hall. And it was the Sixties.

Games People Play

Board games ruled. They provided hours of entertainment and enjoyment, and were safer than dangling my feet off the Eichler rooftop. I was, and am, a restless soul, much like my father and much like the fidgety pebbles on our roof during a hammering rainstorm. My father became disinterested easily and quickly. I too get bored frequently, but board games never made me bored.

I was a board-game geek and master. Whatever boxed game I didn't have at my house, I would uncover at a friend's house. The king of all games, Mouse Trap, was one that Julie, my friend-by-proximity, had housed in her closet. I had a game that was similar and made by the same firm, the Ideal Toy Company. It was called Crazy Clock. The aim of the game was to get the man to jump out of bed to a blaring alarm clock. That seemed to be more fun to play with than rodents and traps.

Both Mouse Trap and Crazy Clock had colorful plastic parts that you'd snap together before playing. We spent more time assembling them than actually playing the game, but that was a joy in itself. In childhood, needs were few, pleasures plenty. Ultimately, the mouse would get caught in the mousetrap or a man would pop out of the plastic bed after the imagined alarm clock started buzzing.

I had already put in my time with youthful board games such as Candyland, Go to the Head of the Class, Chutes and Ladders, Chinese Checkers, and even the elementary Cootie. But now I was in my prime and ready for some complex and cultured pastimes. Enter the sophisticated magic of Lie Detector by Mattel.

My father wandered into my room after work one night and tossed this odd-looking game onto the floor, then walked out. It was exciting to receive such a treat, especially from my father, a man who was not a giver of gifts. Was it Christmas? My birthday? My father didn't celebrate holidays, but when his mood was on the upswing, he would bring home some offbeat random item. This game fit the bill.

The Lie Detector game came with a kid-friendly black plastic lie-detecting machine that came alive when the cards from the game were inserted. Players would identify the criminals by their heavily exaggerated features on the game cards. Each card showed a different possible suspect, and they were all shifty characters. There was the headwaiter, hat-check girl, playboy, taxi driver, trombone player, laundress, night club singer, and racketeer. I had no idea what a racketeer actually was, but I spent more time focusing on the comical faces on those cards than playing the game. Several characters sported a large forehead; others were bald or a redhead. Some had monstrous ears. Did the suspect wear glasses? Did he or she have a bulbous nose? I was fascinated with the game and especially the plastic lie detector machine itself, mainly because it didn't need to be plugged in. The needle would magically move from left to right or right to left to determine guilt. I couldn't figure out how it functioned without batteries or a power source. I still don't know. Maybe you have to be a true detective to figure it out.

Chutes and Ladders was a lesson in frustration and a preview of the ups and downs in life. You were nearly at the top and then ... oh no! You'd land with your game piece on a square with a slide right back to the beginning square, landing squarely on your backend. Suddenly, your unworthy opponent was traveling up a ladder and beating you to the finish line even though you'd been winning in the game for the past thirty minutes. Life isn't fair, a vital lesson, but hard to digest in youth.

Games like Monopoly or Life that went on for hours—and sometimes days—were not my first choice. I wanted something short and sweet. Clue. Trouble. Checkers. Twister involved action, so I enjoyed snaking, rotating, twisting, and turning on the white plastic sheet with the gigantic red, blue, green, and yellow dots.

Monopoly felt more like work than fun. With the roll of the dice, you moved ahead, went back, trotted off to jail, acquired property, and built hotels, and charged tenants astronomical rents until you bankrupted them. My brother would always fold up the board or dump the money back at the bank when he suspected he was going to lose. The cheater—and there always was one—hid a few blue fifty-dollar bills under the table or slipped under a knee when no one was looking. I became bored with the whole scene and didn't have the perseverance. High finance was not my thing. Monopoly taught me how to be patient, or more accurately, it taught me that I didn't have any patience. The game required a commitment that was difficult to manage. There was no immediate gratification or sense of completion with Monopoly. Monopoly equated to monotony. It was more like The Game of Life.

The few times my family sat down together to play Monopoly, my mother always chose the iron token, which I found perplexing as she never ironed. I always chose the dog because it had four legs and looked like my cat. My father wouldn't play. Not a chance. He was too busy pacing and loading his pipe from the yellow and black tobacco tin. My brother chose the car every time, but got bored easily and rode out of the room early on. The game went on too long, no matter how many people were playing. Park Place. Reading Railroad. Rotting in jail. Who cares?

The Game of Life was another torturous board game. It seemed too mature, and I certainly wasn't. This particular board game began with a car in a color of your choice, or a blue or pink peg, depending on your gender. Everything was about gender in the early Sixties. As the game moved along, you went through college, marriage, kids, and even played with the possibility of having twins. In The Game of Life, you held a job or had an exciting career, earned some sort of income, drank scotch over ice before dinnertime, held stocks and bonds, and had life insurance. Yawn. It was all about traditional life. I didn't see a lot of that in my own household, so I couldn't relate to it on a game board. I closed the lid on The Game of Life and went back to playing jacks.

One of my favorite board games was Barbie's Keys to Fame game. Players had to be females, as Mattel cashed in on half the population. During the game, girls were able to decide what we would be when we grew up. In 1963, the choices for women's careers were slim. You could become a ballerina, stewardess (waitress in the sky), mother, teacher, fashion designer, or nurse. Working in the medical arena or being a bookkeeper or homemaker didn't hold any appeal for me. But there was one occupation featured in Barbie's world that broke the glass ceiling wide open. I could grow up and be an astronaut. In 1963, everyone was fascinated with all things skyward. In the mid-Sixties, occupations such as "woman in space" were pure fantasy. We couldn't imagine it. Maybe Gloria Steinem could, but we couldn't.

I spent playtime hours enjoying cat's eye marbles, comics, red rubber ball and jacks, balsa wood planes, and a borrowed Barbie. Ah yes, Barbie and her collection of plastic shoes and plastic friends. The most monumental decision most girls had to make in the early Sixties: Bubble Barbie or Ponytail Barbie. I would have opted for Ponytail Barbie. There was no contest. Bubble Barbie had a hair bonnet that reminded me of my mother's 'do, but she was a generation removed from my friends and me. Bubble Barbie looked much too mature to have any fun with, but Ponytail Barbie fit the bill. Her yanked-back ponytail strained and twisted into a rubber-band looked more like my hair.

In my household, thriftiness came first. Whatever "extras" we enjoyed were purchased with a handful of S&H Green Stamp books. I spent hours licking and putting Green Stamps and Blue Chip Stamps into little booklets so that Mom could redeem them for merchandise. I wish she could have redeemed them for Ponytail Barbie, because no matter how hard she tried, Babette couldn't hold a candle to Barbie.

Babette had thick limbs and couldn't fit into any of Barbie's high-fashion clothes. Babette's feet were too big for plastic Barbie shoes, and Barbie had plenty of footwear. Babette had no sense of style, and as a result, she had no plastic friends.

And Babette couldn't hang with Barbie and her stuck-up friends and relatives Midge, Skipper, and Ken. Amazon women like her stood out from the malleable crowd. Yet the two of us, Babette and I, moved through significant passages together. We dealt with body image issues, felt like outcasts, and became invisible to the masses around us. I obsessively brushed her long, golden plastic hair and placed ill-fitting outfits on her as I tried to stretch the fabric to fit her sizable limbs. They rarely covered her appendages. I tried to shove those tiny Barbie shoes onto her massive feet. No success. She didn't have an orange dream car or a dream house ... or a dream boyfriend. Neither did I. She didn't have a little sister or a love interest. We were clones.

After a while, I started to study Babette's anatomy, which looked very different from my own. Her smooth, strangely shaped hairless crotch, the permanently arched feet awaiting heels that would never fit, the miniscule waist, the mile long legs. I had a Ken doll on loan from a neighbor. He seemed namby-pamby to me, but Babette seemed entranced. The couple went skinny dipping in my bathroom sink. That's when all hell broke loose. So did the toilet paper used to create makeshift swimwear. As the pink toilet tissue dampened and came loose in the liquid, Babette and Ken and their expressionless faces began to kiss. Now things were getting serious. Their lean limbs became intertwined. Babette and Ken didn't quite fit (think disc jockey Casey Kasem and towering wife, Jean), but I helped them network and commingle. Soon limbs were becoming so bent and rearranged so often, Babette suffered a compound fracture, and her leg popped out of the socket. Playtime was officially over, and that was the end of the further adventures of Bodacious Babette and the Wrath of Ken.

I quickly outgrew plastic dolls. But getting to know them and their antics in the sink informed me about distorted views of perfection. Over the next couple of years, I would learn that my female area would never resemble Babette's or Barbie's, my feet would never be comfortable in tiny plastic shoes, but my breasts would be bouncy and weighty with rosy nipples to attract pleasure, unlike the two colorless mounds on female dolls. That was something to celebrate.

My friend Julie not only had a Barbie doll, but also Barbie's Dream House, and her dream mode of transportation, a sports car, along with Barbie's wide-ranging dream wardrobe. My dream house remained the Eichler, and Julie's house was the identical layout as ours. Even so, everything situated in her home seemed like it had just landed there from a completely different time period. Her furniture was dark and traditional and seemed to be battling the contemporary lights and light of the Eichler design. Julie's mother, Irene, dressed in flowery small-print prairie dresses that came to the middle of her calf. Irene cooked, cleaned, and looked like she had stepped out of the Time Tunnel from another age. I always thought she must have landed in the Sixties by mistake. Irene was a pioneer, a passenger in a wagon train on the Oregon Trail. Housed in an Eichler with her traditional furnishings and traditional husband, Irene was living a different sort of struggle in her pioneer gear. But instead of starting fires, she was putting them out. Burdened with her depressed husband, who was unable to work due to his mental health and the aftermath of shock treatments, Irene was rustling up whatever traditions she could maintain in her household. Her pale complexion was makeup free, and her wispy unkempt reddish blonde hair was always disheveled. Her eyes looked worn and ready to close at any given moment. I imagined Irene's life was exhausting, and her world was worlds away from my own mother's choices.

The kitchen truly was the heart of Julie's home. Julie and sister Marlene's artwork from school was Scotch-taped to every kitchen door. The cabinets were a gallery of A-plus papers and whimsical crayon drawings, and the house had a fragrant soup-pot perfume hanging in the air from bubbling vegetable stock chock-full of herbs and spices. It was so unlike my own house, with its potpourri scent of Folger's coffee grounds and burned Eggo waffles slathered in Imperial margarine.

An assortment of fruit sat in a basket on Julie's kitchen table, not stashed in refrigerator doors like in our kitchen. Cabinet doors were left ajar, and the countertop was littered with salt, pepper, and flour in a complicated but alluring mess. Julie's home was always an efficient jumble, never antiseptic. It smelled like home, but not my home.

Julie's father had worked as a horticulturist, but now that he was unable to work, he sat under his dark cloud of depression.

He was the first person I knew, or knew by association, who had shock treatments performed on a regular basis.

One day, Julie described his treatments, and it made me think of one of my favorite horror show monsters. *Did they anesthetize and tranquilize him too, while fastening electrodes to his head and temples and flipping the switch to the ON position while loud claps of thunder filled the sky?* She gave the answer most kids gave to any question regarding the adult world: I dunno.

Whenever her father would come home from the mental ward, I'd watch him from across the atrium. He would rock in a wooden chair in their den and stare at a television set that wasn't turned on. There, he would sit sedated, chin dropped, mouth open. I didn't know what was wrong with him. I only knew that Julie's dad and Dr. Frankenstein's monster were twin brothers from different mothers.

Julie would tense up in visible frustration and anger, shake her fist in his direction, and tell me how much she despised her father. It was clear he was incapable of fathering, working, or doing anything else. She'd squint her eyes and lower her brows in an angry stance. "I hate him. I HATE HIM!" Sometimes the intensity of that resentment scared me so much I had to leave Julie's Eichler and run home to my own horror show.

It's impossible to say how much of her father's memory and cognitive ability was burned away and for how long. He'd evaporate into that TV screen for days, sometimes for weeks, vegetating until he didn't. It was the Sixties, and they hadn't perfected the art of shock treatment or managing depression. I felt sad for this shell of a man, yet I didn't truly understand what was wrong with him or if it would ever improve. It seemed that most of the time, Julie's mother, the pioneer woman, was running the entire household, prairie dress, apron, chapped lips, and all.

In 1968, I was sitting in the back seat of Julie's car on our way to San Francisco, studying her mother's straw-like hair as she took command of the wheel. Julie had won tickets on KYA radio to a premiere of the Monkees' new (and only) movie, *HEAD.* The film went on to become an avant-garde commercial flop, but we were excited to attend anything that had to do with anything musical.

On the car ride to "the City," which is how we always referred to San Francisco, the radio wasn't playing songs by The Monkees. It was playing the Beatles' new *White Album*. There were thirty terrific tunes on that prized double album, and every song was significantly dissimilar from the last. When the song "Julia" came on, Julie became mesmerized. "This is my favorite song," she declared. Two decades later, she officially changed her name from Julie to Julia. I don't know all the reasons, but I'm sending out this song, just to reach you ... Julia.

Julie came to know popular music in her teens, but much later than I did. I had a red Emerson transistor radio plastered against my ear from the moment we landed in San Jose. With few friends, no toys, and a lot of extra time to kill before first grade began, music became the soundtrack of my first year in San Jose. Over the next few years, tunes like Percy Faith's "Theme from A Summer Place," Brian Hyland's "Sealed with a Kiss," Chubby Checker's "The Twist," Johnny Crawford's "Cindy's Birthday," Nat King Cole's "Ramblin' Rose," Ray Charles' "I Can't Stop Loving You," The Brothers Four's "Greenfields," The Tokens' "The Lion Sleeps Tonight," The Tornados' "Telstar," Gale Garnett's "We'll Sing in the Sunshine," Dusty Springfield's "I Only Want to Be with You," Freddy Cannon's "Palisades Park," and The Exciters' "Tell Him" were my joy. I lived for and lived in that red transistor radio and the pink clock radio that sat at my bedside. The songs played in my ear and conjured up images of romance, locations, situations, and what adulthood and falling in love might look like. I could hardly wait to grow up and discover what they were singing about.

I would often dance, or attempt to dance, to every record I had in my small collection. My favorite was "Mashed Potato Time" by Dee Dee Sharp. Another song on the same record was a tune entitled "Gravy (For My Mashed Potatoes)." The first line? "C'mon baby, I need gravy." We had low expectations in the Sixties. That was Exhibit A. Here is Exhibit B: "Hang on Sloopy, Sloopy hang on…." And Exhibit C: "Yummy, yummy, yummy, I've got love in my tummy." Enough said.

✳ ⚛ ✳

My most beloved possession was a record player with a dropdown lid. You'd have to prop the lid straight up when you wanted to spin records, which in my case was all the time. "Stranger on the Shore" by Acker Bilk was my first 45 record. He had a name that always seemed like it should be Bill Acker ... or William Acre. Acker Bilk not only had an unusual name, he played a silky smooth clarinet. My father played clarinet, and I suspect that's how the song endeared itself to me. I let it spin over and over again. It was a wordless tune, and I rarely was drawn to wordless tunes, but "Stranger on the Shore" was one of the exceptions. The song always made me envision a calm, watery, wondrous tropical paradise. Bilk not only recorded the tune, but also he wrote the music. I played this song so often that the record skipped, clicked, and did a long jump near the end of the record. I never knew how the original ending of the song was supposed to sound until years later when I heard "Stranger on the Shore" played on the radio. I managed to memorize the song with the skip and jump. Records were notorious for having pops and clicks, sounding more like bacon frying than a melody.

A not uncommon practice in the Sixties was having two separate artists or bands recording the same song, resulting in not one, but two hit records. Both Marvin Gaye and Gladys Knight had a hit record with "Heard It Through the Grapevine." "Keep Me Hanging On" was a hit for both The Supremes and Vanilla Fudge. "You've Got a Friend" brought fame and fortune to both Carole King and James Taylor. "Proud Mary" went to the top of the charts for both Creedence Clearwater Revival and Ike and Tina Turner.

I became giddy about my favorite artists or groups putting out a new record. When lyrics first began to appear on the back or inside of album covers, I read every word on the sleeve before popping the actual record onto the player. The Beatles' 1967 early concept album *Sgt. Pepper's Lonely Hearts Club Band* was one of the first to feature lyrics on the album jacket, and other artists followed quickly. On Laura Nyro's album *Eli and The Thirteenth Confession,* Nyro insisted that the album's lyric sheet (which was still a rarity for records in 1968) was perfumed. Even today, fans have reported that it still has a pleasant scent.

I scoured and absorbed each album cover and sleeve, front and back, even those without printed lyrics. I reviewed and reflected on the cover design of each album and processed every aspect of the record with a visual embrace.

Brotherly Love Punch

I cannot imagine growing up in a big family of siblings, uncles, aunts, and cousins. My family tree had four branches: father, mother, brother, and me. I always thought it would be fun to forge through childhood with multiple siblings as built-in playmates, confidants, partners-in-crime. Even my extended family tree was on the small side, more like a bonsai shrub that sits on a coffee table. Most of my relatives lived on the right coast while I was sprouting on the left coast. New York seemed light-years away from California. Yes, the East Coast had better deli items and Italian ices, but in sunny and new California we had milder weather, endless quantities of dried fruit, and Baskin-Robbins.

My older brother was tall and lanky, lackadaisical in the classroom, and aggressive with his punches. He projected toughness and tenacity, while I was graced with over-sensitivity and delicacy. In short, I crumbled easily and often. I must have looked like a tetherball to Harold, as he would punch his fist in the direction of my stomach for no apparent reason. Since I had a tummy like soft pastry, I gritted my teeth and took it in the gut. My stomach continued to be a punching bag for my brother's fists of fury for several years, his blows often knocking the air out of me. I couldn't breathe for several seconds that felt like hours. He didn't need a reason. Like my father's verbal outbursts, Harold's angry fits and fist sprang out of nowhere. While walking down the hallway at home, and without forewarning—BAM!

"You'd better watch out, Sis, or I'm going to pound you."

Naturally, my parents were never around to witness these one-sided boxing matches. Didn't his drum lessons release enough adolescent angst onto those defenseless animal skins? Maybe he was getting beaten up in school. Kids often jumped and tussled with the uncool or unpopular students after school. It was a hazing ritual, and like all hazing rituals, it was crafted of equal parts of boredom and nonsense in those tiny, teenage lizard brains. Maybe they sensed he was a *schlemiel* (a weakling) and picked on him. Harold and I had grown up together, but we never talked about why he got beat up at school, the dynamics of our parents, void of care and affection. We coexisted, but didn't communicate about such matters. We didn't know how.

I inherited my brother's taste in music and borrowed a good portion of his record collection, mostly when he wasn't looking. Cream, Tower of Power, Coltrane, Blue Cheer, Janis Joplin's Big Brother and the Holding Company. On his bedroom wall was an oversized poster of Jefferson Airplane. Each member of the group was dressed in appropriate Sixties era fashions with cool glasses and vacant stares. They all held different musical contraptions in their hands. Paul Kantner held a small stringed instrument at his eye and let the neck curl in front of his glasses. Grace Slick smiled, bangs stylishly dipped to one side of her forehead and covering a good portion of her eye. There were hieroglyphics plastered on the wall behind them. Who the hell knew what it all meant? It didn't matter. It was bitchin'. The photo would become the cover design for their classic album *Surrealistic Pillow*.

A short time later, my brother added a gigantic poster of Janis Joplin to his bedroom gallery. Her mane of unruly, enthusiastic hair fell to one side of her face and, again, covered one eye. Didn't anyone need two eyes to see in the Sixties? One of Janis' breasts peeked out of her black velvet embroidered shirt and fell between the strands of her necklace. Unless you had an eagle eye, you didn't see the nipple, but it was there, waiting to be discovered by adolescent boys everywhere.

Grace Slick wrote "White Rabbit" in late 1965, well before she joined Jefferson Airplane. She could never have imagined that song would pave the way for psychedelic rock. The music she came up with was based on a slow Spanish march, or *bolero*, that builds in intensity. She had always had a thing for Spanish folk music. One day she and her then husband took acid, and she put on Miles Davis' *Sketches of Spain*. She adored the album and listened to it over and over for hours, particularly "Concierto de Aranjuez," a hypnotic tune that takes up most of the first side. That album inspired "White Rabbit." Grace Slick said she identified with Alice and celebrated her fearlessness for following the white rabbit down the hole. But once down there, Alice didn't have a Prince Charming or any other sorry schlub to lean on. As Slick put it, she had to "save her own ass while going through all the insane hallucinogenic stuff."

Grace too was a product of America in the Fifties. She grew up in nearby Palo Alto, where she witnessed women as housewives with hair piled high on their heads in programmed roles that were carefully orchestrated. They didn't dare step over the line, but Grace did. She went from the planned, bland Fifties era into the wicked world of rock 'n' roll. It was her own Alice in Wonderland era, as she headed down the rabbit hole and into the unknown. But we all did that. Most people didn't realize that "White Rabbit" was a song aimed at parents who drank and told their kids not to do drugs. The hypocrisy of that time was reflected in the lyrics, but most of us missed that meaning. We were too busy tripping.

Harold took up the drums at an early age and put together his first group, Night Raiders. But the only thing they raided in the evening was the refrigerator. The entire population of The Eichlers could hear him practicing the single paradiddle and other rudimentary routines in the late afternoon and on weekends. One day, when my father wasn't thinking too clearly, he invited my brother's band to play at one of their very adult parties. The cocktail crowd tolerated shaky renditions of "Wipe Out" and "Wild Thing" for about thirty-five minutes before they made the boys break down their instruments, pack up their amps, and go straight to bed.

Night Raiders wasn't the only band to cover such garage band classics. Other renditions of "Wild Thing" surfaced, including one by Jimi Hendrix, and others by Hank Williams Jr., as well as every pimple-faced sixteen-year-old who'd ever picked up a guitar. The song was defiant, powerful, and primitive, and everything rock 'n' roll ever wanted to compress into a two-minute, thirty-second masterpiece. Legend has it that the song had its start on an afternoon in late 1965. Musician Chip Taylor went to a New York recording studio, sat down with his massive Kay guitar, and started strumming away on the strings. Out came "Wild Thing." It made my heart sing. My friends and I turned up the volume when that song came on the radio. We never knew why. It was our own brand of head-banging music.

* ⚛ *

Harold and his pal, Bad Brad, the Eddie Haskell of the cul-de-sac, would tear out the centerfolds of my father's *Playboy* magazines, Scotch-tape them to a diamond-shaped kite and fly them high in the sapphire skies over the ten homes in our cul-de-sac. When the wind died down, those kites with their torpedo-shaped breasts and come-hither stares would shimmy and shake downward like a stripper on a pole and land. They'd land on roofs, telephone wires, and fences. That's when the fun and loud parental bellowing began. The two snickering boys would run faster than a speeding bullet as soon as the kite landed. They would run as far as their legs could take them, far from parental outrage, but not too far from the glee and enthusiastic applause of their peers.

That's what you did in childhood. You ran. You ran to play. You ran to school. You ran from punishment, you ran, and then ran faster ... because you could. Later, we would become adults and have to stand tall, stiffen our upper lips, face the music, deal with the consequences, and explain ourselves. And when someone said to you, "Ah, go fly a kite," you dug your nails into your thigh, toughened your skin, and tried not to take it personally. But in the Sixties, with kites designed and flown by my brother and Bad Brad, we didn't take a helluva lot too seriously.

The Art of Chokes and Other Sixties Fare

Most appliances in the Sixties were finished in avocado green or harvest gold, replacing the cheery turquoise and red of the Fifties. Even though many appliances remained white, colors of that decade bloomed to include cadet blue, wood-tone brown, petal pink, and canary yellow. But cadet blue and wood-tone brown proved to be unpopular and were quickly discontinued.

We had coffee-colored appliances in the Eichler kitchen. The freezer in our refrigerator required defrosting on a regular schedule when it became overstuffed with frost, and we'd practically need a trowel to free the stalagmites and stalactites from that small compartment. It was like being back in New York shoveling snow.

My mother rarely bought ice cream. It was too expensive. Instead, she would purchase imitation ice cream, or even worse, imitation ice milk. No one would touch them, as those unimpressive bricks would lean into the back of our freezer until they sprouted icicles or came down with a serious case of frostbite.

In the Fifties and Sixties, grocery stores contained many products labeled IMITATION, such as lower-fat "imitation" ice cream made with milk rather than cream. To avoid the dreaded term *imitation*, some ice cream manufacturers began naming these preparations "ice milk" rather than "ice cream." We defined ice milk as a flavorless slab that was square, hard, and cold, and soon emptied into the sink.

There were many foods I found revolting as a child, but now find delicious. I was repulsed by rhubarb. I didn't like the way it tasted, looked, or was spelled. Today, I like my slices of rhubarb pie as large as possible. Other foods that made my taste buds revolt included mushrooms, black olives, and zucchini. Now I enjoy all of these flavors and stuff them in my omelets or dribble them on my pizza. And somehow, I managed to be late to the ball when it came to eating apple pie with a slice of melted cheddar cheese. It seemed like an odd, nearly nauseating prospect. Cheddar cheese melted on fruit? Absurd. But now, I thoroughly enjoy the textures and tastes. I don't know if I crave it because it is such an unlikely mesh of consistencies or because the tastes collide in such a way that it feels terribly wrong, yet oh-so-right.

Willi Hastings once said, "Eating an artichoke is like getting to know someone really well." True. Artichokes looked strange to me as a kid—like something we shouldn't touch, so we didn't. I didn't eat an artichoke until I was in my twenties. It was one of many food items that was nowhere near my family's culinary orbit. We tended to dine on minute steaks, "chopped meat" (hamburger), pork chops, lamb chops, Shake 'N Bake chicken, peas, and pot roast. Mexican food, other than what could be found at Taco Bell, was non-existent. Thai, Vietnamese, Greek, crepes, Indian stews, or anything exotic was not on our menu. It wasn't even on our radar. Chinese food was about the only "foreign food" people ate in great abundance in Northern California, at least in that era. It was ubiquitous and qualified as comfort food.

Spicy flavors like red pepper or curry were not considered child-friendly in the Sixties. Perhaps we don't develop our sense of taste early enough to appreciate having holes burning through the middle of our tongues, or hot peppers creating forest fires in our tummies. Mexican parents sometimes give their children packets of sugar mixed with red chili powder in order to build their spice tolerance. Such exposure to small amounts of spices at a young age desensitizes nerve endings. But the fare at our house was bland as beige matzo balls. Spicy food always seemed adult and off-limits.

Sleep of Faith

The only countertop appliance we owned was a hot dog maker my parents won as a door prize in a raffle at Hawaiian Village, a local restaurant. They were so excited to win anything, let alone this plastic steaming contraption. It took ten minutes longer to cook hot dogs in the hot dog maker than it would in boiling water, but who cared? It was food and food machinery, both winners in my father's eyes and therefore in our household. The hot dog maker was proudly displayed on the kitchen top. It gathered more dust than the abundance of nondescript junk displayed on the family room shelves.

* ⚛ *

Since my mother was not a homemaker, she had to find a way to break out of the confinement she found herself in. Domesticity was not in her comfort zone and she hadn't grown into it, even in the Eichler tract, a suburban paradise. Initially, she sought out part-time jobs at Penney's Department Store and later at Breuner's Furniture Showroom. My mother needed to be out in the adult world, even if that world was a boring showroom of Barcaloungers.

Eventually, like many of her peers in the Eichler neighborhood, Mom returned to night school to complete her bachelor's degree. She was out of the house several nights a week. Those evenings turned into nightmares before I even closed my eyes to sleep. I was alone with my father. He was a risky mix of unpredictability and anger. What would he do next? I never knew. I imagined the Creature from the Black Lagoon seated in the living room watching TV. My goal was to remain out of his sight. Since my bedroom was catty-corner to the living quarters of the Eichler, this was easily accomplished. Lying in bed at night in some catawampus position, I remained in a state of hyper-vigilance, soaked to the skin in sweat, unable to sleep, listening with every fiber of my being for my mother's car pulling into the carport and her keys jingling at the front door. Only when I heard that familiar "click" could I breathe again. My muscles would soften. My brain would quiet. My eyes closed.

At some point in childhood, insomnia whooshed into my life like a dark vapor and never left. I'd lie awake and wonder how strange it was that in order to fall asleep, I'd have to lie still and pretend to be asleep. Sleep equated to death. What's the difference? You'd lie there and let go into some unknown state, not knowing if you were going to wake up. How could that late-night darkness be trusted? It couldn't be, certainly not by me. My mind twisted up like a candy wrapper in the wind, or some long receipt from the drugstore that got away from its bag. A storm of past, present, and future worries whirled and twirled and never quite landed or resolved.

I soon found myself envying others who could fall asleep easily and sleep throughout the night. Their brains seemed clearer, the floorboards of the skull swept clean, and all the little goblins of the past or future locked up tight in a dusty trunk at the foot of the bed. If there was a way to overthink some event or idea, I would.

As I lay in my dark room prickling with panic, I prayed to an unknown God for the sunlight and shuffling sounds of morning activity. I wanted to hear the plumbing come alive with early showers and repeated flushing. I needed to know I was still alive and prepared for another day in this repeated drama, or whatever I was in. I bet Theodore and Wally Cleaver, tucked in their cozy bedroom surrounded by Mr. and Mrs. Cleaver's night sounds, never worried or had a racing heart. And if they did, it was about tomorrow's test in Miss Landers' class, or some football player who might beat them up after school. Big deal. My worries had to do with the universe, the existence of God, and the non-existence of me in my family.

My mother continued her night classes, and I continued to have nightly episodes of sleeplessness. Even when I did fall asleep, my dreams were full of stress. I often awoke with my face contorted in some pose of horror, eyebrows furrowed, lips clenched tight. As I lay awake, I could hear the faint murmur of the television droning on or my parents in the kitchen. *Okay, I'm not the only one awake,* I'd think to myself. Good! Relief. When the low talking ceased, and the lights began to dim one by one, and I couldn't locate any brightness at the opening under my bedroom door, panic rushed through every cell in my body. Pitch black! I'm alone! Everyone went somewhere else (yes, to sleep!) and I'm still here, abandoned in a conscious state no one else occupies. It was like that *Twilight Zone* episode where there was only one person left in the entire world. But that person wasn't Burgess Meredith in his sole existence after a nuclear holocaust takes out every other human being on the planet. It was me.

At the time I didn't know what was happening to me. My heart would race, and I began hyperventilating and sweating until my pajamas were sopping wet. I'd examine the hands of the clock across the room and dread the lateness of the hour. I had to get up for school the next day. If it's 11:30 p.m., how many hours of sleep will I manage if I get up at 7 a.m.? I'd start doing math in my head, which was fine if it didn't involve fractions, long division, or multiplication tables. How would I manage to be alert in class, or walk, or function if I'm up all night? Why can't I sleep? Why won't my brain turn off? What's wrong with me? AGGHHH!

I began to play little games and invent secret scenarios to help me drift to sleep. My thoughts were active when my head hit the pillow, but if I turned them off immediately and concentrated only on clearing my mind or clouding my thoughts into a mental blur, I could fall fast asleep. But if I began to run the mental film-roll of fantasy episodes, sometimes starring Elvis with his licorice black hair, or a beautiful horse I was given to ride, or lying under the stars with some nameless, faceless prince holding me in his arms, I would lie awake for hours. Once the tales went into a tailspin, they wouldn't stop. The fantasies played on and on as the night grew later and later. My brain went into a hyper-active state with swirling thoughts, like busy bees swarming the mind's nest. No matter what I did or didn't do, I couldn't control it. Nothing could soothe me to sleep. I would finally succumb to exhaustion.

When I awoke to familiar morning sounds coming from the kitchen, I could finally relax. I had made it through another fitful night. Maybe I would be able to stand on my own two feet today, at least for a while. I had lost so much sleep in my childhood. I decided that, in adulthood, I would make up for it and sleep in until noon.

Playboy and Penthouse and Oui, Oh My!

Our Eichler was bursting at the seams with girly magazines. Each issue was a Holy Bible of sorts. It set the standard for what I thought men desired and women should look like—glazed and glossy. I thought it was the only version of sexy on the planet.

Playboy magazine regularly featured interviews with well-known personalities, such as Frank Sinatra, Miles Davis, Marlon Brando, Jack Nicholson, Vladimir Nabokov, and Norman Mailer, as well as advice columns, faux letters, sexually oriented cartoons, and airbrushed faces, breasts, and shoulders leaning against doorways or semi trucks, or in other unlikely locations. The other magazines my father subscribed to—such as *Penthouse, Oui, Mad, Cracked,* and *Evergreen Review*—explored different regions and open landscapes.

At this time, *Penthouse* was still soft porn, but more explicit than *Playboy,* focusing on genitals and uneasy close-ups, while *Oui* was out there, wild 'n' woolly and flapping in the breeze. *Oui* got right down to business. No come-hither stares. No sexy lingerie. Just labias, freckles, irregular areolas, and triangles of kinky hair waving the viewer in like checkered flags at a racetrack. Their audience had to pull open the pages and take a peek. They couldn't help themselves.

I was embarrassed to open *Penthouse* and could barely convince myself to turn the pages of *Oui* magazine with its outstretched thighs, naughty bits, and droopy breasts pointing southward. In a 1977 issue of *Oui,* an interview appeared featuring a then twenty-nine-year-old emerging actor named Arnold Schwarzenegger. He openly discussed sex, drugs, bodybuilding, and homosexuality. A quarter of a decade later, that interview produced some embarrassment for candidate Schwarzenegger during the 2003 gubernatorial campaign in Kah-lee-foh-nee-a. But at the time, he was making history in another way ... with his steroid-enhanced limbs.

While *Penthouse* was revealing all, *Playboy* hid or airbrushed imperfections out of sight, including blemishes, cellulite, pubic hair, and smallpox vaccine scars. The women seemed softer and more idealized; a delicate mix of sweet and saucy. My brain became wired with the convincing thought that I had to be airbrushed, full-busted, and coquettish in a short plaid skirt, but no blouse. The problem was, my body didn't approach the figures on the pages of *Playboy*. My breasts were small, and I had boyish hips. Even when I began to develop, I didn't have enough to fill an A cup, let alone a B, C, D, or DD. I wanted DD. I wanted to be one of the idealized images whose only imperfection was a staple and crease across her abdomen, courtesy of the page fold. When boys began to pay attention to me, I couldn't figure out why. My nickname was Carol Swizzlesticks because of my slender limbs. Could female allure even exist without curves? I was convinced it wasn't possible.

In addition to soft porn scattered around our living room, there were numerous ballpoint pens featuring bikini-clad women on the side of each writing instrument. Whenever you turned the pen upside down, the woman would miraculously become undressed. Their conservative swimsuit would slip right off to reveal nothing but a birthday suit. If I accidently picked up one of my father's special pens to do math homework, my face would turn crimson red. Dad!

Our family room featured two three-shelf bookcases, both painted jet black with a brilliant chartreuse trim. Chartreuse was all the rage in the Fifties, so we decided to drag it into the Sixties. Our Eichler home was filled with chartreuse and orange hues. When did IKEA begin ripping off my parents' palette?

Although my parents' furnishings were purchased in New York City shortly after they were married, all of their décor soon became ours, in fully screaming carrot orange and bright green. While we were pulled kicking and screaming to California, my parents dragged the nice quiet furnishings along to fill our new home on the West Coast. Those two bookcases, now positioned in the dining room, were crammed with paperback books. My mother always read two or three books at one time. She would get lost in the fictionalized, complicated lives and small tales of non-existent individuals. I approached reading differently. I preferred biographies and autobiographies and learning about the real world around me. That included butterflies, insects, philosophies, and artwork.

Even though my mother's interest didn't lie in the real world, she filled the bookcase with a handful of non-fiction books. One was by Dr. Benjamin Spock, a book on babies and childrearing that was a mainstay resource during that era. The *Baby and Child Care* paperback was popular with everyone but my mother, unless she needed a coaster for her cup of Folger's coffee.

The other non-fiction book was *The Shape of Content* by Ben Shahn. Shahn's name always looked like a puzzle to me, with all the h's and n's leaning against one another in an uneasy fashion. His book featured whimsical sketches, line drawings placed alongside philosophic blurbs and rants on art and artistry. I was charmed by his drawings and would gaze at the pages for hours. Those drawings ended up having more impact on my later interest in art than anything else. Strangely enough, it was a book I never actually read. I wish I had, as I learned later that *The Shape of Content* included writing on artists' thinking in a time considered the height of modern American painting. Having a book full of essays by someone so likable, artistic, and seemingly accessible as Shahn made this book an easy read, but I looked at the drawings instead. I was at an age where only hide 'n' seek, four-square, and gazing at pretty pictures held my interest. I wasn't too interested in his words, but his simplistic line drawings spoke volumes to me.

Our house held a few other odd black pieces of furniture. My father's desk was fashioned from thick black steel wires. He had matching Fifties artwork of abstract fish twisted from wire on the wall above the desk. The desk and fish sculptures meshed perfectly, but they were the only things in our house that did.

The living room's tweed chartreuse couch stood out to the eye. It had a secret compartment on the far right side of the seat that could be discovered only by lifting the end of the couch cushions. Inside this special compartment was a space for sheets, pillows, and pillowcases. My parents had transported this heavy couch-bed out from New York only to reupholster and replace it. It was where my grandparents slept when they came to visit us on Long Island. With its secret compartment and enchanted ability to turn itself into a bed, the brand name should have been Houdini. I thought that couch was a magic trick in itself. My brother and I slept on it in the family room of the Eichler when we first moved out to California. The mattress was rock hard, but when you're a kid you can sleep anywhere—on the floor, on a shoulder, or with your head banging against the car window.

Our furnishings were modest, and our rooms had a lived-in aura. Several of my schoolmates had roped off living rooms with plastic pieces covering the couch cushions and chairs. They were allowed in the room a couple of times a year, or on special occasions like a baby christening or a celebration of the tortured death of Jesus Christ. Otherwise, the space sat unused, antiseptic, and useless. The rooms and furnishings in our Eichler were thoroughly used and abused. We had to have our green couch recovered at some point so that it would last another decade. The new fabric was a bright gold tweed. Later, my parents replaced the sofa with a Naugahyde butterscotch couch that was as uncomfortable as it was hideous. It's hard to say which couch assaulted the eye more. Let's call it a three-way tie.

I never knew what Naugahyde was. I knew it was noisy, and I kept sliding off of it. It turned out to be an American brand of artificial leather—a combination of knit fiber backing and an expanded polyvinyl chloride (PVC) plastic coating. Whoever sat on it sounded like they had a bad case of gas from an omelet with too many onions. In equal parts durable and hideous, it acted as a substitute for leather in upholstery during the Sixties. A marketing campaign of that era proclaimed, with tongue firmly planted in cheek, that Naugahyde was obtained from the skin of an animal called a Nauga. The campaign emphasized that, unlike other animals, which had to be slaughtered to obtain their hides, the Nauga could effortlessly shed its skin without any harm to themselves. The Nauga doll, a pudgy, horned monster with a devilish grin, emerged from this myth and is still sold today. Some things refuse to die, including the Nauga and their wicked marketing campaign.

Our family always included a feline and an abundance of its fur embedded in each couch, chair, or loveseat. We worshipped Pushka, a perpetually shedding white cat with dazzling green eyes. Dad became a kitten when he played with that cat. He made up songs about Pushka and sang them out loud as he pursued her around the house with outstretched arms. "Pushy, Pushy," he would croon like a love song as he chased her down the hallway and around the corner. In the evenings, my parents would go out for their nightly walk around the block, and Pushka would follow them, always a few steps behind.

Mom chose to feed Pushka Friskies cat food from the tall green can. I was certain they chose Friskies because there was an illustration of a white cat on the label. Since my parents' policy was to overfeed everything and everyone in the household, Pushka ballooned to twenty pounds. She lived one year for every pound she carried. Twenty years of catastrophes and, as my mother often pointed out, grace. I can't remember a time in my childhood when Pushka wasn't ever-present, or when my mother wouldn't point her index finger at her and mutter, "Look! She has cat dignity."

After catting around the neighborhood and howling on the fences, she gave us litter after litter of exquisite fluffy multicolored kittens. I watched her give birth, I followed each kitten around the house, took them outside to explore the front lawn, fell in love with them, and cried when they were given away to people not worthy of their greatness. We eventually kept a couple of the white kittens and named them Roxanne and Marty. Soon they were nowhere to be found. Mom gave them away when they hit adolescence. Cats and kids no longer cute were banished from the Eichler in record numbers. But Pushka was the queen. She paraded around the house like she owned the place. And she did. She thought she was a dog. But she was Pushka, the first feline who made my heart flutter. We grew up together in a perfect storm of drugs, sex, rock 'n' roll, and Friskies Buffet.

Cooking 101

I felt like an extraordinary cook when I opened my first package of Chef Boyardee Pizza Mix. The box featured a drawing of the mustached chef with the words "with cheese and Italian pizza sauce" beckoning consumers to grab a box off the grocery shelf. I was a pre-teen who wanted to emulate June Cleaver.

My friends' parents cooked. Their homes smelled like stew, meatloaf, and sautéed carrots and peas. Mine smelled like Lysol. I set out to change all of that as I ripped open the bright yellow box of Italian fare. Inside was a petite can of sauce, a minuscule packet of dry and dusty sprinkle cheese, and a dough mixture that created a s-t-r-e-t-c-h-y thin tasteless crust. I added water and did everything it instructed, and although I was often poor at following instructions, for Chef Boyardee I would make an exception.

But, even when I followed the instructions carefully with their water to powdery crust mixture ratio, the sticky dough never quite fit the pan. I would stretch it as far as my fingers could reach, but it kept pulling itself back to the center, or worse yet, adhering itself to my fingers. There was so little tomato sauce that it covered only a third of the pizza, and the enclosed sachet of cheese, the size of a sugar packet, was an insult to cheese lovers everywhere. Ah, but the aroma of pizza in the oven—even a poor excuse for a pizza like this built-from-a-box pie, was divine. The end result was a pizza pie with craters in the elasticized dough and the face of an aluminum pan poking through. This ragged paper-thin crust was topped with a watery red sauce.

My favorite food group was cake, so I tackled the boxed variety offered by Duncan Hines. I was convinced Betty Crocker and Duncan Hines were real people baking cakes all day in their kitchenettes, just as I was convinced Aunt Jemima was a real person who happened to be shaped like a curvy bottle of maple-flavored syrup and who actually moved and spoke phrases about pancake breakfast, like the ads told us. The Madison Avenue marketing machine knew how to push their propaganda. They had us believing Aunt Jemima was like Mother Earth with her substantial arms and sparkling smile, always wearing a colorful kerchief over her massive head. She was like Grandma Mae if Grandma Mae had been black, sweet, and kind.

Pancakes had always been a treat, but cakes were even better. My mother kept two round cake pans in the cupboard and one of those one-speed handheld mixers. I would gather the pans, butter 'em, pour flour in them, and shake them until every crumb stuck to the grease or to the floor tiles, mix up the batter with the chug-a-lug beater, and—voilà!—dry cake.

The most challenging step was maximizing the boxed icing mix. There was never enough provided, so you had to struggle to cover every zone of the cake surface without making it look like it had some dreadful ailment. What a rip-off! When they eventually came out with rich and creamy icing in a can, it was an entirely different adventure. There was always a bonus amount of frosting in each can for licking off the spoon.

Friends of a Kind

The Irackis are coming! The Irackis are coming!

My parents' closest friends were an eccentric bunch with names that made them seem as though they'd been transported here from another era and galaxy: Nan Mann. Gigi and Grattan. Cookie and Al. Augie and Bunny. Billy and Betty Nudd, whom I fondly referred to as Billy and Betty Nuts.

The names of my parents' friends could have easily become titles for a Sixties sitcom or variety show. My mother's address book was filled with: Florence, Selma, Rose, Mitzy, Frances, Edith, Dee, Lil, Tola, Gladys, and Heidi. Then there was my father's work friend Bill Wikstrom, whom he called Wee Willie Wikstrom because of his place of origin, Sweden ... or because it sounded catchy.

There was also my father's colleague Doc Roberts, and his boss and the CEO of FMC, Mr. Hait. The names of my parents' friends sounded like they were from some dime-store novel. But above and beyond the Nudds, nuts, and Manns, were the Irackis.

In 1966, a comedy film directed by Norman Jewison was released. It was titled *The Russians Are Coming! The Russians Are Coming!* Whenever Bill and Mary Iracki and their sons would visit us at the Eichler, my father would yell at the top of his lungs, "The Irackis are coming! The Irackis are coming!" until they arrived at our front door.

It's an understatement to say that my parents' friends, Bill and Mary Iracki, were a peculiar pair. They owned a laundromat in San Francisco, so Bill would go back and forth to collect coins from the washer and dryer machines on a daily basis. This is what he did for a living. He never worked a day in his life, but he was damn good at collecting quarters. My father, a workaholic, would go on frequent rants about how Bill was "a bum" because he never held down a job. Strangely enough, my parents thoroughly enjoyed the company of both Bill and Mary, the odd couple.

Mary Iracki began teaching English as a second language in tough-as-nails schools to tough-as-nails kids. She taught kids in one of the most impoverished and gang-ridden hubs of San Francisco. On numerous occasions she was beaten up by her students or their friends during her walk home. She would show up to lunch with my parents sporting a black eye or bandaged head. City of

Love? Not for Mary Iracki. My parents were horrified, but even more horrified that Mary kept teaching there and that Bill continued to stuff his pockets with quarters and never looked for a job.

Bill was a wall of a man with broad shoulders, a chiseled face, fair Scandinavian coloring, and apparently no work ethic. He looked like Superman, but without the super paycheck. Soft-spoken, he hovered around Mary like a massive catcher's mitt, as if he were anticipating her next fall. I was certain neither one of them would survive without the other. Mary and Bill were the yin to each other's yang.

I remember a visit to their home on one gray San Francisco afternoon. Most afternoons in San Francisco were gray. Bill, Mary, and the two boys lived in one of those pastel Victorian duplexes in San Francisco, which to me was like an adult-sized dollhouse. I couldn't contain my excitement. What fun it would be to live inside this bold, but traditional house—so radically different from the sleek lines and plentiful glass of our Eichler.

Mary was the mother of two delicate boys, Tom and Paul, who seemed, in a word, slow. They spoke very deliberately. I was around eight or so when I met them, so I didn't really understand the wide spectrum of learning and mental disabilities. I only knew they seemed to function at a slower speed in their speech and movement than my brother and me. Tom and Paul were in their own world much of the time, unaware of our presence or anything else that was happening around them. The only time I saw their power of concentration was when one of them was playing the accordion and the other was tolerating it. I later learned that Tom committed suicide in his early twenties. Paul later became Paula, long before Bruce Jenner became Caitlyn Jenner, and long before it was fashionable.

As unusual as the name Iracki was, the queerest name with the queerest friend attached was my father's work colleague, Benjamin Schnapp. Benjamin rode a bicycle everywhere. He rode it to work, to play, and to his ex-wife's house. She couldn't stand bicycles, or Benjamin. After his divorce, Benjamin became a weekend dad. He would pick up his kids on his bicycle, and they would all pedal down the road. Sometimes it was a ten-mile route. Other times, twenty or more.

Another recently divorced work friend of my father's, Bob Engler, wanted to compile a cookbook titled *You CAN Cook*. Every recipe included a can of Campbell's Soup. My father thought this was an extraordinary idea. I thought it was absurd. Yet when my father asked me if I would type up the entire manuscript and come up with a book cover design, I obliged. I never said no to my father's whims. The power to please was my fuel.

Each nonsensical recipe seemed to have only two or three ingredients. A can of tomato soup with added sliced apple. A can of cream of celery soup with a sprinkling of coconut. A can of tomato soup with a big bonus: a meatball. To quote *MAD* magazine, "Blecch!" I suggested to my father that his friend rename the book *The Clueless New Bachelor Non-Cook Cookbook,* and subtitle it *Everything Tastes Like Tomato Soup.*

Bob eventually dated every inappropriate young woman in Santa Clara Valley. He then left FMC to sell real estate in Portland and date every underage woman in Oregon. He managed to have a different girlfriend for each month of the year. He was a wildcat. One year, he came to visit my parents with a different girlfriend on his arm from the one he had the week before. These sex kittens rubbed up against him as if the fabric on his flannel shirt were soaked in catnip. Or perhaps they were purring about the possibilities of what was in his wallet.

My parents' frequent dinner companions were Gigi and Grattan. Grattan was movie-star handsome with a pile of hair that rivaled Kirk Douglas, with Charlton Heston's chiseled jaw. Upon closer inspection, Grattan possessed a pair of eyes that were going a bit ... well ... cockeyed. He was slowly going blind. His wife, Gigi, would lead him around on her arm while his hand fumbled for a wall or chair or any familiar and comforting horizontal object.

Gigi would often forget Grattan as he stood waiting in the hallway, or she would leave him sitting at the restaurant table after she got up to leave. Gigi was a bit ditzy, but she was elegant and well coiffed. She always wore enormous pieces of colorful costume jewelry around her neck, dangling from her earlobes, and draped over her wrist. The bright red, yellow, and green beads were as large as billiard balls. She looked like she had raided the Woolworth's fine jewelry counter.

My parents would often share tales of Gigi and her impulse to pocket silverware whenever they would go out to eat. My mother would watch in astonishment as the restaurant flatware would slip under Gigi's carefully manicured fingers, off the table's edge, and into her colossal purse that looked more like a suitcase. My father found it amusing. I can only imagine the collection of cutlery this woman had stored in her kitchen drawers.

Years later, my parents named their cat Gigi after their kleptomaniac friend. Gigi-the-cat didn't care for silverware, unless it was shoveling out Fancy Feast tuna-flavored cat food into a plastic dish. It's surprising the Flatware Police never came knocking on Gigi's door to haul her off to Flatware Jail.

Another one of my parents' friends was a TV repairman named Jim Quinn. His kids, who were around my age at the time, used to answer the home phone with "Jim's TV Repair. May I help you?" They seemed so professional and cool, much more so than my brother and I were. At eight years old, they had a job and responsibility. My only job was getting in trouble and detangling my frowzy hair.

Jim Quinn didn't have an office. He took all of his service calls at home and ran out to make house calls with a suitcase full of clanging TV tubes in all shapes and sizes. He seemed to make a decent living. They owned a modest house and had a dilapidated Doughboy pool in their backyard that was always filthy. I loved swimming in it.

Jim's wife, Cala, was full-on Greek, and their house always smelled like moussaka and baklava. It's no wonder I enjoyed going over there. I was convinced their bed sheets were made of phyllo dough. The two of them were a bit mismatched in appearance, much like Laurel and Hardy or the cartoon strip characters Mutt and Jeff. Cala was a short, stocky woman who was forever rumpled. She had a noticeable, raised, boil-type protrusion on one cheek, and her skin looked like it had once been invaded by a fierce firestorm of acne. Jim was twice her size, with thick limbs and even thicker black hair. In all his virile handsomeness, he hovered over her like a persistent waiter, attending to her every need. The lovebirds had a Ph.D. in PDA (public displays of affection). They cuddled, they cooed, they shot each other smoldering glances. His laughter was loud and filled every room. I always imagined their lovemaking would match the vim and vigor of his deafening guffaws. Those two were like a stewed pot of sex. Kisses, hugging, hand-holding. Opa!

Comic Relief

My brother collected *Superman* and *Batman* comic books, and I did the same for *Archie* comics. I kept my collection in a treasure chest, a bent and beaten cardboard box that sat in the corner of my bedroom. Those thin colorful books were my treasures. I could always tell when a different artist was drawing characters for the various books. There was only one genuine artist for each character, at least in my mind. Superman only looked like Superman when so-and-so drew him. Archie and friends looked properly drawn when one particular artist produced them with his pen and ink. The others were hacks. When some understudy or new artist stepped in, the heads suddenly appeared too round, features were too slight, eyes drawn too large or small and very wrong.

The love triangle between Archie, Betty, and Veronica was the Sixties version of Jack Tripper and his blonde and brunette female roommates on *Three's Company*. I don't know why I liked *Archie* comics. None of my friends looked like Betty, Veronica, Jughead, or Reggie. And I never did find a redheaded friend with a checkerboard on the side of his head or covered in immense orange freckles that looked like small continents. Archie was based, in part, on the *Andy Hardy* movie series that starred Mickey Rooney. And when Andy Hardy wasn't rejecting girl-next-door Betsy Booth (Betsy/Betty, get it?), he was dating a slew of Veronica-like girlfriends that included Lana Turner, Donna Reed, and Ann Rutherford. Like Archie, Andy was an average guy who somehow attracted girls who were way out of his league. The same seemed to be true for the eight-time married Mickey Rooney, whose love interests included the luscious Ava Gardner.

My parents always had another place to go. Their respective jobs were laid out for the day like clothes on a bed. They each had an office waiting for them filled with adults and adult conversation, adult play, and adult purpose. They would be there come rain or shine. They liked regimentation and being somewhere for nine hours a day. Or should I say somewhere else. Anywhere else.

My father's boss was named Mr. Hait, although I always thought he was saying Mr. Hate, and so I assumed that my father didn't like his boss. Nothing could have been further from the truth. My father was Mr. Hait's right arm at Food Machinery Corporation. They admired the hell out of one another. An extraordinary engineer in his own right, Jim Hait was best known for his work developing FMC's amphibious tank. Like my father, he was born in Brooklyn, New York, and eventually worked at Peerless Pump as chief engineer. When FMC acquired Peerless in 1932, Hait remained chief engineer, developing pump designs and irrigation devices along with my father. He filed more than twenty patents in his lifetime.

At FMC, Hait ultimately served as president and chief executive officer. In 1983, he was inducted into the Ordnance Hall of Fame, one of the few civilians to be so honored. In 1999, he was inducted into the Silicon Valley Engineering Hall of Fame. He earned everything but an Oscar and a Tony over the course of his career.

The first time my father met Mr. Hait, he was troubleshooting one of their food machinery inventions designed to make milk cartons and then fill them from a valve. But the machine wouldn't seal the containers. It misfired and spilled milk all over the floor.

"We're having a bit of a problem here," my father announced to his colleagues. My father didn't know who Mr. Hait was yet and pushed him aside as he tried to attend to the faulty machinery. Little did he know he was shoving FMC's biggest muckety-muck into a soggy corner of milk. But Mr. Hait took a great liking to my dad, as everyone did. He admired the fact that he was focused and knew what he was doing when so many others were stumbling and bumbling around.

Hait and his wife had acquired a great deal of acreage in Idaho around this time and were having trouble with the irrigation pump on their property. To hear my father tell it, the arms on the machine were so long that they kept knocking the cows in the field over on their sides. A slight exaggeration, I'm sure. Mr. Hait asked my father and mother to come out for a mini-vacation and to troubleshoot the pump mechanism. Where my brother and I were hiding out at this juncture, I have no idea as I've never been to Idaho, nor have I seen cows fall over. Dad managed to solve the problem—one of many that Mr. Hait dropped on his desk—and so began the love affair between Mr. Hait and my father.

It seemed as though everyone had a love affair with my father, or at least with his skills or humor. The other machines he had a hand in were the FMC broccoli machine, milk machine, and desalination machinery. My father even appeared in an instructional movie for a meat-slicing tool. He stood there, like some TV spokesman, but he was dressed in a long white apron. The film co-starred a huge slab of raw meat.

Dad and his ever-present pipe.

Life of the Party

My father had razor-sharp focus when challenged with fixing something mechanical, building a structure, working on his design and drafting projects, or trying to learn a new tune on his shrill soprano sax. But he could also be quite irresponsible. His temper would zoom skyward at the most unexpected times, or his racing thoughts would lead to erratic moments and unplanned escapades. He would isolate himself from others and remain spooky, silent, and sleep-deprived for days.

But on numerous other occasions, he was the life of the party. When he walked into a room, all eyes were on my father, with his whimsical observations, sharp wit, and absorbing tales. He breezed around to every corner and spoke quickly, like Groucho Marx on cocaine. The pictures he painted were vivid with a full brush of well-placed adjectives. His tales always started out slow, laced with pregnant pauses and dramatic facial expressions. He had perfect timing and always an award-winning punch line. But his wide mood swings, keen insights, rapid-fire wit, obsessive mind, and impulsive risk-taking adventures were all signs of a chemical blizzard in his brain.

But we didn't talk of such things in my household, even when we suffered the severe sharp turns in his disposition, and all that came with them. It was as if we were all riding in the same car with dad at the wheel, plowing down a rocky road, but the doors were locked and windows jammed. We were his passengers so we had to figure out a way to manage the ride. We didn't have a name for it. It was his norm, and dancing around him became our own norm.

Mood disorders come in a wide spectrum from soft milky gray to extreme darkness. In hindsight, my father's highs were particularly high. His excitement soared when it came to flashing and colorful lights and unusually useless objects, or anything to do with forbidden sex. He'd perform disappearing acts in the middle of the night, driving down to Mexico on a whim or flying in a private plane to Reno while my brother and I were fast asleep in our beds. If this wasn't a tinge of manic-depression, I don't know what was.

Dad bounced about in the high-altitude winds of mania. He was silly, magnetic, and childlike. But his downturns, frustration, and anger that came with the other end of the continuum were often released in my direction. I had no idea that the cause of his distress had nothing to do with me. I was convinced it all had to do with me. When I was a kid, I was at the center of the universe, so if someone was unhappy, I was the one to blame. Being a convenient punching bag and easy target for his outbursts, I assumed I must have deserved it all. Sometimes there wasn't anything that ignited his mood shifts. They could strike at any moment, day or night. He'd awaken in a state of distress and pace like a lion in the cage shaped like an Eichler. When he threw his verbal punches, my self-worth would shrink to the size of a pea. My confidence and likeability would collapse and crumble to the floor like some weary wrestler. I saw myself through his eyes and tones, and I was, in a word, insignificant. Then the countdown would begin: 5 ... 4 ... 3 ... 2 ... 1. She's ... out!

When I looked at my father, I didn't actually see his diminutive physical form. He had been a slight man most of his life, and his height and features were not threatening. Yet I saw him through a hazy filter of fear and dread. I never quite saw what others did. They saw his clear blue eyes a million miles deep, tight black curls, mischievous, cartoon-like smile as it held his curled pipe in the corner of his mouth. Instead of seeing him, I "felt" him, as if an uncomfortable twister had spun into the room and picked me up with it. His formidable aura filled every corner, and that overwhelming power of his presence, charisma, quick mind, and wit spun 'round like a tornado. I never felt his fondness for me. I only sensed resentment and his desire to not have me nearby. He was a fireball of furious energy, sometimes light and humorous, other times as menacing as a monster that stood ten stories high. In one way or another, my five-foot, seven-inch father was colossal and devastating.

One night, when my brother was nine and I was seven years old, and we were both lost in a dead stage-four sleep, my father sneaked out of the house with my mom around midnight.

"They'll never know we're gone. We'll be back in a few hours."

They boarded a small private plane piloted by my father's colleague at work who was learning to fly. Was he a licensed pilot? Not a chance. Shortly before 1 a.m., they took off during a rainstorm in the rickety plane, filled with hard liquor and inexperience. My father's coworker flew them to Reno that evening while my brother and I were in dreamland.

My mother and father downed a few vodka and tonics at the casino, then a few more, gambled and caroused and flew home at 5 a.m. to ready themselves for work. My father told me this story years later, adding that the plane nearly crashed on the return flight. Of course it did. It was fueled and flown by Jack Daniels.

While all of this action was going on up in the air and down on the ground in noisy casinos, my brother and I were fast asleep in the house unaware of such parental shenanigans. We woke up in the early hours of the morning, drank our Tang, chomped down an Eggo waffle, and were off to school none the wiser. My father did wonder out loud years later what would have happened to us if we'd woken up to find the house parentless. It was a thought that never occurred to either my dad or his copilot, my mom, before taking off into the friendly skies.

On another occasion, my father got a sudden notion to take a long drive from San Jose to parts unknown. It was the middle of the night. My mother was always keen for a new adventure, especially when it meant running away from home. Their friends Betty and Billy Nudd were on board for the mischief, so off they went, kids asleep and unaware. They ended up in Tijuana. Billy Nudd was a significant influence on my father. This manic duo was like a nonstop Lewis and Martin routine, except these adventures involved transportation in planes and all-night car rides south of the border.

Another day, Dad came home with a box of small black, white, and red tiles. He had woken that morning with a crazed notion to cover the living room coffee table in multicolored tiles. Why? Because my father had gotten the idea into his head in the middle of the night. As our family of four sat cross-legged on the floor, each assigned an area of the table top, tiny ceramic tiles of black, red, and white in our clueless hands, we carefully set each small square and gooed it up with some mush that sank between the tiles like warm oatmeal. We then moved on to the surface of the end table. "It all must match," he commanded. My father was at the reins and riding high. We were just trying to keep up.

Sometimes we were embarrassed by his pranks, but most of the time we chuckled at his goofiness. At other times, we'd run for cover as his disposition turned on a dime and sent him on the steep downward track of the roller-coaster. If we didn't clear out of the way, he would take us along with him on some bumpy ride. The time spent serving as a soldier in WWII had something to do with his mental state. But at the time, I didn't know why he did the things he did. He was our father, this was our norm and our home, and hyper-vigilance was the armor we wore.

My father rarely spoke of war except with other men who had also served in WWII. Then they would all chime in, tell stories, glorify and glamorize where they had been and what they had seen. Dad would mention the quick photo he took of Mickey Rooney when the celebrity flew overseas to visit the troops. He'd watch newsreels of shaky gray footage from the battlefields on our TV screen, but seldom commented on the heroic and horrific images. He'd watch *Combat!* with my brother, and they'd cheer on Vic Morrow. He'd laugh at the Nazis on *Hogan's Heroes,* especially Colonel Klink, whom he seemed to know personally. But war seemed to have a lasting effect on my father's psyche.

Dad's photo of Mickey Rooney, taken during WWII when the actor visited the troops.

As George Carlin famously observed, the labels for soldiers' psychological problems changed over the course of the major wars during the twentieth century. In World War I, severe reactions to experiences and visual episodes of war became known as "shell shock." Honest and direct language, like a bomb going off. Two syllables: ka-boom!

By the time World War II rolled around, it was referred to as "battle fatigue." The term made the condition sound like a minor discomfort. "Oh, I'm a little battle-fatigued. I'll take a power nap and be good to go." Fatigue sounded much softer than the term *shock*.

During the Korean War, the authorities came up with the expression "operational exhaustion." Carlin's take on this label: "The phrase was up to eight syllables now, and any last traces of humanity had been completely squeezed out of it. It was absolutely sterile: *operational exhaustion.* Like something that could happen to your car."

But it didn't happen to our car. It happened to my father and millions of other young soldiers. Whether it was "shell shock," "battle fatigue," "operational exhaustion," or finally, "post-traumatic stress disorder," war-related trauma created enormous discomfort for years after soldiers returned home. Those challenges often lasted a lifetime. They certainly did for my father, who witnessed things a twenty-two-year-old should never witness and did things a twenty-two-year-old should never be asked to do. The things he saw and did during the war turned to nightmares that haunted him and unleashed themselves in the form of wide mood swings, and he would disappear for hours, sometimes days, either mentally or physically. My father could run, but he couldn't hide. Those inner battles were always chasing him, then beating him up. Then he'd beat on us, the links on his chain.

Many civilians like my dad don't read the scenery accurately after a wartime experience. They see the world from their inner vision. The recollections are unclear, but they surface as surely as a dead body eventually washes to shore. Insomnia, flashbacks, anger, and depression plagued my father as they plagued and continue to plague millions of veterans. PTSD was and remains overwhelming and damaging not only for the individuals carrying the memories and nightmares, but also to those around them.

My father dreamed of events that he couldn't manage or digest in an awakened state. The pain talked to him in his own language and colored pictures in his own palette of colors with dreams and sometimes nightmares. They told him everything that his conscious mind couldn't.

* ⚛ *

On the one hand, my father was extraordinarily burdensome to live with. He was overly critical, unpredictable, and short-tempered at times. On the other hand, he was comical and charismatic. One side of him was always cancelling out the other, even to me. There was no one who didn't love Joe. He was not a tall man, but women flocked to him as if he were a ten-story tall building jam-packed with masculine vim and verve. They wanted to hear him tell his tales, and he delivered them like no other. They couldn't wait to flirt with his aura of boundless energy and his ability to make them fall on the floor howling in laughter.

Some of my father's impulsive decisions were wonderful, like the times he came home with some electronic gizmo that no one else had heard of yet or purchased some artwork for the wall that had blinking lights that twinkled all night as they poked out of the canvas, or when he tossed a unique toy or board game onto my bed; one that had just hit the market. Then there were those other times.

One workday, my father and mother decided to call in sick to work and drive down the coastline nonstop to Ensenada, Mexico, as my brother and I hurried off to school. With no sleep, but a mountain of frantic energy, my father purchased an empty lot of beach property right on the spot. It was dirt cheap. Without sleep or stops, they drove home and realized what a mistake they had made as they had received no paperwork that held any weight this side of the border. It was too late. The Mexican government kept their deposit and their dignity. Lesson learned? Not bloody likely. My father was already on to his next adventure.

* ⚛ *

One night, Dad came home with a strobe-light device that was unlike anything my brother and I had ever seen. A few years later, they would be commonplace at concerts and in poster shops, but then it was like bringing home a Martian from Mars. My brother and I would prance through the living room, hands and legs flailing, bathed in flashing lights and my father's laughter. He would finally join in, jumping and running around like a child with uncontrollable giggles trailing behind him. There was nothing I enjoyed more than my father's howls of delight. I felt like we were all on top of the world—my father's world. And for a moment, we were. Then my mother stepped in and shut down the whole operation. "You'll fall down in the dark. Joe. Turn that damn thing off." Off it went, and off we went running to our rooms to try to contain our elation.

I was often the butt of my father's personal jokes. He would promise to take me here or do this or that with me, then joyfully pull the rug out from under my feet at the last minute and laugh at my foolishness and blind belief in his words. He thought that teasing and dangling carrots was funny. It didn't feel funny. In fact, my brother and father were gifted at ridiculing me until my bottom lip began to quiver. That damn lip would not follow my repeated commands to remain still.

Don't let them see you're hurt. Don't!

My brother was not immune to the wrath of Joe. In Harold's later teen years, he was kicked out of the house on a regular basis. Several days later, Dad would let him back in. We were both easy targets. Hate is a strong word, but I was convinced my father hated me, not my brother. The two of them sometimes went off and did things together. My father and I seldom did anything other than go to Thrifty Drug Store for ice cream. When we did, it was in silence. Often his words were weapons fired in my direction, but I took them like little bullets, feeling weak and meek for not having the strength or proper tools to care for or about myself. These blasts came out of nowhere, like a storm cloud that appears out of the clear blue sky; the sky blue eyes of my father. I couldn't relax if he was anywhere in the house. And when Dad began yelling about nothing in particular or there was a dark shadow drifting the hallways shaped like his silhouette, I would scamper to my room with my music, magazines, board games, and books.

Perhaps the most impulsive, irrational, and irreversible decision my father ever made was to depart prematurely from his job at Food Machinery Corporation. It was a job that defined him, where everyone knew and enjoyed him and placed him high on a pedestal, where his work and jokes were prized and appreciated and where he was the star of every office party and everyday antics in the workplace. But he retired at age fifty-five on a whim. My father and mother had gone for a short vacation to see Billy and Betty Nudd who had, also on their own whim, moved from San Jose to San Diego. My father saw a cramped one-bedroom condo overlooking Coronado Bay and put a deposit on it right then and there. It was a done deal. "That's it. We're moving. I'll give notice next week."

I don't think Dad thought that decision out for more than five seconds. After all, he had thoroughly enjoyed working at FMC, and all of the people who worked there revered him. But off he went a full decade before he had planned to retire. As soon as he unpacked his boxes in that small condo, he went searching for a new job in San Diego County, an area of California he had visited only once.

An *escapade* was always the carrot dangling on the stick in front of my father, and my mother, always up for an adventure, hopped on for the ride. My father mentioned years later, in the months before he passed away, that he regretted making that decision to retire early and move to San Diego because his life in Santa Clara, his job, and the people there, were the framework for his glory days. He would never be that happy, admired that thoroughly, or as firmly rooted as he was in San Jose and Food Machinery Corporation. His identity, and an appreciation for who he was and what he did, lived there.

Dad's retirement party with mandatory "Joe Sveilich" T-shirts.

To celebrate his final days at FMC, his colleagues and every secretary in the company had dressed in a brightly colored custom T-shirt that read "Joe Sveilich" with a silhouette photo design of my father and his trusty curved pipe and navy blue beret. They gave him a roast presentation that lasted most of the day. He was King Joe at FMC, but he never would be king of anything again. Certainly not to such a degree. He realized his miscalculation, but much too late. Not that he didn't enjoy living in San Diego. But retirement came too soon for a ball of erratic energy like my dad.

In his retirement years, my father began to collect all the kitchen gizmos advertised on late night infomercials. Of course, that included Ron Popeil's Chop-O-Matic and Veg-O-Matic, Inside-the-Shell Electric Egg Scrambler, Dial-O-Matic, Solid Flavor Injector, and other mind-numbing products, such as the Hand-Held Stick Mixer. My father had to have an Inside-the-Shell Electric Egg Scrambler socked away in his kitchen drawer. He was an infomercial junkie, but he never cooked and barely set foot in the kitchen. He wouldn't even remove the products from their hard plastic containers or cardboard boxes. He was fascinated with them and wanted them nearby. They were like his marriage in that way: close in proximity, but nothing to interact with. I always saw my parents that way. They required each other's distant presence in their marriage.

Dad would often buy duplicates of "As Seen on TV" products. They'd eventually end up in my kitchen drawer. One time he purchased a dozen of the Hand-Held Stick Mixers. I had no use for it, but never mind that. When I did take one out of the package to use it, he yelled, "Don't turn that thing on! You'll slice your finger off." I could have it, but not use it, just as he had a kitchen full of products he'd never use. But, somehow, I had grown accustomed to my father's illogical logic. I slid it into my kitchen drawer where it sat unused for years. We were prohibited from using these new-fangled products but not from filling up our junk drawers with them. In my family tree, that made perfect sense. And that tree was filled with more kitchen gadgets than Bed Bath & Beyond.

Putting the High in High School

The Black-Light Special

There was something particularly magical about stepping into a room bathed in black light. This captivating, magical, ultraviolet lighting changed the room's personality and created a distinct atmosphere that even seemed to tamper with the temperature in the air. Everything felt cooler as you stood there looking at the cool colors on even cooler posters. And suddenly, you too were cool. Groovy.

During the Sixties and into the early Seventies, black-light posters were everywhere, covering the walls and ceilings of teen bedrooms, dorm rooms, hippie pads, and even some businesses. Drug-related posters and political posters were tacked alongside the psychedelic designs on black-light posters. The ultra-intense colors on phosphorescent posters grabbed everyone's attention. This otherworldly glow beckoned the viewer to enter into their own three-dimensional inner sanctum of peace. Standing in the dark with a mist of blue cascading up from the narrow fluorescent tubing—our new guiding light—could make anyone and everyone feel like an astronaut circling a new solar system. This special lighting turned most white things to a bright blue and skin into anything but flesh color. Wherever the black light was, was the place to be, and be seen.

Record stores began to feature wall art and exhibits of posters in a special area of the store known as the Black-Light Room. These spaces had a mysterious and dream-like ambiance and were usually separated by an Indian print bedsheet, tie-dyed curtain, or hanging strings of beads. The air was smoky and filled with the scent of sandalwood. Most of these stores and a wide array of head shops carried black-light posters. The designs varied: couples making love, primitive figures riding ornate purple stallions, mountain ranges with vivid hues, waterfalls of bright orange and green, fantasy castles and buildings not yet discovered or invented, women turning into trees, men mounting women, women mounting men, men mounting jungle creatures, geometric wonderlands, Viking ships. Some featured a variety of sexual positions, drug references, rock 'n' roll gods and goddesses, utopian visions, Black Power, and astrology. *Make love, not war.* Hang posters and Escher prints, not paintings.

My friends and I frequented Paramount Imports in San Jose, a head shop in the heyday of Sixties paraphernalia. I would hitchhike to this special sanctuary during my high school years and gaze with the other patrons wandering around in a foggy haze of incensed air and patchouli-oiled shoulders. Paramount had a massive black-light room display that was dazzling. They also had a variety of other kinds of artwork. I remember one poster in the window of Raquel Welch from the film *One Million Years B.C.* She was standing in a skimpy loincloth, breasts heaving, with a determined stare. It all made perfect sense at the time, and the time was 1966.

My father's sister, Evie, who remained on Long Island, reminded me of Lucille Ball, or Lucille Ball reminded me of her. Lucy's life force and lips always seemed a bit more Technicolor than the rest of us, and so did everything about Evie. The pretty mouth, bright orange hair, heart-shaped face, delicate chin, and smart-ass delivery stitched them together in my mind. Both women had a wisecrack lodged in the corner of their mouths at all times, waiting for the perfect moment to be sprung loose.

When I was fifteen, Grandma Anna from New York came out to live with my family. My grandma, with her thin bowed legs, duck waddle, and floral frocks was suddenly homeless and husbandless. My grandfather had passed away without warning in their Brooklyn apartment, and Anna needed somewhere to live. First, she filled an extra bedroom at my aunt's home in Bethpage, New York. But after a few years, my aunt had had enough of Anna's micromanaging her children and her. One Sunday afternoon, Evie called my father and begged him to take her. "It's your turn, Joe. We can't take her anymore! She's driving our kids mad."

Grandma Anna took her first plane ride and came out to live with my family in California. She had been banished from the state of New York for terrorizing my two young cousins and driving my aunt and uncle to drink. Mostly Manischewitz.

Cousin Amy couldn't wait to help Grandma Anna pack. Amy had spent her entire childhood running from our grandmother the same way my dad had run from her. One afternoon, Amy took Grandma Anna to the theater in New York to watch the film *Gone with the Wind.* The scene appeared on screen where the child, Bonnie, falls off her horse and dies. Grandma Anna shrugged and bellowed in a voice so loud it echoed off the theater walls, "So why did they have to let her on the horse?" My young cousin slithered into her plush theater seat. She wanted to die right then and there. That moment of embarrassment is etched in Cousin Amy's mind forever.

My father had grown up under his mother's overprotective regime and neediness for her family close by. Soon Grandma Anna was ruling over me. One day, my friend Heather and I observed my grandma grabbing the kitchen phone from my father's hand to speak to her only daughter, my aunt, in New York. Grandma Anna turned her entire body and faced east as she began yelling loudly into the phone's mouthpiece. It was her unwavering belief that one had to face the direction of the caller on the other end of the phone and speak in a booming voice in order to be heard from so far away. After all, we were in California, and she was talking to New York. That's a long way for "How's the weather there?" to travel. My friend giggled at the sight of her standing there, facing due east out the window, and speaking in deafening tones for ten minutes straight.

When I was visiting with my friends in their cul-de-sac homes, my grandma would settle herself in the middle of the street and yell at the top of her lungs, "Carol. Come home! I'm so lonely. Aww. Come here. Where are you? Carol!" I wanted to crawl under my friend's living room rug, as her ear-piercing hollers would turn my cheeks red and make me want to run in the opposite direction of home. Soon I was playing games with Grandma Anna nearly every day after school. I would hide, she would seek.

The Weight

My mother's weight fluctuated in frequent and enormous swings. There are old family photos of her showing my svelte and smooth Mom rockin' her Sixties Piet Mondrian A-line shift, and others where she looks like Fat Elvis. But unlike Elvis, who remained at his ballooned form until his final days, my mother's weight bounced up and down like a kid on a pogo stick. Heavy or thin, she moved slowly through the world with graceful calypso hands and sure footing. Nothing rattled my mother ... except Republicans.

I'd study the gathering of tiny dark freckles splattered over her rolls of tummy fat. They were lost in a sea of waves and creases. I wondered if I would have similar rolls at some point in my life. Mom's elastic waistband compressed and expanded on a regular basis, and her weight would balloon up to Totie Fields' size. Then she would wrestle it back down by starving herself or guzzling some liquid diet drinks that came in cans and lined the local grocery store shelf. One month she would lose too much weight. Then the scale would ratchet up at a record rate and leave her pleasantly plump once again. Up, down, up, down. Our refrigerator was stocked with low-cal drinks like saccharin-sweetened Tab. A study eventually found saccharin was a possible carcinogen and suddenly the soda companies were scrambling for a new and less fear-provoking artificial sweetener. They always seemed to find one. Then another. And yet another. Sweeter, safer, superior, they told us, and the millions of overweight men and women trying to collectively lose millions of pounds listened.

My mother preferred to live on, then off, Metrecal or SEGO and other SlimFast-type products of the era. She was also on the cabbage diet, pineapple diet, coffee diet, and cottage cheese diet. She ate Ayds "reducing plan" candies, a diet product and appetite-suppressant that came in chocolate, chocolate mint, butterscotch, and caramel flavor. Later, a peanut flavor was added to the diet smorgasbord. The active ingredient was originally benzocaine, presumably to reduce the sense of taste to reduce eating. Later, they changed it to phenylpropanolamine, an even more frightening and much longer hunger numbing agent. Ayds was the diet plan with the unfortunate name. But these low-calorie candies came in an attractive box and tasted like Tootsie Rolls. I know because I snuck piece after piece when my mother was out of the house. She'd eat the entire container in one sitting like it was a Whitman's sampler. I don't think that was part of the Ayds diet plan.

Jack LaLanne was trying to get Americans off their Barcaloungers and to move with him through his exercise routines aired on morning television. He always had his trusty two snowy white dogs by his side, Happy and Walter (the name Walter standing for We All Love To Exercise Regularly). Housewives of the Sixties found it easier to pop a diet pill. And these pills became a helpmate around the house in the Sixties era. Physicians prescribed diet pills, or what were sometimes referred to as rainbow pills. But let's call a spade a spade, or a diet pill, what it was: an amphetamine. Speed. The high from amphetamines was generally followed by a long slow comedown, making many people feel irritable and depressed. This class of drugs also put a strain on the heart that sometimes led to heart problems or even death.

Obetrol, a brand of amphetamine, was approved by the U.S. Food and Drug Administration in January 1960. Amphetamine and methamphetamine were viewed as utilitarian drugs that men and women could use to increase energy, meet performance goals, and lose weight rapidly. It was that last one that women wanted … and they wanted it immediately—because let's face it—what they didn't want was muffin tops puffing out of their capris.

In the Sixties, various forms of speed were beginning to emerge. Even in the 1950s, some energy-enhancing, weight-dropping substances were available. "Lifts" or "pixies," as they were called, started entertaining the mainstream youth movements under the names Black Beauties and Bennies. Stories of amphetamine use by high-profile individuals began to be covered in the press. Artists such as Charlie Parker, British Prime Minster Anthony Eden, entertainers like Lenny Bruce and Judy Garland, authors like Jack Kerouac (who was reported to have written *On the Road* under the influence of amphetamines in twenty-one days on a single scroll of paper) and even John F. Kennedy, who received frequent injections of Benzedrine for his back pain, were a few of many who relied upon amphetamines for endurance and cognitive enhancement. "Bennie and the Jets" indeed. But did my own mother take them? She was a boozy broad who would try them, but I don't remember a steady diet of prescribed diet pills. She had a variety of over-the-counter diet supplements geared at fast but not necessarily lasting results.

The Mail Persuasion

I've always enjoyed the intimacy of handwritten letters. My mother wrote letters to all her friends, even the ones who lived close by. Later, she would write and send letters to me when we lived twenty minutes apart. She reported on the weather, what she ate that day, what the cat ate and how much. I picked up on that ritual and did the same thing for decades.

The process of writing, sending, and receiving letters, placing the address label in the left corner and sealing the letter with sealing wax or a kiss was time well spent. Often, I would melt those wax seals onto the closure of the envelopes, especially when I wrote to Ricky. With a match flame to the wax, and hovering over the flap, the wax would drip onto the paper. Then I would press the design from the stamp into the paper flap while the wax was still warm. It seemed an important and caring personal touch. Signed, sealed, waxed, and delivered.

Around this same time, I received chain letters in the U.S. mail. Why did we bother the mail service with our inane need to harass and threaten each another with bad tidings if the sender didn't cooperate and send the letter to ten to fifteen of their friends? Now people do the same thing on email and Facebook. Chain letters used to be a waste of paper and stamps. Now they are a waste of time. Such letters prey on people's superstitions and fears, much like a powerful, knee-shaking sermon. Out of all our long-standing traditions, chain letters have held fast, sufficiently wasting time and annoying plenty of us for decades.

My first love Ricky continued to write letters, and I continued to respond to them. My feelings for him grew deeper and were genuine. If Romeo and Juliet could have a love affair at fourteen and fifteen, why couldn't we? One day, after we had known each other for several months, instead of writing my letter out longhand with my awkward cursive left-handed handwriting, I decided to use the family typewriter that sat on a desk near the kitchen table. Unfortunately, when I got up to go the bathroom, my mother found my letter to Ricky sitting in the typewriter. In this particular letter, I told him, for the very first time, that I loved and missed him. I also mentioned that I had just hitchhiked to downtown San Jose by myself. When my mother's eyes fell upon the words "I love you" she preceded to flip out and forbid me to see him again. When she saw that I was hitchhiking, her head nearly exploded.

"Too much. Too fast. Too soon. You're both too young! And hitchhiking? Are you trying to kill me?"

She yelled out in her five-octave range when she saw that I was hitchhiking. It didn't stop me. I hitchhiked from age thirteen to nineteen. The incentive to stop arrived when someone who lived down the block from me sliced up his mother like a ninety-pound salami and made lunchmeat out of female hitchhikers around Santa Cruz, the college town where I was living at the time.

Ricky and I remained a long-distance couple for a year before I broke up with him and broke his heart. That's when Curtis Gonzales, a boy from a different school, entered the picture, and I experienced how deep a kiss could travel. The curse of the deep kiss went straight to my curled toes. Curtis, a dashing fifteen-year-old football player from a large Mexican family, was the spittin' image of Tony from *West Side Story*. Curtis flirted fearlessly, and I took the bait, despite being Ricky's long-distance girlfriend. Little did I know I would sink faster than Tony in that final rumble scene.

But before the tragedy came the kissery. Curtis Gonzales hovered ten stories above me as he took me in his athletic arms and planted a slow kiss on my lips that ran deeper than Jane Mansfield's cleavage. In that one quaking moment, everything inside me that was woven tight came undone. We lingered on my front lawn in the summer sun, my toes curled around and through the blades of grass. Curtis whispered something sinful and sweet in my right ear. French writer and philosopher Voltaire once said, "The ear is the avenue to the heart." That was one astute fellow. A soft whisper, a moan, a word or two of French, and I was toast. French toast.

I knew it was wrong to kiss Curtis. After all, I was going steady with Ricky. But as Curtis took control, my limbs dangled from his embrace like one of those wooden toy figures with the string pulley that makes the legs and arms dance. I was dancing, then floating. Long, passionate kisses with the wrong person are unforgettable and stubborn. They refuse to be dismissed. They will be the last memories we release before our death. That night as I rubbed my feet together under the covers, I whispered to myself and to Pushka lying beside me, "This is real, this is real. And this is really happening ... to me."

I had to let Ricky know. The Dear John letter to dear Ricky had to be written.

I broke up with Ricky that very evening with a wordy note and moved on to Curtis, whom I failed to realize had already shared his teasing tongue and fabulous technique with a dozen other wobbly-kneed girls. I had made a grave error in judgment and learned a lesson about lust and hearts. They don't always mix.

I broke up with my first love, Ricky, because of a schoolgirl infatuation over Curtis Gonzales and his kissing skills, popularity, and bad-boy hipness. It was a grave error and lesson best learned only once. Ricky was from San Francisco, where black slacks were the norm and considered hip, rad, bitchin'. But this was not acceptable attire in the Willow Glen Eichlers. Curtis had Levi's hugging his athletic thighs and tight end. Next to Curtis, Ricky was a citizen of Dorksville, U.S.A. at a time when the coolness factor meant just about everything. I regretted my infatuation with Curtis and quick dismissal of Ricky, but I learned a great deal about the high price paid for fleeting passion. I managed to hurt the first boy I truly loved. It seems even more unforgiveable today than it did back then, if that's possible. Sometimes it takes a lifetime to forgive, even ourselves.

Getting in Touch with My Mescaline Side

The enchanting launch of my psychedelic drug experiment happened on the weekend my parents went to the Asilomar Conference Grounds near Monterey. It was lush with evergreens and enlightenment. They had joined a group, *Challenge for Change*, a now defunct touchy-feely higher consciousness encounter-type group that had gotten its start around 1969. Getting in touch with feelings was so unlike either one of my parents, and although they returned from that weekend with their first big hugs and what they called "tremendous love" for us, those expressions quickly faded over the course of a few days. By the following weekend they were back to their Tom Collins Happy Hour. But for a few precious days, my brother and I got to have warm and affectionate parents. I always cherished those fleeting days of warmth and wondered how my life would have differed with a steady diet of it.

On that same weekend, my brother decided it was time for me to experience my induction into psychedelic drugs. Harold handed me a tab of acid as we drove off to pick up his girlfriend,

Jackie, a thirteen-year-old whose voluptuous physique had bloomed several years too early.

I was riding in the seat behind them. On the way home, I muttered, "I don't feel anything, I don't feel anything at all." Two hours had passed and … nothing.

"Here, take this."

Harold handed me something different, a full dosage of mescaline. As quickly as I swallowed it, however, I began to "come on" to the earlier dosage of acid. I don't know where I went for the next few hours, but I'm afraid it was a bit of an Alice-down-the-rabbit-hole escapade. Geometric patterns in the form of spidery webs appeared in my mind's eye, and I was plunging down into the tunneled core. I couldn't stop tumbling off the precipice of the tangible and into the pit of this shadowy hallucination. The combination of drugs was turning my brain into an M.C. Escher design with moving parts as I drifted like an unanchored ship in and out of the mighty waves of chemicals. A surge of hellish tremors washed over me. I couldn't locate anyone or anything other than this overpowering and hideous image of tumbling down the patterned symmetrical tunnel. That is until I opened my eyes. I was in a dreamlike state that felt like actuality. These closed-eyed visions were strangely mesmerizing. Like a dream that you're certain is actually happening, I was convinced that it was reality and my previous life was a dream. I continued to draw philosophical conclusions by the hundreds in each passing second. In this place, no time existed. Harold had vanished along with his car and the Eichler. I quickly learned that two mind-blowing drugs were not better than one. Lesson learned.

How I landed in my bed wrapped in tangled sheets, I have no idea. Somehow, I had managed to time-travel from my brother's car to the cul-de-sac street where some kids were playing what seemed to be a metaphysical game of tetherball, and then to the safety of my room, where, in some otherworldly state, I locked the bedroom door and collapsed into a Stanley Kubrick passageway from *2001: A Space Odyssey*.

As I was pulled out of the web that existed only in my mind, my brother, the consummate alarmist, screamed from behind the bedroom door, "You've ODed! Open the door, dammit. Carol, open the door, or you'll die." I finally made my way to the bedroom door, but I was living in a dream state and moving in slow motion against a fierce wind. Harold mumbled something about a potion that would bring me back to the here and now. "You have to drink tons of orange juice. Gallons of it! It will wash the drugs right out of you."

Of course, this was ridiculous. I don't know where he learned this technique, but I ended up taking the glass of Donald Duck orange juice and pouring it over my head as I bathed in sunlight and citrus in the Eichler atrium. Then, although I wasn't hungry, I wandered into the kitchen and ate a half a block of sharp cheddar and some Lucky Charms. The ritual of eating seemed beastly as I detached from my physical being and watched the ritual from outside of myself. I was a lion, not a teenager. As the hours wore on, the overabundance of drugs that induced this massive and rather nightmarish trip wore off enough to allow the experience to be manageable.

We were supposed to see the music group The Youngbloods perform that evening at Santa Clara University. My friend Denise was planning to come along. When we picked her up, I leaned against her shoulder and whispered in her ear, "I'm on something."

Denise didn't take psychedelics and had no idea what that meant. She thought I was just stoned from multiple joints and didn't have a clue I was in another dimension where there was no time or space. I sat next to her on the drive to the concert, fully embedded in psychedelic chaos with existential insights coming a mile a minute—a minute that seemed like hours. Her mouth smelled like Coors.

My brother dropped Denise and me off in front of the auditorium and took off in his car. "I'll pick you up after the concert."

Off he went into a cloud of multicolored, oddly patterned smoke. I wondered if we'd ever see him again. Perhaps we would spend the rest of our lives in this auditorium. Would that be so bad?

As we sat cross-legged on the floor waiting for the music to start, I whispered, "It would be so much cooler to be outside."

We listened to one or two songs, then gathered ourselves to our feet, hurried to the exit door, and walked outside to study the sidewalk and breathe in the most refreshing air I had ever captured in my lungs.

Denise was stoned on weed, and I was flying high on dueling psychedelics that were clashing in my brain like Cassius Clay and Sonny Liston battling for the belt. Naturally, we began scrutinizing the sidewalk lines beneath our feet. Denise was on a contact high, and I was the contact. She was stoned, but not in the same dimension I was in. Still, we managed to meet and share utterances like "far out" and "wow" with each step. We were as one, seeing with only one pair of eyes, at least for those few minutes. I was convinced she could hear my thoughts, and she seemed to make the same assumption. I thought she saw everything I did. *So this is what it's like to feel connected to other beings,* I thought to myself.

I don't know how long we were walking. Time was not wearing its usual face. It had on a mask that distorted the usual perceived measurement of tempus fugit: irretrievable time. I asked Denise if Earth was trying to shake us to get rid of us, scorch us with wildfire, or drown us with its wide wild oceans. Was the planet mad at us for taking up residence? She smiled slyly and chuckled.

"But I'm serious! I really want to know," I pressed.

My mind was churning with random thoughts. The tall evergreens around us seemed pleasant enough, but did they secretly wish we weren't turning them into Christmas trees in December, or giving them haircuts, or gathering their pine cones? The loud crows circling above us were having discussions amongst themselves. Were they talking about us? Laughing at us? Were they wanting to dive-bomb Denise and me like they did in Hitchcock's movie? "Maybe we should duck and cover. Duck and cover, Denise!" My head was filled with thoughts, images, questions, but mostly conclusions. Denise seemed to be following her own personal Pied Piper. Were her conclusions different from mine? How could they be? Mine were correct.

When we arrived home, Denise began her mile-long walk home. My brother went to bed. I crawled inside the swinging rattan chair that hung in our family room between the now relocated massive Voice of the Theater speakers. I pulled out The Moody Blues albums *Days of Future Passed* and *To Our Children's Children's Children.* Justin Hayward and John Lodge seemed to know exactly what I was feeling and seeing in this altered state. Their conclusions were identical to mine! I was convinced of it. I became fully meshed with the songwriters' insights, while I stayed awake most of the night listening to the wisdom spilling out of the massive speakers and hoping they were gleaning a bit of mine from afar. Justin, John, and I were joined in consciousness. Soulmates.

It was now 3 a.m. I slipped on singer Melanie's album and cranked up "Beautiful People" to full volume. Neighbor's eardrums be damned. She too seemed to share my secret and silent thoughts about wanting to be "close to it all." I knew what she was talking about. I wanted to be close to it all … and now I was. Sure, it was drug-induced, but in that moment, I didn't think so. If I could reach this dimension one way, I could get there another. It was all within my own determination and power. I was close to it all. Everything. Everyone who had ever lived at every period in history. We were all unified in this particular moment. Okay, I didn't know bupkis.

I took the lengthiest, most sensual, drug-induced shower of my lifetime. It took five minutes that felt like five days. I crawled into bed around 5 a.m. Two hours later, the drugs had quieted down in my frontal cortex, and I was back on planet Earth.

"When can I do that again?"

As a budding and brave teenager, I was gifted at repeat offenses.

I awoke to a familiar face hovering above me like a waiting helicopter. As I opened my eyes to reddish lips, eyelashes like vibrant peacock plumes, pale green lids, and miles of Rapunzel-like hair, Denise's voice cut the air.

"Good morning. I thought I'd check on you after last night."

That's what good friends did. They checked on each other. Her colorful beaded necklace fell into my face as I rubbed my eyes. Was I back to my original perception of reality? I was.

"All is well now."

And it was.

The San Francisco Treat

Many songs have been written about San Francisco, and for good reason. The city is simultaneously small and massive. There is so much substance, activity, and diversity jam-packed into one unique population and landscape.

The first field trip I took in junior high school was to Golden Gate Park. We visited museums, the Japanese Tea Garden, and a few other touristy landmarks. On the bus ride over, I developed a crush on my classmate Neil Wright. Neil was our class clown, with a head of golden curls and a mouth like a truck driver. We gazed longingly at one another at the Japanese Tea Garden, brushed shoulders in Chinatown, and shot glances at one another from afar as we made our way through echoed hallways of one majestic museum after another.

On the trip home, our bus driver decided to go renegade. He drove down side streets and through an unusual area of the city called Haight Ashbury. The juveniles on the bus with me stuck their heads out of the windows and pointed their stubby fingers at the people in the loose bohemian fashions with bold flowers, feathers, and leather. The men on the street wore long manes gathered into ponytails. Many of the young women wore white peasant blouses draped softly off their shoulders. Colorful beads and peace signs hung from the necks of both genders. San Jose had none of these lively characters.

"Hey, you hippies! Freaks! Hi, weirdos! Look at that guy! Is he a girl?"

My classmates laughed and ridiculed the crowd of peculiar pedestrians. Did they think they were hollering out to oddly colored animals at the San Francisco Zoo?

I wanted to die in my bus seat right then and there, but I have to admit, taking a slow bus ride through Haight Ashbury was like traveling through another country. Were we on the Marrakesh Express?

In 1967, alternative lifestyles were beginning to percolate in San Francisco. Incense, psychedelic drugs, loud music, sheer tops, hip-hugging bell-bottoms, long hair, and anti-war politics were sifting through the air like a Maui Wowie blend. We were at the start of an era we couldn't quite fathom … yet.

Meanwhile I was stuck in the bus with thirteen-year-olds doing what thirteen-year-olds do: being obnoxious. The bus ride home was unforgettable. Without our realizing it, that bus driver was ushering us through a small section of history in the making. We were being showered with flowers and flower children before they came into full bloom. Welcome to the Summer of Love.

My junior high experiences were a bit tamer than Jimi Hendrix burning his guitar. My days consisted of field trips, daydreaming about boys, hitching rides, drugs, Teen Club dances, volunteer work, and learning a foreign language.

I was offered my first opportunity to learn a foreign language, and I chose Spanish. I was told it was the easiest to learn and that was good enough for me. As I sat in class with headphones on, attempting to learn how to send someone to the library or order meatballs in another vernacular, the teacher filed her nails. I had problems with memorization, so the words, phrases, and especially grammatical rules would stick for mere seconds before they fell away like Scotch tape that had lost its stick.

My name in Spanish class was not Carol; it was Carola. Classmates pestered me and called out, "Crayola!"—as in Crayola crayons. Their taunts were always followed by giggles. Not mine—Carola Swizzlesticks'—but theirs. There was no shortage of teasing in junior high. It's what teenagers excelled at outside the classroom.

Like a Rolling Stone

Bob Dylan had an oddly androgynous, delicate, and innocent quality that was terribly appealing to females. We all wanted to run our fingers through his soft curls, take care of him, fatten him up with stews and bologna sandwiches, and kiss his shy sideways mouth. No danger lurked around the aura of this man-child. But he was no innocent, certainly not when it came to word choice and phrasing. Dylan's words seemed simplistic enough on the surface, but … surprise. His lyrics ran deceivingly deep. I remember studying and discussing each line for hours with fellow Dylanians. In the Sixties, we didn't settle for surface babble. We dove deep and needed to understand the words put to music and the evidence of deeper meaning. Today, we just struggle to decipher them.

Bob Dylan's lyrics are woven into the fabric of my early teen years. When I was fifteen years old and just home from school, I couldn't locate my cat, Twigger, a small Siamese cat who had become my constant companion, my sleep mate, my new best friend. Dawn, mother of my first love, Ricky, had nourished my enthusiasm about Siamese cats. These creatures seemed like comical human beings who were always gearing up for a standup routine. Her nine (yes, nine) Siamese cats roamed around her house, sat on top of appliances, and cuddled up against couch pillows. The first time I entered her home, I thought I had died and gone to feline heaven. Dawn had become my role model in many ways. I envisioned myself growing up to be like her: house full of cats, independent, spunky, and definitely outspoken.

That dream was dashed when I arrived home from school one day, and the house was sans Siamese. My mother had quietly decided to give my cat away. She said we had too many cats. Uh, two. I was distraught. Teenage girls are capable of enormous love, and I loved my constant companion, Twigger.

When I learned the news, I decided to hitchhike into downtown San Jose by myself and escape this hellish home that seemed to dispose of anything that carried emotional weight. I sat through a rerun of *West Side Story* in a second-rate theater ... twice. I cried, even during the joyous love scenes and intricate dance numbers. I made up my mind right then and there never to forgive my mother. I would avoid her at home, stop speaking to her, and quietly and cerebrally vilify her alongside my father. No more mentally protecting her from him. I cut her loose. She was on her own now.

I stayed out as late as I could that night. I never wanted to return home. When I did arrive at that familiar orange door, it was well after dark. I took long strides straight back to my bedroom and listened to Bob Dylan's *Greatest Hits* album for hours.

I was at one with "Rainy Day Women" while I sat cross-legged on my bedroom floor with damp eyes, gray mood, broken heart. "The Times They Are A-Changin'." Were they ever. I'd never speak to my mother again! She was mean. She was heartless. She was no longer Mom.

"Positively 4th Street" was the greatest "fuck you" song ever written. In my head, I changed the lyrics to fit this dismal situation. *You've got a lot of nerve, to say you are my mom.* I played "Mr. Tambourine Man" over and over again. It was a four-chord tune I taught myself on guitar for melancholy evenings like this one. I had no idea what the lyrics meant, but in my despair, I was still on board with every word. Dylan sounded miserable and more than a bit angry. We were the perfect pair. If we had a baby together, that child would be as pitiable and pathetic as we were. Two glum bums against the world. Bob and Carol. Ted and Alice weren't invited to our party of two.

Dylan made me want to write a poem about the rain, so I did. I grabbed my secret notebook that no one would ever read and wrote:

WINTER PASSES LIKE A FREEZER DEFROSTING
Winter passes like a freezer defrosting
and dripping from overhead,
turning oily streets to rainbows,
turning green corduroy fields
to thick syrup.
But I'm no hero ...
Running from the elements, galoshed
from head
to foot.
Making my way through fast breaths and fog ...
A locomotive puffing on a sidewalk track,
cursing and praising nature for falling
without my permission.

I didn't even know if "galoshed" was a word. It wasn't. I didn't care. I drew a small childlike picture of an umbrella, closed the book, and fell into a deep merciful sleep.

Losing My Religion

I never understood religion and what purpose it served, what went on in a church or synagogue, and what was behind the many elaborate rituals and rites of passage. My religion was and remained "I don't know" because I didn't—and still don't. I'm not about to adopt any faith now, and I'm still not certain of anything. No one knows for sure, yet everyone sounds convinced when they talk about what they believe and what they pretend to know. I don't. A good part of this life is and will remain a mystery to us no matter how we try to ritualize it to meet our needs and desires.

That didn't stop me from wondering or philosophizing about the meaning of existence or prevent me from taking psychedelic drugs to explore it. There were many late evenings spent reclining on the floor of my bedroom with Denise, our blitzed eyes gazing at the ceiling, discussing the paradoxes and mysteries of our very being while the vapors from sandalwood incense lingered in the air. The universe seemed small compared with our lengthy conversations, but oddly enough, that's what we discussed more than anything else: the cosmos. Why are we here? Why were we born? What is the purpose of life? Could you pass me that joint? I was never quite certain who I was or why I was here, or there. My life was filled with examination and no concrete answers.

In one of my favorite science fiction films, *The Incredible Shrinking Man*, the main character pondered the same philosophical questions and the same wonky answers that Denise and I focused on in my smoky bedroom. "I had thought in terms of man's own limited dimension. That existence begins and ends is man's conception, not nature's." As Deepak Chopra would later say, "Everybody thinks that what they see is what's there, but what you see is merely a representation of the human brain. A mosquito's brain wouldn't see that. An insect with 100 eyes wouldn't see that." Exactly.

And if an insect with multiple eyes couldn't see it, why was what I was seeing valid? Wasn't I simply a victim of my own brain's ability to perceive? What was I not seeing that was there? Something? Nothing?

My friend and I would go back and forth with philosophies and possibilities. In my stoned state, I would offer up a theory about opposites.

"Denise, everything in the universe has an opposite. Dark-light. Rich-poor. Wet-dry."

I would give a hundred more examples as Denise drifted in and out of her own daze. It seemed, at least to my blitzed self, that I was making perfect sense, having a breakthrough moment. I quoted Vladimir Nabokov so that every star in the universe would hear me.

"How small the cosmos (a kangaroo's pouch would hold it), how paltry and puny in comparison to human consciousness, to a single individual recollection and its expression in words." (Vladimir Nabokov; *Speak, Memory.*)

Perhaps I didn't say it out loud, but my mind spoke it. It was my own *a-ha!* moment.

"So, what is the opposite of space?" I asked my bleary-eyed friend who was now sinking into my paisley-patterned bean-bag chair. "How can our brains comprehend an endless universe? We can't. So, does that mean it doesn't exist? What if time can be folded, like a flimsy rug or a piece of paper, on top of itself. And what is reality? That depends on who's observing it, what kind of brain they are employing, and what sort of questions they are asking. Beyond everything we perceive lies reality. And that's what we can't wrap our minds around, right? Denise? Are you listening? Just because we can't see further doesn't mean we can't believe in what's further out."

"Far out, I can dig it," muttered Denise with a chuckle as she took another hit, miles deep in her own theories and conclusions. Or not.

A Concerted Effort

My friends and I didn't have to travel too far to see and enjoy impressive musical acts. Fortunately for us, popular bands often took gigs farther afield than San Francisco and Oakland. Although I don't recall Big Brother and the Holding Company or Jefferson Airplane coming to our sleepy cherry orchard bedroom community, the Santa Clara Valley Fairgrounds attracted the biggest and best rock groups and pop music performers of the Sixties and early Seventies. For a three-dollar entrance fee, one could see a major headliner and two opening groups. I remember sitting cross-legged on the ground, passing joint after joint, and scratching my head over The Moody Blues' opening act, Norman Greenbaum. First of all, why was he opening for The Moody Blues, clearly a band cut from an entirely different fabric?

Greenbaum had only one hit record, "Spirit in the Sky." It was a strange assembling of psychedelic rock music and gospel featuring loud drums, distorted electric guitar, tambourines, and clapping hands. The Stovall Sisters, an Oakland-based gospel group, sang backing vocals. His line about having a friend in Jesus was baffling because he was a practicing Jew. I may not have known a helluva lot about religion, but I knew one thing: something was wrong with this picture. Oddly enough, the Reprise label had their all-time, best-selling single with "Spirit in the Sky" as it became a world-wide hit, so perhaps I was the only one on the planet who was puzzled.

The same groups seemed to open nearly every Bay Area concert. Over time, some even managed to work their way up to the headliner position. But the ever-present opening acts for nearly every band coming to town included: Tower of Power; Moby Grape; Cold Blood; The Loading Zone; Santana; The Elvin Bishop Band; Sons of Champlin; Spirit; Dan Hicks and his Hot Licks; It's a Beautiful Day, with their FM song "White Bird" in heavy rotation; The Steve Miller Blues Band; and Boz Scaggs. There was no shortage of local garage bands like Count Five, The Syndicate of Sound, and The Chocolate Watch Band. I was a fan of horn bands, and I never tired of Tower of Power or Blood, Sweat & Tears. I tended to lean towards the more bluesy or jazz-infused sound.

Even today, when I hear anything by Led Zeppelin, I'm transported back to my teenage bedroom, lying on my back on the cool tiled floor, massive headphones strapped over a head of chaotic hair, Robert Plant and Jimmy Page pounding in my left ear, then right ear, then both. Audio bliss. Little did I know that the song "Babe I'm Gonna Leave You" was an old folk song by a woman, Anne Bredon. But Zeppelin made it their own. Jimmy Page, seasoned guitarist for Led Zeppelin, got the idea to cover this song after hearing Joan Baez's folk version. Both Plant and Page were massive fans of Joan Baez. Anne Bredon was not credited for the Zeppelin version until 1990 when her son brought it to the attention of the band. Some may argue that Led Zeppelin was at its peak with "Stairway to Heaven" or other Zeppelin tunes, but for me it's this little folk tune by Anne Bredon, turned rock classic.

Stoned in Glass Houses

Shortly before my experimentation with psychedelic drugs, I smoked my first joint. The instructions on how to best get stoned were provided on the floor of my brother's bedroom, with one butt cheek on his navy blue bedroom rug and the other on the Eichler's cool asbestos-infused tile flooring. Harold's bedroom sat directly across from mine and the household washer and dryer were positioned between our bedrooms. I'd come to his room to talk about this or that until he would announce, "You're so stupid, Carol," and I would be off to find other avenues of play and discussion. I never knew what he did with the hours in his day or what made him tick, but he was continually lecturing me on what I should do and how to do it.

On one particular day, we sat cross-legged on the floor with *Fresh Cream* playing on his record player. Harold proceeded to instruct me on how to get properly stoned.

"Okay, inhale as much as you can without coughing. Now do that ten more times."

After several minutes of coughing, we ended up smoking two joints. These were the days you could do that without seeing monstrous hallucinations. Pot was mild and required repeated inhales. Before stumbling out of his room on my first official high, we had a heady discussion about our purpose in life.

"You have to find a way to assist other people, Carol. Otherwise your life, your very existence, is pointless. You might as well be dead. You have to volunteer somewhere to give your life meaning. You have to help others."

This from a person who never helped an old lady cross the street or did any volunteer work of his own. Harold was gifted at doling out advice he would never take himself. But I was naïve and listened to my seemingly wiser brother who was forever propped up on the older sibling pedestal. Additionally, I was stoned out of my mind. I quickly agreed to everything he said. My brother, like my father, was good at giving instructions to other people. "You need to do this and do it now." They never did it themselves, but they were the Commanders in Chief of all that should be done by every other person on the planet. Years later, my first husband would refer to my father as "Sergeant Joe." If my father were a sergeant, then my brother was Lance Corporal Harold. Apparently we soak up our parents' behavior patterns like a kitchen sink sponge absorbs mucky water.

I had two heroines in my youth: Joan Baez and Jane Fonda. Both possessed the self-assuredness and focus that I craved. Both women knew who they were. And they were not only talented; they were passionate about their cause. They knew what was right and what was wrong in the eyes of universal law, not biblical law. There was authority and confidence in their voice. There was no question what to do, and they went about doing it. I wanted some of that.

I quickly set my sights on Joan Baez. I would be her invisible protégé. After all, if you're the only woman in the world who's seen both Bob Dylan and Steve Jobs naked (although not, as she says, at the same time), you're none other than Joan Baez.

Baez was my hero when I didn't have any heroes. She founded the Institute for the Study of Nonviolence, which turned out to be the first of many non-profit agencies I would volunteer for and work in. I was filled with the exuberance of youth and righteousness, and ready to do this—whatever *this* was. And although I found her singing voice grating and too high pitched for my liking, her body of causes was impressive. So I quickly volunteered for the organization she had founded when I was around fifteen years old.

The organization had its hub in downtown San Jose near San Jose State University. One day, my girlfriend and I cut school and showed up at the front step of their office. We had no problem cutting school if there was something more important to do, like volunteer, smoke marijuana, or watch soap operas on television. As we entered a closet-sized office with a crooked sign that read "Institute for the Study of Nonviolence" taped on the entrance door, I summoned every bit of adult conduct and tried to quiet the anxiety. Two men greeted us through a cloud of heavy smoke. One was a hippie with long auburn hair and an even longer beard; the other had a mustache. Both were wearing paisley shirts that smelled like pot and jeans so worn they looked like they had served in the Vietnam War. They were both nice-looking by 1960s' standards, in their early thirties, and they didn't seem to belong in an office of any sort.

"We want to volunteer. We want to work for nonviolence," I said in my lowest register, trying desperately to have the self-assurance of Jane Fonda or Joan Baez. "We believe in this cause," I continued.

"Oh, okay, okay. That's great, gals. But first we have to make a run to our headquarters down the block. Come with us?"

We left the small office and walked a couple of blocks to their so-called headquarters, which turned out to be the apartment of one or both of the long-haired gentlemen who worked for

Baez. "This is your headquarters?" I muttered. "It looks like a one-bedroom apartment."

They led each of us inside by the hand. What we found was an assortment of characters sprawled out on the sofa and chairs. One was a mature Mexican man. A few young people around our age were also scattered about. A couple of elderly male adults were seated on a small couch and were staring off into some distant landscape we tried to see but couldn't.

"Don't worry about them. They're tripping." The mature Mexican man began to sob like a lost child. "He's on his first trip. He'll be fine. It's all mellow."

Suddenly the people on the couch started to disperse. Heather was lying on her side on the small rug in this small apartment with the mustached hippie. The other fella with the beard, the one that I fancied, was leading me into the one bedroom like he had something there he wanted to show me. Once inside, he brought out tray after tray of colored pills in every shape and size. "Want one of these? No charge. Acid? Mescaline? 'Shrooms?" He sounded like some high-flyin' steward on TWA.

"Uh, no thanks." I declined the assorted delights from the buffet, and we jumped in the bed, talking, touching, and hugging, with me beating his hands off my thighs. I didn't want to sleep with this stranger. I wanted to save the world from violence … or something. Anything. I was a rebel in search of a cause.

Going to this hangout became a tradition for me and my friends. Sometimes I cut school and hitchhiked downtown with Denise. Other times I ventured there with Heather. Sometimes Heather went there alone, but I never did. It always ended up the same scenario, going to their apartment and seeing a variety of young and older people on the couch, tripping, staring, crying, or laughing uncontrollably. One day their cat was literally bouncing off the wall.

"Don't mind Bonkers. He got into the acid this morning. He'll be fine."

But Bonkers didn't look fine.

In the initial meeting, it never occurred to any of us girls that this organization on nonviolence was a front. At that time, we didn't even know what a front was. We thought these bodies draped across the furniture were stoned buddies. Unbeknownst to us, their apartment did turn out to be a headquarters of sorts:

the most massive drug headquarters in the country. My young heart was in the right place, and I was sure Joan Baez's heart had always been. But this time, both of us were naïve.

One Sunday morning, as I was picking up the newspaper off the driveway, I spotted several recognizable faces and a photograph of a familiar room on the front page of the *San Jose Mercury News.* In fact, the article took up the entire front page. This was a whopping news story, and my girlfriends and I knew the cast of characters intimately. These characters were high-level dealers who were all going to jail for life. The entire operation was shut down after being caught in a colossal sting operation. My knees began to buckle. I knew these guys. Were some of those tripping people on the couch who looked so ordinary and "off the street" really narcs? What if we had been there when the bust went down? Holy shit.

Naturally, we didn't know this organization was a front for a house of dealers even though we had hung out there dozens of times and had seen hundreds of drugs in every color of the rainbow displayed in little compartmented trays throughout the living room. It was a psychedelics buffet. The wide array of colorful capsules should have tipped me off. It never did. I was too busy fighting off the grabby hippie with the long beard, probably the head of one of the nation's largest drug cartels at that time. I thought we were going to make the world a more peaceful place. I thought we were going to infuse nonviolence into society. Unfortunately, we fell short. But the work Joan Baez was doing back then, the passion she exhibited, and the certainty she seemed to possess were all things I had aspired to. I just didn't aspire to go to juvenile hall.

Joan Baez played another pivotal role in my life. In 1970, Joan wrote an autobiography titled *Daybreak,* an easy-to-read account of her youth in Palo Alto, her family, her faith as a Quaker, her beginnings as a singer, and her eventual work in the area of nonviolence and other humanitarian causes. Baez's father, Albert, was a physicist. His avoidance of the Bay Area's lucrative defense industry jobs influenced Joan's political activism in America and in international civil rights, as well as the antiwar movements from the early Sixties on. Her inspiring story in *Daybreak* mentioned her neighbor Ira Sandperl. He was a teacher, Gandhi scholar, and outspoken advocate for people and nonviolence. Not long after reading the book, I would bump into Ira's estranged son, Mark Sandperl, at Seacliff Beach while flying high on a tab of acid.

Ira Sandperl, a pacifist and scholar, not only mentored Joan Baez, but also was a political ally of Rev. Martin Luther King Jr. He introduced a generation of draft-age men to nonviolence during the Vietnam War. An enthusiastic follower of the principles of Mahatma Gandhi from the late 1940s, Sandperl met Joan Baez at a Quaker meeting in Palo Alto in 1959, shortly before my family left the East Coast for San Jose, and when Joan was a senior in high school. The two developed a deep bond and shared a number of interests, not the least of which being political causes. Sandperl helped Baez found the Institute for the Study of Nonviolence and became its first president.

The organization had a lasting influence on both the civil rights and antiwar movements into the mid-1970s. For a period, Dr. King would send members of his organization, the Southern Christian Leadership Conference (SCLC), to their institute for training in nonviolent organizing tactics.

"I began accompanying Ira to places where he spoke," Ms. Baez wrote in her autobiography, *Daybreak*. "I heard more about Gandhi, love and nonviolence and a brotherhood of man, which he said didn't exist yet."

But Ira's young son, Mark, hadn't embraced any of his father's philosophy. Ira left him, Mark's sister, and their mother when Mark was quite young and took off with Baez before her career blossomed.

Joan Baez wrote of Mark when he was a young ragamuffin of a boy, before Ira left his two children and ventured into the world with Joan and an amalgamation of causes. In *Daybreak,* Joan had written some prose about Mark's soft blue eyes and long dark lashes. She also wrote that Mark always beat his fists against Ira's arm, wanting to play guns and war games and begging his father to get a TV set so he could watch westerns. Ira was a pacifist and wouldn't have it. Perhaps this begging and teasing was part of Mark's anger at his father. He never called his father Dad or Daddy. Only Ira.

Years later, Joan would sing a song titled "Turquoise," written by Donovan. But I always wondered, did she ever think of or concern herself with the young Mark Sandperl when she sang it? He was the boy with clear turquoise eyes whose father pulled away from his family to lift Joan up on her wings.

Fake It 'Til You Make It

In junior high school, my inner life had suddenly become larger, much more interesting, and valuable than my outer activities. One early Saturday morning, Heather and I hopped a Greyhound bus in Los Gatos anticipating a fanciful weekend at the beach. By this time, I was well-versed in the world of psychedelic drugs, having been introduced to them by my brother. But Harold's lack of knowledge about dosing nearly resulted in disaster when I took my first trip. Remember, he gave me a tab of acid. Less than an hour later, he handed me a dose of mescaline because the acid hadn't kicked in yet. The two drugs mixed together garbled my brain and took me into a part nightmarish, part blissful dimension I didn't recognize and have not visited since.

Heather had not yet partaken in any type of psychedelic drug experience. I had explained to her about how it somehow opened your consciousness and let you walk through the otherwise sealed door (with apologies to Aldous Huxley) into a much deeper perception of the world around you. When it came to drugs in this class—peyote, mescaline, acid, magic mushrooms—I was fearless and more than a tad gullible. I took whatever was handed to me and assumed it was a pure potion provided in loving kindness and goodness. But some of it turned out to be horse tranquilizers. And sometimes it was cut with speed. Still, I survived and thrived on these mind-expanding adventures, fully equipped with profound thoughts and perception.

To my way of thinking, psychedelics were not for those who wanted kicks. They were for the intellectually curious, and I certainly counted myself in that category. I was never drawn to heroin, coke, uppers, reds, or any other category of drug. The music group Paul Revere and the Raiders had a hit record called "Kicks." But for me, dropping acid or mescaline was not done for kicks. Not in my case anyway. I didn't take drugs for recreational purposes. That's like saying you want to take an advanced organic chemistry exam just for the fun of it. Tripping on mescaline, acid, or peyote was not like riding a fancy-free amusement park ride. The brain on psychedelic drugs was a mental minefield to maneuver at times, but quite mesmerizing at others. It was never a buzz. It was always a profound learning experience.

Heather was not a deep thinker, but she was somewhat curious and recklessly bold. Heather wanted to try acid or mescaline, and what better place to "come on" than the soft sand at the beach. We placed our respective mescaline tablets on our tongues and went off on our trip via Greyhound bus.

Twenty minutes into the ride I asked, "Are you feeling anything yet?"

"No," she muttered, disappointed. "Not a thing."

I felt like a failure. What if the drugs weren't potent enough? I gazed out the tinted window of the bus for the next few minutes and watched the trees whizzing by. Suddenly I noticed I was seeing trees in vivid detail. Plus, they were breathing. I could see their trunks rise and fall with every one of my own breaths. My mind examined the veins and the life force throbbing out of the atoms and molecules of the foliage and bark. The greenery out the bus window seemed so alive and active as it began speaking to me in the language of trees and nature. And I understood every word. I looked down at my hand, and the fingers splintered into broken number two pencils. I looked over my other shoulder at Heather as she muttered something that sounded odd in my ear, then didn't.

"If I wanted to, I could rotate my head 360 degrees ... twice," she whispered. Heather's eyes and facial expression said, "Wow. I feel it!"

And we were off.

When we arrived at the Santa Cruz Greyhound bus station, my brother greeted us with his latest "beater" on four wheels. He had trashed his first two cars, and this was his sixth or seventh. I had lost track. This time it was an army green station wagon. By this time, my saliva tasted like the color teal.

"Shhh," I whispered to Heather with an urgent warning. "Don't tell him we took anything. Don't say a word." Then I muttered the one instruction everyone who has ever been high has uttered or has had uttered to them in mid-flight. "Maintain!"

We crawled in the back seat harboring a two-person secret that for some reason we weren't allowed to divulge. It didn't seem to matter that the driver, my brother, was the one who had turned me on to psychedelics in the first place. But for today, this was our little secret universe—mine and Heather's.

A dog on the sidewalk morphed into a serpent. "Look," I whispered to Heather as I pointed out the window. "That man is my grandmother in disguise." She nodded. Everyone nods when they're on psychedelics.

She smiled a knowing smile, but in hindsight, I don't think she knew what the hell I was referring to. She was too busy giggling and studying the pattern on the upholstery.

"Oooo, look. Paisley. How did they know?"

"Know what?"

We were in the same hemisphere and no one else was, so we shot each other knowing glances even though we knew very little about what the other was feeling or seeing.

"My fingers are Parker Brothers Pick-Up Sticks!"

We both giggled, these two astronauts on a spaceship going nowhere, but everywhere.

When we arrived at our destination, we were dropped off at "the little room" which was attached to the apartment four-plex. There was no bathroom, and no room division. It was a small rectangular space that would serve as housing for our cerebral expedition. Heather crawled on the floor beside me. We silently stared at the walls for minutes that felt like hours. She was dazzled by the patterns in the popcorn ceiling. We fell into it, lost ourselves in the white stucco and the geometric universe it provided like it was a planetarium dome. The ceiling texture morphed into patterns and became our inner space manifested in outer space. I suddenly launched into teacher mode, and poor Heather was my student.

"I know it's tempting to stay inside and stare at the ceiling all day, but we need to get ourselves out," I instructed. "We need to get ourselves outside. We must. You'll see why when we get outside."

I had no idea what I meant or what was outside, but it seemed like a good idea to get out of that little stucco universe where the ceiling topography was overwhelming our senses. As soon as we stepped into the sun, our smiles expanded, so much so that our cheeks hurt. The feel of spongy springs had been planted on the soles of our feet, propelling us up and down as we bounced down the street.

We marveled at this strange new sensation and new way of being in the world.

"My feet are cushions! My toes have springs! I could fly if I wanted to."

We could have. We already were.

Side by side, we wandered down to the beach as if we were poised on a magic carpet and our sense of oneness with the sand, sun, and sky carried us there. Suddenly, I morphed into Heather's mother, and she was my child.

She kept saying, "Yes, Mother. Yes." Then her tears started flowing, followed closely by laughter. Our newly defined roles were fully understood by the two of us. We were tripping and tripping hard.

As we walked along the sandy beach, we were greeted by a nice-looking young man at the water's edge. Soon we'd learn his name: Mark Sandperl. I hadn't yet made the connection between Joan Baez's book, *Daybreak,* her mention of Ira Sandperl, and this new Sandperl, named Mark, on the beach. Soon I would come to know him much better. As he watched us playing Mommy-Baby or whatever the hell we were doing, he started a casual conversation with me. One by one, he began to share eye-opening facts about himself and his experiences and family, confessions breaking like wave after wave. Why was he being so candid about himself? The tidbits started coming faster, as if he were unraveling his entire lifetime like the seam that frayed near the ankles of his Levis. One of the first revelations he uttered was, "My dad has met the Beatles."

Yeah, sure. But it turned out to be true. Mark's father, Ira, estranged from his mother, was living a different sort of life; a political mentor and spiritual advisor for Joan Baez. "Joan Baez, my idol?" Joan, my doppelgänger when my eyes were weary from too little sleep? My parlay into nonviolence and massive drug busts? Yes, it was the same Sixties goddess.

Mark resented the hell out of his father, Ira, who rarely, if ever, contacted his kids. There was pain in his eyes when he spoke about Ira. Mark soon became a friend, then an occasional boyfriend, and later a pleasure pal when he was on leave after joining the military. I wondered if that's why Mark joined the Navy. His dad, king of everything nonviolent, would not have been proud of his military stint.

Run for Your Life

When my father's mood swings became unmanageable, I ran away from home. I ran away a lot, only to return at twilight. But as a young teenager, despair trumped fear. I put my thumb out into the air and hitchhiked from the on-ramp to Highway 17 in the direction of Santa Cruz. I was picked up by a nice enough looking middle-aged man on a motorcycle. Off we went as I experienced my first motorcycle ride ... with a total stranger. As we curved around the winding mountain road leading to the beach area, I wrapped my arms around the mystery man in front of me with the intimacy that comes with a two-year relationship. I was hoping our relationship would make it as far as the Santa Cruz border and over the rock 'n' rolling twists of Highway 17. For the first time, I began to question my wisdom about trust ... and about thumbing rides. But such worries were fleeting. The man on the motorbike dropped me in Santa Cruz, and I stuck out my thumb a second time, this time destined for Aptos and Seacliff Beach, the beach town twenty minutes south of downtown Santa Cruz. It never took long to get a ride. I never worried about who would pick me up. I felt fully capable of taking care of myself. I was a fool.

On one runaway adventure, I wandered to a pathway that led from the neighborhood of summer beach homes to Seacliff State Beach. Before the climb downward, I dropped to a step on the pathway, sat with arms wrapped around my knees to shake off the cold and wondered what I would do next ... or more urgently, where my next meal would come from. I hadn't brought any money with me on this impulsive departure.

"Hey, I know you." Suddenly, from out of nowhere, he appeared again. Mark Sandperl, son of Joan Baez's spiritual mentor and absentee father, Ira Sandperl, lowered himself beside me on the walkway step. The last time I had laid eyes on Mark was when I was flying high on the wings of windowpane acid. It turned out Mark lived up the road and was out for his usual stroll down to the beach. His clothes and hair smelled like saltwater. For the first time, I noticed that his lashes were dark and unusually long. His eyes were crystal clear turquoise, like the blue waters waiting for us below on Seacliff Beach. We ended up talking on the steps as he dried my tears and hugged away my homesickness. Later, we shared Italian food at Aptos Pizza, then tangled our bodies and lips together in the "little room" like gooey mozzarella. Later, he ran off into the night and back to his own bed. I went to sleep in the "little room"—the closet-sized, shower-free sleeping quarters at the ground level of my father's four-plex rental building in Aptos.

The next morning, while I was still foggy from confounding dreams, my brother's voice blared like a car horn through the darkness and damp air. He was standing over me.

"What are you doing here? You need to go home. Mom and Dad said so. Come on. They sent me to get you."

Harold was no longer living at home. He had been kicked out yet again because his hair was too long. I'd only see him when he'd patrol by my bedroom window at all hours of the night asking for a new supply of socks and underwear from his dresser drawer. He was now living in his bandmate's garage.

"I can't go home. Dad is out of control," I protested. "I won't!" But I did, and without a bit of sympathy from my brother.

"Get in the car. Let's go. I've got other stuff to do today. The band is learning a new tune."

And with that, we headed back down the winding mountain highway, back to Santa Clara Valley and Willow Glen, back to a glass house that was being rattled too much and too often by my dad's frenzied and random quakes.

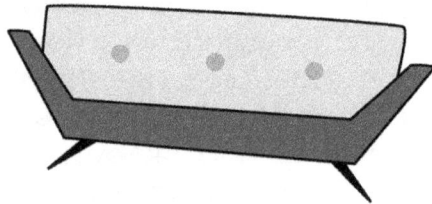

SECTION VII:

Babes in Boyland

New York, New York ... Again

On my sixteenth birthday, my mother and I flew back to New York City to visit relatives and wander the streets of my birthplace and hers. It was quite an education for a young girl who thought she knew this from that. I didn't know squat. The two of us came off the plane and took a bus to visit my grandparents in the Bronx, to spend time in New York City, to visit my aunt, and to take in some of the sights I was too young to absorb before our move to California. After showing my grandfather how to turn on the television, then it was just the two of us, my mother and me, hopping buses, strolling the city streets, noshing on pastrami, kosher pickles, Italian ices, hot pretzels from street vendors, and bland sandwiches from the automat. Once we were nourished, we covered multiple blocks of our old stomping grounds by foot, bus, and subway.

My mother took me to Radio City Music Hall. It was such a treat. I had never been there in my younger years. Before they showed the film *The Out-of-Towners* starring Jack Lemmon and Sandy Dennis, a new film that was an appropriate one to watch, seeing as we were out-of-towners ourselves, the Rockettes—the world famous Radio City Music Hall dancers—hit the stage. They hit the stage hard. All those sparkles and sequins. All those legs and high kicks. All that razzle-dazzle.

We stayed with my grandparents, Mae and Murray, in the same basement apartment my mother had grown up in and that had inspired daily runaways to her friend Joyce's brownstone so many years ago. At nighttime, our roommates were assorted rats that ran along the pipe-work on the ceiling. I tried to sleep while I watched and listened to them scurry back and forth, as if they had somewhere to go other than back and forth. Curling up beside my mother in her parents' double bed was a new experience. I liked it. My mother and I were never really close, but now we were, as least in the physical sense.

We slept in my grandparents' bedroom while they shared the ghastly floral couch in their small living room. I breathed in the scent of Downy Fabric Softener from the bedsheets and pillowcases, while my mother shared stories of her girlhood. She talked to me like one would talk to a friend, not a daughter. She shared stories about her desire to get out from under her parents' roof. Their constant verbal combat was the soundtrack of her childhood. The dampness of the rooms and the close confines of that tiny apartment were her hell. I felt honored she was confiding in me. If I couldn't be her daughter, perhaps I could be her friend.

Mom frequently fantasized about the day she would escape. This was one of the few times we talked about something meaningful, something other than the humidity or the amount of rain outside. It was like a slumber party, but the nights consisted of my mother's voice and stories, the honking taxis and frequent police sirens blaring outside the bedroom window. There was an occasional gunshot. I tried to imagine a childhood there. I couldn't. I suddenly felt enormous empathy for my mother. I had new insights and understanding of what made her so different from me. I could finally see why home didn't mean to her what it meant to me. For her, it was something to run away from. For me, it was something to hunker down in, grip tight, and never let go.

Those late nights with the pitter-patter of rats and my mother's ramblings are forever locked away in my memory. My grandparents slept and fought in the living room on the other side of the wall while we chatted in their bedroom. I listened to their howls and hollers and the little trifles they quarreled about for hours. What nonsense, I thought to myself. Do they even like or care about one another? The room was the size of a postage stamp, and their amount of patience was not much bigger. My grandparents carried on with their verbal battles in Liz Taylor–Richard Burton fashion, housed in the barracks of that dreary basement apartment in the armpit of the Bronx. Who's Afraid of Virginia Woolf? Not me. I was afraid of my grandparents' grand fights and constant discord. Their inharmonious coupling hurt my heart. I wanted to bury my head in the bed pillow to dampen their furious exchanges. But first, I wanted to cover my mother's ears.

My first friend on Long Island, before my family moved out to the West Coast, was a round five-year-old girl named Patty Lufrano. We grew up on the same block, where all the houses looked alike. She was chubby as a rock, and I was skinny like a stick, so we looked like Laurel and Hardy when we'd pal around together.

Patty wore a sailor hat on her head at all hours of the day. For all I knew, she slept in it. Maybe her father was in the Navy. When my family left New York State, I was six years old. I missed Patty and would send her letters in my big script 'n' scrawl. We stayed in touch for a while with crayon drawings and letters. Then we didn't. But ten years had flown by. On this, my sixteenth birthday, and our trip back to New York City, my mother called Patty's mother, Rosemary, and we all agreed to meet for lunch. I was feeling anxious. Who was this first friend I had so long ago? Would we have any commonalities? Did she like the same music groups I liked? Did she watch the same TV shows, wear the same fashions, have the same sensibility? How could she? She had grown up on Long Island, and I was a long way from Long Island now.

We met up briefly with Patty and her mother in New York City and went to a movie at a grand old theater where my grandfather was working as an usher. His job in retirement, because for him there was no retirement, was tearing tickets and greeting theater-going guests. He loved his job. He loved having someplace to go, preferably far away from his wife. He loved life and New York. He radiated glee unlike anyone else in my family tree.

After my grandfather smiled a smile as wide as the candy counter and tore off half our tickets, we entered the darkened theater with the two-story red velvet curtains, plush seats, and ornate carvings on the wall. But I noticed something about this enormous old-world elegant theater that was peculiar. There was no one filling the seats. We were the only four people there when the massive curtains parted and Katherine Hepburn, Peter O'Toole, and Anthony Hopkins began to entertain us in *The Lion in Winter*. There was no one in the theater except Patty's mother, my mother, and two young old friends who hadn't seen one another since swing sets. I wondered what my grandfather was doing in the lobby to keep his mind occupied. He seemed overjoyed and proud to be there and to simply have a job in such a lovely theater. But where were the moviegoers? The shame of it was many of these old New York City theaters were sitting empty.

The movie began, and we fixed our eye on the lush curtains as they parted, and then we took in the magnificent broad screen. I heard my stomach growl above Henry II as he ruled a world in which kings still kicked aside chickens on their way through the courtyard and wore heavily layered costumes that would be ideal for New York winters. My mother, Patty, her mother, and I piled out of the theater and discussed the best places for lunch, then found ourselves at the automat, where you could pull sandwiches, burgers, pies, pastry, or whatever you desire from the food doors. Patty and I reconnected over egg salad sandwiches, sour pickles, and a couple of Dr. Brown's Cel-Ray sodas. I soon learned Patty enjoyed Joni Mitchell's music just as I did. Suddenly ten years fell away. We both had plenty to say and share about everything. Clothing, music, books, boys! What else is there when you're turning sixteen? We were rekindling our long-lost friendship as teenagers living on different coasts, but we now had even more in common. When I got home, Patty and I exchanged letters again, catching up with everything that was going on with us. We stayed in touch. Then we didn't. Sometimes the final curtain falls on a friendship, even when you're Laurel and Hardy.

My grandmother warned my mother and me to hold onto our purses in downtown New York. "I've had the straps cut off of my purse six times now! They are everywhere, those hooligans. Watch out! Hold your purse against you when you walk." Both of my grandmothers had been mugged, and my Grandma Anna had once been brutally attacked in the process. Both women were afraid to walk the streets in their own neighborhood, even in the daylight. They never ventured out at night. The New York City streets were lined with threats. "Watch out for strangers!" was built into our Ashkenazi DNA.

While my mother and I were wandering through Alexander's Department store in New York City, I spied a bright yellow songbook for *Clouds,* the new Joni Mitchell album I had just purchased at home. It was as though I had spotted an angel, and I had: Joni Mitchell with her angelic yellow hair. I stopped in my tracks, turned to my mother and said "There's only one thing I want for my birthday, Mom. That songbook! That's all I want. Please?" She was agreeable, and I was over the moon with excitement. I can still remember my heart bouncing hard beneath my blouse—thump-thump—like a rough ride in a New York cab. I purchased the book and held it under my arm the rest of the day. I would never let it go.

On another afternoon, as my mother and I were wandering the streets of downtown New York, I had to use the restroom, the result of too many iced tea refills at lunchtime. "Well, if you have to go, let's go in here," instructed my mother as we strolled Rockefeller Center by Saks Fifth Avenue, a store we otherwise never shopped in or even considered browsing in. We certainly had never purchased anything there. My family shopped at discount department stores such as Gemco, Disco, and White Front. J.C. Penney was a luxury store as far as we were concerned, and we visited it only once to purchase barbecue tongs.

As my mother and I stepped into the Saks Fifth Avenue elevator, we both took a deep breath and inhaled the scent of money and competing perfume fragrances circulating in the air like a high-priced brothel. As I stepped through the elevator doors, I studied the list of floors and departments listed beside buttons on the wall. The restrooms were listed alongside lingerie. "Which floor, madam?" asked the elevator operator, who was dressed like one of those tall uniformed nutcrackers you see at Christmas time. *I'm a madam now?* I had never been in a store with an elevator operator. "Uh, lingerie, please." That must have sounded funny coming from a sixteen-year-old dressed in jeans, a peasant blouse, love-beads, and a belt featuring multicolored peace signs.

Before arriving at our destination, the elevator stopped to let in other customers. I caught a quick glimpse of a dark-haired gentlemen dressed in a fluorescent blue one-piece jumpsuit. He stood to my left as I stared straight ahead along with the rest of the elevator passengers. As I peeked out of the corner of my left eye, I could see his face was caked in heavy makeup. Eyeliner surrounded his lower and upper eyelids, and white powder covered his checks and forehead. And was that orange lipstick on his lips? Who was this character? Suddenly his identity came into view.

Oh, my gawd, it's him! I said to myself in a loud and enthusiastic inner voice that only I could hear. I nudged my mother, but she was busy fishing for something out of the bottom of her purse. My mother always carried a purse the size and weight of carry-on luggage. All she ever carried with her was one orange lipstick, a wallet, and a three-inch stack of two-for-one coupons wrapped in a rubber-band. She didn't notice the subtle barbs to her waist coming from the direction of her only daughter.

"Lingerie. Ninth floor."

Which floor? And there's one more above this? Where are we shopping, the Statue of Liberty?

As my mother and I stepped out of the elevator car to search for the ladies' room, I hurried to tell her about what she had missed.

"Didn't you see him? That was Peter Sellers!"

I had recognized him from my father's favorite comedy film from 1968, now my favorite film: *The Party.*

"He must have just come from a movie set. Did you see him? DID YOU SEE HIM?"

By this time, I was hopping up and down like a hyper kangaroo—a kangaroo in the middle of the lingerie section of Saks. My mother's interest in my discovery seemed slight as she peered around the wall-to-wall robes, panties, and nightgowns. She was being pulled to the merchandise, and there was nothing I could say or do to break that mighty force.

"There it is. There's the Ladies' Room. I thought you had to go. I'll be browsing around at the clearance racks when you get out."

My enthusiasm and glee from my brush with greatness, or at least a great actor, were shrinking as my bladder was filling. I was off to the latrine.

After ten days in the Big Apple, I packed my bag for our rapidly approaching departure, stashing the newly purchased Joni Mitchell songbook into my suitcase. I couldn't wait to get home and examine its pages, read both sides of each page, and study every chord and lyric. It was my first songbook. I still have it, along with my memories of bus rides in the rain and walking the streets of downtown New York with my mother until we were both ready to collapse and drown ourselves in a chocolate phosphate.

My memories from that trip back east were very different from my mother's recollection. At the end of the trip, her only thought was "I've got to get the hell away from my parents again!" Mine were of that bright yellow book filled with Joni Mitchell's powerful poetry and music mixed with the scent of lavender sheets in my grandparents' bedroom. By the end of the week, I was ready to get away from the commotion of the city and return to our suburban playground. I wanted to bring my new sixteen-year-old body home to the Eichler. I was having a heavy and crampy period that began the day we left on our trip. It was so heavy I had to wash out my blood-soaked panties in my grandmother's sink and hang them in the shower one by one, a sorry replacement for a washer-dryer set. My grandparents washed all their clothing in a basin and hung the soggy pile of shirts, blouses, and undergarments on a clothesline draped outside their living room window. It hung over the alleyway to the next apartment building. And now, so did my crimson panties. I couldn't go an hour or two without soaking myself. This was not an impressive case for womanhood.

House Calls

Once back in San Jose and safely at home in our Eichler, we found my brother's thirteen-year-old girlfriend, Jackie, living there. My father had allowed her to move into our fourth bedroom while my mother and I roamed the streets of New York City. This bedroom, sometimes den, was used for many purposes while we lived in the Eichler. Initially, it was my father's study, which consisted of a drafting table and an amalgamation of strangely shaped drawing tools. Every one of them appeared peculiar and whimsical. They were unlike anything else we had around the house. Some of their shapes reminded me of the Paul Klee print that hung on the family room wall. In a shoebox with the top cut off, which is how my father stored everything from nuts and bolts to Q-Tips to cans of sardines, sat triangles of every size, a compass, rulers, drafting paper, and paperclips. It seemed like a mysterious world, this one of right and left angles. I wanted to use the slanted wooden board he called a desk. I wanted to know what to do with the instruments, even though I didn't have a clue what they did ... or even what my father did for a living. I wanted to be a part of his world, but I had no idea how to mesh my childlike hemisphere with his adult hemisphere.

One year, my parents announced that they were renting out the fourth bedroom. I was stricken with anxiety. What? Another person—a perfect stranger—living in our house, sharing my bathroom, taking up precious Eichler space? But it turned out to be one of the best experiences of my young life. A college student moved in and befriended me in a big sister style that I didn't expect. She taught me how to knit as we sat on the slatted bench in the living room. She talked to me, encouraged me. I was suddenly visible. It was a new and precious sensation. I mattered. But after one semester at San Jose State University, she blew far, far away never to be heard from again. It was the closest I came to having a sister and an attentive friend all rolled into one. I welcomed such a kinship with open arms. But her stay with us was brief.

Later, my father would shout, "I never had my own bedroom when I was living with my parents. I want my own room! I claim the fourth bedroom." He moved in and slept in the fourth bedroom for a couple of years, then slipped back into the master bedroom when he got that out of his system. But for a while, my father had his own bedroom for the first time in his life. He used the kid's bathroom, as the fourth bedroom was located at the end of the hallway surrounded by my brother's room, my room, and the washer and dryer. Late at night my father would break out in some nonsensical song with a familiar melody, but one that he put his own lyrics to. Or he would simply chant one word to a well-known song. He would often sing the singular word and name, "Hayakawa! Hayakawa!" over and over again until I thought my head would explode. He likely saw a local news story about famous Californian S.I. Hayakawa, and his rhythmic name made its way into my father's brain.

I never knew what went on in my brother's room. He had his own friends, his own records, his own comings and goings. I was seldom included, and that was fine with me. But now my brother's young girlfriend, who was a child of the foster care system, was taking up residence in our fourth bedroom. My mother wouldn't have it. The yelling began to swell and suddenly Jackie was out of the house, back with another in a series of foster homes, and the fourth bedroom was back to being my father's den. Harold was in trouble, not from my father, but my mother. My father didn't care if Jackie was only thirteen years old. To him, it was fun having someone else in the house. My mother was fuming, however. But trouble was an ongoing production at our house, especially for my brother. His hair was too long, he wasn't supposed to be driving, he wasn't doing well in school, his music was too loud. "You're a BUM!" That was my mother's favorite word for everyone she didn't like, and sometimes she didn't like my brother.

Harold didn't have many girlfriends before moving out of the Eichler and heading off to Santa Cruz for college, playing music, and meeting chicks, but shortly after he moved into his beach town apartment he met Bridget. She was statuesque, and below my brother's six feet one inch height. Bridget sported a delightful, juvenile-sized button nose, sizeable breasts, and a high, rather unique lilt in her voice. She was everything I wasn't. She had all the attributes "The Girl from Ipanema" described. Furthermore, you could have fit two of me into one tall, tan, young, and lovely Bridget. Her straight, glossy black hair looked very much like my mother's. But her pussycat nose looked like no one in my family tree. She had a contagious giggle, an intense interest in everyone and everything around her. Bridget was an Amazon woman full of natural beauty and poise. She was a clone of Linda Carter's Wonder Woman. They were twin sisters from different mothers.

Bridget's majestic frame was voluptuous, her spirit freewheeling and unguarded. In contrast, I was a timid stick figure sporting soft bones and dull, russet brown, unmanageable hair. I wondered what it was like to be her. What was it like to walk down the street and have every man's head click to the side and turn like Robby the Robot? They watched her sashay down the sidewalk runway. Our boobs never kissed when we hugged, which was often. They were much too mismatched in height. Her bosomy chest sat so high and mighty on her nearly six-foot frame that my forehead would sink into them like cushiony couch pillows. Bridget had more curves than San Francisco's Lombard Street.

Flights of Fancy

As I was ruminating on various escape plans from my current home life, my friend Heather couldn't have been happier with hers. Her name might as well have been Polly, as in Pollyanna.

Heather suffered from a significant case of Pollyannaism, a tendency to remember pleasant events and push the unpleasant ones aside. Nothing was complex, discouraging, dire, or dark. She was walking in the light, open and hopeful, always disgustingly pleasant and pleased with people and situations, while I leaned back in the dark and dove too deep, pondered too long, dissected and examined until there was nothing left in the petri dish.

Heather, in her tailored gold sweater and plaid skirt, was radically different from me in my black velvet home-sewn jacket and dark olive pants. One night, she and I decided to sneak out late at night and go to Georgio's Pizza for some dinner. When we arrived, the restaurant was crowded, and the owners were busy tossing dough, bussing tables, and making change. Instead of hanging out in our favorite pizza café, we wandered to the Jolly 5 & 10 Store to pick up some packets of square stale bubblegum packaged together with Beatles cards. Then we strolled to the grocery store where we finagled the purchase of a pack of Viceroy Filter Kings.

"Let's smoke the whole pack on the way home."

It sounded like a good idea. Between the two of us, we smoked all twenty cigarettes on the fifteen-minute walk home. Not once did we inhale. We puffed on stick after stick like they were sooty candy cigarettes rolled in sugar dust.

On one particular jaunt to this strip mall, at age fifteen, I walked into Georgio's Pizza Parlor, and one of the owners, John, asked me my name.

"Hi, I'm Johnny Cash" was my rapid-fire reply.

And so began our love affair. Georgio's Pizza Restaurant was owned and operated by two attractive Italian brothers, John and Frank. They would flirt with my girlfriend and me, and we would eat up their compliments like slices of pepperoni pizza. I was partial to John and would sit on the stool for hours, talking with him and watching his hands kneading the flour, water, and salt. His eyes looked odd in a Sammy Davis Jr. sort of way. One of them was glass, but I didn't care. There was an attraction rising like a ball of fresh pizza dough, and nothing could stop it. I knew John was too old for me. At the ripe old age of fifteen, every man seemed too old for me, but terrifically alluring and deliciously dangerous.

John and I were kindred spirits, lovers of tomato sauce, mozzarella, and mortadella, and masters at flirting. I would make clever quips while John created mouthwatering masterpieces. A jukebox sat next to the stools. I'd always punch Chicago's "Color My World" while gazing at John working behind the counter. Would he cook for me if we were married? Would he make pizza for breakfast, lunch, and dinner? It sounded perfect to me.

Heather and I would frequently hang out at the restaurant after school let out for the day. The banter and baked calzones were intoxicating. John finally shared the saga of how he lost his eye and had to have it replaced with a glass eye.

"I was cleaning the toilet and some VANISH liquid bowl cleaner splashed into my eye." And with that one random spray, John's sight had vanished and was lost forever. Truth in advertising. Heather and I gasped and sat back in horror. Poor One-Eyed John! Despite the round glass object in his socket, he was a handsome devil, and I still had my eye on him. Both of them.

✳ ⚛ ✳

My father's moods always came in unpredictable waves. We were doing this, but suddenly … no … we were doing that. The roller-coaster ride of his highs and lows carried with it many passengers. I was always seated in the rear car feeling the brunt of the rotations, never once throwing my arms high over my head and enjoying the turbulence. In those days, I required a mild ride, something along the lines of It's a Small World. My father was the Matterhorn.

Dad was always trying to shed his restlessness like a snake that couldn't quite shake its skin. The summer before my junior year in high school, on an arbitrary whim that arrived like a sudden gust of wind, my father decided we would move to a small apartment in Santa Clara. The decision came on as suddenly as their impulsive trip to Tijuana or a night flight to Reno, or the way his anger and joy blew up and down like a paper kite. My brother had already moved out of the house or had been kicked out. I can't recall. His long hair made my mother's blood pressure soar, and my father usually ended up taking him by the arm and escorting him out the door and to the sidewalk.

"Get a haircut, bum."

Off he went with his pound of hair and a paper bag filled with underwear and T-shirts.

All of a sudden, a new plan was laid out before us—my father's plan. He wanted to get away from the Eichler biosphere for a while, so he rented out our Eichler to our next-door neighbors, Frank and Barb Barrington and their nuclear family of four that, based on appearances, was the most well-adjusted household in the cul-de-sac.

The plan for me? I was to move with my parents and be thrown into a different high school in a different biosphere called Santa Clara. But I didn't understand the soul of Santa Clara. Bookser High was radically different from my school in Willow Glen, and Santa Clara was a profoundly different community from the Willow Glen Eichlers. I would be forsaken in this new city. My parents had derailed me from our comfortable tract house and dropped us, now a family of three, into a small apartment in a foreign region several miles from Willow Glen and too far from John and his glass eye. Could life get much worse?

The original proposal to save myself from the dismal year ahead was to live with another family in our Eichler neighborhood and continue my junior year at my usual school, sleep in my usual bed, and hang out with my usual friends. The most logical choice was to stay with the Barringtons who were going to rent our home. They were more than agreeable with the arrangement. Frank Barrington had been a probation officer and was considered "cool" with the cul-de-sac kids as he spoke our language: adolescence. He swore in front of us and talked to us like we were already adults. He was hip, and more importantly, he was fun to be around. I could remain in my room and even keep my two cats there while I continued to go to school at Willow Glen High. It was a perfect arrangement.

Not so fast.

Boys Gone Wild

I had been the babysitter for the Barrington's two kids a couple of years prior to this arrangement. The two half-pints were fast asleep the entire time I was in their home, so I watched *The Johnny Cash Show* on television and thumbed through the paperbacks in their walnut bookcases.

I was never one to run out and buy the latest Johnny Cash record. But in 1969, I was front and center at Frank and Barb Barrington's house watching Cash's variety show on TV. It featured an eclectic menu of musical genres and musicians, such as Joni Mitchell, Bob Dylan, Linda Ronstadt, Kris Kristofferson, Mickey Newbury, Neil Young, Gordon Lightfoot, and James Taylor. It also featured musicians such as jazz great Louis Armstrong, who died eight months after appearing on the show. I began paying attention to the show and to this phenomenon named Johnny Cash. He seemed to have an open mind and heart, and didn't give a shit what you thought of him.

Cash's show had a somewhat rocky two-year run, occasionally making network executives nervous when, for example, he refused to censor the word *stoned* from Kris Kristofferson's performance of his self-penned "Sunday Morning Coming Down." Cash also brought on Pete Seeger, despite the uproar over his anti-war views—views that caused some of Cash's audience to tune out and turn off the program.

But for me, the show was beyond my wildest expectations, especially when Joni Mitchell played "Both Sides Now" from her second album, titled *Clouds*. She was already a rising star, and Dylan was, well … a phenomenon. Cash was an admirer of Dylan, and Dylan admired the hell out of Cash. The year *The Johnny Cash Show* debuted, both men recorded more than a dozen songs together, one of them was the rocky "Girl from the North Country," which appeared on Dylan's *Nashville Skyline* album, despite the two vocalists singing a different lyric at one point during the song. To me, that miscalculation was endearing. On Cash's show, Dylan sang another song from that same album titled "I Threw It All Away," a song that left me in tears in front of that snowy television set. Dylan, who had famously walked off the set of *The Ed Sullivan Show* in 1963, set aside his distaste for American television and sang both songs with Cash. It was a mutual admiration society.

Another musician had a big breakthrough on Cash's show. He happened to be the cousin of Frank Barrington's wife, Barb. His performance in front of a national audience on Cash's show led him to a long-term recording contract. A few months later, and to top his extraordinarily good year, one of his songs was broadcast back to Earth by the crew of the Apollo 12 moon mission.

With his previous notoriety limited to his home region, this musician had now become known in mainstream America. On one particular summer night when Heather was babysitting the Barringtons' two small children, Frank and Barb arrived home with Barb's musician cousin from their evening outing to San Francisco. It was around two in the morning. The intoxicated musician offered to walk her home.

"That's okay. I live across the street," she said. But he insisted.

As soon as they were out Barringtons' front door, the musician slipped Heather's fifteen-year-old hand into his and clutched it tightly. Too tightly. He held her grasped hand down straight at his side with subtle force and no bend to the elbow. Instead of walking her to her door, he guided her around the cul-de-sac, hand in hand. She thought it was odd, but he was the adult, and she was a teenager who had gotten her first period and was trying to maneuver her walk so that the oversize Kotex pad didn't give away her secret. When they moved through the gate to her front yard, Heather spoke up, but timidly. "My door is right there."

But he insisted that they walk into the backyard instead. It was past Heather's bedtime. She was sleepy and not sure what was appropriate or not appropriate, so she obliged.

"Let's have sex," he muttered as he began touching her back and front in places a fifteen-year-old would rather not be touched by an older and rather repellant relative of a neighbor.

She took a whiff of his neck, which smelled adult and wrong. "I have to go inside. Now!" Heather was tired but managed to push him away and steer her way inside the safe harbor of her Eichler where her parents and sister were fast asleep. In the mid-Sixties, even adults didn't know where the line was drawn or when they had crossed it. And for some, it was a dotted line begging to be crossed.

Frank Barrington was personable with teenagers. He spoke to me and my friends in shorthand—the kind you use with close colleagues. We didn't understand most of it, but we puffed up our feathers around him because he made us feel as though we were in his league. My friends and I often felt he was the only adult who understood us. Frank even spoke our slang. In our eyes, he was beyond cool. We trusted him. He pulled us in with his peacock blue–colored eyes and began sharing his experiences about working with adolescents. When he suddenly switched careers from probation officer to insurance salesman, we thought it was a bit odd, but none of us were looking for red flags. We should have been, but we were not yet savvy in the ways of adulthood.

Frank's wife, Barb, was an effervescent elfin blonde with a perpetual smile. She seemed continually happy and was exceedingly approachable. She too seemed like one of us: goofy, childlike, fun-loving. The Barringtons' two kids were both under the age of six but were well behaved and well adjusted. They seemed to be raised with equal parts iron fist and soft touch. From all outward appearances, Frank and Barb were the ideal parents. When they agreed to let me live with their family, I exhaled a sigh of relief that would fill a hot air balloon. I didn't have to move out of our Eichler! I didn't have to uproot myself, my life, my cats. I was safe. I was home again, or still. And I was going to live with the hippest family in the area: the Barringtons.

My parents moved out, and the Barringtons began to move their furnishings and boxes into our home. My home. It felt strange to have so many foreign furniture pieces scattered about the family rooms of my Eichler. They placed their traditional grandfather's clock housed in a walnut cabinet in the living room and hung pictures of strangers on the walls, my walls. But there was no other way to win this war. The thought of being away from my parents, my father's mood swings, and my mother's apathy, seemed like an all-expense-paid vacation won as the grand prize in the Publisher's Clearing House Sweepstakes.

My parents moved out. Every piece of blond wood furniture, each modern art print of Klee and Picasso, every music book and trashy novel had been cleared from the rooms. The night the Barrington family began loading their final boxes from their house next door into my family's house, their kids were already fast asleep in my brother's room and in my room. My friend Heather and I were in Frank Barrington's old kitchen helping him pack the final dishes, pots, and pans. We had never had alcohol before, but Frank soon began plying us with drinks that he announced were like chocolate shakes. "Try these Kahlúa and cream drinks. You'll love them. Come on. Drink up!"

Heather didn't want to and said she needed to get home. Off she ran into the dark and across the street. But I couldn't run home yet, even though it was just next door. I needed to help my new friend, my confidant, my cool father figure who would be living in my house for the next year. I started sipping this small amount of chocolate-colored liqueur out of a lowball glass. My friends and I had never tried alcohol before and had no desire to do so. We smoked marijuana, dropped acid, took mescaline, and gagged on peyote buttons. Alcohol seemed like something that belonged to my parents' generation, not ours. But tonight, with the urging of this new friend, this man-of-the-house—soon to be the man of my house—I felt I should oblige. The beverage tasted sweet and pleasing.

"Here, have another," he urged.

Before I knew it, my head was spinning and so was my stomach. I had been drinking what tasted like Hershey's syrup and milk. Frank Barrington couldn't wait to give me another ... and another.

It was soon closing in on midnight. My mind and body were beat and ready for sleep.

"I need to go out for cigarettes," said Frank in an insistent tone. "Come with me."

I was weary, but he was treating me like such an equal, such an adult, that I didn't dare reject his invitation. I hopped in the car, but quickly realized he too had been drinking all night, and not sweet drinks. Whiskey. Lots of whiskey. He was plowed. Soused. Smashed. In short, Frank Barrington was as dangerous as a kicking mule, especially behind the wheel of a car.

It was so late, there were few other cars on the highway. Frank's driving was full of swerves and sudden jolts, but more importantly, I didn't know where we were. It was not a familiar landscape. We were climbing up hill after hill. Soon we were high above San Jose looking down at the sleepy valley from the hilltop. I looked out my passenger side window into the darkness and wondered how to turn the car around with my mind. Where were my magical powers now?

Frank picked up a couple of packs of cigarettes at a convenience store, crawled back into the car, and made several attempts to slide the key into the slot. He kept missing. Finally the engine turned over, and we made our way out of the parking lot. Good. Let's get home. My eyelids were heavy and ready for some sleep. But instead of turning right and heading home Frank turned left. We were heading down winding roads that were farther and farther from our cul-de-sac. Panic was beginning to race my heart a bit, but … was he not an authority figure, a model father, and more importantly a friend? Of course. He was a buddy, a chum. He treated me like one of his pals, and I felt like one. Sort of.

Suddenly Frank was weaving and winding all over the country road and driving straight into a grove surrounded by pine trees. It was pitch black. I couldn't see anything out the car window, but I could smell his whiskey-infused breath all the way from the passenger's seat. I wanted to trust him. He was an adult. He was a father. He was our trusty neighbor. He was renting our house from my own father. He wouldn't do anything inappropriate. He couldn't. Not so fast. Could he?

He tried. He reached out and grabbed at my blouse with his pudgy, paw-like hands. I wrestled him away from me. Frank's thin lips pushed into mine, but I held my mouth firm and closed.

Everything about Frank was severely circular. His face with puffy pink cheeks, his protruding tummy, balding head with baby fine hairs, were all rounded. He had a matching round bald patch on the top half of his skull that I could clearly see as he fumbled towards me with his groping hands and gaping mouth trying to force a French kiss.

Nausea set in. I was terrified. I could clearly see this housing arrangement was quickly twirling down the toilet.

"Take me home!" I insisted, as I wiped the goopy saliva from his thin lips off of my lips. I insisted he drive us back, even though he was incapable of driving in a straight line. He mumbled something or other, and we began weaving back down the hilly two-lane road.

We made it to the safety of the cul-de-sac. My stomach was in knots as the inebriated father figure opened the orange door and stumbled to the master bedroom to join his perky wife for a deep sleep. I stood in the hallway of my old home, my unshakable shelter that was now shaken and stirred. It had been my escape hatch, but no more. It was now walls of glass and wood with strangers snoring inside.

I crawled into the lower bunk in the son's room—my brother's old room—and wondered what the hell I was going to do in the morning. Wait. It *was* morning. I looked at the clock on the nightstand. It was 4 a.m. What was I going to do come daylight? I tried to soothe myself, quiet my mind and nerves, fall asleep. The more I tried, the more hyper-alert I became. What if he came into the room? Maybe he didn't even care that his son was sleeping in the bed above. Maybe he will come after me if I fall asleep. I couldn't find a way to quiet my thoughts, and I couldn't think of a sensible way to remain under the same roof as a man with two faces, one of them clearly sloshed.

But where was I to go? Clearly rattled, I felt a familiar wave of dread. I didn't know if I had any other options, but I knew one thing. I couldn't live with this family whose father could not be trusted.

I lay in that child-sized bed, thoughts fidgeting. Just when I believed I had a solution, it flew out the window. My brother's bedroom window. I barely slept that night in that bottom bunk that belonged to some strange kid attached to a warped and inebriated father. The Barringtons' basset hound was breathing at the foot of the bed, his short rhythmic inhalations and long exhalations conflicted with the rapid tick-tick-tick of their walnut grandfather clock in the hallway. What was that old-fashioned timepiece doing in a modern home? My home.

I now knew I had to move to that cramped Santa Clara apartment and join my parents. I felt dread, but by morning, I felt resolve. With my small packed bag in one hand, I walked past the cheery Mrs. Barrington in the family room of my Eichler where she was folding freshly laundered bath towels and shirts. I left the perfect nuclear family behind.

I never uttered a word about my encounter with Frank Barrington. At that time, such events were buried, not discussed. I didn't think my parents would believe me, and frankly I didn't think they cared enough to listen. Although I didn't know it at the time, that was likely the typical response to many girls and women, not only in the 1960s, but in all the decades leading up to the #MeToo movement. By this time, my brother was already living elsewhere and not at home. If he had been available, I still wouldn't have said anything to him or even to his girlfriends. There was a kind of hush all over the world, and it had to do with inappropriate and unwanted carnal lunges, not Herman's Hermits.

Lost in Eichler Space

My mother and father didn't seem happy about my return to their domain. In fact, they wouldn't have it. None of it. Their fantasy about living in their own apartment, recreating some earlier slice of their New York City life and the bloom of their relationship did not include a teenage girl. My mother's eyes gazed skyward as she rifled through her massive mental Rolodex of friends and doorsteps where she could drop me like a fruit basket. We drove silently back to our old neighborhood where she dragged me from Eichler to Eichler, and to all her neighborhood friends to see if they would take me in for the school year. She did everything but wear a sandwich board that read: TAKE MY DAUGHTER ... PLEASE! But no one was interested. Even my friend Heather's mother turned us down. Who could blame her? I was a slightly disheveled sixteen-year-old wearing a torn black velvet jacket in the middle of summer. And I was carrying a secret about their tenant that would never leave my lips.

We finally uncovered someone willing to let me live under their roof. It was the neighbors who happened to have their own bomb shelter, the Ludwicks. This couple had a young boy of about six or seven years old. Suddenly I was part of their silent family. Neither parent talked to me or to one another. I was to fend for myself, find my own meals, and hide in my new room when I came home from school. I was familiar with these house rules. There was no one to converse with or fix me breakfast.

I may have been living in an Eichler again, but it didn't feel like my Eichler, except for the part where the parents didn't seem to be aware that I was there. The Ludwicks' home was identical to my Eichler except that every bedroom closet in the home had at least one gaping hole in each sliding door. I couldn't imagine why or what caused it. After several days in this haunted house of avoidance, I asked the young boy, "Why all the holes in the doors?"

"Oh, my dad gets angry and kicks them in."

That evening I called my father, tears streaming down my face. "Can I come live with you? I can't stay here."

No! My mother was off to find another family for me to stay with for the school year.

Adults, M.I.A.

My next "home" was with the Lewis family, my father's best pal who happened to be recently divorced.

Hank Lewis was in the midst of *The Dating Game.* No, not watching it on television, but living it. His wife had recently left him and his three children, and Hank was left to fend for himself and find a new mate. Two of his three children lived at home: Tommy and May, who was my age. We were to share May's bedroom. I had never shared a room before. It was sort of fun, except that she was on a strict schedule and went to bed long before I was even the slightest bit sleepy.

Tommy Lewis and I had already managed to engage in a pillowy lip-lock inside the giant pipe at a local playground about a year earlier. He had come by on his bicycle one evening to see my brother. I happened to be home alone after a verbal beating from my father that, as usual, came out of nowhere and left me in tears. My father left the house, and I ran to my bedroom, hitting the pillow harder and harder in frustration and confusion. Why did he pick on me so? I didn't know. I never knew.

When the doorbell rang, I ran to answer it. Despite tears rolling down my cheeks, I opened the door and looked into Tommy's beautiful dark eyes, his face, as Janis Ian once sang, "clean and shining, black as night," his square jawline and thick lips asking what was wrong. All I could manage to release between sniffles were the words "my father" and nothing more. I must have looked like Bambi who had just lost his mother to a hunter.

Tommy urged me to hop on the back of his bike and off we rode down the suburban streets and into the night, not knowing where we were going, but knowing we had to go, go, go. We crawled inside one of those giant cylinders housed on the playground and held one another. Both of us had emotional battles with our fathers, but we didn't discuss his nor mine. Our hands wandered and caressed as we comforted one another like lost children. Janis Ian sang about raising up her glistening wings to fly. We agreed and decided we would raise our wings and soar once we were out of our parents' domain, and out of adolescence.

In the late hour of darkness, in that school playground shelter, I was Society's Child and so was Tommy. We were stuck. We couldn't scratch our way out. Not yet. A year after our playground rendezvous, I was moving into Tommy's home to reside with the rest of his family. Well, the rest of his family excluding their mother, who had run away from home in the middle of the night and headed back to Philadelphia without her three children and her husband. Rarely do mothers physically run away from home. My mother ran away from home in other ways, but Tommy, May, and Gail's mother ran far, far away on two low-heel pumps, one suitcase, and no solid escape plan other than continually wanting to flee.

Tommy was at odds with Hank, who, rumor had it, was not his biological father. They had fist fights—real ones—even in the kitchen. They glared at each other and never sat down to eat together. Where in the world had I landed?

The Lewis house was the identical layout to our Eichler. They even had Les Lambson paintings splashed on the living room walls. A lot of our neighbors did. But I stayed out of the living quarters and lounged in my single bed in the corner of May's bedroom, eyes wide open when they were supposed to be shut, my ongoing worries bubbling, then boiling. I could see straight through the glass wall and atrium to the dimly lit living room area. That was where Hank brought date after date. This is where the kissing, fondling, drinking, dipping, swirling, and twirling ballet of love took place. This is what kept me up most nights. Hank's dalliances.

After a few days in the Lewis home that seemed like weeks, and after too many dinners that consisted of Chicken à la King over toast, I made the timid call to my father once again.

"May I come home?"

This time I was allowed back into my parents' domain to set up camp with my two cats, my three psychedelic posters, one sagging mattress, and the familiar furnishings. I was home. Sort of. Except that I wasn't. I was in some minuscule apartment in Santa Clara, and school was about to begin. I was facing and dreading a new landscape filled with new high school kids, a new array of teachers, a new cosmos called Santa Clara. This was going to be my year from hell. No more One-Eyed John, pizza, or flirting in my neighborhood pizzeria. The strip malls would look different and feel like a foreign country. This new universe was called Santa Clara.

Where the Boys Are

I attended Bookser High School for a couple of weeks. The classes were not in sync with my previous high school. The lesson plans and students seemed much more advanced in Science, Math, and Reading. I felt stupid. I was falling miserably behind and felt miserable doing it. The worst, of course, was gym class. This school didn't provide the familiar blue shorts and crisp white blouses with snaps running down the front. Instead, we had to wear a bright green uniform in the style of a one-piece jumper. What? Absurd. I felt completely alienated from the students, the teachers, the layout of the school, the gym wardrobe. It was as if I had set up camp in another country where none of the residents spoke my language, and I didn't speak theirs.

Until that time, I had been a pretty decent student. I received mostly high Bs and As. But at this new school, this new cosmos of challenges, I was slighted and snubbed. I was going to fall miserably behind—and be miserable doing it. I began smoking a lot of dope before and after school. I have no idea where I got it as I never bought any weed or psychedelics. An array of drugs was always supplied to me by others and seemed to appear out of nowhere. Before the move, I had smoked marijuana just to be sociable or to enjoy music. In Santa Clara, I smoked to numb myself so I wouldn't feel like an alien.

But even with my head in the clouds, I still felt like an alien. In my previous school, we had classes like Existentialism, Humanities, Lyrics as Poetry. But this new school offered nothing but Biology, Algebra, and Physics. I was floundering. I was adrift on a raft in the middle of Santa Clara. My mind gratefully took a hike as I inhaled my reefer, dropped acid and mescaline, hitchhiked here and there, and tried to soothe the ache of being nothing like my new classmates.

In the evenings, I crawled into those big gray pipes in playgrounds near the apartment complex and canoodled with any passing stranger. I let boys put their fingers inside my panties. I didn't care. I needed an escape hatch. I needed to feel better. I needed to feel wanted. I was nothing but a colossal ball of need. And inside those concrete cylinders, between the swings and the slide, I felt chosen and desired. I felt something other than gloom and hopelessness. I was no longer dissimilar and shunned, which is exactly how I felt in Bookser High's schoolyard and classes. No one talked to me in or out of class. I started walking home during the lunch hour and after a short while, didn't go back for the second half of the day. After a few weeks, I stopped walking to school. I'd leave for Bookser High, flying high from smoking pot, circle the block, and walk back home. I painted in my bedroom with a box of acrylic paints and a wiry brush. I mimicked Peter Max's style of painting and copied the covers of books such as *The Stranger* by Albert Camus, where the crowds of faces looked vacant, abnormal, and foreign. That was me ... a stranger in my own home, my school, my new city. I lost myself under my headphones, reading books, or painting.

Who needs this new school? Not me. I was going to educate myself.

Uh, not bloody likely.

One night, out of desperation, I wandered away from my parents' apartment, put a coin in the slot at the pay phone on the corner, and called One-Eyed John from Georgio's Pizza.

"Call me if you want company," he had said.

Did he mean it? I didn't know, but I wanted to find out.

Bathed in misery and feeling homesick for any home but that apartment in Santa Clara, I made the call from the booth. I had told John a few months earlier that I would be moving away. He handed me his phone number on the back of a matchbook cover with the instructions to call him anytime I needed to talk or wanted to meet. Summoning up the courage to call after smoking an entire joint, I dialed his number.

"Hi, this is Carol. I'm the girl who talked your ear off as you tossed pizzas in the air. Hi, I'm Johnny Cash? Do you remember?"

"Of course, Carol. How are you? Where are you?" He seemed somewhat standoffish in tone. Cold. Were all men distant? Was he busy or was he wondering: Who is this teenager calling me at the restaurant? Carol who? What does she want from me?

If only I could communicate clearly what I was feeling, but my words were a fumbling mess, a Scrabble game of mismatched letters and words on wooden tiles. What I needed was a little warmth, a sense of belonging, or to nuzzle a shoulder or any body part. I needed to nestle, but I couldn't find the words.

"Wanna meet?" I was falling apart faster than a newspaper in a rainstorm. But John seemed to have lost interest in this sixteen-year-old with an unsteady home life who was now as unsteady as a donkey making its way down the Grand Canyon.

Take me away from here, I thought to myself. *Anywhere but here!* He made an excuse to hang up, and my lifeline was gone in a blink of one eye.

I never called John again ... until I was sixty-two years old. We reconnected, and I found out that he really liked me at the time, but because I was a teen, he didn't dare drive over and rescue me that night. How life would have turned on a dime if he had. I wanted to reach through time and gently move that young girl into the arms of the one-eyed pizza guy.

As soon as my parents discovered that I was ditching school, they would have none of it. "Please let me go back to my high school." My mother gave the administration office at Willow Glen High the address of her friend as my address and off I went, back to my old school to rejoin my comrades, turn the combination lock on my old locker, and pick up where I left off. It wasn't going to be easily accomplished, however. For one thing, I was entering six or eight weeks into the semester. And I didn't have a ride back to our new apartment home that was anything but home. The journey would require three different buses in the San Jose City Bus District in order to arrive at my front door by 5 p.m. I would have to rise very early each morning so my father could drop me in the school parking lot before he went to work. I would loiter around campus, alone, for ninety minutes before classes began.

I was determined to make this new approach work, but it was an exhausting process, even for a teen. The exhausting part of this new ritual was sitting beside my father on the drive to school. I'd assume the crash position again, not for protection from an Atomic War, but from the apathy that radiated from the driver's seat. His silence cut the air like a razor. *I'm right here, Dad. Look at me. Yoo hoo!* But he never would utter a word to me. It was as if I wasn't there. I was Virginia Bruce as Kitty Carroll in *The Invisible Woman*.

My father wasn't mad. He had just managed to tune me out. This was nothing new, but somehow, seated beside him, the two of us in this five-day-a-week morning ritual, it felt more dispiriting. I tried not to personalize it. But how could I not? He detested me. I was certain of it. I was shrinking again, getting smaller with each mile. I was vapor. I couldn't wait to release myself from his car when we arrived at Willow Glen High. I'd wave, smile, and say, "Have a good day, Dad!" but he never replied. How could he? I was a ghost. Over the last several years, my father had become as cold and hard as yesterday's Bisquick biscuits. He didn't see me, so why would he respond?

In those years, my father came after me, not with an angry foot or tight clenched fist, but with indifference. It was like a faulty thermostat. Shivering and cold to the bone from too much chill radiating from my father's direction, I shriveled further into the bench seat. My father silently stared as he lost himself in the road ahead. He lost himself in Bach, Beethoven, and Brahms on his favorite classical music station. Those pieces of music became the soundtrack of those endless rides. I'd catch him out of the corner of my eye, squinting through his pipe smoke, pondering the past, and missing in action. Perhaps he was lost on the battlefield, or reminiscing about Times Square, or stuck in the Catskills in his bathing trunks, long before we were born, long before his youth vaporized. I didn't know the contents of his thoughts. He wouldn't speak. He was stone-faced, and I was stoned with a mouth full of sawdust. Being in an altered state was the only way I could endure this endless icy winter and time away from the Eichler.

As I sat beside him, aching like a rotted molar and longing for contact or some sort of recognition, he tuned in and turned up the radio, seemingly to tune out my presence. I was seated right next to him, but I needed a first-class ticket and a suitcase stuffed with secrets to break the code that would reach my father and open him to me. That half-hour drive filled me with more anxiety than an investor watching the stock exchange plunge. I felt insignificant in his enormous automobile, hushed in Dad's presence as the music of Vivaldi's "Four Seasons" filtered into my ears. I was the smallest star in his sky, ready to dissolve, descend, decrease in speed, and perish. In my father's presence, I did just that. To paraphrase Strother Martin and Paul Newman in *Cool Hand Luke*, what we had here was a failure to communicate.

Our constant soundless war continued. In my home, the family members worked hard to appear as though we didn't give a damn about one another. I avoided my father like a mouse in a house with an angry cat. This was nothing new. By the time I was ten, my father had tuned me out. He unfriended me, like a disinterested Facebook friend. It's not that we didn't see each other, pass in the hallway, share the same dinner table and Eichler airspace. We did. He didn't BLOCK me. We could still view one another's activities if we wanted to, but he seldom looked in my direction or even seemed to be aware that I was there. If I spoke, he only heard silence. There was no response or recognition of my words or presence. He no longer picked me up and flew me around the living room in his arms like he had when I was much younger and light as a cork. I treasured those airplane rides. But now he seemed not to recognize me or want to be playful around me. Nothing I did was adorable, smart, or worth commenting on. He didn't want to hear about my day or about my opinion on this or that. He stopped joking with me. He had even stopped teasing me as that would require some recognition. I wasn't there. I could glance over and see all the activities going on in his world and view all the friends he commiserated with, but he didn't seem to want to see me. He had checked me off his list and checked me out of his life. And soon my friends and Harold's friends would be checked off the list too.

"I don't want any kids in my house. This is my house! Get outta here. No one is allowed into my house." And my friends didn't come in, except when my parents were at work or at Happy Hour, which was always. As soon as my parents' car pulled up in the driveway, Heather, Denise, Jane, or whoever else happened to be over had to quickly hurl their bodies through my bedroom window and into the bushes on the side of the house. As my parents moved from the car to the front door, my friends shot like firework sparks across our front lawn and to their own homes.

There were a few close calls, a few moments when my parents saw them, and we were all busted! "What are you doing here?" my father hollered. "Get outta my yard!" was meshed with a few warnings that we'd better not have anyone in our house again when they were not there ... or when they were there.

My brother and I would still invite friends to our respective rooms. We became more practiced with our timing and escape plan. We plodded through the terrain of that sleepy valley of bedroom communities and located survival tools to deal with the hazards of adolescence.

I repeatedly tried to understand my parents and brother so I could feel connected to them. I mentally molded them like Play-Doh into a family I could pretend to be a part of, but ultimately it felt like I needed them more than they needed me. I longed to be visible, this feral child I had morphed into who felt misplaced and misaligned with the rest of the family.

I'd look to boys and men to hold me and provide a sense of value. I'd look for intimacy, but even after the first time I had sex, it was like waking from a dream to indifference. I had to find something new, something that felt like caring. It had to be something that didn't radiate rejection, humiliation, and desperation. There was only one problem; I didn't have a clue what it felt like or where to find it.

No Place Like Home

The apartment complex in Santa Clara was a cold space in an unfamiliar neighborhood with an uneasy ambiance. It was surrounded by open spaces that had been cleared but not yet filled with family-oriented apartment complexes. Our apartment, with its lackluster white walls and small rooms, was devoid of charm. Across the street sat Kaiser Hospital with its constant siren soundtrack. Seven days a week, loud construction noise echoed around us. Santa Clara was growing up. Was I?

Looking for some form of escape, I found it in various forms. I responded to the continuous flirting with small waves to the construction workers in the field outside my bedroom window. Those quick winks made me feel wanted. I smoked joints and placed psychedelics on my tongue. I made a gazillion mistakes and found multiple methods of flight without actually leaving the premises. I wanted care and warmth. I settled for caresses.

When I first arrived at my parent's apartment complex, I would take long strolls in the evening to hang out in the local park, smoke weed, and exchange glances with boys who seemed to be around my age. It was easy for me to meet and burrow into the shoulders of perfect strangers. It certainly beat hanging out in the frosty rooms of that apartment filled with my father's Dixieland Band music, pipe smoke, and blaring WWII documentaries on the television set.

Around this time, I had developed an addiction of sorts, but it wasn't for weed or sex. In my junior year of high school, my addiction was Pepsi-Cola. I needed a swig of the stuff every few hours. In the middle of the night, I'd find myself standing in that small kitchen, lit only by a yellowing nightlight bulb. I'd open our apartment-sized refrigerator, grab the bottle of carbonated liquid, and take several gulps so that I could go back to sleep. Although caffeine was supposed to keep me awake, it teased away the anxiety and allowed me to drift off to dreamland. However, in those days, I could have used the caffeine jolt. I was taking three buses to get home from school and always arrived at the front door exhausted. I would collapse onto my bed and fall into a deep sleep. I don't think I did any studying that year. Dazed and likely depressed long before I knew what a beast depression was, I felt disillusioned with life, or at least my life. My grades plummeted.

I missed the Eichlers, and particularly my Eichler. That structure had become a family of sorts. During that year away from that neighborhood, I was a nursing baby pulled away from its mother. I wanted to return, at all costs, and reach back for the comforts of my previous home rather than for my parents. They didn't want me, but I was certain my old room did, as if it was a living, breathing being. That house began to represent not only security and safety, but a dwelling where I could feel content and protected.

Without a physical structure as my base, I was suspended, anxious, and homesick. To make matters worse, Frank Barrington, with his drunken and unsavory behavior, was living in our house. Throughout my entire junior year, while feeling broken and misplaced, I catapulted into drug use and failing grades. More and more, I became a sexual tourist, which included light, medium, and heavy petting, and falling into any available and open arms in this chronic storm. I promised myself that someday, as soon as I was able to do so, I would seek out a shelter to call my own and hold onto it with both hands. I would never release it no matter how hard circumstances tried to pull it from my grasp. If I lost the means to maintain it, I would sell my possessions, and my soul, and hold onto the framework of home. For me, becoming close to a person was not a possibility. I didn't know what it was like to feel cared about or to have trust in another person. Finding a warm structure with a corner to crawl into was a much sounder and more appealing proposition. The Eichler had managed to become not only a shelter, but a family of sorts. The other people residing inside, however, were aliens.

Leave the Driving to Bus

Riding city buses may have seemed grueling to some, but it was a joyful experience to me for a multitude of reasons. In New York City, public transportation was a way of life. I must have inherited the nonchalant manner in which one climbs a handful of steep stairs onto the platform of the bus to the coin drop. My parents were gifted at it; I followed in their footsteps.

I took the bus everywhere around San Jose. Downtown. Uptown. Across town. I would study the back of people's heads and imagine who they were and what types of experiences they had encountered. I would marvel at the way skilled bus drivers would magically maneuver sharp turns and corners. It was a special gift passed on to a precious few. Who among us mere mortals could manage such a massive vehicle on city streets? The fumes that coughed out of the back of the behemoth filled the sidewalks, streets, and our nostrils. It remains one of my favorite scents. When I catch a whiff of it on the streets, I'm immediately transported back to my bus seat in those oversized, slithering caterpillars on wheels.

During my junior year, the ride home was an entirely different adventure from the ride to school with my father and his Cone of Silence, where I sat on the outside of his bubble even though he was seated beside me. The return trip made me feel mature and independent of anyone's resentment or regulations. On the bus, I was the adult managing my journey homeward. I was the head astronaut on my own rocket ship.

After my final class finished in the afternoon, I would blast out across the lawn in front of the school, and on to the bus stop, as fast as my sandaled feet could carry me. My classmates ran or bicycled home or to the closest shopping center to hang with their friends at nearby ice cream parlors or the Woolworth's counter. But I'd hop on my *Magic Bus* with The Who playing in my head. Off I'd go with the elderly and the homeless, the forgotten and concealed population hidden in the lint-lined pockets of San Jose. In 1970, I was one of them.

The San Jose city bus made two lengthy transfer stops on the way back to Santa Clara. On the first stop, I would exit the vehicle, seat myself on the splintered bench, and wait for the second bus ... then the third. Each juncture required a wait and more coins. Often, I'd have to wait for a half hour to an hour. At the first stop, I'd run into a small convenience store and pick up a treat for the ride home: packages of crackers 'n' cheese with a plastic red utility stick to scoop out the cheese. I began to crave these treats, which became part of my ritual for the ride back to the apartment. I became addicted to the rubberized cheese, the rectangular utensil, the stale soda crackers. Those little packets were my daily reward. But there were never enough crackers for the cheese, and there weren't enough hours in the day. By the time I arrived home, my tank was on empty. There was no drive for homework. Dinners were grab and go, and then go to bed.

Bus drivers often had to switch vehicles or take a bathroom break, so there was a lot of time spent sitting on the bus while waiting for the driver to finish his Pall Mall and coffee or empty his bladder from the previous cup of joe. The second bus stop provided the greatest scenery. Our driver stopped in front of the landmark J.C. Penney department store in downtown San Jose. Like many historic downtowns in the United States, downtown San Jose was the city's primary shopping district until strip malls started to pop up in suburban communities. Saturday was the busiest shopping day, so the downtown area was relatively quiet during my school week. It housed the homeless, the handicapped, the hobos—or "bums," as my mother called them. It was territory claimed by the prostitutes and the disheveled souls who carried on a continual conversation with themselves. Occasionally someone talked directly to me, a timid teen trying to become comfortable on the splintered bench in her splintered world during eleventh grade.

I always felt comfortable in downtown San Jose and spent a lot of time there. First Street was the principal commercial street, starting with J.C. Penney at Santa Clara and heading south to include Woolworth's and Sears, Roebuck and Co., south of San Carlos Boulevard. There were also several substantial historic hotels, one of which was the first hotel we stayed in when we first moved to California: the De Anza Hotel.

Many of those who shopped in downtown had far less discretionary income than those who lived in the surrounding suburban areas. Downtown—with its department stores, Orange Julius stand, movie theaters, and 99-Cent stores—was San Jose's very own Times Square until retailers led an exodus from which downtown San Jose never recovered. All of the major department stores closed (Hart's in 1968 after 102 years in business, J.C. Penney in 1972) or moved to one of the new malls. The retailers that remained were primarily furniture and jewelry stores.

In time, buildings were demolished and businesses closed. Blocks were left unfinished, filled only with vacant lots, and some of the existing downtown culture was pushed aside. But I wouldn't stick around to see San Jose's future beyond the early Seventies. I was sitting on a bus stop bench in the midst of downtown San Jose's glory days and sharing my seat with other souls who found themselves adrift. We were all homeless in a sense, although I was beginning to feel like one of the fortunate few. After all, I had a room in an apartment waiting for me. Many of those I brushed shoulders with on the bench had nothing. We were all, in our own way, trying to get through, get by, get to the next stop on the path.

My final bus stop on the ride home was near Santa Clara University. The bus driver would hop off the vehicle, grab a smoke on the sidewalk, and stand in place to shake out the creases in his pants. He would take his fifteen or twenty-minute break while my fellow nomads and I would twiddle our thumbs. There were no cell phones to deliver us from boredom and fill the gaps, just dirty windows to gaze through.

In addition to enjoying dry crackers with cheese on my ride home, my other delight was watching the bus driver's arm in action as he spun that massive steering wheel. There was something about the curve of an upper arm muscle peeking out from the short sleeve of the driver's uniform that sent shivers and quakes to my limbs. I had developed a fascination with men's arms. Even as a young girl of seven or eight, I studied my father's arm at the dinner table like it was a map. I memorized every freckle, the thick directional hairs on his forearm, the places where the darkest hairs grew, and his upper muscle as it crawled under his sleeve. I was in awe of the strength and power it radiated. Masculine arms meant everything would be secured, protected, and everyone—even me—would be taken care of.

Men would go out in the world and bring home a paycheck. They would fix the annual leaks in the Eichler roof to make sure we were safe from the elements. They would drive us about in vehicles with the supernatural knowledge only adults have about spinning a piece of metal around curves and through inclement weather. Muscled arms would move mountains of dirt and mow acres of green lawn. That's what men did. That's what fathers in the Sixties did. They did all the things I couldn't do. Men were gods with coarse hair on their limbs.

Even in my early youth, I was fascinated by Hercules, Samson, and any man, real or mythical, who exhibited enormous strength and a substantial circumference around their biceps and triceps. I would visually examine every man's upper arms. I was looking for protection, an umbrella from the outside world. Surely I would find it burrowed under the muscled mountain range of a male appendage.

Bad Boys

A few weeks into my return trip to Willow Glen High, I began seeing a boy who was a year my senior. He was friends with my friends in Ecology class—a class I was too late to enroll in. His name was Rich Spooner. I would often go to his house after school and listen to Neil Young's *After the Gold Rush* album, drop acid, and watch him crunch his fingers together, which in my altered state translated to fingers breaking apart and falling to the carpeting in his bedroom. He'd laugh, I'd hit him on the shoulder, and we'd playfully tease each other, then flip the record to side two to hear a wobbly Neil Young sing *"Oh Lonesome Me."* Then I would run to the bus stop to head back to Santa Clara.

Every time I would visit Rich's large house, which compared with an Eichler seemed more like the mansion on *The Beverly Hillbillies,* both of his parents would scatter like billiard balls into their own corner pockets. Rich seemed to rule the place, and without competing siblings, he did. His parents were mere tenants. My home was the polar opposite, where I would be the eight ball shooting off to my corner of our home while my parents loudly ruled the roost.

One afternoon, as a last-ditch effort, I begged Rich to ask his parents if I could stay in a room in their expansive home. "They won't even know I am here," I begged. Surely they would say yes. It would be the perfect solution to spending my life on a bus route and with my parents. "Tell them I wouldn't be any trouble.

My mother will give you money for my meals." In my mind, it would be like the Eichler where I was never seen or heard. I would be a silent boarder in my assigned room, doing homework, occasionally making out with their son, while the parents could collect a paycheck from my mother for their trouble and take me, her daughter, off her hands. But Rich's parents said no to the request, and with that refusal, I was back on the bus.

✳ ⚛ ✳

In that junior year of high school, Monday through Friday were protracted hours. The day began at 5:30 a.m. with a long and uncomfortable ride to school beside my father's silence and the Brandenburg Concertos, followed by hours to be killed before homeroom class began on a schoolyard with no other dwellers. In those cool early morning hours, the janitors cruising the hallways and banging the locks against the metal were my only, albeit unwitting, companions. The ride home was even longer, delivering me to my final bus stop and the three-block walk to the front door of an apartment I didn't want to enter.

My parents were often working late, doing their Happy Hours, or simply avoiding the return home. I started to smoke more and more joints; I dropped acid and mescaline. I continued to glare out the window at construction workers who stared back at me with their crooked smiles while providing cat calls and wolf whistles. Those hoots 'n' hollers were music to the ears of this insecure and anxious girl.

One particular early afternoon, I had left school in the middle of the morning. I wasn't feeling too well, so I hopped the city bus for home. Three hours later I arrived at the bus stop and walked home past the usual whistles from burly men in sweaty T-shirts. I looked out my bedroom window at the open field where cookie-cutter apartments were being constructed. Every day, the construction workers would spot me peering out the window and throw kisses or employ various other flirting methods. I would hurry away from the window, embarrassed, but intrigued.

One day, there was a knock on the apartment door. It was the sun-toasted dirty blond construction worker who was always working outside my window in the open fields.

"If it's not too much trouble, may I get a glass of water?"

He took a seat at the kitchen table, and we chatted for a while in the breakfast nook of the kitchen. He flirted, I blushed, I flirted back. He grabbed me by the waist and pulled me onto his lap, facing the same direction as he was. I didn't see his face as he slipped his hand between my legs and began to move his hands on my jeans. His fingers seemed to know things nobody else knew. They grazed my inner thighs like feathery wings. I was terrified he'd detect the rapid pulse on the surface of my skin or radiating through the baby fine hairs on my upper legs. As he explored, I became drowsy, then inebriated. The multiple tingles produced a feeling of being high. He offered quick breaths on the back of my neck. In that instant, we were one. I couldn't see his expression, but I could imagine it as I smelled the light cologne of beer breath. I closed my eyes tighter and lost myself as he continued to stroke me. His breath quickened. He never asked for anything in return as he kissed the back of my neck. He whispered sweet nothings I couldn't quite decipher, which made him all the more alluring.

At the time, I thought he was being respectful for not lowering my head to his lap, for not maneuvering me to the floor, or to my bedroom, for not insisting on those things an attractive construction worker would ask for from a girl who had just turned sixteen. He only wanted to touch me, soothe me. I interpreted that touch and attention as caring and sweet romance. Touching equated to caring. I liked it. I liked it too much. I let him put me at ease and caress me long enough to become lost in a haze of pain-killing endorphins, oxycodone, and passion. It successfully killed the psychic pain of displacement. I had found a cure for what ailed me in my junior year. It was passion.

After that afternoon with the dirty blond construction worker, I hid behind my curtain, never to make an appearance at my window again. When I walked by them on my way home from the bus stop, I didn't stop or look. I had played a lot of hide-and-seek in my youth, but not this type of hunting game. The flirting game was new and smelled like afternoon sweat, testosterone, dirty T-shirts, and curious fingers. It smelled like my youth.

The Art of the Matter

One weekend at the Santa Clara apartment, I decided I would create a painting. I had never painted in my life, but I needed to do something to move me out of my current mindset. It didn't matter what I painted on that canvas board in my bedroom: the mere act of putting paint to canvas soothed me. It was like Valium in a paintbrush. This creative act took me out of my head and into a different, more pleasing sort of moment.

There were plenty of other escapes at this time, in addition to painting and the caresses of a construction man. There were psychedelics. There was plenty of marijuana. I always had it on hand. Most of it came from my brother or friends at school. I never questioned the contents of the pills. I popped them and hoped for the best. It was what my brother and his friends were doing, and I wanted to do it too. I wanted to see the patterns and colors, but much more than that, I wanted to feel the profound warmth and pulsation of the sky. I wanted to feel peace. I wanted a fuckin' break. And for a few hours, I had it. I wanted to feel at one with the universe, a universe that didn't include my parents. Artwork, writing, and taking trips and tokes took me out of myself for awhile and transported me to a more delightful destination.

As a result of entering my old high school a few weeks into my junior year, I was hastily assigned classes that had available seats, ones I never would have chosen, and the types of courses I wouldn't excel in. Physiology was one of those classes.

The classroom was occupied with frogs, their legs spread-eagled by our lab instruments and pins as the scent of pickle juice wafted through the air. I was partnered with a classmate who was as clueless as I was about which bone was connected to the hip bone and how to hold the instrument. We couldn't even cheat off each other's papers as we were both clueless. Both of us were geared toward the arts and literature, certainly not science. But I was determined to study hard and make this grim year and my coursework work in my favor.

The best thing about Physiology class was our instructor, Mr. Stump. He looked like a mad scientist, with kinky hair like Ben Casey's colleague, Dr. Zorba. Stump's long, weathered face and missing thumb were legendary on campus. Yes, there was a stump where Mr. Stump's thumb used to be. He told the class it was shot off in the war, and he didn't want to hear any jokes about it. But being sixteen-year-olds, muttering sarcastic remarks about Mr. Stump and his stump was in our job description. He also had an odd mouth that puckered like it had ingested an entire lemon. Maybe it was from being around all the formaldehyde and jarred frogs.

I would have preferred to attend a class like Ecology. That's where all my friends were. They were excited to learn about how to save the environment and the planet, so I learned about it through them. I could have bloomed in such a class. I could have recycled, reduced, reused. Instead I rolled joint after joint, took a long bus ride home, and collapsed on the bed.

Moving to the Rhythm

Andy Christakos and Mike Abbott were in the Ecology class with my classmates, even though they were a year ahead of us. They seemed to enjoy our company and conversations, and we enjoyed theirs Monday through Friday of each school week. But one weekend, we broke out of our schoolmate relationships and took a ride together to the beach. Andy, Mike, and several of their friends along with Julie, Heather, Denise, and myself were now officially weekend as well as weekday friends.

It was an overcast day, too cold to swim, but not too cold for flirting and pairing off. Andy was shy but kept trying to start up a conversation. His voice would always drop into a lower register whenever he approached me. Everyone was planning to sleep in the little room at the beach, the space with no windows or bathroom, while I would sleep upstairs in my brother's apartment. That evening, my friends canoodled with one another in the little room. My friend Julie, who later realized she was a lesbian, lost her virginity that night to one of Andy's friends. Everyone was sleeping in the same room when this happened, so the quiet grunts and groans became material for giggling and jokes later.

During that beach weekend, Andy and I forged a romantic relationship that would last for two years. He was a slight, quiet dark-haired Greek boy with long black eyelashes and swift nervous movements. Andy was always lifting one leg behind him and cracking his knee. "I have arthritis. I'm falling apart." He was only seventeen, but Andy sounded like an old man taking up residence in a young body.

I didn't have a strong attraction for him, but he was a savior in that sordid year. I no longer had to take three buses home from school. Andy would now drive me back to my apartment in his blue 1967 Mercury Comet the size of a living room. Not only did it have long, comfortable bench seats, but it housed a decent radio that was always tuned to my favorite AM rock stations: KYA, KFRC, and KEWB. I was in heaven.

Elton John's first hit song, "Your Song," would play over and over on the radio. As I sat beside him and snuggled up to his shoulder on the bench seat, I was certain Andy had somehow transferred his heart to the lyrics of that song. "Your Song" was now our song. He didn't have much money, but if he did.... And when my new boyfriend took ownership of me by placing his hand on the small of my back as he led me through a doorway or into a fast-food joint, it felt good. In high school, this was called love.

The songs beyond Elton John's first hit were incoherent. I was a fan, but my preference was to learn more about the unassuming man behind the lyrics—Bernie Taupin. Here was a guy creating all the words to the songs Elton performed, while Elton sang them in some distorted unrecognizable fashion. *Words shouldn't be treated so carelessly in the mouth,* I thought.

Andy's best friend, Mike, was taller than Andy, firm-bodied, hairless, and delightfully sarcastic. He had a bit of a baboon face, but his satirical wit and tall stature were charming and charismatic. A year later, I would be lying beside him in my parents' bed after school let out, soap operas blaring on their portable television at the end of the bed. With the tick-tick-tick of sprinklers out the bedroom window, I slipped my palm and fingers down Mike's pants to find a massive attentive rod like one of those sherbet-on-a-stick Missiles in creamy orange and pink swirls. I could barely wrap my hand around his rocket. How many times I had slipped my hands into a stranger's pants, fantasized about being in a sleeping bag with Elvis, his waiting lips before me, or dreamed of riding a fast-moving horse on a path that led far from my family's orange front door. Mike, Elvis, the glistening black horse running down the road. In my mind, they all cherished me as they carried me off and away.

After that impulsive act, Mike and I managed to remain friends throughout high school and to this day. He eventually became an attorney, but back then he was a teenager soaked to the bone in testosterone. We never spoke of that late afternoon when we rolled around under my parents' blankets. We never told Andy. We never wanted to be a couple. We only wanted a diminutive slice of love in the afternoon, like the daytime television characters that appeared at the foot of the bed.

Andy and Mike were both passionate about the law, and both were planning to attend law school. The enormous book *Clarence Darrow for the Defense* was Andy's bible. He carried it under his arm and placed it near him at all times. There was no shortage of heroes for both boys. Andy had colossal posters of the Kennedy brothers on his bedroom wall. They were his idols. Pictures of John, Bobby, and Ted were pinned up with four mismatched colored tacks. Like deities on high, the Kennedy brothers observed all activity in Andy's boyhood room. But Mike and Andy didn't idolize the Kennedys so much as they idolized their ideals.

Mike would eventually work at a law firm in Santa Clara Valley as an attorney while Andy would turn his after-school job at Orchard Supply Hardware, a local hardware chain, into a career as store manager. He remained there for decades as he cruised up and down the aisles, attending to customers until his own retirement. The two boys took dissimilar paths, but they never lost their idealism, strong political views, liberalism, and ability to argue both sides of an issue, even if it was to decide if the moussaka was too salty. And they remained best friends through the next several decades. There was something special about these schoolyard friends.

Andy's entire house smelled like pastries. He came from a Greek Orthodox family, and when I met him, his father had already been married and divorced. He remarried a stout woman who looked like she should be aproned and roasting something in the oven at all hours. That's exactly what his bride did, except instead of roasting beef or chicken, she baked sheets and sheets of gyros. Andy's stepmother couldn't speak a word of English, but she was the diminutive Julia Child of Greek cookery. You could find her in the kitchen all day, every day. Pans of Greek pastries; acres of casserole dishes filled with bubbling eggplant, ground beef, and phyllo dough; and dozens of sweet wedding cookies with essence of almond covered the countertops. Andy's entire house was rolled in confectioners' sugar, or so it seemed. Throughout my junior and senior years of high school, Andy and I would binge on his stepmother's baklava. I never wanted to wash the scent of those baked goods out of my hair and skin.

One afternoon before Andy drove me back to my apartment in his massive Mercury with the blaring radio, he brought me to his house. Next to the couch sat his family's piano. Andy had sheet music to Linda Ronstadt's "Long, Long Time." I sat at his living room baby grand and tapped out the notes one by one like I knew what I was doing. I didn't. But I loved that song, Ronstadt's voice, and the odd way her last name was spelled. Before Adele there was Linda, wearing her heart on her sleeve and belting out hit after hit. Girls wanted to be her, with those massive gold hoops, button nose, little girl smile, and cool bangs; men wanted to date her; everybody wanted to play her music on their turntables.

As we lay down on his Victorian-style floral couch in the living room, so different from my home's modern furnishings, we would assume the spoon position. The afternoon sun was washing out of the room like a receding tide. Like a brush loaded with grey paint, the darkness of late afternoon in winter poured over the living room rug and walnut coffee table. Andy's home felt and smelled so different from mine. His smelled of cookies and felt like the pictures depicted in old-world fabric. Mine smelled of Naugahyde and the Jetsons lived there. But the couch in Andy's living room was small, so we had to cuddle up tight. As the room grew darker, I knew I had to head back to my parents' apartment. But as I lay in front of Andy, the afternoon shadows grew longer and so did his curiosity and manhood. His hands slowly crawled through the opening of my blouse. He fondled my breasts for what seemed like days, but was likely an hour. I became aroused by his light touch. That was as far as our intimate activity went in my junior year. During my senior year, we would habitually head to my home after I got out of school, wash one another's back in a unvaried shower routine, climb into my single bed, and have missionary-style vanilla sex until he climaxed. Where was mine? The female orgasm didn't seem to be on the menu.

We went from showers to baths together, but it didn't help the monotony of our relationship. After reading Richard Brautigan's *Trout Fishing in America, Rommel Drives on Deep into Egypt,* and

In *Watermelon Sugar,* where Brautigan's prose all turned to poetry, I even tried writing poems to Andy in Brautigan's freeform style:

LOVE LIKE A BATHTUB DRAINING
Your toes like walnuts,
wiggling when excited,
and wrinkling from too much
bubble bath.
Let me smother you
in terrycloth
kisses,
and collect all of your love
like a bathtub draining.

But the poems and baths and showers didn't help. Being with Andy during my senior year was anything but arousing. It was routine, predictable, and for me, lacked passion. But he was in my orbit and a part of me needed that steadiness and reliability—a consistency lacking in my world.

In the teen years, sex is at the far end of the spectrum. Either your knees are wobbly while you're kissing a Curtis Gonzales, the boy who first made my knees buckle with his penetrating tongue, or you're doing your history homework in your head as someone rhythmically thrusts his manhood in and out like the fast-ticking timer on a bomb ready to blast. There had to be something in between.

But attracting the wrong guy was a skill I started out with early on. I had an inner compass for finding partners slightly off-center. If they were smoking cigarettes alone, looking downcast at the ground, or kicking some object in front of their foot like they were training a rock to skip, I was pulled to them like metal to a U-shaped magnet. It's not that I didn't want a compassionate, loving, gallant Prince Charming. I couldn't find him, so I settled for what I stumbled upon. There were no "Dating for Dummies" books in the late Sixties or early Seventies. There were certainly no "Fucking for Dummies." We could have used them.

✳ ⚛ ✳

Andy and his school chums were slightly obsessed with Bonnie Raitt's music and Leonard Cohen's lyrics. I quickly moved away from my usual Motown fare and rock favorites to newer lyrical and bluesy artists. I was nothing if not impressionable, especially when it came to finding new musicians and their tunes.

When Joni Mitchell's first album, *Song to a Seagull*, was released in 1968, Heather's sister, Jane, loaned me her copy. There was something comforting about girl-with-guitar music. I read all the lyrics as Mitchell meshed her poetry with catchy melodies. Her songs, although enchanting, personal, and bursting with wisdom, were accompanied by a vocal that seemed as though it were captured in a poorly recorded space or through a hairnet. The production stunk. It reeked. Musician David Crosby had produced this first Mitchell effort, and he must have smoked one too many doobies. The recording had a muddied echoed quality, as if Mitchell were performing in a bar and someone had propped up a reel-to-reel on the stage.

Side One of the album was titled "I Came to the City," and the flip side was labeled "Out of the City and Down to the Seashore." This folk-rock concept album unified the theme of moving out of the city and back to nature as an allegory for moving on in personal relationships and discovering different and more satisfying ways to love and live. It was inspiring, especially to the aspiring young poet and songstress in me. Her fingerpicking had an intimate Simon & Garfunkel vibe. I dug her.

Even though she didn't attend Woodstock, Joni Mitchell created an anthem for an entire generation—ours. We were stardust, we were golden, but we needed a compass or a GPS to find the garden in all that East Coast mud at Woodstock. Mitchell didn't get to go to the massive music festival. I didn't attend either. I did stand in line for an hour to see the movie at the Century Theater when it was first released. I also had the two Woodstock soundtrack albums. But I didn't even know about Woodstock until *LIFE* magazine published an entire issue about the mud, music, magic, and mayhem. Oh yes, and the nakedness and bad acid. We all wanted to be there to see Jimi Hendrix's guitar screech out his bombs-bursting-in-air rendition of "The Star-Spangled Banner," watch Richie Havens strum his fingers to the bone, get high with The Lovin' Spoonful's John Sebastian in his tie-dye shirt, and go home with Ten Years After. But my friends and I were too young for such freedom. And according to my father, freedom only came after you retired with a pension and a medical plan.

Joni Mitchell was an astonishing storyteller. Her songs were little novels, and her narratives featured a distinct plot, theme, and a cast of characters. When I first heard her sing "Night in the City" on late night FM radio, I envisioned the hustle and bustle of New York's Times Square. When she performed her songs about the seashore, I envisioned myself at Seacliff Beach near Santa Cruz. Each song and story resonated with me. I'd close my eyes and trace each word and phrase with my mind's eye. I studied her artwork on the front cover, with its title "Song to Seagull" spelled out in small and delicate inked birds. I used to call seagulls beach-birds. Now I had a song for them. It was clear to see that Mitchell was well above the average singer-songwriter, even in the late Sixties when our airways were flooded with them.

I'd bury my ears under a pair of massive headphones. Bob Dylan, our new Pied Piper, provided the prophetic voice and moral soundtrack for our generation. While my parents were ringing in the New Year with Guy Lombardo, I was listening to the countdown of the top 100 hits on AM radio and wondering who would make it to the number one position. Every year I stayed up until midnight to hear it announced and played. While my brother and friends had already fallen fast asleep before midnight, I remained glued to the radio. It seemed important and almost urgent, like finding out the results of some imperative election. In the morning, I'd tell my brother what the song was, and with the least amount of astonishment on his face, he would utter a familiar response.

"You're stupid, Carol. Who cares?"

Getting the Willies

One weekend afternoon while I was huddled in my room at the apartment in Santa Clara, my dad announced that it was time to move again. He had found yet another two-bedroom, lackluster apartment in a new complex and wanted to live there instead of the small apartment complex we had settled into. I thought he was joking, but when it came to impulsive moves, my father was never kidding. "This complex has too many kids. Pack your bags. We're moving next week." And as usual, my mother went along for the adventure. She thrived on large and small changes, so in that regard, Dad was the perfect partner.

We packed and readied ourselves for the second new residence during the middle of my junior year. Without the aid of Andy's massive Mercury Comet, it would have taken a fourth bus from Willow Glen High and another hour to finally arrive home to this new apartment complex. Our new smaller apartment was now located upstairs. I couldn't figure out the allure of this apartment over the other, but I had given up trying to figure out my father's strategies. It was like some complicated chess match. My father was not making eye contact with me at this time, let alone talking to me, until one Saturday afternoon.

"You should meet up with my friend from work, Wee Willie Wikstrom. He's a writer too. A poet. You two will have a lot to talk about."

What? Why would I want to meet up with my father's coworker? Sure, he was a nice-looking, middle-aged man with a thick mane of wavy auburn hair, a bronze face, and perfect physique. But he worked with my father. He was his colleague. And why would he want to go out with a sixteen-year-old girl? The suggestion made me feel queasy, but my mom agreed that it would be a fine idea. Well, she agreed by not weighing in. I didn't care what my mother thought. She had checked out of motherhood long ago. But I still wanted to please my father. I wanted him to not only notice me, but also to like me. Perhaps this would score some points in my direction, and I could finally win his approval. "Okay, I will."

The next weekend, the Swedish coworker, Bill Wikstrom, who my father called "Wee Willie" was picking me up in his mid-life crisis vehicle. I was still wondering, *Why do I have to go out to dinner with this guy? What in the world do we have to talk about?*

Wee Willie handed me a small yellow poetry book titled "Things and Throes" as we drove off to a restaurant. "Here's what I did," he said with pride in an accent I had never heard before. We never actually arrived at the restaurant. Wee Willie was pulling into the dark parking garage of his apartment complex in Santa Clara and opening the door for me.

"We don't need to go out. I can make you dinner, and we can talk about poetry in my apartment."

Whatever. I looked at my Timex watch and calculated how long it would be before I could go home and catch my favorite show on television.

As soon as we entered his scantily furnished, second-floor bachelor apartment, a flashing red warning sign passed through my eyes that sounded like the robot in *Lost in Space.* "Danger, Will Robinson. Danger!" Although in this case, I was the one in danger from Will … or Bill … or Wee fuckin' Willie whatever.

Wee Willie's apartment was even smaller than ours. It smelled like a bachelor pad: burnt toast, overflowing kitchen garbage can, dead coffee grounds. Before I knew it, I was being pulled to the ground and wrestled to the floor. His wet Swedish lips found my mouth and drool was running down my cheeks. Do men born in other countries learn to kiss differently? I wondered to myself. Is it in their genes?

Now his tongue was being shoved so far down my throat that I thought I would choke. Soon he began sucking on my lower lip like it was a Lifesaver. Parental instructions and approval or not, I had had enough. My lip was sore as I pushed the rough parchment skin of his cheeks into the palm of my hands and pushed him away with every ounce of strength I could summon.

"Let me up!" He wouldn't. "Let me up. I want to go home!"

Did I ever. His hands continued to wander north, under my blouse, then south, down my pants. Not knowing what else to do, I began to whimper and then shout hoping the volume of my voice would scare him enough to loosen his grasp. I knew my father would be displeased. I was flooded by feelings of failure; failing my father. It was a familiar sinking feeling.

"Please, please, let me go."

Willie Shit-for-Brains finally did. "What about dinner?" he asked.

Did he have SpaghettiOs in his ears?

"No, I need to go home! Take me home."

The drive home was a blur, but I vividly recall the look of disappointment on my father's face as I walked quickly down the hallway in Santa Clara apartment number two.

"Why are you home so early?"

I didn't respond. What could I say? I slipped into my bedroom wanting to lock the door and never emerge. But this door didn't have a lock. I wanted to curl like a bay shrimp on my bed and die right there. I felt confused, worthless, dirty, lost. I called Andy to say goodnight. I wanted him to take me away from everything. I didn't love him, but I was fond of him, and I certainly needed him. Andy felt like the safest corner of my life.

As I put the new Graham Nash album *Songs for Beginners* on my record player and turned down the volume so it wouldn't disturb my parents, I listened to the record play as I drifted off to sleep. Every kiss and callous maneuver was washed away by dreams. As my head hit the pillow, Graham Nash's "Sleep Song" played on.

The next thing I knew, morning light was spilling into my room. It was time to ready myself for school and tuck away the baffling events from a few hours ago as I tucked my pillow under the comforter. I stood at the bathroom sink, the one I shared with my parents, as this apartment had only one bathroom. I tried to put on a mental survival suit so that I could endure the long drive to school with my father's silence and quiet judgments. How I wished someone, anyone, was kissing my forehead. There was no soft corner that existed, except the content of my records, Andy's upholstered seats in his Mercury Comet, and Pushka the cat.

You Can't Go Home Again

When I was a young girl of six and had just arrived in San Jose, I would dream big dreams. I had a small pink jewelry box with a rotating ballerina under the lid and a small round mirror beside the slim spinning figure to reflect her grace and those slightly jerky rotations. I would lift that lid up and down to expose the spinning figure over and over again, as if I were watching and re-watching a few precious moments in a choice movie. I didn't house any jewelry in the box, only Bazooka Bubble Gum comics and long carpenter nails I had found in the open field and construction sites around our Eichler.

The contents of my treasure chest shifted as time moved on. Nails and gum wrappers would be replaced with notes passed in class, ID bracelets, and plastic charms from bubble gum machines. Eventually there would be anniversary necklaces, colorful jangly bracelets, and rings of gold or silver with glistening rocks, sophisticated settings, and heartfelt promises strung or infused into their metal. The final gift we want to sock away inside that precious box is time. Much more time. But as young girls, we want a prince, protection, and the promise of love in a sparkly shower of pink and lavender petals falling from the sky.

In my youth, I read fairy tales. In fairy tales, the young girl meets Prince Charming, and he has everything she ever wanted. He offers her security, safety, and a lifetime of beaming smiles. In fairy tales, the bad guy is very easy to spot. He's always wearing a black cape, a cockeyed hat, and scary mustache so you can quickly see the trouble he carries under his cloak.

Then we grow older and learn that Prince Charming is not as easy to recognize as we thought. We realize the bad guy is not wearing a black cape, and he's not easy to uncover; he has a clever tongue; he makes us laugh; he has clear blue eyes, massive muscles in his arms, and a Pepsodent smile. The grown-up world of sorting out the good from the bad, the men who were for you or against you, had begun. But one thing was for certain ... Wee Willie was not going to stuff his wee willy inside of me.

By the end of my junior year, the Barringtons who were living in our Eichler home had stopped sending rent checks to my father. It seemed Frank Barrington couldn't hold down a job. The payments stopped rolling in, as did the excuses for their delays, and my father became even more agitated than usual. I don't know if it was Frank Barrington's struggle with alcohol, or his inability to keep his job and earn a living because of his drinking. Whatever it was, I didn't care. The day my parents announced we were moving back to our Eichler, I thought my heart would burst from excitement and my head would explode like a giant box of Red Devil Fireworks.

It was unbelievable news. I was finally going home. I was ecstatic. Surprisingly, my anxiety wouldn't cease when we moved back into the Eichler. I remained uneasy, even within the comfort and safety of my bedroom and the Eichler armor. It didn't end when I no longer needed to take three buses home from school and crawl into my bed, too tired to eat or even care about sustenance. My junior year had become a one-day-at-a-time exercise in survival. For those nine long months, I had been floating on a spacious unsettled sea called Santa Clara. It contained no anchor or sense of self. I had numbed my brain with various substances to get through the day and sleep through the night. I struggled to feel at home in the world for that entire academic year. The only sustenance I had came in the form of hermetically sealed cheese and soda cracker packets.

My father's unpredictable behavior continued, as did his avoidance of me. His apathy was palpable when it came to my whereabouts or what I had to say. He had shaken off all signs of domesticity and parenthood, just as he had once tried to shake off my brother as he ferociously clung to my father's pant leg. I could never fathom what I had done or not done to bring about such disdain or to cause such evading. It was a mystery that would permeate the next few decades of my life.

Was It Good for You?

Teenage boys were seldom erectile-challenged. They seemed to wander around in a perpetual state of arousal with a collapsible stick leaning behind the teeth of their zippered Levi's. Those needs never quite accommodated an adolescent girl's desire for a prince, a heart-stopping romantic kiss, or being asked for the first dance at a bar mitzvah, wedding, or Teen Club dance. Thanks to the school system's sex education program, young girls were groomed to be virgins while we learned the fine art of cookery. We were also given the goal of finding a husband who would bring home the bacon while we fried it up in a Teflon-coated pan. My no-nonsense Home Economics teacher instructed us to "learn to cook and please your husband." After all, boys only wanted two things: bed and breakfast meat.

But we paid little attention during our sex education class. The films seemed outdated, even back then. They were geared more to the prudish and traditional Fifties than the swingin' late Sixties. Girls were being pulled in two radically different directions: the traditional role of the Fifties housewife and mother or something radically different. We didn't know whether to crawl into bed in a modest two-piece nightgown or in a flimsy tank top hiding next to nothing. With one foot on the platform of motherhood, hearth, and home, and one on the rapidly moving train towards a future of fresh possibilities, it took a while to find our collective footing. Women of the Fifties had been commanded to sit down and shut up, but the women of the Sixties were gathering themselves to their feet to march, shout, and soar.

I lost my virginity … twice. Once to Chuck, a sandy-haired beach bum, and the second time to a Kinney Shoes salesman. I wasn't certain Chuck had fully penetrated the entrance gate to my castle, so I have to give the trophy to the Kinney Shoes salesman, who, to paraphrase The Rolling Stones, made it bleed. I started my adventures rather clumsily, certain I would never learn exactly what to do and how to do it, or even how to touch a boy with the proper pressure and method. I wanted a "quick-start" guide to sex. In 1969, there was an urgency to gather skills swiftly.

Chuck was the first beach boy I was taken with and taken by. He looked like an unmade bed and his vocabulary consisted of five or six expressions. Four of them had to do with swells and surf wax, and none of his vocabulary contained fully realized words. Most were muttered in stoned lingo that only surfers and dolphins could hear and comprehend. Every other word was "bitchin'."

But despite his vast lack of verbiage, I thought he was adorable, with his hickey-covered neck and an unbuttoned shirt flapping in the breeze. He smelled like a day at the beach. Unfortunately, the charming "Aw, shucks" Chuck didn't have any notion about how to kiss. His tongue stayed lodged in his mouth, much too shy to emerge, but he was appealing in a Jeff Spicoli, *Fast Times at Ridgemont High* kind of way.

As we were sprawled out on the soggy couch cushions in the little room, he crawled on top of me, pulled his sweatpants down to his knees, and attempted to trespass into my open field. Unfortunately, his ejaculate got caught somewhere between the moon and New York City, or between my legs and the now soggy couch cushions. He tried pushing and pushing, but ... was he fully inside of me? I was tighter than a securely wrapped kosher kishka. His manhood, still boyhood, couldn't manage to penetrate more than two inches at best. Did that count? Was I still a virgin?

I was attracted to boys and mischief in equal parts, and my pair of Hush Puppies took me in the direction of both. They brought me to strangers' cars while hitchhiking. I willfully threw myself into the passenger's seat. It's not that I was drawn to risk. I truly trusted the outsiders who opened their car doors to me. It was the Sixties. We were all supposed to love one another, right?

Hush Puppies. They sound like the quietest shoes in the whole world. And perhaps they were. I had a pair in beige, the universal shade for humdrum footwear. I had recently turned sixteen when I slipped them on and hitchhiked to a nearby Kinney's Shoe Store.

I had been hitchhiking around Santa Clara County for two years. But on this day, a nice-looking shoe salesman, who at nineteen seemed terribly adult, took one look at my puppied feet and started to crouch down in front of me. He slowly slipped a pair of new leather sandals on my feet, and I started buying what he was selling. Mostly, he was selling himself. After some world-class flirting and one shoe purchase, we made plans to meet for a date, even though I wasn't allowed to date.

The second door in the bathroom was key. That escape hatch near my bedroom was my own clandestine tunnel to freedom. It took me from the porcelain lavatory to the great outdoors. After I turned the doorknob and crept slowly through the side yard to the outside fence, I jumped in his cherry-red Chevy Chevelle with a damaged fender and more dings than a church bell. The night sky was splashed with soft sherbet hues of peach and pink. I had never felt so alive and so adult. Off we drove to the nearby theater, the Campbell Twin, where we sort of watched a movie as the shoe salesman tipped his head sideways in my direction and leaned his head against mine.

The movie M*A*S*H had just been released in theaters. We settled into our plush movie seats, and Kip reached out to place my hand in his sweaty palm. It was all quite romantic. There was popcorn and Pepsi and ear nibbling involved. And later, I'm nearly certain he was my first fully formed sexual encounter. Surfer boy Chuck had tried, but I decided that time didn't count. When it came to Chuck, I had a locked gate with a missing code or something. But things with Kip the Kinney Shoes salesman progressed differently.

We left the theater and peeled out of the parking lot in his Chevelle towards some rolling hills surrounding Santa Clara Valley. The entire county could be seen from this new vantage point, even though we couldn't quite see each other's faces through the darkness. Kip suggested we throw a blanket on the roof of his car and study the stars, which by this time were filling the night sky like a planetarium dome. We crawled onto the roof from the car hood and lay together under the stars, while the radio blared Bread's "Make It with You."

Kip did want to make it with me, and in the worst way. And I wanted to be familiarized with this new world. After a bit of clumsy wriggling and initial timid resistance, we wrapped ourselves around each other, and I yielded to his advances. It hurt like hell, but much differently than I expected. It wasn't a stab of pain like a penetrating sword, but rather a dull ache like when someone steps on your toe and it throbs for a few hours. No matter how romantic the evening and my date seemed, the after-party now consisted of a throbbing hunk of burning love in my Petticoat Junction. Bathed in soreness and sexual awareness, I finally felt less awkward, more desirable, and rather extraordinary. Now I was special. I was a woman. Nah. I was a tender girl whose cage had just been properly rattled.

When I finally crawled through my bedroom window back at the Eichler, the hands on the clock sat at 1:30 a.m. My brother swung open my bedroom door and chuckled, "You're in so much trouble, Carol." And I was. He giggled and pointed his finger at me while he danced around my doorway. I wasn't amused. Suddenly I was distracted. I ran to the bathroom. My brother was still carrying on in the hallway about the whuppin' I was about to get from my parents, but all I could focus on was the blood dripping into the toilet when I urinated. The Kinney Shoes salesman had penetrated the gizmo that gets broken. It was official. I was no longer a virgin. So, this is what it's like? Chuck couldn't manage to tally the point, but the older and wiser Kip the Kinney Shoe salesman did. He scored. Hymen ruptured. I was elated, yet terrified. My thighs began to quiver as my brother stood on the other side of the door chortling like a court jester or, more appropriately, the village idiot.

"Mom and Dad called the police! You're so stupid, Carol. What an idiot."

Maybe I was. One of my parents must have checked my bedroom at some point that evening, something they rarely did. So much for quiet shoes. Apparently Hush Puppies weren't so hushed.

Long after 2 a.m., my mother and father were still out conversing with the local police in parental panic. Harold couldn't wait for my parents to get home and give me a talking to, which they never really did. I got a slap in the face, my mother christened me a whore, and then off to bed they went. I never saw Kip again.

The first time a boy thrust back and forth, I thought there was something horribly wrong with him, something that might require a medic. A mechanical malfunction perhaps? He moved rapidly like some crook rushing to hop a train while experiencing an epileptic seizure. More importantly, he seemed to turn into some beast with no brain, only odd, quick movements and a determined stare and focus on the end goal. He didn't speak. He was strangely possessed. Only his fingers did the talking. When these gyrations were accompanied by deep kisses, I thought it was love. But it was sex.

The great mysteries of manhood took years to decipher. Eventually I would visit the museum of widths and lengths. Love Pipes seemed to come in all shapes and sizes. Some were soft like a stick of butter that had been sitting at room temperature too long, while others were like a slab of concrete formed into the shape of a baseball bat, always at the ready. Each one had its own personality and headgear—a combat helmet of sorts, like the one that sat atop Sergeant Schultz's head on *Hogan's Heroes* or Vic Morrow's on *Combat!* Sometimes the head looked like one of those knitted pull-down ski caps. I soon discovered that sex was hard, even when it was soft.

I buried my face in boys' shoulders and rested my nostrils near their necks. Some boys had an aroma that was garden fresh, like a spring shower. Others smelled like a pile of week-old T-shirts. Some lovers' hands would guide me to the bed and gently turn me on my stomach, while others crawled on top of me like they were mounting a beach blanket. My only job was to lie there and wait for the big finish. Sometimes it was a quick sprint, other times calculated and slow like a marathon with a distant finish line barely in sight.

My girlfriends and I would eventually count lovers like vacation destinations. Each intimate experience was radically dissimilar. Each boy or man had his own tang, identifiable caress, and precise kissing technique. All grunted and groaned in their own fashion. Each new partner was a new country with different scenery and a distinct aroma. Some lovers grew silent as their erections sprouted, while others murmured and moaned as if they were giving birth or were cheering for their favorite sports team.

My friends and I cringed when we saw how well traveled we were.

"How many did you get on your list?"

"You tell your number first."

"I'm not telling. You have to!"

It sounded like a Life cereal commercial, only in this case, one of us was Mikey and the other was the annoying brother egging us on. Not one of us revealed our true number. To do so would have teased up feelings of being cheap and small, used and damaged goods, not at all sophisticated. Just well traveled.

Were we too needy in our youth, too available and hungry? For me, sex was the only affection choice on the menu. Like train cars, one after the other rattled our track, and not one of us had arrived at a worthy destination. But we never stopped hoping that our ultimate endpoint, and a conductor to help us get there, were around the bend. We didn't need quantity, just quality, and preferably a boy equipped with an accessible heart.

Sex Marks the Spot

Sexual activity became a surreal circus of emotions and physical sensations. I felt like I was dancing across high wires, flying gracefully from trapeze to trapeze, engaging all of my female regions and fluffing up my self-worth, which was at an all-time low. I continued to misconstrue sexual approach as affection. If a boy wanted to touch my arm, my face, my breast, he adored me. If he wanted to take me to his bed, I assumed he was taking me into his heart, safely locking me in behind its protective walls, cherishing me forevermore. If his fingers tip-toed down to my thigh and between my legs, he was falling even more deeply in love with me. Touching and desire were getting all mixed up with affection and concern.

As a teenager, I seemed to require enormous quantities of that care to fill a fuel container that was always hovering in the EMPTY range. But the Sixties were all about touch. Encounter groups and love-ins, both tactile and emotive expressions of connection. The Sexual Revolution. Free Love. Express yourself! Release your inhibitions. Reach out and touch someone. Give yourself over. Surrender. Thanks to Madison Avenue, even Coke had every race, creed, color, age, and sexual orientation holding hands and singing in perfect harmony. It was the real thing all right, but for many it was really about sex and getting it as often and in as many positions as possible.

My parents showed little affection for each other, and none for my brother and me. I saw my mother grab for my father's arm while walking, slip her hand through his bent elbow, and stroll alongside him. Beyond that gesture, I can't remember a hug, knowing glance, or passionate kiss between them.

The yelling. That, I remember. My mother was supremely tranquil, until she disapproved. She used a different voice with my father than she did with my brother and me. With us kids, she would start with a low-register snarl that gradually built to a growl of annoyance, an angry wolf's low moan, or a cat beginning a catfight, teeth gritting to the right side of her cheek, bottom lip trembling, jaw slung like a bulldog. The quarter-notes and half-notes of disgust and seething phrases would progressively rise and fall, then explode to a loud roar, her mouth open to maximum expanse, expletives bouncing off walls and breaking the sound barrier. A slow build-up, then a blare that would fill a football field, no loudspeaker required. The megaphone voice was Mom's specialty. It would amuse my brother and me, inspiring us to imitate, but never duplicate, her gift for the dreaded crescendo and bellow from low C to high G.

Decades later, I would see a movie that featured an astounding performance perfectly capturing my mother's dissatisfaction with us. It was Mary Tyler Moore in Robert Redford's directorial debut, *Ordinary People.* Moore's character in the film is so tremendously repressed that you want to stick a pin in her balloon of inhibited emotions and release them into the ether. She buries so much disappointment and grief by constantly changing the subject and the location that she can barely handle a silent moment or conversation with her own son. Her performance startled me and made me cringe. I didn't know why until I realized I was watching Mary Tyler Moore portray my own mother, who masked her inner sterility behind a masterful facade of cheerful perfection.

This was a difficult realization. I'm talking about my one and only mother. Hello, years of therapy. To realize your own mother doesn't care or know how to show affection for you, but can embrace a perfect stranger or neighbor and give them her undivided attention and talk for hours was a startling observation. She was trapped in the role of mother, a shoe that didn't fit. Like

Babette trying to strain her plastic foot into one of Barbie's shoes, motherhood and my mom weren't a suitable match. She had centered her life for years on superficial presentations and an avoidance of emotion. It was much easier to dance around things than to dance.

The Summer of Gavin

While posing for my senior picture, I accidentally flared my nostrils when the shutter registered its first click. An unfortunate occurrence was officially frozen in time to mark my seventeenth year. I looked like I'd just caught a whiff of Limburger cheese on a Ritz cracker. The senior class photos were taken on Blossom Hill Road. My mother's name was Blossom. No connection. The portrait studio photographer, in a display of uncommon astuteness, took both scholarly and pseudo smile poses of each classmate. In the serious pose, I appeared to be deep in existential thought. I probably was. I had completed a course in Existentialism in my senior year with Mr. Ferry. No sense in letting it go to waste.

In each pose, I wore a delicate pearl suspended from a gold-filled chain, part of the Gemco jewelry collection. A rare moment of conforming to a traditional adornment. Nearly every girl in my class was wearing the same elegant, understated necklace. Perhaps the photographer loaned it out to each of us to contrast with the black V-neck faux half-top supplied by the photographer and his lovely assistant.

In one scholarly pose, my eyes are bulging like Peter Lorre's in *The Raven.* I look terrified, as if I had just seen a ghost, or was one. In the other, I was Sylvester after swallowing the canary. My mother didn't want to buy any of the graduation poses or packages.

"They're too expensive," she declared. "Besides, your father takes too many pictures as it is." I finally collected enough coins that had been squirreled away in pockets to purchase the bargain mini-package: two poses in sepia-toned wallet-sized snapshots.

Every classmate, whether male or female, parted their hair in the middle, which made us nearly indistinguishable in the pages of the annual yearbook. How Morticia Addams became the poster child of the hip hairdo, I'll never know. Everyone looked related except my black classmates, most wearing an Afro hairstyle, some with 'fro pick combs sticking out of their hair. The Afro comb and hair pick of the early Seventies was worn in the hair not only as an adornment, but also as a political emblem and a statement of a collective identity. It was a fashionable way of saying NO to oppression and racism. Wearing the comb led to a form of camaraderie amongst my classmates whose hair grew up and out, not down. Since the Afro comb hadn't been widely visible before the Sixties, it was assumed that it was invented in the early Seventies. In actuality, more like the 3070s BC in Ancient Egypt, where it was popular with the aristocracy. As much as you might like them to, some things never go out of style.

But my hair wouldn't hold a comb or any particular style. It was as unruly as a kid on a sugar rampage. I had a few kinky hairs, but other than that, my hair was uneven soft waves, the sort that had my contemporaries placing their heads on the ironing board and firing up the steam iron. My friend Denise ironed her hair, as did many of my classmates. It wasn't something I was willing to try, or singe.

I had always suffered from that syndrome where your neutral expression makes you look like you're an angry serial killer or deep in melancholy. My mom wore the same unintentional appearance when her face was relaxed. It was the curse of our gene pool, certainly not a choice. Through the intervention of some anonymous high school student, I became aware of my expression and how it was being interpreted. As part of an assignment in my senior year Humanities class, we had to scribble an anonymous note to one fellow classmate and tell them something we liked about them, but never divulging our identity. I still have the note. I saved it in a large green scrapbook of odds and ends. It reads:

"I've noticed you many times before because there's something rather interesting about your face. This is what it is. You look so melancholy and sad when you don't smile. But when you flash a smile it changes your entire face and the energy around your being. I've never seen such a dramatic shift in someone's appearance with a smile. Smile, Carol!"

I remember being startled by the note. I had no idea I came across angry or glum. It caused me to make an effort to smile at every occasion, especially when it wasn't warranted.

Even my parents commented on my perpetual sorry expression.

"Stop pouting!" they'd chide me.

But I wasn't pouting. It was the way my eyebrows sat, my lippy lower lip jutted out, and the contours of my cheeks sat on my face. This perpetually pissed appearance was entrenched in the barbed wire strands of my DNA. My resting face, despite its best intentions, conveyed melancholy. I'm afraid it still does. I look pouty when I'm not annoyed. I look gloomy when I'm not sad. And I look melancholy while pondering happy thoughts. Unless, of course, I smile. Then the Earth shifts a few degrees off its axis, at least according to the anonymous high school senior who slipped me that note.

Despite my perceived perpetual pout, when I had to choose one pose for the yearbook, I chose the one featuring my sober expression. In it, I appeared scholarly and contemplative, with the wisdom of Methuselah … parading around in a black V-neck faux top.

Prototype Cast

In my early school years, I met prototypes of all the other people and personalities I would ever encounter in my lifetime. They sat next to me in third grade, and I found them again when I was twenty-seven … and fifty-seven. Characters and personal styles from high school days never vanish. Someone always reminds me of someone else. It was the curve of their cheek or their spine as they hunch forward, the way they carried themselves, their aura and energy, their lack of security or great abundance of it. It was their manner, the register of their voice, the curl or fall of their hair and lift of their eyes as they met mine.

I never felt like the cool kid in school, nor the nerd, nor even a fully fledged hippie chick. Naturally I wore the hippest attire and carried adolescent angst around my shoulders like a champ. But my label wasn't clearly defined, at least by me. To some, I was the class clown constantly telling stories and jokes like my father. To others, I was a peasant-bloused hippie smoking dope, but not in plain sight. But for the most part, my body and face felt invisible to the student body. In school, and at home, I was an island. I was hungry to be seen. Famished. I wanted to reduce the space between my classmates and me by wiggling my nose like Samantha on *Bewitched* or nodding my head forward like Barbara Eden on *I Dream of Jeannie.* But I had no magic up my sleeve or my spine. Every clique of hoods, preppies, hippies, troublemakers, jocks, stoners, intellectuals, and even the flawless and the fractured had its own force field. I didn't have the password to any of them.

I was bony, like one of those wooden puppets on strings with the jangly legs and arms. I was awkward inside, razor sharp on the outside. I was the girl who was convinced that cars and plants had feelings, the girl who worshipped cats like an Egyptian, the girl who had few friends at school and too many complications at home, the girl who loved The Beatles, Batman, and Barbra Streisand. I didn't want the coolness of the prom queen, the haute couture of the popular girls, or the stylishly disheveled. I didn't want to be them, but I would have given anything to be acknowledged in the hallway with a smile, a knowing glance, or greeting. It never happened. I felt as invisible in school as I did at home. The three friends I had were invisible too. We were the Casper Quartet, one another's friendly ghost, as we locked translucent arms and took on adolescent challenges together.

No one wore nametags in elementary school, middle school, or high school, but we managed to learn everyone's name through osmosis or something. There was not one kid in my elementary school, nor in my high school class of 586 students, whose full name I didn't have memorized. I immediately knew which clique they belonged to, and each group cultivated its own distinct persona. Surfers, druggies, jocks, hoods, theater geeks, band folks, photographers and writers who worked on the class yearbook, creative types who took an abundance of art classes, the class klutzes and the class clowns, hippies and brainiacs were posses that maintained their own brand of uniform and tribal rituals.

Everyone labeled everyone else and stayed far from the other groups immersed in their own culture of like-minded friends. Spaz McFarland was the brainiac. Bart Reynolds was with the theater department and would star in every high school musical. Moondoggie Schwartz was a surfer dude. Quaalude Quinton hung with the druggies and rode a Harley. I knew them immediately based on their outfits and their particular brand of panache, stance, aura, and that small swirl of hair at the nape of their neck. I could identity all of these cliques from across the student parking lot, but I couldn't identify fully with any of them. I was my own island.

There was no one whose approval I wanted more than Mr. Trevor Ferry, except perhaps my own father. In my senior year of high school, Mr. Ferry's Existentialism class was life-altering in every way I needed my life altered that year. I dove into a cavalcade of intoxicating writings and new concepts and a genre of books I hadn't known existed until I found myself seated in this man's class. Mr. Ferry not only introduced me to a stunning array of literature, he expanded my ideas about how to embrace my loneliness, my philosophy, my viewpoint, and my life experiences. And, yes, my misery.

We discussed the many facades people wore and what it felt like to be an outsider, always one step removed from the crowd. I could have written a set of books on that particular topic. We delved into philosophy, psychology, and matters of life and death. We discussed the meaning of existence. More importantly, his feedback on my essay papers made me higher than a reefer and worlds removed from my sniveling, gossipy, low-consciousness classmates. He often cited my papers and ideas in class, much to the uneasiness of my shy self. Mr. Ferry's glowing comments were noted on the edges of my papers. He prompted me to read parts of my own essays out loud. I thought I'd die as I stood there bathed in anxiety, damp and dripping with perspiration and embarrassment. But I wanted to please this new father figure.

Instead of taking my usual spot in the back of the classroom, I gradually moved to the front row. My first essay received an A. Score! Then ... A+. Score again! A++. What? SCORE! Mr. Ferry plumped up my confidence like he was a bicycle pump and I was a threadbare tire. He made me want to go further, strive harder, reach deeper. No one had ever inspired me in this way, and I wanted to maintain my ability to please him.

"Very insightful of you, Carol," he jotted down in blue ink at the end of a paragraph on my essay exam. The singular word "Yes!" sat beside another line. "Nice job, Carol!" he wrote at the top of the page. Oh my god! He was writing my name. My heart pounded harder as I read the words scribbled along the top of the page in masculine cursive. The fact that Mr. Ferry was married to a rotund Asian woman, a fellow intellectual, and had a small son at home made him even more captivating. He was always clothed in a casual tweed jacket layered over his black turtleneck knit sweater and corduroy pants. He was supremely settled and secure within himself, something I longed to be. If only his raves and reviews of my work could cancel out how insignificant I felt at home.

I had never received an A+ in any class and didn't realize teachers could assign such a grade. But he wrote the letter and plus sign on my papers and presented it as my final grade. Initially, I felt shock, then pride, and later … giddiness. If Mr. Ferry thought I was insightful and capable, maybe—just maybe—my own father would notice me as well. Wouldn't my high grades please him? Perhaps I was not pathetic and bothersome after all. Maybe there was a place for me in the world. There certainly was in Mr. Ferry's class.

The bearded Mr. Ferry radiated intelligence, inner calm, and wisdom. He was a Buddha of Literature. He had all the answers. Mr. Ferry was as confident and serene as Lord Nelson on the bridge of the HMS Victory. Beyond all that, he shivered my timbers. Those warm brown eyes were like a blanket from the discomfort I felt at home and out in the world. I couldn't wait to sit in his classroom and be in his presence.

One evening, as I was dreamily fantasizing about Mr. Ferry, I realized how foolish and futile it was to do so. He was married. He was older in every way possible. To him, I was a teenager who thought too deeply about everything. I didn't want to think about him, but I couldn't release him from my thoughts. I scratched out a quick poem for Mr. Ferry in my journal, a poem I would never show him:

FOSSIL
How I want my impressions of you to decay,
like the fading fossils
in my cheek and breast,
from a bunched-up Burlington sheet,
and a restless night's sleep.

Go to the Head of the Class

Since Mr. Ferry's heart was unavailable to mere mortals and high school seniors, I set my sights on my studies and smoking more pot. My senior year was clouded in billowing smoke as I drifted through classes like Existentialism and Lyrics as Poetry. I was enthralled with books by Nabokov, Dostoevsky, Hesse, Camus, Maslow, and Moustakas and short stories by Tolstoy, but drunk with desire for my new Creative Writing class instructor, Mr. Gavin Moore. It was his second year of teaching, and he was handsome, with his Seventies porn-style mustache, long wavy auburn hair, and swashbuckling good looks. He was the star of my daydreams and considered one of the coolest teachers on campus. There were only a handful of teachers who were decades younger than their elder colleagues. Cool teachers taught the profound and heady classes and looked a bit more like us than the rest of the stodgy faculty. Mr. Gavin Moore was only twenty-five years old and wasn't terribly cerebral. He was more of a grinning jock, which normally wouldn't be appealing to me. But what he lacked in brains, he made up for in eye appeal. He was the Rhett Butler of Willow Glen High.

Although Mr. Moore had taken too many handsome lessons and had a vast mountain range of charm, he wasn't an inspiring instructor, and his creative writing assignments weren't all that creative. He couldn't tell his iambic pentameter from his haiku, but he scrawled atop my poetry assignment that he thoroughly enjoyed mine. And that he was envious. "You're my hero," he wrote in red ink in the margin of my paper. Mr. Moore had never written poetry and wanted to try it "because of you," he once scribbled in red pen on the last page of my exam. I was flattered, but baffled. I assumed he wanted to know more about the poems, not me. I didn't know how to take a position in the spotlight, so I didn't take it anywhere. I decided he meant nothing by it, that the flattery was something he offered every student to tease them out of their shells.

Poetry, for me, began in the secrecy of my diaries and journals and far from an audience. My scribbly verses appeared only on the paper hidden behind a diary cover or in a hardbound notebook labeled RECORD from Rexall Drugstore. I poured my thoughts and emotions into lines of analogies and descriptive prose as though I were on a sinking ship and writing to stay afloat. Privacy was where my poetry was born, but how marvelous it was to have it move another human being. There couldn't have been a better gift. Not in twelfth grade. But Mr. Moore's class continued to be one unimaginative exercise after the other. The only project we were given with some substance was the instruction to pull a page out of a current magazine and write a short story around it. As he handed out the magazines to pass around the class, I smiled. That was an easy task. I could do that. In fact, it was enjoyable. The storylines that poured out of my pen were vivid in detail and laced with humor. I was beginning to think that I might be good at something. But my confidence remained a closed flower that would take decades to bloom.

One day, Mr. Moore marched our entire class next door to join with the students in the adjacent classroom. We were instructed to sit on the back counters behind the class that was already seated and watch the movie *Picnic*, a 1955 film starring William Holden and Kim Novak. I had no idea what that had to do with creative writing, high school studies, or anything else, certainly not in the year 1972. The movie appeared dated and trivial, hardly relevant to my education. But the important thing was we got to spend the hour giggling, swinging our legs, and doing something completely new in a different seating arrangement. And we got to do it in someone else's classroom. Cool. Yes, Mr. Moore, fresh off his own college degree and barely into his teaching career, was randomly splashing about, flailing his arms, and treading water. He punched the clock and picked up his paycheck. For that fifty-minute class, we were all playing hooky with Mr. Moore.

The day of my high school graduation was a turning point. Yes, we were finally finished with our mandatory secondary education. None of us knew what was in our future. I certainly didn't see Mr. Moore coming. I had signed up for his class simply because I enjoyed writing short, silly poems about everyday life. Writing was the only thing that came easily to me. I never had to push the words out. The ink released from the pen and leaked prose. If you're fortunate, life might endow you with a talent. If you're even luckier, you might get two. I had been given two: fellatio and writing.

On graduation day, at seventeen years old, I walked out on stage at the Santa Clara Fairgrounds in well-worn leather sandals and bloodshot eyes from too much cannabis. It was a hot afternoon in Santa Clara Valley—hot in so many ways. Mr. Moore was standing in the receiving line as my classmates and I filed off the stage, one by one, diplomas in hand and futures as foggy as a brain on Vicks NyQuil. With my fine-tuned radar, I located him immediately. He wore dark-rimmed glasses, and even at a distance I could see his grin. A flirty devilish glint sparkled behind his spectacles, and despite his thin lips and straight line for a mouth, he looked like a handsome prince. Uh-oh. I recognized the look, even at thirty feet away. I had seen it several times before on the faces of the men twice my age. I wondered why Mr. Moore was suddenly wading into the same cesspool. And where was my own moral compass? Why couldn't I locate it? Why did all this behavior seem familiar and flattering? Maybe James Brown was right, "It's a Man's World."

Mr. Moore loitered at the stage exit, now smiling broadly like a Cheshire cat. His expression communicated that he knew something the rest of us didn't. He took a quick photo of me with his Kodak Pocket Instamatic camera. I was scrunching my mouth into a sour lemon pucker while my eyes beamed at him like the headlights of a skidding Chevy Corvette before a head-on collision. He handed me a single crimson carnation. I was dumbfounded. For me? What? Why? But I couldn't ask any questions or manage any response as I continued falling in line with the parade of classmates, now graduates.

His smile trumped not only the long-stemmed bud, but the diploma in my right hand and washed away any wise words that were uttered on stage mere moments before. Every detail of that late afternoon dissolved like Alka-Seltzer in water. Fizz. Gone. The only thing I knew about my future was that I would daydream of Mr. Moore and imagine many a romantic rendezvous that were all out of reach. I was drawn to him like Madge to a bowl of warm Palmolive Liquid … and I was soaking in it. But … he was my teacher. My ex-teacher. He was off-limits. Wasn't he? Did I make up this attraction in my overactive mind? I must have. Did he give a long-stemmed bud to all of his A students? Did he genuinely like my poetry? More importantly, did he like me?

That evening after the graduation ceremony, I went out to celebrate with Andy, who by this time had been my boyfriend for nearly two years. We were still a couple, terrifically bored, yet comfortable together. But this evening felt exceptionally empty. I was still flying high on the attention from my Creative Writing teacher. My attention to Andy began to fade as he was drowned out by loud music and chatter in a neighborhood pizza parlor.

I finally arrived home around midnight and began readying myself for bed. Slipping on my lightest summer nighty and curling up on my single bed, I started drifting to sleep with images of graduation marching through my mind. I was startled back to wakefulness by the ringing of the telephone beside my bed.

"Hello," I answered.

"Carol? It's Gavin."

"Gavin? Gavin who?"

I was barely awake, enough to realize that I wasn't dreaming, but it still felt like a vivid hallucination. Or perhaps this was a pre-dream drift.

I don't know how he got my number, but on the other end of the line was my high school Creative Writing teacher pouring out his heart and asking me the question I had been obsessing about for months:

"Now that you're no longer my student, would you consider going out with me? There's an end-of-the-year faculty-student potluck coming up at Mr. Robertson's house. May I escort you there?"

I could barely speak. My heart jumped into my throat, and I could scarcely form sounds or even catch my breath.

"That sounds nice," I managed.

Our first adult conversation went swimmingly, I thought. But when I hung up the phone ... BANG! I was shvitzing from head to toe and couldn't remember my own name. I smiled a sweaty smile and drifted off to dreamland with thought bubbles starring, you guessed it ... Mr. Moore ... now Gavin.

Married once already, Gavin later explained he had not yet experienced either true passion or true love. He stayed in a conventional marriage to his first girlfriend, a pleasant enough unambitious blonde, until he realized he didn't want to be married to her anymore. Throughout my senior year at Willow Glen High, Mr. Moore was moving through his first divorce from Blondie, and I was writing poems in class about how downcast and distant he appeared to be. I wanted to soothe him, restore him, turn his attention my way, but I didn't know how, and I didn't dare tell him. It turns out I didn't have to. He began moving in my direction before I was aware of it.

I had never dated anyone who had ever been married. Hell, I had barely dated anyone who didn't have acne. Gavin and his wife were in the midst of a divorce. The position of wife sounded so adult. Had he made a home with her like Rob and Laura Petrie on *The Dick Van Dyke Show*? Why was it being cancelled? Whatever his marital status, we were off and running to the Summer of Gavin, to the thrill of a budding romance, and to this singular teacher furthering my education. There would be deep discussions, book recommendations, and exposure to an adult world and social mingling, the likes of which I had not yet experienced other than at the distance and through the glass of the atrium when my parents held gatherings.

Teach Me Tonight

Gavin and I were on our first date, the curious twosome teaming up against the other partygoers in Mr. Robertson's end-of-the-year potluck. We quietly took our positions at the end of the patio's ping-pong table. Suddenly, we were a team. Or were we a couple? Gavin and I hard-slammed every ball bouncing towards us with the gusto of Billie Jean King and Jimmy Connors. Our host, Mr. Robertson, was the dreaded Lyrics as Poetry teacher in my senior year. I had just graduated from his class. He gave me my only A-minus grade that year. Everything else was an A+ or an A. Mr. Robertson was an ill-informed, unlikable, and reluctant instructor, but the class and the students who attended were curious and motivated. Basically, we would dissect the word salad of popular songs. One person suggested we tear apart YES's song "Roundabout." We tried, but concluded it didn't mean anything in particular, which was a rather rude awakening for those of us who looked forward to unearthing the deeper meaning in all things. Didn't everything have to have meaning? I thought so ... until I took Lyrics as Poetry.

Mr. Robertson didn't like me. Lyrics as Poetry was my first class of the day. I arrived each morning after rolling out of bed, rolling some joints, rolling off the sidewalk, and collapsing into the front row of his classroom. With red eyes and a stimulated mind, I exchanged sideways glances with my classmates and giggled in the inappropriate moments. If looks could kill, Mr. Robinson would've massacred me. And I couldn't blame him.

"Carol, if you don't control yourself, you will be heading to the principal's office."

But I couldn't stop chuckling. The world was finally looking like a tolerable place behind all the smoke and mirrors of marijuana. Besides, I was pulling straight As without even trying. Mr. Robertson was being stuffy, conventional, and uninventive. I, on the other hand, was reading and dissecting Dostoevsky's *Crime and Punishment*, Albert Camus' *The Stranger*, and Tolstoy's *The Death of Ivan Ilyich*. I was exploring the great texts of Clark Moustakas and discovering Herman Hesse's *Siddhartha, Steppenwolf*, and *Demian*. And in my spare time, I would curl up in bed and feast on J.D. Salinger's *The Catcher in the Rye*, William Goldman's *The Temple of Gold*, and Joseph Heller's *Catch-22*. I knew that the music group Steppenwolf took their name from Hesse's book. What did Mr. Robertson know? Bupkis.

But at Mr. Robertson's end-of-the-year party, the new teacher-student couple was receiving stares and unwanted attention. The faculty didn't know what to make of us showing up together, and the students who attended were baffled as well. Mr. Moore and I won every round of ping-pong despite the scrutiny. We filled up on lukewarm appetizers and Orange Crush, then hopped in his car to retire to his one-bedroom bachelor pad to listen to music and talk all night.

"I have something to confess to you," he meekly muttered as I sat down on his apartment floor. "I want to tell you the first moment I noticed you." What? I thought he noticed me in his classroom.

"You caught my attention in the school quad one day," he explained as he paced back and forth before lowering himself into a ragged leather chair. "You were seated on a bench and the sun was hitting your hair in such a way that it formed a halo around your head. You were stunningly beautiful in that moment. You *are* stunningly beautiful." I hung on his every word like a monkey on a tree.

I didn't feel beautiful, but I basked in his flattering praise and absorbed his cascading compliments like an O-Cel-O kitchen sponge.

Easy now, I commanded myself, as I sat on the carpeted floor. *He's not Wee Willie Wikstrom*. Sure, I was in distress most of my junior year, but it had been over a year since that incident with my father's coworker. *This is a vastly different setting and situation. Nothing to be fearful or uneasy about here,* I told myself. *In fact, Mr. Moore might swoop in and save me from villains like a caped crusader.*

Suddenly there was a knock at his apartment door. It was one of his former students, Angie Kamloff. I recognized her from one of my previous classes.

The sounds of Angie's sobbing spilled into Gavin's small living room as the door opened. Soon the dreadful wailing reverberated off his apartment walls. I stepped back, hiding myself in the kitchen, not really knowing why I was hiding.

"Excuse me, I need to take care of something here and calm her down," he said softly.

Gavin stepped out into the hallway and closed the door behind him. I could only make out muffled and unrecognizable words. But from the tone of her voice I could tell Angie Kamloff was upset. Very upset.

I paced back and forth in that small kitchen, turning over kitchen timers and placemats to kill time. Why was Angie Kamloff upset and crying, and how did she know where Mr. Moore lived? I never found out.

He returned to the living room with a flimsy explanation. "She had a crush on me last year. I guess she's upset you're here," he surmised.

In that moment, I nodded and accepted his explanation, but quietly I wondered. *How did she know where he lived? And why would she be jealous of me?*

The Kamloff factor was always the big matzo ball sitting in the room. But the jolt of her knocking and sobbing soon fell into the background along with the music from his stereo system. He climbed back into the chair, and I crouched nearby on the floor. Gavin touched my cheek with the back of his hand that was covered with soft black hair, smiled that charismatic smile of his, and made his first move. Knight to queen four. He pressed his thin lips to my full ones. I was certain I heard bells chiming, birds chirping, fireworks exploding. Either that, or his apartment fire alarm had gone off. We were off to the races and our summer of amorousness.

Gavin assumed I was a virgin. I know because before we actually pressed our clothed bodies against one another for that first steamy evening of dry humping, he mentioned his hesitation. It was based on my age and some sort of angelic halo hovering above my freshly shampooed head. The Halo Shampoo must have been working. He assumed that my cherry was still sitting on my sundae and the deflowering bell had yet to ring. He assumed wrong. I had been with several lovers, and he had bedded one maybe two other women. It showed. For all the pre-bedroom bravado, ear nibbling, and sweet talk, I discovered that Gavin had little to offer under his freshly laundered sheets. The poor fellow was panting and wheezing and trying to keep up. Beyond Gavin's mouthwatering kisses, he struggled in bed in those early weeks of our bedroom romps.

Crawling on top of me like a bear and lowering his weight onto my frame, he mechanically moved in-and-out, in-and-out, until he completed his mission. Show over. Eventually I schooled him in lovemaking with a sprinkling of depravity. But Gavin wasn't in my life at that moment to be a pleasure pal. For all intents and purposes, he was my boyfriend.

I ran home and wrote in my journal:

ZOO
Your skin after loving me; slick as a seal.
You grunt
like an elephant.
throwing up his trunk to the sky.
And getting it.
And getting it.

Gavin valued novelist Kurt Vonnegut's wordsmithery above all other literary masterworks. He deified the writer, cut his veins and sacrificed his soul on the altar of Vonnegut's *Slaughterhouse-Five* and *Cat's Cradle*. He wanted to catch the current in Vonnegut's slipstream, or at least mimic his crafty keystrokes.

Gavin yearned to write compelling fiction, but more importantly to be a charter member of AAA. Not the American Automobile Association, but the group of accomplished, acknowledged, and applauded novelists. I know this because he told me so—every day. Gavin wanted to write that sweeping novel that would leave even Vonnegut at a loss for words. Like a whispered promise, one he was making to himself, Gavin stated with great certainty, "I'm going to write the Great American Novel." He said it like it should appear in all caps. He said it like a daily prayer or incantation so that it would manifest before him.

He was working on several new manuscripts that he insisted I read and offer feedback on.

"Me? I'm just a kid. What do I know?"

Here's what I knew. Gavin's earlier writing efforts read beautifully. They were clever and had genuine promise. I thoroughly enjoyed reading every short story he slipped into my hands. Then he presented the big beast, his new baby, the so-called Great American Novel, Mr. Moore's Opus. The manuscript was only forty pages long, but he had been working on it for a full year. Gavin always used writing stock that had tiny bits of dusty gray lint imprinted like threads of wool in satin. It was not at all like the flimsy onion skin typing paper I used at home on our electric typewriter. But Gavin's heavily textured and complex paper stock made every word and paragraph seem impressive and important.

He was beaming with pride as I curled up in one of his living room chairs and began reading. As I moved through pages one, two to twenty-two, and finally to page forty, I noticed something peculiar about the content of his Great American Novel. It was as if Kurt Vonnegut himself had written it. The sentences had the same cadence, clever vibe, and wordage. Vonnegut was his god, and now Gavin was writing with the same voice, style, and substance as the Almighty. He even used Vonnegut's language, special words, and phrases. I didn't say anything. I didn't dare. After all, I was the student, and he was the seasoned writing instructor. Right?

Gavin even began to call me "sparrowfart," a pet name which I always assumed was from Vonnegut's play *Happy Birthday, Wanda June.* Or perhaps it was from Vonnegut's *God Bless You, Mr. Rosewater.* For no apparent reason, Gavin insisted on referring to his place of employment, Willow Glen High School, as "The Plant" and that I call him Uncle Gruffy. He also attached the phrase "and his orchestra" to nearly every paragraph in his book.

Gavin always saw himself as my teacher, long after he no longer was. He had lesson plans throughout our Summer of Love. He whispered in my ear about why certain films and books were important. We had dinners at grown-up Mexican restaurants, and he gave me book after book to read. He introduced me to every Vonnegut book he had ever read and reread. In the dead heat of The Summer of '72, he took me to see the just-released film *Slaughterhouse-Five.* Not since Olivia Hussey played Juliet in Franco Zefferelli's *Romeo and Juliet,* or Laura Mothrup unsnapped her gym blouse in the girl's seventh-grade locker room had I seen such impeccable breasts. Valerie Perrine had them. Her C-cups filled the wide screen. Gavin shifted nervously in his seat.

On my birthday, which fell a week after graduation, Gavin came to my orange front door bearing gifts. Still determined to educate me, he handed me Walt Whitman's *Leaves of Grass,* apparently to inspire a model for my poetry, and a hardback version of *Three Little Kittens,* to perpetuate the young girl in me. We jumped in his white sedan and rode to San Francisco so that he could single-handedly continue my cultural tutelage. Gavin escorted me to Hippo's Restaurant, a colorful San Francisco landmark that featured dozens and dozens of different types of hamburgers and a whimsical wall mural of painted hippos splashed onto bright orange walls. Orange booths. Orange flooring. Orange menus. I was thrilled with the decor. This was my kind of birthday.

But two weeks into our budding relationship, and a mere week after celebrating my eighteenth birthday with Gavin at Hippo's, he drove me to Redwood City near San Francisco to introduce me to his college buddies. It was vital to have his new love interest accepted into the sacred fold of fraternity friends.

All the men there had a Mickey's Big Mouth malt liquor in one hand and well-coiffed girlfriends or wives in the other. The women sauntered between the kitchen and living room in brightly colored halter dresses, cleavage, and matching earrings. Every one of them seemed several generations older, more scholarly, and certainly much more knowledgeable about sports. With no common interests shared with this group of ex-college roommates and friends, every reference and term sounded foreign to my ear. His college pals had nothing to say to me, and I had nothing to say to them. Drat. I was disappearing again. Poof! Some of them didn't even look at or acknowledge me, while others rolled their eyes at this nymphet that their college chum had dragged in from the street, or in this case, the classroom ... and the cul-de-sac.

Gavin's eyes unexpectedly turned from flirty and warm to scrutinizing and disapproving. I was his girlfriend, but my years of sloughing off schoolwork and inhaling reefers began to show in this mature mainstream setting. I was not well read enough to keep up with the inane cocktail and beer conversations swirling around me, and I certainly couldn't talk sports. Gavin's friends were jocks and contemplatively discussed every aspect of every sort of game. The terminology was like a foreign language. The only games I understood were board games from Parker Brothers. As I disappeared into the wallpaper, I realized I had nothing in common with these middle-aged (okay, mid-twenties) married folks who owned homes in the Bay Area hills and talked babies, broken furnaces, the latest football scores, and suburban fix-it woes. My social skills were not attuned to such small talk, nor did I want them to be. That was my mother's territory. She was the small talk queen, and I was the shrinking violet in a room full of blooming cherry trees. I tried to blend in and hold my own, but I could see I was near drowning as I paddled ferociously and tried to keep up during Adult Swim.

The next outing for Gavin and me was to an imposing Mexican restaurant, El Burro, in San Jose. I had never been served Mexican food before, other than an occasional dripping grease pocket from Taco Bell. I was not used to spicy food, I was used to bland matzo balls. Unaccustomed to red chili and hot salsa, the chicken enchiladas burned my tongue. Was this another area where we were not going to mesh well?

A few weeks later, we dined at a Japanese restaurant where they placed a piece of teriyaki salmon in front of me shaped like one of the contiguous states. I told the waitress, who didn't speak English, that my dinner looked like Florida. Gavin didn't crack a smile, but the waitress laughed in Japanese.

Gavin and I seemed to be living in different countries. I wanted him to fall deeper in love with me so that our differences would drift away like icebergs, but he was too consumed with his friends and their opinions while he fidgeted with the raw egg atop his udon noodle. I was disappointing him. I was certain of it, even though he never spoke of his dissatisfaction. I felt lonely in his company, especially when we ventured out beyond his apartment in Campbell, a suburb of San Jose, or found ourselves dining at some new café. Eating sad is the worst. Yet it felt familiar.

Mealtime with my father had been sad. There was a distance growing between us. I needed a 747 airplane to reach him, even when he was sitting right next to me. It felt as though the Great Wall of China stood between us. In our case, it was the great wall in Campbell.

The next couple of summer months consisted of a multitude of games with Gavin: playing pool in the garage; playing with each other in the Eichler's backyard above-ground swimming pool; and teasing games in my bedroom under the yellow floral quilt. One afternoon in August in the middle of our May-September romance, I rode my one-speed bicycle to Gavin's new rental in downtown San Jose. He had moved from the one-bedroom bachelor pad in Campbell to a small but enchanting cottage with a half-acre yard. San Jose State University sat a mile or two down the road. The bike ride was long, but there was a pot of gold at the end: an afternoon with Uncle Gruffy. His modest red-tiled rental had old-world Spanish charm, and nothing like the sleek, contemporary lines of the Eichler.

Lunch and learning chess were on the afternoon menu at Casa de Gavin. As he leaned into the tiled kitchen counter preparing egg salad, Gavin announced in an authoritarian voice that the instruction for his new girlfriend, the chess virgin, would begin after lunch. Until then, he took particular joy in nourishing me with a steady stream of Mickey's "Big Mouth" Malt Liquor in its trendy wide jar. I watched him boil eggs while I took baby sips. Later he planned to plow me, so perhaps he thought beer would assist in irrigating my trough. This beverage was his favorite brew. He rotated it and black coffee as if hot and cold liquids would lubricate the cogs of the wheels that ground out the prose, like Hemingway did with his steady supply of dry martinis and Bloody Marys. But malt liquor wasn't for me. I never could work up affection for the bitter taste of malted barley, hops, and yeast.

Gavin took great pride in preparing his egg salad, adding plenty of relish, a splash of lime, and even a few shavings of celery stalks and carrot curls. I was impressed with his skills in the kitchen, but I didn't know what to do with myself while he cooked. I strolled down his short hallway, looked at the pictures on the wall and made pleasant conversation and comments. I felt uneasy. I was turning into my mother. Then I looked at myself in the mirror on the back of his bedroom door. I always looked like a different person in someone else's mirror. I looked like the person I was trying to be, but wasn't.

Gavin considered himself not only a teacher, but also a connoisseur of chess and a grand master of game-board maneuvers. He boasted of his keen knowledge of the game and couldn't wait to "learn me." I grew up with Milton Bradley and Parker Brothers, but chess was a game I had never tackled. I didn't have any interest in strategizing so profoundly in order to win a game.

But strategize I did to please and persuade him in my direction. After a few key instructions, the chess tournament commenced. Seventeen moves. Checkmate! Carol: 1; Gavin: 0. Yes, I quickly beat him at his own game, so to speak. Thinking it a fluke, he challenged me to a second round. Fifteen moves. Checkmate! Carol: 2; Gavin: 0. A frown came to his face and forced the corners of his mouth in a downward position. I instantly knew that I had made the worst misstep of my gender and generation. I didn't allow the man to win. I could almost hear Gloria Steinem cheering in my right ear.

A strange hush came over Gavin. I wasn't quite sure what had happened, but after he put the king, queen, and knights away in the waiting open box, he steered me to the kitchen to gobble up his egg salad masterpiece. Soon after, we stumbled down the narrow hallway and into his small bed, leaving a trail of garments and footwear. As I stretched out on his miniature mattress, contented and fully savored, I felt enough joyfulness to start my own religion.

Gavin was recovered and was fully loaded. He crawled on top of me again, but everything about him shifted, including his mood. His skin felt different, and his movements, grunts, and sighs suddenly were housed in a different beast. My ex-teacher had disconnected and was a million miles away even though he was lying right on top of me. As he moved through his usual bag of tricks with a newfound vitality, he threw in a few new moves that I assumed he read about in the newly released *Joy of Sex*. But Gavin and eight million other readers were still studying the many salacious illustrations; not fully comprehending that passion, the key component superior to varying positions, came from a different erogenous zone: the mind. Surely the real Kurt Vonnegut wasn't this sexually inept, with or without a manual.

Still, I managed to enjoy my time with Gavin under the sheets as we giggled and grabbed and made love with a new buoyancy. My concern was not technique. I was single-mindedly fixated on him, on us. But, today, his thrusts and grasp felt furious. As the afternoon ticked away, Gavin transformed into a fireball of sexual experimentation and lust. He breathed harder, moaned louder, and enveloped me with a fervor that felt fresh and mildly erotic. Perhaps it was because he was in familiar surroundings, I reasoned. Or maybe he was falling deeper in love with me. When I was with him, he became an uninhabited animal in some forbidden forest. I didn't want a stitch of clothing on my body, or on his. I only wanted to hear my lover's grunt and growl. I wanted to be his prey.

As Gavin remained ridiculously erect for the remainder of the afternoon, and for several go-rounds, he was beginning to look a bit like Coit Tower. Gavin's engine and other parts were revved up and raring to go again and again, but he wasn't particularly caring. He had stopped saying my name. A few minutes after his final release, Gavin settled back into the sheets. There was a somber instructional quality to his voice, like a parent trying desperately to sound detached as they lectured their child about some unpleasant business.

"You need to move away from home, grow up, have experiences," he lectured in monotone speech. "I'm much too mature for you."

As my post-coital mindset began to sober up, I sensed the bomb bay doors opening. He took a long breath as he held me and whispered in my left ear, "It's not working."

Huh? What did he say? Am I being dumped? We had just banged the chalk out of our erasers! He's breaking up with me? I was bewildered.

"Now?" I managed. "But you just fucked me. Three times!"

With his now flaccid love pipe still dripping, I pried myself from his arms and out of the bed, gathered my garments previously shed like some steamy scene from *Valley of the Dolls,* held back my tears as he held me one last time—a long, long time— jumped on my bicycle and rode off into the hottest day in Santa Clara Valley history.

But this particular afternoon, Santa Clara Valley was no *Valley of the Dolls.* It was more like Valley of the Malls, and I was riding past dozens of them. I was too many miles from home as I pedaled down busy main roads, marinated in sunshine, with tears streaming down my face like one of those sad Save the Children orphans or a Keane painting.

I couldn't wrap my mind around the events of the day. During the course of my endless bicycle ride home, I kept reliving each word, replaying the day over and over again like a phonograph needle skipping over the same scratch on a record. Gavin was delighted to see me at his front door. He held me longer, kissed me deeper, smiled more often, made me lunch. He was playful and content. Then the chess game followed by lovemaking and ... bam! Hasta la vista, baby.

Vonnegut wrote in *Slaughterhouse-Five* "How nice—to feel nothing, and still get full credit for being alive." If I could have looked Gavin directly in his two dreamy eyes and delivered those words to him with panache and conviction during my exit, I would have. But with weak knees and a heart aching like a rotting tooth, I pedaled my bike towards home. It was a hellishly hot jaunt. I was convinced I was going to melt right into the pavement, a root beer Popsicle baking in the sun. Sweat and teardrops were pouring off of me like rain off of an Eichler rooftop during a fierce storm.

Arriving back at the Eichler, I walked straight out to the Doughboy pool my father had assembled a few weeks earlier, dropped my sweaty clothing to the ground, climbed in, and pulled myself down into the four-foot water with knees bent in a fetal position, my head submerged into the cool blue chlorinated liquid, arms curled around my knees, toes gently tapping the lower lining of the pool like some sad ballerina. I was poised at the bottom of the world, and the rest of humanity was marching on above the waterline. I couldn't join in. I had been jilted. It seemed to come out of the blue. I was reduced to nothing by another man—first my father, now Gavin. I was unlovable. I had looked for adoration in the eyes and care in the arms of men, but I hadn't yet learned to retrieve it from myself, for myself. I had been everyone else's girl, not yet my own.

Soaking in all those tears and blue water, I couldn't escape the fact that the pool's liquid felt comforting, blissful. Almost protective, like amniotic fluid. I stayed under the waterline for what felt like eternity. I filled the circular vinyl pool to the waterline with the weight of tears. I swam short laps, bouncing back and forth from one side to the other like a puck in Atari's Pong game, feet and palms slapping the water. No one had ever broken my heart before. I was a heartache virgin. That moment would have made a good country song. But the song that kept playing in my head was Otis Redding's "I've Been Loving You Too Long," even though Gavin and I had only had a ninety-day love affair.

✳ ⚛ ✳

My final summer in the Eichler was turning from bad to worse, and from oral sex to oral surgery. The week after Gavin threw a curve ball and sent me back to the dugout, I found myself on the end of a scalpel and a pair of pliers wielded by Dr. Handel, the Tormentor in Chief of dental surgery. All four of my back molars had to be evicted as there were new teeth growing in, anxious tenants wanting to move into the currently occupied units.

The surgeon extracted all four of them, sewed me back up, and sent me home in the custody of my inconvenienced father. I stumbled to the car with a written prescription for penicillin in one hand and for codeine in the other. On the drive home, my father puffed at his pipe and was silent. Pumped full of laughing gas, I sat beside him on the bench seat and tipped against his cold shoulder when the car took the curves. Normally I wouldn't allow myself to penetrate his personal space, but with dental drugs still fogging my brain, I took the liberty to allow a gentle shoulder bounce. I couldn't help myself. I was continually being pulled back into a hazy state.

Dad stopped on the way home to pick up a tin of his pipe tobacco and to drop off my prescriptions. I was supposed to go straight home and rest as I was still flying high on anesthesia. I remember my unsure footing that afternoon, simultaneously stumbling and floating through the drugstore wondering if this was the best high I had ever been on. Yes, I decided, it was. And it couldn't have come at a better time, just after a shattering heartbreak, and during a car ride with my father, a different sort of heartbreak.

My father moved sluggishly through the store. He was a butter knife stirring a jar of gooey chicken fat. His footsteps dropped leisurely, like slow-moving syrup off buttermilk pancakes. As he tucked the tobacco tin under his arm and wandered up and down the aisles of the store in slow motion, he managed to examine and turn over every item on the shelf. Time moved like a glacier as the overhead speaker played The Chambers Brothers' "Time Has Come Today." I wanted nothing more than to lie down in bed and pull my yellow quilt over my spinning, dopey head. It seemed as if my father was delaying the return home. Up and down the aisles he sauntered, over and over, unaware that I was in the store, or in the world.

I assumed the delay had something to do with me. Perhaps if I needed to get home and rest, that gave him a perfectly good reason not to rush there. I was being punished with silence in a corner drugstore. Why? For what? I didn't know. Needing four wisdom teeth removed? Having my cheeks stuffed with cotton and blood? Hell, I wasn't Typhoid Mary. I didn't have the plague. Was there a special island for those like me? Would Alcatraz do? Perhaps a leper colony? But I strongly preferred the Eichler cul-de-sac. I was exhausted from the guessing game that was my father. I wanted to find a foam pillow for my head, take a month-long nap, and escape my broken heart that needed stitching, and my newly sutured gums.

We finally walked to the car, although I was stumbling more than walking. Back we drove to the familiar streets of Willow Glen. We pulled into the Eichler carport and made our way to the familiar front door with the bright orange face. My cheeks were red.

When you can sing all the lyrics to the *All in the Family* theme song and you've seen each episode of *Adam 12* four times, you know you've been too long in recovery. It was during this period of squandered hibernation that I received a lengthy letter from my ex-teacher, ex-boyfriend, ex-lover, ex-egg-salad-chef, Mr. Moore.

"I care deeply about you," he wrote on that familiar dust-infused stationary, "but you need to go out in the world, experience it, grow up."

Again with the go-out-into-the-world-and-grow-up speech? Enough! His words lurched off the page and stabbed like the healing pain of a deep wound. I was still weak from the recent surgery and from a youth jam-packed with insecurities and disregard. The directives and excuses written out in longhand were offensive. The words stung. They stung, but they were bearable. Well, just barely.

Clutching a shaky Bic pen, I responded to Gavin with a multitude of probing questions awash in adolescent bewilderment. Whenever someone conveyed how little I meant to him or her, something compelled me to move in closer, like some sort of pathetic punching bag provoking yet another blow. And that's what I was doing with this wretched letter and appeal to "please reconsider me."

With every frantic plea I wrote, I began to feel worse, and mean less ... to myself. "What did I do wrong?" I wrote. "Am I not good enough, pretty enough, smart enough?" First my father turned his attention away, and now Gavin? Perhaps I did have leprosy. Neither one of the men whom I had lifted high on a pedestal wanted me around.

For several more days, my mouth and cheeks remained swollen. Tired of looking and mumbling like Marlon Brando in *The Godfather*, I decided I needed a diversion. It was either divine intervention or mind-numbing boredom that inspired me to find a creative outlet. *That's it! I will paint again ... and I will make Gavin an offer he can't refuse.* The gift of framed art. Not the warmth of the physical, but the cool and warm colors of expression.

My paint box was my Pain Starter Kit. With cotton in my mouth soaking up the still draining ooze from missing teeth, and still looking like Don Vito Corleone, I hastened the healing process by applying pigments of cerulean blue, burnt sienna, cadmium orange, aqua green, and dioxazine purple to canvas. Three paintings were rapidly created for Gavin. I didn't know if I would ever see him again, but I painted with great fervor and a slightly elevated fever from a dental infection.

I painted the hell out of those canvases. The bristles of the brushes were practically smoking. With all that comingling of wrath and affection, I'm surprised I didn't burn a hole through the white gesso surface.

One of the artworks featured the two of us, Gavin and me, locked in a passionate kiss in an impressionist style that I had seen in artworks by Claude Monet. *Perhaps I will become a painter!* I thought to myself. *I will turn my pain into artwork.* And faster than

Van Gogh lost his ear, I lost what little dignity I had left. I was not a natural artist, so the results were not ready for the Louvre, but I enjoyed the act of putting paint to canvas. It helped calm and transport me out of my body and into an entirely different altitude. I felt lighter, like a smooth brushstroke of arctic blue. I had found an escape hatch from sorrow. It was an artist's messy palette. It was the perfect outlet at a perfectly miserable interval.

> *Just yesterday*
> *when you said you were leaving,*
> *my palette bled,*
> *Painting a blue sky*
> *with watery red eyes.*

Around this same time my previous boyfriend Andy began showing up at my bedroom window at all hours of the night, tapping on the glass with tears streaming down his cheeks. "Take me back. I love you, Carol. Please?" He had become as desperate, undignified, and unattractive as I had become to myself.

For an hour or two he would stand there like a woodpecker, gently tapping on the side of the house and the glass on my bedroom window. It was like some sort of mind game designed to drive its victim bonkers, like Anthony Perkins stalking Janet Leigh in *Psycho,* but without the knife, messy shower curtain, or mummified mother.

"Go away! I'm trying to sleep."

But Andy wouldn't leave. My stomach muscles were turning into one twisted knot of tension. In desperation, I wandered down the hallway and clicked open my mother's medicine cabinet. Instead of sneaking a few crumbs of her Valium medication from the bottom of the prescription bottle, I swallowed three or four full tablets. Not enough to do harm, but enough to soften the edges of the world around me and to help me sleep through the tapping, moaning, and pleading in late summer.

Andy remained at my window, an unmovable oak. He was Romeo, long-stemmed rose in hand, but with no willing Juliet to receive it. I wanted to sleep for weeks and wake up to a world without Andy or Gavin or the emotions that accompanied either of them. There was nothing worth waking up to in the late summer of '72.

Pain continued to throb like the low beat of a bass drum housed in my jaw. Despite a slew of prescribed antibiotics, my cheeks went from the marbled puffiness of Marlon Brando to the eye-popping blowfish expansion of Louis Armstrong hitting an E-sharp on the trumpet. My friends gasped at my appearance and suggested that I looked more like a chipmunk than a horn player.

"Which one?" I quipped. "Simon, Theodore, or Alvin?"

I not only looked misshapen, I felt weak and sad from head to toe. Nothing, not antibiotics or pain pills, could touch the sting of my trampled heart.

It was at this precise moment that my father instructed me to move out.

"Now!"

"But I was going to move out at the end of summer with my two friends. We're going to live together and go to school in Santa Cruz," I stated, but with no force or mighty words to make my case. "They can't move out of their parents' home until then."

"Get out of my house," he demanded. "It's my house, not yours! Get out!"

Everything was more colorful and bold in the Sixties, particularly my father's language when he was anxious or angry. But wallpaper, furnishings, clothing, and cars were vibrant and pulsated in new shades. Even the AMC Gremlin was green and the Ford Pinto, my first car, was what I referred to as Play-Doh blue. It looked like a wind-up toy. Today, you can't locate your car in the parking lot because most cars are black, silver, or gold. Once in a blue moon you'll see a red car, maybe a green one. Otherwise, it's a sea of beige and blah.

But there was nothing blah about my father's language when he had his mind set on something. He wanted me out, raging dental infection or not. Not only was his timing imperfect, he always referred to the Eichler as his house. Such statements had been made since we were seven or eight years old. He had a lot of rules for his house. None of our friends were allowed on the premises—his premises. No bare feet in the house—his house. No nails in his wall to hang pictures or posters.

My mouth still thumping with infection, cheeks swollen, and knees wobbling from the fear of living away from my familiar bedroom with the warm mahogany walls and the small pink rug beside my bed, I was told to pack my bags sooner rather than later. I had never lived away from home or cooked a full meal on my own. I had never driven a car outside of Driver's Education class. With wisdom teeth, virginity, and innocence lost, I gathered every ounce of willpower I could muster and stuffed it into the front seat of my car. I packed up everything except Pushka, who sat at the entrance of my bedroom watching me grab everything I could carry. My mother was at the end of the curly kitchen phone cord chatting away with a friend. My father was standing in the backyard lost in thought and puffing on his pipe. I assembled my clothing, dishes my mother no longer wanted, and boxed LP records and books.

With wisdom teeth lost and wisdom gained, I unhung my hat from the hallway of my parent's Eichler and slipped on my new minidress and matching pumps. I had one more stop to make before I got the hell out of Dodge in a Ford Pinto.

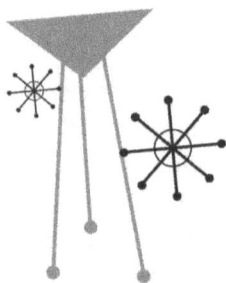

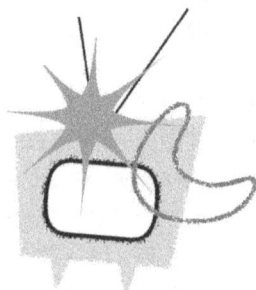

The Next Level

Open Roads

M y family of four had moved from the East Coast to the West Coast, and into a peculiar house of glass and wood that provided comfort and a sense of belonging for twelve years. The Eichler had become a touchstone for everything positive I clung to during the exasperating and isolating times of feeling unwelcome, trampled on, and dumbfounded at home, and in the world. That mid-century manor provided armor. Now I was leaving that cocoon and felt ill-equipped. For what, I didn't know.

On my way out of town and to my next home, a one-bedroom apartment shared by three girls in the Santa Cruz Mountains, I was dressed in a newly purchased polyester black and white minidress. My hair was freshly washed and fancied up after a full hour of careful attention at the mirror. My eyes were heavily lined and mascaraed to appear more sophisticated than I felt. I headed towards Mr. Moore's gingerbread house near downtown San Jose after phoning to alert him, in nonchalant tones, that I would be stopping by oh so briefly to drop a few things off on my way out of town. I didn't tell him what I'd be unloading on him.

As I drove, Brando's Corleone whispered in my ear, "Revenge is a dish that tastes best when served cold." I was the dish that was going to coldly kiss Mr. Moore's ass goodbye. As I maneuvered my blue Pinto through the grid streets of San Jose, sweating into that Size 4 polyester outfit that was shorter than a station break, I turned on the radio to drown out my unsteadiness. As I sank into the seat, sticking to the vinyl from the humidity, and fidgeting in apprehension, my flattering dress felt light as a feather. He could belittle me, lecture me, toss my emotions like a mixed salad, but he wouldn't have me. Not this time.

There it was: his block. His house! I turned down the radio station while I looked for his address. I was convinced I could see better without music playing in my ear as I searched out the numerals. Trotting the Pinto up to the curb outside Mr. Moore's home, I emerged from the driver's seat wearing a whole lot of very little as I mustered up as much pseudo confidence as I could manage. I felt a little woozy standing on his doorstep, thinner than oxygen, heart beating like a jackhammer. The last time I was there it was the end of our affair.

I knocked on the door. My chipmunk cheeks had decompressed significantly. Those same regions were now covered in soft pink rouge. Corleone continued to whisper sweet nothings in my ear: "Why should I be afraid now? Strange men have come to kill me ever since I was twelve years old." A truer statement was never uttered, although in my case, it had been since I was ten years old and had to do with the slaying of my spirit. Yet somehow my will had seen me through the most difficult days of youth and brought me to this moment on a front step in downtown San Jose.

I tried to remember a quote from Vonnegut's *Mother Night*: "We are what we pretend to be, so we must be careful about what we pretend to be." I would pretend to be confident. The door opened too quickly. When our eyes met, I was suddenly someone else; someone who could stand my ground.

"I am leaving town for college in Santa Cruz but wanted to give you a gift I made before heading over the mountain," I announced in self-assured tones, sweat flooding into my polyester pits like a broken dike.

"You're going … now?" he managed, as he cranked his head up, then down, scouting out the dress, or me. I wasn't sure.

"Yes, right now."

I handed him the three paintings that were barely dry, each one wrapped in different colored paper. As he sat on his couch, a couch I knew much too well, I gazed at him as if I was seeing him for the very first time. He was a stranger and back to being my teacher, not my lover. I examined his attractive profile. Had he really been mine for a precious few months? As he slowly opened each gift-wrapped mystery, he looked up at me, then up and down at me again. He was impressed with my artwork, but he was more impressed with the new sultry edition of his ex-student and ex-girlfriend in a short dress. The bohemian girl-child had been made over and transformed into a confident woman.

"You have grown up in a matter of weeks. I'm impressed." His eyes were nearly drooling. "You look so sophisticated. Carol, you're so damn beautiful." He hesitated for a moment before he said, "Very, very sexy, dear. Can't you stay longer?"

All my careful preparation and faux confidence had won. I was in charge, not Mr. Moore. Finally I had secured the upper hand. The ruse had worked. I was elated.

"You look drop-dead gorgeous," he continued, with wolf whistles sounding out of his steady gaze. "Where did you get that spicy dress?"

The words drooled from his thin lips. *The Godfather* had been released earlier in the year, and *The Family* and their words of advice were spinning around me. Corleone muttered something new in my ear, this time almost indistinguishable. "Never let anyone know what you're thinking." Thanks, Marlon.

I struggled to keep my facade erect and lifted like the backdrop during a stage play, but it was beginning to tear and become wonky. As we strolled out to my Pinto, tank already filled and ready to gallop over Highway 17 to my new college town and fresh start, I allowed Mr. Moore to give me a long kiss goodbye. I carefully maneuvered myself into the driver's seat of the car, pulled down my skirt as far as it could reach, and lunged my car away from him still standing at the curb. I pulled away from Mr. Moore, from San Jose and the sticky Valley floor, away from the Eichler neighborhood and our house on Fairgrove Court, and away from the boys and men who whispered promises to help me escape the turmoil that was rattling around in my own body. Only I could lift myself out of what had been.

"Forgive. Forget." I heard Corleone once again in my ear, spouting wisdom like a fountain. "Life is full of misfortunes." Was it ever.

I felt intoxicated with power as I waved a final goodbye from the car window. I felt adult. Was this happiness? Was it my first inkling of confidence? Was it adulthood? Had it crept in when I wasn't looking? I didn't know what it was, but it was the first time I had felt an invigorating mix of pride and control. I liked it. I felt unfettered as I drove up that winding mountain road to my new residence.

Rebirth

I was born, not once, not twice, but three times. First as a six-pound rosy baby in Flushing, New York. I was born again when Curtis Gonzalez lifted me in his arms off the front lawn on the California coast and transported me with his warm lips and soulful kiss. And perhaps there was a third birth when I drove away from my parents' home as fast as they had left their own sets of parents and ran again from the icy state of New York. I refocused my compass in a different direction, away from the Eichler and a neighborhood that was a house of cards. It had served as my shelter for twelve years and the beams and warm walls hugged and held me. But those cards were now crumbling.

I knew the name of every street in that Eichler neighborhood, every kid in my class and on the block, every rock group that recorded. I knew every groan of the floors, walls, and foundation in earthquakes and throughout the countless verbal battles. I shoved my fears and doubts into my closet, in the back of drawers, and under rugs, and scribbled them down in diaries and journals now demolished. From the facade of the home, it looked safe and sound, but underneath it was perilous.

I drove away from my room filled with Beatles music, the atrium full of black sky with flecks of light and wonder as we stood with our necks cranked upward to witness the first moon walk on that clear summer night. Armstrong spoke his famous quote, which he later explained was slightly garbled by his microphone and meant to be "that's one small step for a man, one giant leap for mankind." He then lowered his left foot on the powdery surface, took a cautious step, and every one of us took a leap forward on the enigmatic face of that moon.

That entire home of glass and wood was my kith and kin, my blanket of protection, my rock where I rolled with the punches. I wondered if it knew I was moving on. I wondered if it would miss me, or if Pushka would miss me. As my car wound its way out of Santa Clara Valley and snaked through the Santa Cruz Mountains with their blind corners and tall pines, where nothing was visible until you came upon it, I realized my parents had been unfaithful to New York in the same way I was being unfaithful to our Eichler home. We had to leave them in the dust in order to create a fresh start.

I pulled up to the curb in front of my new apartment, a boxy beige building that was nothing like the Eichler. No mid-century modern design in this perpetually overcast beach town. Like the Russian nesting dolls, it was a box that housed four small one-bedroom apartments. For a moment I panicked that the next week or two without roommates and without anyone to bounce ideas off of was going to be intolerably lonely. I thought I'd be overcome with homesickness as I had been on that first night of camp in elementary school. I was certain of it.

I unpacked my small tables, pole lamps, Herbal Essence Shampoo bottle, and jeans, and went about the business of setting up a bed and pinning up posters. As I pushed pins into the wall, something that was never allowed in my father's home, I wondered if this new residence would ever feel like a sanctuary. Would it ever hold the same protection and warmth I found in my bedroom at the Eichler?

I turned on the furnace at night, something that would have sent my father into overdrive calmed only by rapid puffs on his pipe, even in the dead of winter. But in the dog days of summer on the Santa Cruz coastline, the night was still cold and damp. I was in the dark in that small apartment with few furnishings, a poster of Laura Nyro, a wobbly table, and a hard sofa for sleep. I sat cross-legged on a blanket in the shadowy space doing nothing, yet everything in that stillness felt comforting. I felt sheltered. An unfamiliar calm washed over me. It was as if I was in my own space capsule with seatbelt unlatched and set free to wander about the cabin. What if I had been damaged fruit, merely because I hadn't had a chance to ripen yet? I was going to ripen. I was already ripening. I pulled myself to my feet—this Cancer the Crab Moonchild—and walked around a new space: my own newly discovered planet. I put on Laura Nyro's album *Christmas and the Beads of Sweat* and exhaled as her piano sifted into my head through puffy headphones. She was singing something about a white dove coming today. I was home.

Glancing to the right as I entered the kitchen, I saw an empty countertop freshly scrubbed and waiting for new odds and ends, new possibilities. I placed a goldenrod Waring blender and a two-slice toaster on its surface. My Grand Opening had officially begun. There was no spotlight sweeping the sky, only a soft moon beaming light through the coastal fog onto the laminate kitchen counter.

"Italians have a little joke," Corleone whispered again. I thought he was gone, but he was there in the kitchen waiting for me. "The world is so hard, a man must have two fathers to look after him, and that's why they have godfathers." Funny, but I would have settled for one father or half a mother. Now I would need to do the job of both parents. And I would. I could hardly wait for parenthood and to take care of myself, my needs, and my comfort. I turned the heat up another degree with an internal grin.

It didn't take long for some of my earlier concerns to drizzle in again. Beyond the initial angst of being away from the Eichler, the old Willow Glen neighborhood, and all that was familiar, rapid-fire thoughts started orbiting around the certainty that I was ill-prepared for college. Too much dope, dopey boys, and distractions littered the past few years. How does that prepare you for Geometry and Earth Science? Well, maybe Health Science. After all, I knew a lot about sex, or so I thought. I climbed under the covers of my freshly made makeshift bed. It was half of a rigid convertible couch set my parents didn't need any longer, just as they didn't require me.

That night, much to my surprise, I slept more soundly than I had in years, perhaps in all eighteen of them. I woke up feeling the revitalization that comes from deep regenerative sleep. Sitting up on the mushy couch cushion, I exhaled like I was blowing out all eighteen candles on the cake. It was going to be okay. I felt restored, nearly reinvented. This new planet called Santa Cruz felt suitable, and I felt suitable in it. That half-furnished apartment was an astonishing beginning to a new chapter outside of Fairgrove, Fairlawn, Fairview, Fairorchard, Fairglen. Fare-thee-well to all that seemed fair but was disastrous. Hello, gorgeous! I was at home in my home. And so it goes, wrote Vonnegut. And so it does.

Throughout high school and in college, the Boys Club ruled. Men in positions of authority were able to manipulate, flatter, or flatten females who were their students, secretaries, and employees without any real ramifications. In my days in the

Eichler, I had learned the tired history lesson about being female in the Sixties era. We'd come a long way, baby, but we had an even longer way to go before we'd break the glass ceiling and shatter it to smithereens.

Like most young women in the Sixties and Seventies, I excused men's behavior or attempted to wash it away like Mitzi Gaynor in *South Pacific*, who washed her man right out of her hair. I believed anything that happened was my fault, my doing. I had frequently been propositioned by older, certainly not wiser men. As I sat in my apartment, light-years away from San Jose and the cast of characters who performed there, I cracked open *Leaves of Grass* from Uncle Gruffy and read a few lines about keeping my face towards the sunshine, being curious and not judgmental. I closed the book and pulled my knees to my chest. Okay, Walt, my good fellow. I shall try.

Quick as a wink, Mr. Moore turned back into Gavin. He began driving up to see me at my new apartment near Santa Cruz with a new respect, an adult relationship, but not necessarily an exclusive coupling. And in 1972 that was supposed to be just fine.

He saw me differently and told me so repeatedly. And I saw myself differently. I felt I had "won," but I hadn't won a thing except some trivial amount of dignity and a certain degree of respect from this man who was no longer my teacher. He was simply a man with flaws and fumbles. I continued to hold the cards in our relationship. Gavin and I made love in my makeshift bedroom, which by now was part of a small shared kitchen. I had walled it off with a green India print blanket to give the illusion of privacy, but in actuality I had none.

The first evening Gavin came up to visit me at the beach, my brother, his friends, and my two female roommates sat in the living room talking about nothing in particular while Gavin and I quietly made love behind the blanket wall. I had already met and was dating a new boy at the beach. In the fall of 1972, nothing and no one was exclusive. Free love. Love the one you're with. All that crap.

Back in San Jose, Gavin had moved for the third time since I first met him. Now he was living in a granny flat behind Mr. Ferry's main house while taking a sabbatical from his third year of teaching in an effort to complete his Great American Novel. One afternoon while I was visiting him in his new home, Gavin introduced me to Mr. Ferry as his girlfriend. Was I? Or, more accurately, was I still?

"Hey, Trevor! Come inside," Gavin said with a smile. "You remember Carol from your class, don't you?" he asked with a grin. "Well, she's the girl I'm in love with. That's right. I'm in love with her. " In that moment, awkwardness and astonishment crashed over both my previous year's Existentialism teacher and me like the monstrous wave in *The Poseidon Adventure,* a film that had recently hit theaters. We displayed the same stunned expression as we shifted from one foot to the other unable to make eye contact. I was speechless and puzzled. Gavin seemed certain about his giddy declaration.

I drove over Highway 17 and back to San Jose to visit Gavin several times, but eventually I moved on with a different relationship, and he moved on with his, a girl who happened to be another student a year behind me in high school. Yes, an even younger student than me. They married and had two beautiful children, then divorced. Like many of us, he didn't learn how to love until later in life. The majority of us are slow learners.

War Games

My father survived his time in the service, not with a gun in his hand, but with an ever-present camera hanging around his neck. In some way, photography detached him from what was taking place all around him. It gave him the distance to survive and was his personal weapon against war.

Photography served him well. I can't remember a day my dad didn't have a camera at the ready. He had the gift of a great eye for composition and knew which moments to capture and which ones to discount. There weren't too many right moments in WWII, only wrong ones that were beautifully composed with my father's masterful eye.

While he was slight and certainly not muscular, my dad served four years in WWII. He had always been exceedingly thin in his youth, stalks for limbs sticking out of his shirt sleeves and shorts. Dad lugged around a camera during his entire four years of service and captured the good, the bad, and the enormously ugly. Like the calming medicine of his ever-present pipe, the camera was his savior and his way of coping with what was shattering around him. With bombs bursting in air, bodies mangled, buildings blown to bits, he sorted out this jumbled human disorder called war by documenting it.

It is not a pretty picture, wartime. But my father built some significant relationships with his comrades, his fellow soldiers. Those unspoken, deeply entwined links lasted a lifetime. The bonds of men and women on the battlefield are cinched tight, like a knot.

In my youth, I learned that the terror experienced and the sights witnessed during wartime could not be untied either. My father suffered flashbacks over his lifetime due to the scenes he witnessed and what he lived through, although he wouldn't admit to post-traumatic stress disorder or any other name post-war living nightmares had been given. He was part of the Greatest Generation, and they kept mum about much, suffered quietly, but celebrated madly with acres of colorful confetti when the war finally ended.

During the Vietnam War, my brother became eligible for the draft. My father—this four-year WWII soldier—fought hard to help him obtain a C.O. (Conscientious Objector) status. A conscientious objector was an individual who claimed the right to refuse to perform military service on the grounds of freedom of thought, conscience, or religion. During the Vietnam War, a large number of young pacifists pursued conscientious objector status to stay out of the war. He solicited letters from our neighbors and friends in high positions; attorneys, professors, physicians, and anyone who might carry some weight with the U.S. government. C.O. status was not easy to qualify for in 1970 and certainly not during such an unpopular war as Vietnam. Many young men were marching against the war, claiming C.O. status, or packing a suitcase and shuffling off to Canada.

In the end, my brother received his C.O. He had my dad, the WWII veteran, to thank for that and for his enormous efforts to protect his only son. While my brother and I always felt we were a nuisance, a bore, and a burden to the man, my dad went to great lengths to shield his child from the type of battle he had already had to endure. Perhaps my father was detached from us, but he had found his own way to shelter his children—safety from a war zone, and the comfort of an Eichler home.

My father was an overprotected and scrawny twenty years old when he went into the Army. Like most kids who enlisted back then, he was not ready for what he was to see, do, or experience. He returned damaged. My father wore the guise of a comedian, but he was the archetypal sad clown that most of us become when our mind or heart is damaged, even after months, years, decades have passed. As time went by, I began to see a slight and later a profound crack in my father's armor. It caused me to care for him, to love him even more. I had to do it within myself. My family did not discuss or acknowledge emotions. We felt a mountain of them, but we weren't allowed to let the blessings or burdens out. That was our way.

Sin and Sanctuary

After the dust had settled from my move out of the San Jose Eichler and to my first apartment in Santa Cruz County, my parents found themselves contending with something they had not experienced before. They missed me. At the same time, I discovered something I had never noticed. My parents were flawed just like I was flawed, and riddled with quirks, customs, and wavering moods. They were tortured by a past they were determined not to pass on, but managed to do so anyway.

Suddenly, after eighteen years of struggles, pushes, and pulls under their Eichler roof, we found that we enjoyed each other's company, "got" each other, and more than that, cared about each other. We looked forward to our occasional reunions on weekends and weekly phone calls. Even as a non-traditional family, we were happy to be in each other's company, content about the connection we had with each other, delighted about the familiar comfort in the dysfunctional discomfort. Their visits became more frequent than I ever imagined they would be. Perhaps the enjoyment of each other's company could not be expressed when we lived in the same space pod in San Jose. Now that I was out of their shadow, out of the Eichler, and out of their way, we were able to enjoy our togetherness for the first time. In breaking apart, our puzzle pieces snapped together into a much more comfortable fit.

Finally, my parents, without meaning to, gave me what I needed more than anything else: someone to tuck me in at night and stay in the room no matter what. No matter what! When nightmares, fears, or fevers would flare, the person I wanted, the one I needed, wouldn't disappear down the hallway. They would soothe me, place a cool cloth on my fevered forehead, hold my hand, and stroke my cheek with the back of their hand. In all my sweat and grime, and even when I was difficult or pouting, they would still love me. They would never resent me. They wouldn't know how. They would care for me in all my imperfect glory. And most importantly, they would like me and never fail to let me know. That's what I needed. That's what I hadn't had in my youth. That's what was essential to my survival now.

Maslow's "Hierarchy of Needs" should have placed one parent, maybe two, in every level of the pyramid under the following headings: Esteem Needs; Belongingness Needs; Safety Needs. Forget about the Physiological Needs. I needed someone to take my hand, kiss my cheek, show me some concern. I needed fingernails running lightly up and down my back. I required it more than food, water, and rest. In my parents' house, I couldn't have their attention or kindness, even though I waved brightly colored flags. So I went ahead and captured the love and attention I needed in other ways. I tossed my net in another direction of the sea, scooping up inappropriate men who promised substance but delivered little more than short-term affection and sex. But that wasn't unusual. Not in the Sixties where everything was free 'n' easy, casual, and not complicated. Carnal yearnings were woven into the Bay Area Sixties like a wall tapestry from India or a paisley-printed fabric.

In my early years as a sexual tourist, I journeyed the countryside and uncovered every sort of physical sensation and emotional pull and pain. Unrequited crushes on teen idols, classmates, and celebrities didn't compare to the moment Curtis Gonzales found my earlobe with the tip of his tongue and bells chimed that would deafen the loudest rock bands of the late Sixties.

Then along came beach boys, shoe salesmen, classmates, chefs, and countless others. New sensations and newly ignited nerve endings pirouetted through my body as I lost my balance and lost myself to men who were boyish, and boys who were firm and fresh.

Even in today's explicit age, we cloak ourselves in euphemisms. We "lose" our virginity, we "get some," or "do it" for the first time.

But "doing it" needs to be an event, not a continuum. It should be lasting, not a one-time happening. And if we actually lose our virginity, aren't there multiple "first times" and occasions to do so? Aren't we virginal in most areas of our life before we're not? There are so many first times when we are fresh and new, then broken in. For me, it was the first time when I opened my mouth during spin-the-bottle and tangled my tongue with another tongue—a boy whose dried lips tasted like Juicy Fruit gum.

We have many first times, not just one. And they are all milestones, both terrifying and pleasurable, and all marvels of the mating game. When we lie on the couch snuggling, sweating, and spooning for hours; when we first get naked with another person for more than a few minutes; when we first cry in another person's presence; when we first wake up with a new lover; and okay, when our first intercourse occurs involving a penis and a vagina, or a vagina and a vagina, or penis and penis? They used to call women "spoiled" if a man entered their womanhood with their manhood too early in the game, but what does that have to do with true intimacy? It didn't mean much. Sex never did equate to true intimacy.

The only thing I remember about my first kiss from Danny Fowler was that it left me hoping for something better and more. Most people remember their first kiss. You know, the one that fluffs up the brain chemistry and makes you fly higher than a kite in a mighty windstorm. It's life-altering, tattooed on your brain. You'll probably relive it on your deathbed. Like roller-skating, skateboarding, or kicking up wheelies on your Stingray bicycle, kissing made you feel fully alive in every way imaginable. And no matter how often you did it, it was never enough. Although the joys of kissing were off to a rocky launch when Danny Fowler pressed his dry lips against mine, the joy of sexual stirring launched when Curtis Gonzales had his way with my heart on my front lawn, the summer sun beating down on us, toes curling through the blades of grass like little gopher snakes.

There was the colossal crush on Kevin Carroll in sixth grade when we were shoved into my bedroom closet by our two best friends who were hoping we would kiss, hold hands, or hug. Something! We stood there in the dark, both dying of embarrassment, bathed in want and perspiration, not knowing what the hell to do in each other's presence.

Then there was the Marvin-and-Blaine show, where I walked around the cul-de-sac holding hands with Marvin, then switched to Blaine's palm while walking in the opposite direction in that ten house circle. Was that to keep from getting dizzy? Apparently I was already dizzy with indecision.

Dry humping was the foreplay of youth, and as teenagers we enjoyed every bump and grind. But being a sexual tourist was not always pleasant. Sex, drugs, rock 'n' roll. They bent me, but they didn't break me. They made me whacked out for a while, heartbroken, and cautious. Then I picked myself up and got on with the monkey business of adulthood.

Reunification

Over the next few decades, I attended my share of class reunions. At such gatherings, mandatory nametags sported badly reproduced Xerox copies of yearbook photos. Without them, we were lost in a badly lit room full of unrecognizable versions of people, distracting ourselves with appetizers and fruit punch surreptitiously spiked with vodka or windowpane acid by the class jokester or jock. By the time my twenty-year reunion rolled around, my memory had gone to hell in a white woven bicycle basket. For all I knew, I was standing in a room filled with students from another high school altogether, one that I never attended. Too much time, too much weed, too many commercial messages where we zoned out, not enough active brain cells.

Some things looked better from afar, like Woody Allen, Pollock paintings, past romantic relationships, and my years at high school. At reunions, I felt lost in the booming under-lit room until someone tapped me on the shoulder and reminded me that they sat behind me or fidgeted in front of me in homeroom or history class. We shared this class or that class, or we shared gym lockers or a tube of mascara in the restroom. Only then does the past come cascading back like snippets of a misty dream. I look in their eyes and try to uncover the same pubescent face that once appeared at the next desk. Now it's muddied with foundation, more than a few facial lines, an assortment of chins, and a constellation of age spots, but it's still there. They're still there, young, old, and everything in between. I could see it as clearly as the nose on my face, but in this case, the nose on theirs. Everyone's except Donna Bednarski, who had her nose altered at some brave moment in her twenties. I didn't recognize her when she tapped me on the shoulder. I swung around in my chair and peered up at an unrecognizable face. We looked into each other's eyes, searching for the fourteen-year-old girls we once were. *Who are you again? Which class did we have together? Who were you to me? Oh, yes, my best friend in eighth grade. You threw up next to me on a Tilt-A-Whirl.*

Suddenly you remember the color of the classroom floor tile, the cool boys you had a crush on, the horizontal vents on your school locker door, and whom you ate lunch with in the quad, all cross-legged and in proper gossipy position. You remember your own gaze out to the football field filled with uniformed boys you would never get to know, who would never say hello to you in the hallway, who would go on and break someone else's heart.

Two decades after high school ended, I entered the ballroom of a hotel chain for my high school reunion. An attractive gentleman was frantically waving his hand in my direction from across the ballroom. He started to move towards me. His body was toned and thin like a runner, and his hair was slicked back in salt and pepper strands. He didn't look like anyone I remembered from my graduating class, but it was obvious he remembered me, or thought I was someone else.

Dressed in pleated beige Dockers and a colorful Hawaiian shirt, the mystery man rushed towards me as I cautiously moved in his direction, confusion written all over my face. Feeling awkward and slightly foolish for not knowing who he was, I radioed back a closed-mouth smile and waved. I didn't have a clue who he was. As I turned my head to the side, I whispered to my friend Heather, "Who the hell is THAT?"

She quickly responded. "That's Gavin Moore!"

Gavin was with his former student, now his adoring wife. She peered at me for a moment, then turned her head away. Her permed blonde hair was the perfect 1980s 'do and mimicked my own hairstyle. In 1970 straight hair parted in the middle was the thing. We all looked like Julie from the *Mod Squad,* a TV series with a cast of sullen characters running from here to there, with knowing glances and minimal dialog. Everyone and everything was so cool on that show. But now we twisted all those same hairs into a wavy mess of frenzied frizzy curls. Gavin's wife began to converse with other guests. He had lost his oversized, dark-rimmed glasses from 1972 and traded them in for tinted contacts. His beefy build was now svelte and light as he glided across the room to greet and hug me like an underweight bear.

"You're here. I can't believe you're here!" he shouted over the distorted and loud music so that everyone standing around us could hear. I was pleased to see him but baffled by his greeting.

"What do you mean by that? Where should I be?" I asked, half-joking and half-rambling because I didn't know what else to say.

We moved closer through the deafening room, Motown music piped in from tinny wall speakers and dozens of simultaneous conversations echoing off one another. I remained perplexed and wanted to know what was behind his odd greeting. He seemed genuinely shocked to see me, but we could barely hear one another. Was he surprised I attended our high school class reunion? I had attended all of them. I couldn't imagine what else he meant by the greeting.

He grabbed my arm and closed his mouth into the side of my face, nearly touching the rim of my lobe with his lips. His mouth was still shaped like a flat straight line. "I can't believe you're here. That you're still alive," he spoke in measured beats, like a swimmer's strokes butterflying from one end of the pool to the other. His words were strangely gleeful and upbeat. Huh? What a peculiar comment to have shouted in one's ear.

"Why wouldn't I be here? You thought ... you thought I'd be ... DEAD?"

I truly wanted to know why he thought I'd be six feet under by age thirty-eight.

"You know," he managed, above the 120 decibels of chatter. "Well, your home life was so ... so ... wicked. I thought ... Well, I just figured...."

I scrunched my face up and cocked my head to one side. I suddenly felt like belting out Stephen Sondheim's survival anthem from *Follies,* "I'm Still Here."

If our reunion had been part of a musical or made-for-TV movie, and if I had had the guts, I would have sung out directly in front of the chiseled nose on his perfectly carved face with the square jawline. But this was real life, so I silently played a stanza in my head as I wandered off to get a beverage and sample the hors d'oeuvres. Mr. Moore had morphed into a conservatively dressed, middle-aged married man, so different from the long-wavy-haired beefy writer I had placed high on a pedestal. He followed me around the room with his eyes as I wandered about the cliques, away from Gavin's faded charms, tinted contacts, and brightly colored shirt of the sort that hung in gift shops on Waikiki Beach. He no longer appeared flawless or at ease in the limelight. It was my spotlight now.

Dad ... and All That Jazz

My dad's record collection consisted of standard and modern jazz as well as samba music. Big Band orchestras such as Glenn Miller, Tommy Dorsey, and Count Basie resonated with my dad. He favored vocalists such as Billie Holiday, Bessie Smith, Ella Fitzgerald, Peggy Lee, and Julie London. His favorite singer was Anita O'Day, and her version of "My Funny Valentine" was a beloved tune. One particular Anita O'Day album played over and over again in those early years: *Anita O'Day Sings the Winners.* "My Funny Valentine" was featured on the album, and it became one of my favorite standards. My mom played and sang it in the evenings, and my father squeaked out a few notes on his sax. The record played on our living room hi-fi. In many ways, Dad was a "sweet comic valentine" who made me smile with my heart. I thought the lyrics had been written specifically for him.

Twenty years before my father passed away, Anita O'Day, who by now was living in a low-income trailer park in Hemet, the armpit of Southern California, was going to make a rare performance at a quaint beach town near my home, now in San Diego. I grabbed my recently retired parents and took them to the small concert venue. It was a dive bar along

Hwy 101 in North San Diego County. They couldn't wait to hear her perform live. The room of cramped fans was buzzing with anticipation.

Dad in the Eichler family room squeaking out a few choice notes on sax.

Fashionably late, Miss O'Day climbed onto a stage the size of a small dining table and stood with her back to the audience the entire evening. O'Day had had a colorful history of alcohol and drug abuse that had gone on for decades, a likely reason she was now living in Hemet. Her desire for excess was in full view that night, but her front side wasn't. O'Day was in full-tilt inebriated bliss. My father went about telling the story of her singing with her back to the audience for the next twenty years. It was one of those amusing complaints woven into a story that only he could recount and tell well. I'm glad we went, not for the sorry concert, but for the pitch-perfect narration of the evening.

One particularly dreary Sunday afternoon in 1969, I put a newly purchased Roberta Flack album on our living room hi-fi. It was Flack's debut album, *First Take*, and every tune painted a picturesque tale. The song "The First Time Ever I Saw Your Face" was featured on the soundtrack of Clint Eastwood's 1971 film *Play Misty for Me*, and it quickly became the number one song in the country. In contrast to most number one hit records, this one was a moody piano piece.

Another song on the album that I was drawn to was "Ballad of the Sad Young Men." As I lifted the record needle to play side two and heard this somber song begin, my dad lowered himself onto the couch more slowly than usual, as if he were taking in some message coming in to him from outer space. He listened intensely. The lyrics to "Sad Young Men" seemed to touch him personally and deeply. He would play the album, and those particular two songs, over and over again. That wasn't like him. He always listened to albums from start to finish. But with this record, he'd pick the needle up, play "Sad Young Men" and "The First Time Ever I Saw Your Face." Then he'd pick up the needle again to repeat the ritual. I squinted at him trying to see what was going on in the man I could never read easily. I wondered if the song reminded him of the fellow soldiers he caroused with who didn't make it back from their time at war. Although I was pleased that some of my music had bled into his collection, he seemed to become somber, melancholy, and vacant while listening to it. Where did he go? Who was he catapulted back to during those quiet stares?

Music teases up emotions like nothing else. Even a photograph cannot conjure up the sensations that exist in combined notes and musical phrases. I'm swept away to another time when I hear a tune from the soundtrack of my youth, and it's usually connected to a love interest. But when I hear a bar or two of any Dave Brubeck tune, or even the tinkering of Vince Guaraldi's piano keys, I am transported back to my childhood living room with our orange oval shag rug and the full-sized hi-fi console. My father's Brubeck records are playing on the hidden phonograph on top of the cabinet. It's twilight time. The autumn mist hits the glass outside the windowed wall of our living room. An icy temperature is seeping in through the Eichler walls and paper-thin doors. It smells like rain. I can hear the low murmur of my parents at the kitchen table and sense my brother's presence in his bedroom down the hall. For a few moments I am back there, and back there is back in me.

Three years before his death, I bought my father a copy of *First Take*, this time available on CD. He pressed the repeat button and played that recording continuously throughout the day.

A Change Is Gonna Come

It has finally happened. I've become my mother. Her wide hips, short temper, superficial smile, finely tuned skills in denial, and crooked dental work have become mine. Despite attempts to keep the breakers at bay, and for all our conviction to do otherwise, we become like our parents. Or we strive to be the complete opposite of them even when we have similar choppers.

My father had a faster wit, greater charm, and more radiant energy than I would ever possess, and he pulled in audiences with some mystical gravitational force. Eventually I broke off from my father like a square off of a Mr. Goodbar without either one of us noticing. I have my father's gait, quick wit, sharp tongue, enormous highs and melancholy lows, and the tendency to make compulsive purchases of whimsical, useless, but fascinating items.

Those things we run from, rail against, or reject in childhood, we morph into and become in adulthood. It makes perfect sense. We are made up of our parents' ribbons of DNA. It is now ours, even when their physical body has departed from the station for that final excursion out of town. We can't bring it to the Returns Department or exchange it for another set. They are still swimming in us as we try to find our own freestyle stroke and drown out the roars of the ancestors who splashed about and paddled before us.

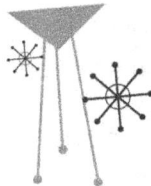

Family Practice

Ships Not Passing in the Night

The idea of having kids was intriguing to my father when he turned thirty, but raising them was another story entirely. Every morning, he'd ready himself for work with a Barbasol shave, crumpled shirt, and narrow tie, then jump in his car and head to the building that offered recognition, camaraderie, raises, accolades for his work, and cheers for his humor and his cleverly told stories. He would philander with the secretaries clomping up and down the hallway. My father was well designed for the adult domain and was a world-class flirt in this production firm of engineering and coffee breaks.

After work, it was time for Happy Hour, some late-night television, usually a World War II documentary, *Joey Bishop,* or *The Jackie Gleason Show.* He would transition to pacing and puffing on his pipe in the living room, then climb into bed around 11:30 or midnight.

My father and I didn't hit it off until a few years before his death, which arrived at age eighty-four. We didn't find the right footing for conversation and compassion until months before he was kidnapped by a stroke. In the 1960s, our ships never crossed in the night or during the day. On the rare occasions when they did, it was a brief brush in the hallway, throwing out a smile to him—a Frisbee that was seldom returned. Many times, he walked around me like I was dog dung on the sidewalk.

I spent my girlhood craving my father's attention and the love or show of affection that he couldn't seem to muster. With each decade, I told myself it didn't matter. I was fine without his approval. Just fine. I whispered it to myself hoping that I would someday believe it.

I stopped having relationships with men whose actions and decision making mimicked my father's behavior. I stopped looking for approval in the eyes of older gentlemen. I wanted to be gifted at the things that mattered most to my father: drafting, math, or anything technical. I never was, as my interests were in the arts. I was neither pretty enough, nor busty enough, like the women in his girly magazines or the piles of porn videotapes he kept in his clothes closet. I could never meet his standards. People told me I was the funniest person they had ever met. My response? You haven't met my father, the man who could fill every room with uncontrollable laughter. I wanted to be capable at something that would make him proud. I tried, but all I could do was write silly little poems and prose, scrawl in my diary, play outside with friends, and daydream through the minutes, days, and years of youth.

My early poems were overcrowded with everything I was feeling but couldn't reveal through any other method. I wrote about isolation, separation, wanting to love, not knowing how to fit in, loving some boy, not loving some other boy, wanting to leave, wanting to stay, wanting to get laid, wanting a Prince Charming to save me from my own wicked fairy tale and a rickety self-image. When the teacher in the classroom used phrases like "indicator of the economy" and lectured about what the stock market was, I scratched out a silly poem incorporating that very phrase instead of taking in the lecture.

You are the indicator of the economy.
The stock market of my emotions.
You bring me up 1.25 points,
And sometimes,
when you forget to call,
I crash.

When my history instructor pontificated about particular wars, I wrote …

JUST AND UNJUST WARS
There are none.
There are many.

Writing was my escape hatch. It gave me a place to unleash the broken spirit bubbling below the surface. The feelings of unworthiness, the feeling of being perpetually unloved and certainly unlovable. I wanted nothing more than to feel secure and safe and to embrace the person I was, but I was nothing like the man I idolized, the man I feared, the man I looked to for approval, and the man who wouldn't give it up.

In my teens and through several decades beyond, I felt terrified and anxious in my father's presence. I withdrew and folded when I was close to him. No one could see that. Nobody knew. He always seemed as towering and imposing as the Manhattan skyline. Later in life I realized what a slight, short man my father was. My mother stood an inch or so over him in height and fifty pounds beyond him in weight. The massive man who panicked and petrified me was, in reality, a small man. As they moved into their golden years, my father was further dwarfed by my mother. He became a thin, fragile figure, but still managed to radiate vitality as he walked briskly, a pipe stuck in the side of his mouth like Mr. Potato Head. My mother, Mrs. Potato Head, would bark back at him throughout their last decade together, unlike the shrinking woman who sobbed at his raised voice in the Eichler kitchen.

I had a fistful of friends, not a crowd of admirers like my father. A small circle of comrades would keep me propped up throughout the teen years. Even though my father's father had quite a few brothers, my immediate family tree was mighty small. More like scrub brush that's been baking out in the desert much too long. You could fit what was left of the Sveilich family on the head of a pine needle. But depression and anxiety had woven a tight and wicked web over both sides of my family tree. What my mother lacked in agitation she made up for with a low-level depression. My father swung high and low, his moods changeable and unstable.

Both of my parents overcompensated for their dissatisfaction with other soothing activities: impulsive shopping and overeating for my mother; hardcore pornography, extracurricular sexual activity, and vigorous flirting on my father's side. Sometimes he seemed to disappear or become hazy, as if he were standing behind a piece of wavy glass, like the glass sheet of the Eichler that stood between the carport and the atrium. His eyes would grow vacant, his mind seemed to travel elsewhere. I don't know where. I only knew that when I asked him a question or talked to him, he was somewhere else, and I was undetectable, my presence faint and unwelcome. At those times the only stimulations that seemed to bring him joy were his cool jazz and Big Band records. His music was ever-present like his pipe, blowing smoky notes into the air and calming him in a way nothing else could manage.

There was always a leaky felt pen in Dad's shirt, making a trademark black or blue stain at the bottom of each pocket in his wardrobe. His shirt looked like a Rorschach test, but he didn't care what people thought of how he looked. I don't think he was aware of what he wore or how he wore it. He was a man of the mind, not of the wardrobe. He marched to his own drummer, all while squeaking out mangled notes on his sax. I came to appreciate his idiosyncrasies and to see that I was strangely similar to him in many ways. I had to learn that being different from the crowd was not something to hide from, but something to celebrate. My father was not only different, but also he was one of the most complicated, charismatic creatures on the planet. He was impossible to get close to, so I took a seat in the audience with the rest of the fans and watched the greatest show on earth.

Eichler Living and Forgiving

For the next two decades, Eichler homes didn't age well. They fell out of favor in the Seventies and Eighties, and bounced back in the Nineties. But despite the embrace of mid-century modern and everything Eichler, some of the features of these once-modern homes were going to have to change, and did. New owners installed better insulation, replaced the transparent walls with shatterproof glass that stopped the outside temperature from coming in, revamped the heating system, put on a roofline that offered a bit of slope so that the water wouldn't pool in the rain, propped up solar panels, flooded the home with LED lighting, and wired the Eichler home for TV, computers, and sound.

Original Eichler models had wooden paneling on the interior, making for dark hallways. Skylights were added in key locations, such as the living or dining area, as well as the hallway to the bedroom and washer-dryer area. New owners installed a second story on their Eichlers, much to the dismay of their neighbors. Eichler people, although a social bunch, valued their privacy and eventually managed to get an ordinance passed to stop such drastic remodeling on a home that had originally earned resounding applause for granting solitude.

As I mature, I long for what's familiar and offers me comfort and pleasure. I reach for what feels like home. Little by little, and without conscious thought, I've been recreating the protective cocoon of my youth over the past three decades. Running up and down the aisles of the local IKEA store is like coming home again. The store stocks mid-century modern furniture and accessories that pepper my current home. Chartreuse vases, splashes of orange in rugs and dishes—colors that evoke a previous era. Little by little, piece by piece, I've replaced my Eighties oak furniture (that replaced my Seventies maple furniture) with contemporary blond birch and beech wood tables and chairs. I've dreamily strolled up and down the aisles of Crate and Barrel stores scouting out the patterns, fabrics, and styles that echo the Eichler nest of my youth. Everything old is truly new again ... and it's now in my living room.

* ⚛ *

Both of my parents were born in New York and never had a car in the city. They walked, took subways, and mixed with the other nuts on the city streets. When we moved out west, my parents took a stroll each night around our Eichler neighborhood. They memorized the front yards and greeted every neighbor working on their car or mowing the lawn. Now I wander the streets in my neighborhood. The homes don't look anything like the Eichlers, but I study the front landscaping, trim colors, and variations of front door designs. None are bright orange. All colors on door fronts and siding are muted. There's not a neighbor in sight. The cars pull into the driveway, the garage door opener is clicked, and just like that ... no neighbor, no greeting, no hello. It is nothing like the Eichler neighborhood where everyone commingled as if they lived in a commune—a commune the shape of a horseshoe.

The Welsh word *hiraeth* is a noun that refers to homesickness for a place to which you cannot return, a home that perhaps never was; the nostalgia, the yearning, the grief for the lost place of your past. Dad was such a massive allotment of my past, and he remains so in the present. Perhaps writing about my father brings him back to me in pieces of a new puzzle, one that snaps together easily as the larger picture appears.

My father was the ruler of his own country. So was Joe Eichler, who helped market a new dwelling to live and thrive in. Society and religion create a paradox. Initially they tell us not to wander too far off from the crowd and not be too distinctive. Then society pays us the big bucks or issues a reward for doing something new that breaks the boundaries and blows the norm to smithereens. Elvis, Pete Seeger, The Beatles, Ben and Jerry, Howard Stern, Joe Eichler. Joe Sveilich. They all colored outside the lines and created their own innovative masterpiece.

There was something inside my father, as well as Joe Eichler, that was not satisfied with the old rulebook. Neither man was particularly good with boundaries. I didn't appreciate my father's uniqueness until it was too late, but I believe he knew how much I loved and admired his cleverness, expertise, and wit. I made damn sure he knew in the end.

In *The Godfather*, they told us, "Time erodes gratitude more quickly than it does beauty!" But my gratitude increased with the passing of time. It grew for both my father and mother, for the Eichler, and the neighborhood I grew up in, for my tightly knit group of friends in Santa Clara Valley, and for the curve of the cul-de-sac as it greeted me after school, drawing me into its U-shaped hug.

Do we ever stop missing our parents? Initially we miss them while we're rolled snugly in a sleeping bag during the first night of summer camp with unfamiliar sounds, far from familiarity, far from home. Later, we miss them while we're lying in the dark on our memory foam mattress, and they have turned to ash and blown under some random wave. It is unending, this missing. For too many years I tried to manage a balance between logic and emotion, pain and comfort, desperately missing or finally letting go. I'm not in perfect balance, like the up-and-down motion of the bird's wing. I want to be and yet, I am perfectly imperfect.

Think Pink

In 1956 Elvis Presley bought his mother a pink Cadillac with plush bucket seats, like the one Bruce Springsteen wrote and sang about in his song. Aretha rode in one down the freeway of love. But why did Elvis buy one for his parent? Because driving a Caddy was a status symbol in the Fifties and Sixties. It signaled the peak of success. A pink Cadillac set you apart from the rest, and in a good way.

Elvis had the car, originally blue, repainted for his mother by a neighbor who designed a customized pink color for him, which was soon referred to as "Elvis Rose." Once the car was finished, Elvis gave it to his mother as a gift. She adored it, likely because she revered her son in some perpetually worrisome way, and deified everything he did or said.

My father drove a very old, massive, horribly pink Mary Kay car for several years during his retirement. He bought it from some coworker he ran into in the parking lot after work. Why? Nobody knew. Nobody ever knew why my father did what he did. But that was the marvel and mischief of his lifeblood. He was as impractical as he was shrewd, and more than a bit eccentric. Driving around town with him in a car the color of Pepto Bismol was downright awkward. Here he was, this slight, silly man behind the wheel of a soft pink dinosaur on four bald tires. You could barely see his head peeking up from the wheel as he muscled down the road in a vehicle that was equal parts monstrous and atrocious. He himself was equal parts turmoil and elation.

I believed my father could do anything. He could drive through the thickest fog and make his way to safety through a torrential rainstorm without a hitch or the blink of an eye. When I couldn't make out the road ahead during a fierce storm, he could. He had special vision or something. All fathers do.

My dad could fix anything, build whatever, and make everything work ... until he couldn't work. He had a heart attack at age fifty-nine and had to stop working. Everyone thought he would decline rapidly once he officially retired, but he didn't. He thrived. He ate out often and ate everything in sight, he walked on the beach, he didn't take any bullshit, he pontificated routinely, and ranted on about everything and everyone. He watched *The Sopranos* and *Seinfeld* and enjoyed his Breakfast Jack at Jack in the Box and Arby's roast beef sandwich that looked like shredded tires. He lived another twenty-five years.

When my parents were in their early eighties, my Jewish father displayed an aluminum Christmas tree in the middle of the family room in their mobile home. And with colored lights blinking, he left it there for two years straight. My dad loved blinking colored lights, and he loved Christmas, even though he refused to celebrate holidays with gifts or other annoyances. I silently concluded that the blinking lights reminded him of Times Square. My mother was perpetually annoyed, but she put up with the Christmas tree in the center of the room and vacuumed around it. She put up with the numerous bare-breasted lady statues from Tijuana and the painting with the blinking lights over the living room couch. She secretly relished it. All of it. My mother was always up for something. She was up for anything.

The last multiple item fixation my father had was with shifting color night-lights from Costco—in packages of four. He spotted them on the shelf and went a bit bonkers. He had to have them, and a lot of them. Like an excited child spotting the perfect toy, he filled our cart with dozens of plastic packages housing multicolored night-lights. I found all of them in his closet and shed after he passed away. They were stored in their original unopened boxes. Perhaps they were parting gifts. I stuck them in every socket of my house. At night, when the rooms darkened, the twinkling of lights switched from blue to green, red to orange, as if the twinkle in my father's eye had reappeared, filling every room.

The afternoon before my father's stroke occurred, he told me how much he saw in his time as a soldier and how trying those four years were for him. He had never before shared these buried treasures and private secrets, certainly not with me, the daughter who was always in the shadows.

He was a proud man, my father. His stories and observances on life were, for the most part, witty and entertaining. His confession about the impact and brutality of war was out of character, but he was no longer himself. He no longer had the armored protective casing sitting across his chest. The words he spoke brought tears to my eyes—tears I couldn't let him see. I finally heard how his time in war had left him with a gaping wound. It's a pity they don't give medals of honor to those surviving such gashes.

Catch and Release

My father never identified with being a senior, and in my mind, he never became one. He always wanted to be around younger people. Besides, he was just a big kid himself. He always wanted to be in the midst of a frenzy of activity, to act silly or inappropriate, never like an adult. He used to call senior citizens "a bunch of old geezers" even when he was eighty-four. He was never a member of their club. But as he grew into his eighties, his body told him otherwise. He was becoming one of them, but fighting it, like the soldier he was, until the bitter end. No assisted living home for him. He wanted to be independent. When he had a serious episode with his heart and the doctors wanted to keep him in the hospital, he checked himself out. When they wanted him to have physical therapy, he shouted at the home health nurse, "Go! Get out!" He was going to depart his way on his terms.

When my dad had a massive stroke in 2008, I was finally able to take care of him and tell him how I felt about him: how much I adored him; how much I appreciated his humor, his spirit, his ups as well as his downs. By that time, he couldn't speak. But I'm hoping that he heard every word, knew I was there, and more importantly, knew what he meant to me. I cared for his shriveling body and damaged mind, and finally, after an arduous relationship and an entire lifetime, he let me.

Parenthood may not have been in my mother or father's job description. But to paraphrase John Lennon once again, they had me, and I finally had them. Not until the latter part of their lives when they relied on me, called for advice and laughs, and wanted to know what I was doing for the holidays, did I feel visible. The group laughter among the four of us—my brother, my parents, and myself—was intoxicating. We became drunk on uncontrollable glee. Humor was the Super Glue that bonded my family when nothing else could.

Four months after my father's stroke, he was gone. I didn't know how to be in the world without him, so I held onto him in the only way I could. I kept his urn in the hallway and walked by it several times a day. Seven years after he was gone, and after not being able to let go of the last essence of him in that dust-filled urn, which I set beside my mother's container, I rented a boat to toss the remains of both parents out to sea. It was nearly impossible to let go, even years after both of their deaths.

I recently read about the time James Taylor's father rescued him when he was in a bad way. During the summer of 1967, Taylor says he found himself going down a dangerous path of drugs while living in New York City. After his band, the Flying Machine, lost their record contract and his bass player quit, Taylor spent most of his time in his apartment, getting high on drugs. "I could have disappeared down the drain really quite easily at that point," he says. "It takes a week or two in the wrong place, and suddenly, very bad things can happen."

One day, Taylor, strung out and stranded in New York City, spoke to his father on the phone. "I don't know if I called home or if home called me, but my father got on the phone and he said, 'How you doing, James?' I said, 'Well, I don't know. Not so good, Dad.' He said, 'Stay right there. Do not leave. Don't go out of that apartment until you see me.' "

At that moment, Taylor says his father, a successful physician in North Carolina, grabbed his wallet, got in his car. and drove thirteen hours to New York.

"He showed up with the family station wagon. He picked me up and took me home, and I recovered for about six months or so until I was ready to start the next chapter."

Reading this story made me reflect on the one time my father came to my rescue. I had recently moved away from home and was living in an apartment and attending college. The boy I was madly in love with had broken my heart. We had been together every day for a year. Then we weren't. I was shattered. My father called me late that night, flying high on a few glasses of J&B or some damn thing.

"How are things going?" he asked, in a general way that usually meant he didn't really care to hear the answer. But this night, deep in the despair of a youthful heartbreak, and feeling like my entire life was hanging in limbo, I told him the truth.

"Not good, Dad."

For once, I took a chance and let him in. I didn't cry. I wept. There's a difference. One is filled with hopelessness. I never wept in front of anyone, certainly not my father. All the walls I had built to protect me from my father crumbled in that moment.

"I'll be right there," I heard on the other end of the phone.

"What?" Did I hear that right? My father lived in San Jose. I was living at the south end of Santa Cruz. It was 2 a.m. He'll be right here? Impossible. But an hour later, after miles of twisty turns on mountain roads at some ungodly hour, and with the scent of whiskey, my father showed up for me.

We lay on the bed, and he spoke about how crappy life and love can be sometimes. He talked to me as though he were talking to a friend, an adult, and not a child. Not his child. I wasn't his daughter, I was his friend. He didn't belittle my feelings. Not once. Not this time. It was the only talk my father had with me about anything, but it was worth waiting for. Sure, he was more than a bit blotto, or perhaps he was on one of the manic highs that carried him over the mountain in record time from there to here. I didn't care why or how we got to that moment. For one night, in the middle of the night, he was my father in every sense of the word.

The "S" Word

The moment you find out your parents are flawed human beings with tempers, and their own individual imperfect temperaments, is life-altering. But when you hear them loosen and spit swear words from their inner cheeks, and at record volume, that's a game changer. The first time I heard my mother mumble a curse word under her breath, she was fumbling through a moment of frustration at the kitchen sink. The plate slid out of her hand, the fork tumbled into the saucer, and—voilà—"SHIT!" It was followed closely by "Dammit!" Suddenly she had the vocabulary of a teamster. I was taken aback. I had never heard such language spew out of her mouth. My mother suddenly slipped out of her parental uniform and became a stumbling, bumbling, short-tempered human being. I was ten years old. She never would have survived the frustrations of technology that still lay decades ahead. Managing a sink full of melamine dinnerware was challenging enough.

The moment my father became fully human in my eyes was much later. When he was eighty-four he had a massive stroke. He was tied to his bed in the Intensive Care Unit at the local hospital. My father was barely alert as he struggled against the belts that held him to that thin hospital mattress. As his face cranked towards me, the invisible daughter who couldn't capture her father's attention or approval no matter what she said or did, he looked directly at me with tears in his eyes. In that moment, he was a frustrated baby in a crib.

I had never witnessed my father weeping. This was the first time he let frustration and sadness bubble to the surface in a stream of tears. He mouthed, "Get me out of here." I finally was being asked for something, but I couldn't rise to the occasion. I can't recall a more painful or helpless moment in my life. It was the first time I had witnessed vulnerability in my father. He was no longer high on a pedestal, shouting out orders like Stalin, or causing hysterical laughter in a crowd of strangers, coworkers, or friends. I wanted to reach out and unleash the howling puppy from the kennel. My heart broke for the frightened child who lay before me, yet I too was helpless. I couldn't do anything for my father. I tried. I begged the nurses to let him out of the restraints. I pleaded with the orderlies to do something, anything, to help him. I talked to him and tried to soothe him with words.

"Soon, this will all be over. It will get better. Soon, Dad."

But my mouth was full of cotton and lies. I could barely speak the words I didn't believe.

I raced to his doctor to see what could be done to make my father more comfortable. Perhaps in the midst of this post-stroke nightmare he was coming off the nicotine addiction that for decades had calmed the nerves—a massive population of nerves that sat so close to the surface you could scratch them with a fingernail. I finally understood the meaning of powerlessness. I was marinating in it. All the king's horses and all the king's men could not put my father together again.

He survived that night in Intensive Care. The doctors told us he wouldn't see the light of day, but they didn't know my dad. Mom wasn't around too often during the hospitalization. She was in a state of shock, trying to gather her thoughts and plans on how *she* would survive without him. Who would pay the bills? Who would drag the garbage can to the curb? Who would annoy her and then make her laugh? Who would walk ahead of her on the sidewalk? Who would light the Christmas tree in the middle of the living room in July? Who would she split a meal with now that he had to be fed?

When Dad was moved to a regular hospital room, opportunity knocked and I answered. I was finally able to tell him how much I loved him as he sat speechless, unable to move or to respond. Sitting by his bedside and playing his favorite jazz records on a dusty boom box, this force of nature was quickly collapsing into a fetal position, unable to utter a sound or walk on his own. But in that quiet stream of music, he managed to move his limbs ever so slightly to the sound and memories of the music. It was the only thing that could tease a smile to my father's face. Music worked its magic, even at the bitter end.

It's been over a decade since my father departed, dressed in that wrinkly hospital gown with tiny blue buds and remnants of juice stains. They wanted me to give permission to "let him go" after the massive stroke took him into a coma. But I haven't been able to let him go at all. Not in all of this time.

That fateful morning, I went for a bland breakfast in the hospital cafeteria and was flooded with waves of competing emotions. I said a prayer for my father, even though he was an atheist and I was his agnostic daughter. I was unsure anyone or anything was listening as I walked around the hospital grounds in a daze and thought of the twists and turns of our intricate game-board existence together. My dad had always entered each room like a ferocious storm. Now he was exiting his ICU room. I sometimes smell the smoke from his pipe. If I catch a whiff of that scent at the shopping mall or on the street, I'm catapulted right back to his side.

My father remained bigger-than-life for my entire life. Even after he passed, I wrestled with the massive presence that was Joe Sveilich. I remember the trivial things he did or the stories he told, and I laugh out loud. All those long, witty, spellbinding stories, all the flaws and unexpected, unexplained furies and episodes have become treasured memories. Living through his moods wasn't easily accomplished, but remembering him and washing him in a bright white spotlight of unconditional love is the easiest thing I've ever done. That, for me, has been the biggest surprise of all.

* ⚛ *

There are dozens of questions I wish I had asked him before he departed, and many things I wish I had done for him. But I did everything I could. In the end, at the only time I was allowed in, I was there. Perhaps that's all you can do for someone: be there when they allow it.

I played his beloved CDs by his bedside, I held his hand, and more importantly, I finally got to say "I love you" because he couldn't dash away anymore. He couldn't glaze over. He couldn't disappear into some faraway land. No, now he couldn't even speak. First a massive stroke had taken that from him. His words were like garbled Scrabble tiles spilled on the floor. Then death clicked the door shut. But his spirit never sailed away. Not from me.

The Key of C

I now have many more years behind me than I have in front of me. The future is shrinking while the past grows longer and more vivid. In hindsight, I wish I had had a better experience with learning music. As an adult, I wanted to know how to read and play music and do it well. My mother played music by ear and played that funky piano nearly every day and evening of my childhood. The final two years of my mother's life were spent in an assisted living residence where she finally was able to live out her dream. She owned the spotlight in that small facility for the aged. Every day, without missing a beat or a date, she would play piano and sing for the residents while they ate their institutional food from the in-house cafeteria. Ladies and gentlemen carpeted with age spots and bent over like reeds fighting an airstream would gather around the piano in the cafeteria and sing all the standards along with her—their own memories rolling back to them, taking them out of this hellhole of final days on a cloud of notes, lyrical prose, and the memories they conjured up. I had never witnessed so much contentedness on my mother's face. She was finally in her element. She was the star of the show.

Mom played piano until the day she died. In fact, she played the very day of her passing. She tinkered out "Tenderly" and "My Funny Valentine" on the keyboard in the dining area and shuffled off to her modest apartment with a waiting cat at her doorway, never to reemerge. In hindsight, that was not only appropriate, it was well played … in the key of C.

Lost and Found

Even after their deaths, I continue to learn about my parents. Not as they were when they were younger, but who they are now that they live on inside of me. I still hear their voices here and there, sense their observations and imagine their clever jokes and rants. But mostly I feel their judgments of my actions, like little devils perched on my shoulders instructing me that I can't, I shouldn't, I won't. Yet, their treatment of me—as a child, as an adult—had nothing to do with me. If they had a problem caring, encouraging, or loving me, it's just that they didn't have a clue as to how to go about doing those things. That was their lot in life, not mine. I, on the other hand, loved too much, held onto people and memories like the tight grip my brother had so many years back when he clung to my father's pant leg as he tried to leave my mother, our family, our Eichler home, our lives. Harold held on for dear life. But I held on tight—too tight—to their judgment, to their disapproval, to their silence as I turned the corner and came into view, but seldom into *their* view. I was invisible, you see. Over time, I had to become visible and matter—to myself.

Heather, who had lived across the street from me in the Eichler cul-de-sac, moved to my current hometown three years ago. Her mother, Betty, a name you don't hear enough these days, happened to be visiting her from out of town. I hadn't seen Betty in over thirty years. I grew up across the street from Heather; her sister, Jane; and her mother and father in our small, ten house snow globe. Her mother was now ninety years old. The first thing she said to me when our eyes met, and before we hugged, was: "Carol! You look like your mother."

Her comment took me by surprise. I had lost my mother several years before, and I was feeling like a different sort of orphan in the world than I felt like in my younger years. Mom died without warning two years after my father. I never thought I came from my mother, let alone looked like her. Our vision, our sensibility, our emotional landscape, our level of comfort or discomfort in the world never intersected. My mother seemed to have landed here from a foreign land. She was born with paper-straight, jet black hair and distinct, heavily lidded eyes surrounded by thick black lashes and a bold sweep of black eyebrows. She always wore red lipstick on her full lips and wide mouth. I had thick, mousy brown hair with a cockeyed wave on one side of my head that never laid itself down in the proper direction. Part of my hair was kinky and part unruly curls. Unlike me, my mother moved in the world with ease and a slow stroll. I was an anxious jumping bean, much like my father. But Mom was at ease with small talk. She socialized, fluttering and flitting around the room like a butterfly, the fanciful party girl; a bright iridescent fishing lure in a crowded room, able to hook and reel in a conversation with anyone about anything. I was terrifically shy in my youth, with a tentative spirit—a mere lightweight with my verbal skills, chronically unsure of my footing, my purpose, my significance on the planet. But my mother ruled the roost.

In the Mirror

Do we take selfies with our cell phone cameras because we're self-centered or because we have no idea what we look like and want to see what other people see? I believe I fall into the latter category. I have no idea. I look in the mirror, but I always see something new and someone different. And sometimes I see my mother from her later years staring right back at me. Her multiple chins, pale complexion, tired eyes, and heavy lids. Hi, Mom.

In the last couple of years, my face has shifted and morphed into the senior version of my mother. I don't know exactly when that happened, but it did. My mother's expression and crinkly eyes are now my own. So are the lines, the dark circles born of Eastern European descent, and the weary appearance that comes with age. Genetics emerge when you least expect them. I'd much rather have her here with me than have reminders of her mature face in my mirror.

My mother had one of those round, mirrored, perfume trays on her bedroom dresser. It had little veins and speckles of faux-gold scratched into glass that gathered dust while reflecting bottles of colored water with labels that promised adoration. She would buy only inexpensive drugstore cologne or splash herself with free samples of Avon, but never Jean Naté. It was too expensive and the bottle too intimidating to manage or justify. Whatever was on sale landed on that perfume tray. The bottles were pretty enough, but the contents smelled like the elderly woman wrapped in a damp wool coat and seated next to you on a city bus.

My mother had one high-end perfume, Chanel No. 5. That bottle sat on her dresser for over two decades. She rarely used it because she didn't want to waste it. Maybe it was her Depression Era mindset. Waste nothing. Better yet, don't use it at all. So, she didn't. It was the only fine-quality perfume she ever owned or had out on display, but she dabbed it on less than a handful of times over her lifetime. A lifetime later the bottle still sat on her mirrored perfume tray, waiting patiently to be used.

Several years before she passed away, I bought my mother a quality perfume whose scent we both liked: Trésor. The bottle was an elegant inverted triangle of glass. Even the name sounded like refinement and allure. She was overwhelmed with joy when she opened the wrapper to find a sealed, pink box housing a delicate bottle of scented water. She put it on that same mirrored tray in her bedroom. There it sat … and sat. She used it in small dabs and only twice. She didn't want to waste it. She was in her mid-eighties, but she didn't want to use too much of it. After all, it was a posh perfume, and it could never be replaced.

That was her conviction. I know that thinking pattern well. I bought a bottle for myself over fifteen years ago, and I still haven't sprayed it more than four or five times. Apparently, I inherited her reluctance to enjoy expensive things: "It's too grand, too nice, too new, I don't dare use it. I'd better save it." For what?

The problem with this theory is this: perfume quality declines very quickly. It should be used within the first twelve months of opening a new bottle. Yes, perfume does spoil. So this theory of saving the good things in life to savor later is not useful practice.

Scents are powerful memories, much like your first open-mouthed kiss, or the first time you sit behind the steering wheel of a car and move it down the open road on your own, feeling empowered and very adult. If we breeze by another person and they're wearing the familiar fragrance of a former boyfriend or relative, we are immediately transported to a precise time and place. My first boyfriend, Ricky, wore drugstore English Leather cologne that came in a bottle with the softly rounded wooden cap. For years, when I caught a whiff of it splashed on the back of someone else's neck or jawline, I was a lusty fourteen years old all over again.

Women seem to have a distinctive history with their perfumes. We remember the first brand we wore, and the next ... and the next. My first perfume was Helena Rubinstein's Heaven Sent. It was marketed specifically to teenage girls, with its soft powdery scent. They still sell it in the drugstore, but it smells worlds different now and is manufactured by another company.

As I moved through adolescence, I shifted from Heaven Sent to the more adult Emeraude perfume, which I thought would tint my surroundings an elegant shade of sparkling green, just like it did for the woman's gown and wallpaper in the commercial, and like the rich emerald color of the bottle. It didn't. It probably carried the scent of soiled socks, but I was convinced it was bottled Christmas, special greenery under glass, infused with glittery green flecks. In reality, it smelled like an atrocious accident at the department store cosmetic counter.

I learned so much from my mother, Blossom. Everything is dirty. Germs are everywhere. Every day we have weather, and we must discuss it. Kids are annoying. Stay away from a draft. Every room has a draft. Marry a doctor, or at least someone with full medical benefits and a dental plan. Don't buy retail. If you do, guilt will consume you to such a degree that you'll never be able to enjoy your purchase. Accessorize. Never buy leather footwear. Instead, purchase plastic uncomfortable shoes. Never stop complaining about them. Ear-piercing causes raging infections that can move quickly to your brain ... and will. If someone coughs, or—God forbid!—sneezes, leave the room, and preferably the building. There may be a God, but there may not be.

"How is that my business?" she would ask in a question that was never a question.

My mother taught me there were countless things to be afraid of in this world, and then she went about the business of being fearless.

Hands are an essential component to one's overall appearance. Mine were small and delicate like Mom's hands. But her fingers and hands were extraordinarily animated while mine sat quietly curled in a bundle on my lap. My mother had a dancer's hands and would use them when she talked ... and she talked all the time. Me? Not so much. But my mother could talk about the weather and do it for hours. Her hands would wave with tremendous grace and point and flutter above and around her head. They were petite and feminine, flying and flapping like small sparrows. I was putting down a coffee mug at a nearby restaurant recently and noticed I have my mother's hands. Without prompting, they glided and rhythmically shifted from this direction to that. My slight, softly gliding birdlike hands matched my mother's finger-wings. I did come from her after all.

Pleasant Under Glass

Twisting the phone cord connected to the telephone in the kitchen was my mother's favorite pastime. It was her link with the outside world, to adult civilization and away from children's needs, meal preparation, dusting, or vacuum cleaners. From an early age, I would listen to her side of the conversation and the slight exaggeration of the current outside temperature, or her latest views on neighborhood happenings and situations at work. She was outraged. She was pleasant. She was opinionated and terribly poised.

My mother expressed her thoughts for the pleasure and entertainment of others, but I would direct myself inwardly with words on the page, or paint on the canvas, or the movement of dance. That was the fundamental difference between her generation and mine. They were the presenters. We were the present ones, mindfully focused on vital issues and deep examinations, not adorning ourselves with glittery words and fashionable deeds, but instead stepping to our own rhythm using our own unique footprint. We didn't blare our trumpets. We didn't sound the shofar. There was no razzle-dazzle. We were after authenticity. At least I was. I would be a humble and righteous being. I would appear as clumsy on the outside as I felt on the inside. I would wear my flaws inside out. I would be true to myself. I would be anything and anyone but my mother.

With that said, my mother's friends liked her very much. Why wouldn't they? She was forever cheerful, personable, interested, pleasant, and talky. She always had a thick address book of superficial friends. She couldn't have approached any of them in a true emotional or physical emergency. They were there to ping-pong words back and forth about the high heat or the most recent downpour.

One of the mom-isms my brother and I heard most often was, "I'm not a doctor!" Whenever we were sick or experiencing any type of physical symptoms, my mother, the queen who wrote the book on denial, would shake her head from side to side, and in a voice that could stop a firing squad, exclaim: "I'm not a doctor!" We could never count on her for understanding, kind-heartedness, or medicine. Those were not her areas of expertise. If anyone, including her children, were stricken with a cold or flu, she had to go anywhere and do anything but care for you.

The only time I remember my mother touching me during my childhood was when she would, without prompting, slip her delicate fingertips under the back of my shirt and lightly run her fingernails up and down my spine. Feather-fingers. This teasing touch would last for a few blissful seconds, then stop. My nerve endings, finally ignited, would feel deflated and abandoned. It was never long enough, this infrequent ritual. I don't know if there's a stretch of time that would have been long enough. I can still see myself sitting on our chartreuse couch in the living room with the green comedy and tragedy masks on the wall peering down on me, my mother seated behind me and surprising me with this unrequested gesture. In one solitary moment I felt cared for, lovable, wanted, worthy. It was the most sumptuous and blissful sensational sensation. I don't know if it was because my mother rarely touched me, or because she had the skill of an angel's touch, but to this day I can recall those featherlike fingertips. I hungered for that touch and a loving sensation throughout my childhood and well into adulthood. Men I have been in lengthy relationships with were always given the stringent order (and okay, sometimes pleading request) to lightly run their fingertips or nails along my back and arms as often as humanly possible. I can't imagine a more powerful sensation than feather-fingers, or one I miss quite as much.

During and after my college years, I learned that touch during infancy and childhood is as necessary as air or water. In order to develop emotional intimacy, children need to be touched and held. It's a way of transmitting care and emotions through our physical beings. A lack of physical affection and emotional intimacy can cause great needs and psychological pain throughout a lifetime. Emotions become suppressed, social insecurities surface, illnesses raise their ugly heads, and one confuses the need for physical affection with sexual desire. Bingo! I could suddenly trace my career of being a sexual tourist back to the human touch, or lack thereof.

Handy Work

My mother always painted her own nails. She never went to a nail salon where millions of other middle-class women allowed others to do the honors. She thought such rituals were pretentious, silly, and extravagant. These types of services simply weren't part of her bumpity-bump, potholed, economy-class block of the Bronx. Yet I can't remember her nails without a splash of drugstore pearly pink or discount-bin sherbet orange from the Ninety-Nine Cent Store or Woolworth's. She would do her nails while seated at the kitchen table, often ending up with more polish on the sides of her fingers than on the nail. These small bottles contained poor quality polish that would crack and peel an hour after application. A day or two would pass and it would be time to begin the ritual again.

I followed in my mother's pedicure-free footsteps. I had a hard time *receiving* manicures and pedicures. I felt like Cleopatra being waited on by servants. It felt wrong. Besides, I was no Liz Taylor. These lovely people made a mere seven to ten dollars for their effort, which takes at least twenty to thirty minutes. I didn't get my first manicure until well into my fifties. I had my first massage at forty-eight. It never felt right to be waited on, except by a man who loved me. That always felt luxurious, unfamiliar, but welcomed.

When my mother was in her mid-eighties, and her brown-and-beige spotted hands were quivering and twitching, she continued to apply nail polish, often to every area of her hand and finger except the top of her nail. Over the decades, I would polish her nails for her with this or that glossy or fluorescent drugstore brand. She cared about such things as looking nice and appearing presentable, and I cared about her.

Now when I do my nails I envision my mother and her small hands waving about like little birds, twirling and whirling and orbiting her head, or waving their last wave. But these days they are transparent hands, waving around my own head, motioning me to sit up straight and use a paler shade of peach. Oh, and to move away from drafts in restaurants ... or put on a sweater, for goodness' sake.

＊ �֍ ＊

One day, I was driving to my favorite shopping mall when I saw a man and woman standing on the curb waiting for the light to change. I was at the stoplight a few blocks away when the old woman, bent over like *Laugh-In*'s Ruth Buzzi heading for a park bench, methodically dropped one foot off the curb, then the next, without lifting her head to see if any traffic was approaching from either side. I held my breath. She moseyed across the street like a slug on Xanax. The man she was with bounded ahead of her, clearly on steroids. Was everyone on drugs? They moved like my parents in their conflicting paces. Wait. What? Those two people in front of me *were* my parents.

I sat in my car watching from a distance, unable to protect my mother or father, or to hurry them safely across the street and away from the college students rushing down the road on their ten-speed bikes or blathering away on their cell phones from behind the wheel. I watched as two vulnerable spirits, who were forever connected to me, but unaware of their surroundings, made their way across the street at radically different paces. I wanted to throw protective bubble-wrap over my mother and father as they moved from one side of the road to the opposite curb. I gripped my steering wheel with a tension that tightened my jaw. It ran down my knotted neck to two stiff arms that clung to the leatherette wheel cover. "Please let them be okay. Please!" I don't know who that prayer went out to, but if they live long enough, your parents become your children and you send desperate prayers out to the ether for their protection.

I couldn't find my previous mother in that stooped figure. Not as she was in her youth: jovial and chatting up neighbors, party-goers, and strangers. She never missed a step in her verbal delivery, even though her physical steps were slower. Now she was an old woman in a highly trafficked crosswalk with that same gap in her two oversized front teeth, the identical dark hair, dyed to mimic her original color. Her lips were still orange-red in her usual shade of Revlon lipstick, which she held onto until she had to scoop the last contents out of the tube with her fingertip. She was no longer a beauty, but she was still my mother, this old woman who was making her way across the road despite the flashing DO NOT WALK sign. My father was still several steps ahead of her, just as he had always been. He was still impatient, rushing forward like some well-oiled machine ready for a race and a rumble. But she was quite Zen, bathed in the moment and in each individual step. She always was.

Both of my parents wore hats often. My father wore the same flimsy and filthy gray canvas headpiece every day for the entire final decade of his life. My mother, on the other hand, had a collection of hats that would rival Imelda Marcos and her shoe collection. She had what I would kindly term a hat fetish. She coveted acres of vibrant berets, beach hats, and boleros. All were inexpensive, and most were those colorful felt toppers that seniors often tip to one side and sport on a cruise. She had oodles of them, more than any one person should be allowed to have, hidden in closets or stuffed into drawers.

During my parents' final move to another home, my mother was going to give away all of her hats. There were too many to keep in storage or use. I stopped her and said I wanted to do something special with them. "Trust me," I assured her, even though she seldom trusted my judgment.

I tacked the colorful berets to the back wall of my parents' bedroom behind their king-sized bed. My mother's colorful array of headwear became a headboard and yes, I put tacks in my parents' wall. (P.S. It was a rental.) Hats of every color and texture covered one full wall of the bedroom. I've never been a hat person, but I find myself drawn to them now. I have three or four hats in my meager collection. Perhaps when I'm older I will cover my walls with a headboard of caps, bonnets, and fedoras.

A familiar scene that remains locked in my memory is my father playing his squeaky soprano saxophone or clarinet on his squeaky butterscotch plastic living room couch. He had a hole at the bottom of each shoe. My father had no fashion sense. His was more like fashion nonsense. He enjoyed a well-worn wardrobe. Shoes. Hats. Jackets. Shirts. The more rips, spills, and ragged edges, the better.

In his final decade, he wore the same thick-rimmed glasses that he had when he worked at FMC. Shop glasses. In all, he wore them for twenty-nine years. The lenses were coated with gunk. He rarely wiped them clean. Several pounds of glass and metal sat on the bridge of his nose, but he liked the sensation of mass on his face. Maybe it reminded him of the Brooklyn Bridge in his old neighborhood. He liked the way they pushed against the upper portion of his nose, never letting him forget they were there. He could have gotten new, lightweight frames. He never did. His old frames reminded him of his glory days at FMC where he was a king, and the secretarial pool greeted him with "Hi, Joe!" or a wink.

Both of my parents wanted to be cremated and tossed into ocean waters clear as the Eichler's wall of glass. The Neptune Society had their money, but for seven years after their passing, I still had their ashes in two different-sized Costco urns. My mother was housed in the larger vessel. She liked her desserts.

I don't think either one of them gave this death thing a whole lot of thought. For instance, my mother always felt a draft. She'd shift from table to table in restaurants because she was certain she felt frigid air traveling through the vent and onto a direct route to her neck. She was sure of it. No matter where she went, she brought a sweater and urged me to bring mine. Like weapons for war, we loaded ourselves with outerwear. It could have been 114 degrees, but ... "Don't forget to bring a jacket." She'd cinch her sweater or jacket tight, pull it to her chin and quiver. "There's a draft! Let's move." Like a colony of ants, we'd relocate to another hill. A better hill. Or in this case, a red padded booth. So, how was I supposed to place them out in the cold ocean waters now?

My parents never even went camping. Why would they? They hated the outdoors as it reminded them of the bitter cold of the East Coast. Besides, they were New York Jews, and Jews don't camp, unless they were camping out for tickets to the latest Broadway production. So, now I was going to put them to bed in the cold night sea? Preposterous. It's drafty out there. There's no tall chrome coffee pot with Maxwell House coffee brewing, no butterscotch couch, no sour pickles, or deli platters. As I said, I don't think they thought this through.

From age six to eighteen and perhaps beyond, I wanted my family to look like the families portrayed in sitcoms. Any sitcom from any era would do, but particularly the 1960s. Yet none of the behaviors or mannerisms of any or those characters matched my parents or my brother. My father's pants were always stained because, doing routine chores while drinking coffee, he spilled paisley patterns of beverages and food droppings all over himself. His attention was always elsewhere, not on spillage. My brother and I wore ill-fitting clothing from the clearance areas of low-end department stores. Wading through sales racks was my mother's special gift. Her hands waved through the fabric like she was conducting a small orchestra. To her, a sale was like a buffet. You could take more than you needed because it was virtually free.

Both of my parents waited patiently and quietly in my hallway for years, in their respective urns. I didn't release them into the indifferent, hard-hearted universe until recently. On my small tabletop in the hallway, I had a shrine erected featuring personal items next to each urn. My father's drafting rulers, WWII Army compass, and other pertinent, yet impertinent nonsense. There should have been a statue of a naked lady. I laid my mother's cheap costume jewelry necklace with fraying cord next to her vessel. The fabric was ready to give at any moment. What do you want? It was on clearance.

Regrets, I've Had a Few

Not everyone thinks about death. Most have religion to fall back on, like a safety net that sits below as we swing ourselves to and fro on life's trapeze bar. Most are assured that once the dirty deed of living is done, they will enter some ornate gate or be reincarnated or go back into the earth as a big scoop of nothing. I haven't decided anything yet, but I'm leaning towards the dirt theory. All I know for certain is that I don't want to outlive my two cats. And I don't want to die from a painful and long drawn-out illness. Let me go quickly. Don't we all wish for that?

Don't we all ruminate on what we'd like to accomplish before we depart through the final exit turnstile? I'd like to write another book. I'd like to meet more people more often who vibrate at the same frequency as I do. That's not easy to find in this twenty-first century. Most of the time, when I meet other people, they are alien beings. I can't find a connection, or perhaps I don't want to. If I did, that would mean my contribution is as valuable or worthless as their two cents. I have to be radically different, like my father. I don't know why. I just do.

I'd like to learn a new craft or learn to paint so that the end result doesn't look like a kindergarten class assignment with boxy homes, stick figures, and swirly shrubs. I'd like to do collage work. This book is a collage of sorts with bits and pieces of a lifetime loosely sewn and glued together. But most of all, I'd like to trust and love in a way that I haven't before, with zero hesitation and in some final leap-of-faith maneuver, like the exercise where you fall backwards and rely on another person being there to catch you before you plummet to the pavement. I'd like to take more chances. I'd like to fall flat and get up and not be fazed by what others call catastrophes. I'd like to call all failures successes and no longer beat myself to a pulp when I walk headfirst into a brick wall. I'd like to be able to eat a half Jamoca Almond Fudge/half Mint Chip ice cream cone and not worry about the three pounds that will adhere themselves to my thighs or the gas that my lactose-intolerant gastrointestinal system has to produce in order to transport it through my colon. I'd like to live long enough to do all of these things.

I wish I had invented a cure for something instead of dating so many wrong suitors or watching too much daytime TV. There are so many good things we can do with one life. We can love those who need our love. Forgive others. Make them laugh. Make them feel special. Make them feel calmer, safer. Adore, honor, respect them. Make them feel young again.

I wish I had learned to dance. Really dance. It's the only thing that feels like a natural extension of my being and a way to clearly communicate. Talking, not with words, but with movement. Not writing but composing with my body that has finally been set free—free of pain, free of the past, free of being told NO when all my limbs want to do is YES, YES, YES! I wish I had mastered a musical instrument and become fluent in a different language beyond being able to ask where the library is in Spanish. ¿Dónde está la biblioteca? And I hope to write a book that resonates with the crowd who always felt like they were from another planet, or paint a picture that stops people in their tracks and connects them to me and to each other, in some mystical way.

But what I really want to do is dance.

Open House

Things I miss:

    a) perusing Tower Records on Friday night

    b) the ability to digest dairy

    c) my mother and father

My parents sold our Eichler home in 1974. It was another impulsive move that turned out to be a blunder, but only if you wanted a massive nest egg. My father purchased our Eichler home, a ticky-tacky box placed in a suburban landscape of other ticky-tacky boxes for around $19K. In 2016, they were selling for $1.4 to $2 million. That's Silicon Valley today. It's not the Santa Clara Valley basin of cherry orchards and modest neighborhoods I knew or the bedroom community of affordable Eichlers I grew up in.

When I was eight, I wanted to be ten. When I was ten, I wanted to be sixteen. When I turned sixteen, I only wanted to be eighteen and get the hell out of San Jose's Willow Glen. Then after that I stopped wanting to be older. Now I go into the doctor's office, fill out a form, and insert my age, which has become even more painful than inserting my current weight. I feel as though I've spent a lifetime wanting it to be further along or earlier in the game's inning. I've never wanted to be where I am or who I am at any particular moment in time. I've spent much too much time wishing for this or that. Wishing I could remember, wishing I could forget. Wishing I had loved this person more, and that person less. Wishing I hadn't ruined countless opportunities because I was so plagued by insecurities. Wishing I had done something constructive during my bouts with boredom. Wishing I had what that person had rather than looking at what was in my own backyard. Maybe my grass was greener, not theirs. How would I know? I never had anything to compare it to. None of us do.

We grow up in a bubble thinking other people exist in the same bubble. They don't. There is always someone with more and millions upon millions with less than what we possess. I had the Eichler. I wish I had had my parents more often. But some people have neither. They don't have the beam ceilings, the globe-like lights dangling from the ceiling, the indoor/outdoor living provided by an atrium, the Kinney shoe salesman on the top of a car at 11:45 p.m.

Now I wish for different things. I wish I had asked my parents more questions. I wish I had found out more about my grandparents and the details of their adventures before and after immigrating to America. Sometimes I wish I didn't know myself as well as I do, but more often than not I wish I knew myself better. I wish I had never cut my long hair to the shoulders as it never grew back, never was as thick or full, never was as shiny or youthful. I spent too much time wishing I was 5'2" when I had a shorter boyfriend and five feet nine inches when I had a taller one. I spent time wishing I'd been more patient, and other times wishing I'd hurry my feet and move faster. I've spent too much time regretting the times I fell down and spent too much time on the ground rather than getting up immediately. At the same time, I wish I had rested when I bit off more than I could chew, which happened too often and was quite detrimental. Moderation was never my strong suit. The same could be said for my father. We'd often overdo and stretch and strain beyond our limits. The result was unfinished projects tossed aside like too many pillows on the loveseat.

"Aww aww, baby,
Momma is a lady.
Daddy is a gentleman.
All fall down."

There should be lullabies for adults. Adulting is puzzling. Planning for retirement, paying bills, watching weight too closely, letting go of people too often are all in the job description of a grown-up. Oh, to be young again, when my biggest concern was trying to hold down the play and record buttons simultaneously on my cassette tape recorder to capture a song without capturing the commercial messages.

I spent more than fifty years observing my parents and the way they moved through the world. My mother taught me to care only what the neighbors think. Life was about presentation and chitchat. My father showed me, by example, never to think about what the neighbors think. Life is a circus and made for living, amusement, and pleasurable experiences. If you're curious, don't sit in the back of the class. Ask questions. If you like or don't like something, spill it! If you want to go through life with funny glasses and a Groucho nose, why not? It keeps the troops entertained and preserves your own youth, and sanity.

I no longer believe in happily ever after, and yet I do. I'm a sucker for a good fairy tale, but as I learned on *The Rocky and Bullwinkle Show*, most fairy tales are fractured. People who have it all together don't exist. They never did.

Ash the World Turns

On Veteran's Day, my beau and I rented a small boat in Oceanside Harbor near where we live and braved the cold and high waves to release my parents' ashes several miles offshore in the indifferent waters of the Pacific Ocean. I asked my brother, Harold, to join us. He was now living fifteen minutes from the pier, but he declined. He had become much like my father and was difficult to get close to without having to endure an accompanying bark or a bite. I had learned to approach my brother cautiously and finally, but sadly, learned to avoid his company. Sometimes we become the opposite of what causes us pain, and sometimes we mimic or morph into it. My brother and I had taken two different paths to make peace with our childhood, our parents, and with ourselves.

For a lifetime, my father and I had gone after one another like two sets of feet kicking at each other under a heavy blanket of uneasiness. It was a blanket that no one could see or feel except us. I couldn't understand or excuse everything my father had done, and I didn't know what it was like to deal with his particular demons. But over time, his judgment of the world around him, and more importantly, of me, had managed to weasel itself into my own head—the head of a child—and followed me through my adult life. With the passing of time and years of intermittent therapy, I had learned that, although neither parent knew how to care for me with warmth and kindness, I could learn to care for and about myself. I didn't have to take on their critical voice and inflict it on myself. I didn't need to absorb their messages of being undeserving and invisible. I could write and embrace my own vocabulary for myself. I had to create a list of "search words" to find and define myself in a new way. This would take decades not only to write, but to absorb.

On the small rented motorboat surrounded by waves reminiscent of *The Poseidon Adventure*, I would release my mother first. That seemed only right. It would be easier, yes? I wanted to stop what was about to happen. I couldn't. It was time. Were they really in there? They seemed awfully quiet.

Blossom: *Could you finish putting polish on my nails first, Carol? And color my hair? I want to look nice. Oh, and can we get an Arby's Beef 'n Cheddar before you shake me out onto the ocean so I end up God knows where? I feel a draft. Can someone turn up the heat? Maybe drop me from the other side of the boat where it isn't so blustery?*

Joe: *Blossom, have you lost your mind? Haven't you had enough heat? How the hell do you think we became ashes in the first place? Carol, tell your mother to get this whole cockamamie thing over with, already. Hey, listen … sorry about all that pipe smoke. I guess you got me back with this cremation business. Yeah, I know, I know. We asked for it. We put it in writing, for God's sake. Be careful what you ask for, Carol. You may just burn like you're in hell.*

I opened the twisty wire at the top of the plastic bag where her ashes had been held for years. It was the kind of closure you get in the produce department to secure your zucchinis and carrots for the ride home from the market.

Blossom: *Brrr. I wish I could stop what you're about to do. Hey, I heard you singing before bedtime the other night. You know, when you were flossing. You sulked about having my limited range. Maybe so. But you don't need my voice, Carol. You've got your own. It sounds … pretty. You have your father's hurried mind. Quick wit. Good luck with all that.*

Mom's ashes fluttered into the breeze, then scattered themselves onto the surface of the cool water. No more costume jewelry, unused perfume, early bird specials, or hoarding of catsup and mustard packets. No more tinkering on ivory keys or Sinatra tunes … or Christmas carols. No more anything.

Blossom: *You have my face and eyes now. Are you going to go eat after this?*

Suddenly an unexpected sound roared up from the depth of my belly, flew through my chest, past my racing heart, fired out my throat like Godzilla's breath, and released itself from the depth of my core like the howl of an unexpected predator. I didn't cry. I didn't weep. I wailed. I couldn't stop what was arising. I tried. The sound wasn't familiar. Where did that come from? I didn't know, and I didn't even know why this sound was soaring out of me. Yes, I did. I didn't want her to get chilled. And what about unexpected predators like sharks or stingrays lying in wait? Was I being overprotective, like my Grandma Anna who wouldn't let me out of her sight? Was I wringing my hands needlessly? What if my parents can still catch a cold out there? Isn't it my duty as a daughter to keep them safe from harm? Or was I crying out because she couldn't? Was she channeling her five-octave hollering sprees in the choppy waves of early morning?

Blossom: *You should have been a dancer, Carol. A ballerina. You can still dance. I can't do a damn thing. Put me back in the baggy. Let's go home and watch* Dancing with the Stars.

She loved that show. She never missed it.

Blossom: *I'll always be watching with you, Carol. We can talk about it tomorrow on the phone, after I tell you about the weather. Oh, wait. No, we can't.*

I composed myself and reluctantly grabbed the second, smaller urn that housed my father.

Joe: *I feel like chopped liver in here. Come on, get on with it. Chop, chop. Oh, when you get a chance, let me know if that nice Obama fellow got elected. And explain to me again—what happened in the finale of* The Sopranos? *Tell me, who was that last guy who walked into the restaurant? Did Tony know him?*

I took a considerable gulp, the sort you take before you give a book report you haven't prepared for—or before you release the chief person in your life. But when I opened the plastic bag stuffed inside to release his ashes, I was unable to shake his remains from the cavity of the urn.

Joe: *Oy mush! Get me outta here. You could get claustrophobic sitting in here for eight years. It's like that* yutzi *MRI contraption. Carol, dammit! Come on. Hurry.*

His ashes had settled for too long a time inside that ceramic monstrosity, or perhaps he was being as stubborn in death as he was in life. I thought I would ooze sorrow, moan, and sob uncontrollably when the moment came to scatter his ashes—ashes likely mixed with the cinders from the bottom of his curved pipe. But instead, I laughed out loud as I clung to the boat with one hand, banging and banging the urn against the edge with the other, trying to loosen his remains and shake his remaining reluctance to budge. I marveled at his determination to stay in the decorative floral vessel. I could feel his fingers and toes holding that congealed ball of powder back.

Joe: *No! I'll stay. It's nice in here. Leave me be, or bring me some nice lean pastrami. Don't forget the Gulden's mustard. What kind of* fakakta *place is this? No condiments? Oh, and dear ... we did the best we knew how. I'm out of time, Carol.*

He remained stubborn. I banged and banged. *NO!* He wouldn't come out.

Dad! Please. Give me a break, if not in life, in death.

He finally emerged, but in chunks. I shook my head and smiled. Dad got the last laugh, but in truth we were both snickering at the absurdity of life, and now of death. It was perfect, and it was perfectly Joe. He wouldn't come out. His immovable nature was at work once again. When I finally saw his ashes glide away and mix with the blue of the sea as it rippled in all directions, I was too dumfounded and amused to weep. He gave me a good tease and chuckle, while he got the last laugh ... as he should. As he always did. Perfect. Curved pipes, straight-edge wooden rulers, metal protractors, inky pockets, Brubeck and Tjader records. Vince Guaraldi's *Cast Your Fate to the Wind* playing softly on the surface of the sea. The fragments of my father were moving away, faster than a Ferrari. Now he was a granulated cheetah, a decaying rocket making its way homeward, plunging into soft dark waters. I watched as both of my parents floated off and away, trembling kites carried off on an indifferent sea. I wanted to turn back time, say something more to them, do something different, warn them to be safe and somehow assure them of safety. I couldn't do a damn thing except watch, then turn away.

＊ ⚛ ＊

Heading back towards the shoreline, my parents now mixed with the splashes of water under my vessel, I already missed my father, the times when he was whole and had me howling at some random and outlandish observance, or telling a common tale with humor and flair as only he could tell it. I remembered the dizzying airplane rides around the living room rug as he spun me loosely in his arms, and we both left a trail of giggles. I thought of the rolled up newspaper fights, the hit and run, the fear and exhilaration of those mock battles. But I didn't want to run from him any longer. I wanted to run towards him. I didn't want to let go of my memories along with his remnants. We didn't hate each other through those decades. We didn't know how to love one another. Finally, we had discovered how to manage that and to let the rest of it release, like a powdery substance on a sea breeze.

With his light witty ways and stories, and just as many dark corners, I suspect my father's psyche was damaged by what he saw and was asked to do in wartime. After years of working in the counseling field, I also imagine he was impacted by a mood disorder even though it was never diagnosed. The Greatest Generation was not eager to seek out mental health assistance. But his massive mood swings, sudden angry outbursts seemingly out of nowhere, impulsive and often inappropriate actions, disappearing acts, and risk-taking shenanigans always fell into the you-know-how-your-father-is column, usually delivered by my mother, and always with an accompanying eye roll. His complex behavior was labeled quirky. But perhaps it fell into the bipolar column. Not that having a diagnosis would have excused the behavior, but it would explain some of it, at least to me, his only daughter.

But lovable, charming, and entertaining doesn't begin to describe this man who both terrified and astonished me. His way of looking at the world was always a bit askew, but it quickly became my approach to living. I adopted his outlook and outrage, his creativity and skill with a camera, and most importantly—and the skill that served me best—his ability to find humor in the most desperate situations. Why not turn norms upside-down, change your name at the restaurant hostess desk, and make inappropriate comments.

I missed my mother too. Who would tell me the weather forecast now? Who would wave her hands like doves sailing through the air? Who would have a remark for everyone she met? And more importantly, who would hum pretend tunes to pass the time? I would.

As my limbs and thoughts flopped back and forth through the choppy ocean waves and back to shore in the rickety rented boat, I found myself hoping that Buddha was right about life and death being illusory. And I hoped that my adoration for my father would now be transparent to him and as clear as our Eichler glass walls looking out to the heart of the house: the atrium. I hoped that he would feel the softness I felt for him in my heart, in all its unguarded glory, like the warm mahogany walls of the home we shared together an entire lifetime ago, moving around each other like the resistant ends of two magnets.

I thought of him traveling in a purposeful manner towards a vague destination, as I mumbled "coddiwomple" under my breath. I said it in hopes he would arrive safely. I realized, perhaps for the first time, that one can easily become transfixed on the glorification of destinations. The idea that contentment or happiness is in the next place, the next relationship, or the next job is a false notion. Until I gave up the idea that happiness was somewhere else, or with someone else, it would never be where I was. I had to find ease and pleasure in the present. I hoped my parents had found plenty of it in theirs. I felt certain that they did.

Act Two
Scene 1

[Narrator: A once-young girl, now decades beyond her youth in the Eichler, steps out of the small power boat and onto the deck, turns, and looks out to sea as the chill off the water blows into her face. She pulls the loose hairs away from her eyes and the corner of her mouth, and looks closer at the surface of the water, as if she's trying to see through it. The two empty, different-sized urns are tossed into the public trash bin so that they can settle with the candy wrappers, wadded-up Kleenex, and dirty napkins. Souvenir stores line the deck of the Oceanside pier. Her boyfriend, Sam, follows her out of the small boat and onto the deck.]

Carol: The out-of-towners are filling the parking lot. Look. They're driving up and down looking for a spot. Maybe we should give up our space so that they can pull in?

Sam: Shouldn't we catch a bite to eat first? How about lunch? I know you're always hungry!

Carol: I am. A little.

[Narrator: She turns out to sea again, eying the landscape as if she can see below the glossy surface of the water. Her hair blows back again, this time with greater force. She lingers for a moment, gazing out at the tide. She cinches her red sweater up to her neck to keep out the cold air as the couple walks towards Joe's Crab Shack, their favorite fish eatery.]

Sam (taking her hand.): What are you going to have today? Salmon?

Carol (fresh tears dragging the black liner and mascara down both of her cheeks): I've got to go fix my face first.

Carol walks to house left, bows her head downward towards the audience, and begins to speak, as if to herself, but out loud:

"Today, it's easy to celebrate my father—a lover of felines, MAD magazine, jazz music, The Three Stooges, bawdy jokes, and good eats. It's true, I come from a long line of lunatics, but that's not such a bad thing. In fact, in a world of same old, same old, lunacy may be the best choice on the menu."

Sam: The restaurant might be warm. Do you want to leave your sweater in the car?

Carol: No. I'd better take it with me, just in case.

[She pulls her red sweater tighter around her shoulders as the curtain falls.]

End Scene

www.ingramcontent.com/pod-product-compliance
Lightning Source LLC
Chambersburg PA
CBHW031143270326
41931CB00006B/121